D1488440

THE LOEB CLASSICAL LIBRARY

FOUNDED BY JAMES LOEB, LL.D.

EDITED BY

G. P. GOOLD, PH.D.

FORMER EDITORS

† T. E. PAGE, C.H., LITT.D.   † E. CAPPS, PH.D., LL.D.

† W. H. D. ROUSE, LITT.D.   † L. A. POST, L.H.D.

E. H. WARMINGTON, M.A., F.R.HIST.SOC.

SAINT AUGUSTINE

THE CITY OF GOD AGAINST THE PAGANS

I

BOOKS I-III

411

SAINT
AUGUSTINE

THE CITY OF GOD AGAINST
THE PAGANS

IN SEVEN VOLUMES

I

BOOKS I–III

WITH AN ENGLISH TRANSLATION BY

GEORGE E. McCRACKEN, Ph.D.

PROFESSOR OF CLASSICS, DRAKE UNIVERSITY

CAMBRIDGE, MASSACHUSETTS
HARVARD UNIVERSITY PRESS
LONDON
WILLIAM HEINEMANN LTD
MCMLXXXI

American ISBN 0-674-99452-3
British ISBN 0 434 99411 1

First printed 1957
Reprinted 1966, 1981

Printed in Great Britain by Fletcher & Son Ltd, Norwich

CONTENTS

INTRODUCTION

No paucity of data confronts the modern biographer of St. Augustine, for the information on his life which has survived the lapse of sixteen centuries since his birth is so rich and so abundant in detail that we run the double danger of omitting the significant or of becoming intolerably prolix. No writer of any period is so completely autobiographical, so frankly personal, permits the reader to enter so deeply into the inmost recesses of his mind. We know as much about the minutiae of his daily life as about his achievements and, if occasionally there are lacunae where the scholar wishes he knew more, these omissions create little difficulty in understanding the mind of the man.

Yet he who would truly know the life of the Bishop of Hippo must himself read the works, especially the spiritual autobiography contained in the *Confessions*, augmented by the letters and by the great work here presented in a new English dress. On the other hand, this volume must have an introduction, and an introduction should attempt a biographical sketch, so, to use the saint's own words, God being our helper, we shall begin.

I

That the full name of our author was Aurelius Augustinus has been generally believed in modern times, but " Aurelius " occurs neither in the *Con-*

fessions, nor in the salutations to the correspondence, nor in the earliest life by Possidius.[1] Born in Numidia Proconsularis at a place then called Tagaste, now Souk-Ahras in eastern Algeria, Augustine was, if not wholly African in blood, certainly African in spirit and in interest. The birth occurred on 13th November, A.D. 354, and he was the eldest child [2] of Patricius by his wife Monica. Though only late in life a Christian, the father was a man of some prominence in the community, a decurion or member of the town council, yet never rich, and, to judge from the little that is said of him, he exercised no great influence on the life or mind of his famous son.

With the mother Monica, however, the opposite was certainly the case. Of all the human factors that formed the boy and youth and made him what he ultimately became, his mother's constant solicitude for his welfare and for his conversion to Catholicism was surely the most powerful element. Reared as a child in a rather strict Christian home, she lived, until her death in her fifty-sixth year (A.D. 387), when Augustine was thirty-three, a life exemplary in its Christian devotion. Her marriage with a pagan was

---

[1] Composed in the decade following A.D. 430. For the text see Migne's *Patrologia Latina* 32.33–66; for the text and translation, see Herbert T. Weiskotten's *Sancti Augustini Vita Scripta a Possidio* (Princeton, 1919); for a new translation based on Weiskotten's text, see F. R. Hoare's work, *The Western Fathers*, in " Makers of Christendom " series (New York, 1954), pp. 191–244; a third translation appears in E. A. Foran, *The Augustinians from St. Augustine to the Union, 1256* (London, 1938).

[2] There were others, including a brother Navigius, who later married, and a sister, whose name is not preserved in the surviving works, though known traditionally as Perpetua, who became a nun.

beset with problems of adjustment, but it seems to have been a happy one, and if her husband at times displayed the defects of a violent temper and occasionally lapsed from marital fidelity, she bore this with patient understanding. There is no reason to suppose that the childhood of Augustine was especially unhappy, despite the impression given by the mature writer of the *Confessions* that, as he reviewed his childhood memories, he found much to regret. Augustine was a normal boy, and the relationship with the mother, unusually close and intimate as it was, had no adverse psychological effect upon the child. It did not in any way thwart his natural development or suppress his individuality. He speaks of his mother only with the greatest of respect and affection. It is from him that we learn of her saintly character.

Shortly after birth, the boy was enrolled as a catechumen: the sign of the cross was made over him and the salt of the catechumens was placed in his mouth, but he was certainly not baptized as an infant. This was no departure from the custom of the times, for even in devout circles baptism was usually deferred until the threshold of maturity. Yet in after years the saint regretted that he had not been baptized as an infant, believing that the efficacy of the rite might have cured the sickness of his soul so much the earlier. Augustine, in fact, became one of the great champions of infant baptism.

As a child he learned to speak both Punic and Latin as native languages. His first formal schooling was in Latin grammar and arithmetic under a master who never spared the rod. His pupil retained a natural aversion to this method all his life. His first

recorded prayer is a plea that this flogging might be ended, a prayer that went unanswered. When, a little later, he began the study of Greek, he was, so he tells us, less successful. He must be accounted one of few students who have not been impressed by Homer, whom he says he could not understand. Perhaps it was the teacher who was at fault. Whatever the cause, he did not drink deep of Hellenic culture, yet this by no means indicates that he was ignorant of it. Much came to him at second hand through the medium of Latin translations. His bent was toward philosophy, not philology.

Though Augustine was naturally so brilliant that his school record would have been outstanding anywhere, out of school he was a healthy boy, delighting in games and pranks, often playing the truant. Those who look in the story of a saint for a childhood without faults, precociously pious and wholly unselfish, will not find this pattern in the boy of Tagaste. Despite the devout character of Monica, he probably had little instruction in Christian doctrine, even though he was a catechumen from infancy. In his day the " Discipline of the Secret " concealed from non-Christians, and even from catechumens until their preparation for baptism, many fundamental truths of the Christian faith, and excluded them from parts of the Mass itself. Yet once, during an illness, the boy showed his awareness of the significance of baptism and eagerly asked for it. His mother seems to have been willing, but his speedy recovery postponed the rite.

When Augustine was about twelve the parents decided to advance the education of their son by sending him to school at Madaura, about twenty

miles south of Tagaste. Here, surrounded by the town's pagan culture, Roman and native, he found no substitute for Monica's Christianity. The education he received, however, must have been the best obtainable in the region at the time.[1] He doubtless mastered Sallust, Cicero and Virgil.

Returning to Tagaste after about four years at Madaura, Augustine spent a year in complete idleness, as his parents were now unable to afford the expense of higher education. He describes this year as spent in sinful pursuits, yet tells specifically only of the boyish theft of some pears. No progress, however, was made. Upon the death of his father about A.D. 370, Augustine was enabled, through the munificence of Romanianus, a wealthy pagan of Tagaste, who was for many years to remain his patron and friend, to enter the rhetorical schools at Carthage and take the training required for the legal profession. The course of instruction, in spite of the name, was not limited to what is now called rhetoric, though that was included, but was more nearly equivalent to present-day liberal education in literature and philosophy.

Residence in Carthage brought enlarged acquaintance with the world and stronger pagan influence to bear. Studies in classical literature, with its double standard of sexual morality, may have been a factor in causing this boy away from home to take a mistress. His later regret for this action caused him to suppress her name but not his guilt. Though she remained faithful to her lover until he dismissed her at Milan,

---

[1] On the possibility that he here made a first contact with neo-Platonism, see G. Papini, *Sant' Agostino* (Firenze, 1930), 37–42; English tr. by L. P. Agnetti (New York, 1930), 38–42.

and bore him a son Adeodatus (" God-given "), she was probably a woman of lower social standing than Augustine, and not even Monica appears ever to have counselled marriage with her.

At Carthage, too, Augustine must have met for the first time, if not earlier at Madaura, the licentiousness of the pagan theatres, which so enticed him by their lubricity that after his conversion to Christianity he became a vigorous opponent of the stage.[1] He soon became known as a brilliant and serious student, not interested in the pranks of the *Eversores*, a student group more given to disturbing the decorum of the classroom than to intellectual pursuits. In his nineteenth year he was first, as he tells us, keenly drawn to the study of philosophy by the reading of the *Hortensius* of Cicero, a work now lost. About the same time he made the acquaintance of certain Manichaeans, followers of the Persian prophet Mani, who lived in the third century of our era. The reason why Augustine fell into this error, he tells us,[2] was that the Manichaeans professed to free men from all error, and to bring them to God through reason alone, without " that terrible principle of authority." This pseudo-intellectual character of the sect, with its twin tenets of rationalism and dualism, thus made a strong appeal to the young man, and he remained under its influence for nine years, an " auditor " or novice who never became one of the " elect " to whom the supposed inner secrets of the Manichaean teaching were revealed. Often he would engage in the polemics of Manichaeism, which

[1] See Welldon's edition of *The City of God*, 2.659–69: Appendix C, " The Church and the Stage."
[2] *De Utilitate Credendi* 1.2.

consisted mainly in negative attack upon their opponents, castigating chiefly the credulity of the Christians and the foolishness of the Jewish scriptures. Neither the Manichaeans with whom he associated nor Augustine himself were close students of the religion that they were attacking. He may have had some slight contact in this period with the Christian church at Carthage, and he did read the Bible without understanding it. Lacking the charismatic gift to comprehend what he read, which he afterwards possessed in such abundance, he soon gave up the practice as a waste of time. He also began the study of Aristotle, but with no better result. Augustine was never strongly influenced by the Stagirite, as his extant works clearly show.[1]

By the year 374 either he had completed the prescribed course in Carthage but decided not to engage at once in the practice of law, or else he failed to complete the training. In any event, he returned to Tagaste as a teacher. As he was now an ardent Manichaean, eagerly preaching a faith of which he did not yet, as a novice, know the inner secrets, if, indeed, there were any, the gulf between him and his mother had greatly widened, for her own Christian faith had grown stronger. She therefore refused him the hospitality of her own home, possibly because to receive him meant also receiving his mistress's son. Her interest in Augustine's welfare and eventual salvation was, however, as deep as ever, and she even begged a certain Bishop[2] to endeavour to convert Augustine. This the Bishop refused to do, convinced that the time was not ripe for such an effort and that Augustine would ultimately discover his own

[1] But cf. *Conf.*, 4.16.28.　[2] Perhaps the Bishop of Tagaste.

error. Among his Manichaean converts at Tagaste were his patron Romanianus and two close friends of later years, Alypius and Honoratus.

As a teacher Augustine probably had no large school, but took only a few pupils for individual instruction. One was Licentius, the young son of Romanianus; another, Alypius, was little younger than Augustine himself, so the teaching doubtless was fitted to the pupil. Among his close Manichaean associates was now an unnamed young friend whom he had known in boyhood. Taken seriously ill, this friend was during his illness, and while unconscious, baptized by Christian rite. Upon the young man's recovery, Augustine began to make fun of this curious baptism of an unconscious man, and was surprised when his friend rebuked him sternly. Such a change of character made a profound impression on Augustine, who could not explain it, and when the new Christian soon afterwards died, Augustine was deeply grieved. In order to escape from the scene of this bereavement, as he tells us,[1] he decided to return to Carthage. Elsewhere he adds[2] that Tagaste offered little chance for advancement. His career as a teacher had apparently not been very successful, and in his native town frequent contact with his mother must have been a constant reminder of the difference between them. So to Carthage he returned in the autumn of 374 and remained there as a teacher for the next eight years, that is, from his twentieth to twenty-eighth year.

Licentius followed him to Carthage and continued his studies under Augustine; so, probably, did Licentius' younger brother, and, after a period of

---

[1] *Confessions* 4.7.12.   [2] *Contra Academicos* 2.3.

estrangement, Alypius. There was also a wealthy youth named Nebridius, much interested in speculative questions. The reputation that Augustine gained at Carthage at this time was long remembered. When he returned to Carthage from Italy fourteen years later, he was met by a former pupil, Eulogius, who told him that some time past he had had a dream in which Augustine had appeared and explained to him obscure passages in the rhetorical works of Cicero.[1] How thoroughly our scholar had at this time mastered his subject matter is shown by his ability, in 410, long after he had ceased to concern himself with profane studies, to pen an extended reply (*Epistle* 118) to a young Greek scholar Dioscurus, who had ventured to ask for assistance in interpreting the philosophy of Cicero.

Like many men of his time, Augustine now displayed an interest in magic, but soon gave it up. For much longer he was impressed by the pseudo-science of astrology. To this period belongs the first work from his pen, a lost poem for which he won the agonistic prize, the proconsul Vindicianus himself crowning him with the garland. Also lost is his first prose work, *On the Beautiful and the Fitting*, written in 380, which, like many another initial effort, created no interest, despite a dedication to the Syrian Hierius, then famous at Rome as a master of Latin eloquence.

Augustine's always lively mind was in this period busy with many philosophical and religious difficulties which he naïvely believed could be answered by his Manichaean associates in Carthage. Yet whenever he sought their assistance, he was put off with the

[1] *De Cura pro Mortuis Gerenda* 13.

promise that when a certain Manichaean bishop, Faustus of Milevis, should come to Carthage, he would be able to provide the answer. The actual arrival of Faustus, long delayed, produced, however, only disillusionment and disappointment, for though Faustus proved to be eloquent and charming, as Augustine remembered when he wrote the *Confessions*, he was not really learned at all, having less comprehension of these problems than Augustine himself. He could give no answer to the fundamental problem of Manichaean dualism which had been pointed out acutely by Nebridius: Why did God not fight with the evil principle? This failure of Manichaeism to answer a crucial problem inherent in its own beliefs doubtless destroyed the hold of the doctrine upon Augustine; but he did not make an open break.

Instead, once again, in the autumn of 383, he decided to transfer the scene of his labours elsewhere, this time to Rome itself. The ostensible motive he gives for the migration was a desire to gain students more tractable than the boisterous young Carthaginians. Moreover, in the capital of the empire new experiences, professional advancement, and contact with greater minds awaited him. It was claimed by hostile contemporaries that fear of legislation restrictive of non-Christians in Africa had provided a motive for the move, but this can hardly have been true, as the legislation was actually enacted after Augustine was in Rome, and he there made no attempt to conceal his non-Christian position, openly associating for some time with Manichaeans.

His mother's reaction to this proposal was at first strong opposition. If he crossed the Mediterranean,

she would again be out of close contact with her son. Failing to dissuade him, she now offered to accompany him to Rome, but, as they were on the point of sailing, he employed a ruse to escape without her. Leaving her to spend a night in prayer at a seaside chapel of St. Cyprian, he told her that he wished to bid farewell to a friend at the port, but instead of returning he sailed away himself, leaving his mother to return in sorrow to Tagaste, where once more she continued to live the life of a pious widow engaged in acts of devotion and works of charity.

Not long after he reached the Eternal City he was seized with a fever and nursed to health by a Manichaean auditor with whom he lived. After his recovery, for about a year he gave instruction in rhetoric at Rome. There is a tradition that the school was in the neighbourhood of Santa Maria in Cosmedin. While the Roman students were less rowdy than those in Africa, they had another and much more serious defect: whenever payment for instruction became due, they would remove in a group to another school, leaving behind them their unpaid obligations. Thus the young teacher was willing to accept an offer from another quarter. When he was in his thirtieth year he learned that the city of Milan had written to the prefect of Rome, asking him to recommend someone for appointment as public teacher of rhetoric in Milan. Augustine was recommended to the prefect, that staunch pagan, Symmachus, and, after a demonstration of his abilities, received the appointment and went to Milan with government transportation provided. Here, at the northern capital, he was engaged for the next two years in his chosen profession and was

financially more secure than he had yet been. With greater repute in the community went association with the first citizens of the city and empire. As official professor of rhetoric in the important northern city, Augustine became well acquainted, to name a few, with the archivist Zenobius, a Platonist; Hermogenianus, a scholar; and Verecundus, a grammarian, who was afterwards to figure prominently in Augustine's life as the owner of the famous villa at Cassiciacum. Augustine knew also the great bishop of Milan, Saint Ambrose, then at the height of his fame, but his acquaintance was hardly intimate. Ambrose was a very busy man, not likely to pay much attention to a new arrival from Africa, particularly one not a Christian and with Manichaeist tendencies. Yet the *Confessions* tell how much our rhetorician admired the rhetoric of the bishop, often listening to his sermons and even visiting his house merely to watch him lost in concentration as he read the Bible.

Among the small group of Africans living in Milan, if not in his own household, at least within his circle, were his beloved friend Alypius, his mother Monica, his brother Navigius, and possibly other relatives, his patron Romanianus, the boy Adeodatus and his mother, and Evodius, a newly baptized Christian from Tagaste.

The disillusionment felt at the encounter with Faustus of Milevis continued to detach Augustine from Manichaeism during the next three years. Two other influences worked to the same end: first, following his reading in Rome of some of Cicero's philosophical essays, he developed a lively interest in academic scepticism, particularly its tenet that

man can know nothing certainly. This undermined the dogmatism of Manichaeist doctrine. Secondly, he had an opportunity, while listening to the biblical exegesis of Saint Ambrose, to discover, as we have seen, that there was another method of interpreting the Scriptures, not literally but spiritually. He saw now that many things in the Bible, hitherto incomprehensible, were at least capable of meaning.

Early in his residence at Milan, an opportunity was offered of marriage to a young woman of suitable social position, and Monica was in favour of this marriage because it seemed likely to cause her wayward son to settle down. The girl was attractive, though not yet old enough for marriage, and Augustine was sufficiently interested in her to come to the point of dismissing, in a manner some have thought callous, his mistress, Adeodatus' mother, who went home to Africa with a promise never to marry another. Augustine, however, soon afterwards took another mistress instead of marrying the young woman as he had planned.

For a time the friends played with the idea of founding a philosophic community in which the members would devote themselves to discoursing on fundamental problems, but this idea never came to fruition, as they could not agree whether or not those who were married should take their wives into the community. History shows that attempts to combine monasticism with family life have been unsuccessful. In 385 he was strongly influenced by the reading of " certain Platonic works," as he calls them, really neo-Platonic, and they helped much to solve for him the problem of evil left unsolved by

Manichaeism. These neo-Platonic writings, whatever they were, opened to Augustine for the first time the possibility of a spiritual realm not provided in the thoroughgoing materialism of the Manichaeists, the Stoics and the Epicureans. These were the only philosophic sects that still flourished among pagans. Then he read again the New Testament, but though he had come a long way from the position of Manichaeism, he was not yet committed to Christian morals.

One day he took his problem to the old priest Simplicianus, who listened in kindly attention but made no attempt to deal with philosophical problems. He simply told Augustine the moving story of the old pagan Victorinus, who, after a life devoted to opposition to the Christian faith, was in old age, at the height of his fame, converted to Christianity, making his profession of faith publicly before all the church at Rome, as Simplicianus himself had witnessed. The effect of this simple story upon Augustine's mind was incalculable, and did much to prepare the way for the ultimate conversion. Augustine burned, as he tells us in the *Confessions*, with the desire to do likewise, but he was now faced, not with a problem of thought, but with a problem of will: " Soon, in a little while, I shall make up my mind, but not immediately." [1]

Then on one never-to-be-forgotten day he heard from his friend Pontitianus, now a Christian, of the life of Saint Anthony of Egypt and of the existence of monasticism in the east, and specifically of two friends of Pontitianus who had decided to become monks after merely reading, in moving circum-

[1] *Confessions* 8.5.10–12.

stances, a life of St. Anthony.[1]   The spiritual struggle
within Augustine was thus brought to a crisis, and in
the heat of emotion, he rushed out of the house into
the garden, followed by Alypius.   There, in anguish
of spirit, struggling to make a decision, he heard
the voice of a child saying " Tolle lege!   Tolle
lege! " (" Take up and read!   Take up and read! "),
and concluding that the voice of the child was the
bearer of a divine message, he turned to the Bible,
where his eye fell first upon Romans 13.13–14:
" Not in revelling and drunkenness, not in debauchery
and licentiousness, not in quarrelling and jealousy.
But put on the Lord Jesus Christ, and make no
provision for the flesh, to gratify its desires."   Having
read these words of St. Paul, Augustine was filled
with peace ; his conversion was effected.[2]

Quickly telling Alypius what he had read, he saw
the latter glancing at the next sentence: " As for
the man who is weak in faith, welcome him, but not
for disputes over opinions."   This Alypius took to
be a message to himself.   Then the two friends went
eagerly to tell the great news to Monica.   While
residing in Milan, Augustine had experienced an
intellectual conversion, resulting in a change in his
method of thinking about immaterial being.   The
scene in the garden produced a second conversion,
this time volitional, the decision to lead a Christian
life ; but he was not yet formally a Christian, and his
Christian education was yet to begin.

An interlude enabled him to make the necessary

---

[1] Translated by Robert T. Meyer, *Ancient Christian Writers*,
No. 10 (Westminster, 1950).
[2] The whole scene in the *Confessions* 8.8–12.19–30, deserves
to be read.

adjustment to his decision. At Cassiciacum, a villa north of Milan, a small group of his friends escaped from the turmoils of the city, partly for recreation, but primarily for philosophical conversations. Besides Augustine himself there were Monica, Adeodatus, Navigius, and two cousins, Lastidianus and Rusticus; two pupils, Licentius and Trygetius; and his friend Alypius. Nebridius was still teaching rhetoric in Milan, and it was through his friendship with Verecundus, the owner of the villa, that the small group were able to enjoy the delights of the countryside. Out of these conversations, carefully recorded by stenographers, came the three earliest of the extant works of Augustine, the dialogues *Against the Academics*, *On the Blessed Life*, and *On Order*, while the two books of the *Soliloquies*, though written later, record the thought of Augustine himself as he meditated on other questions during hours of solitude. The book *On the Immortality of the Soul* was also written before baptism, but in Milan after the return from Cassiciacum.

Augustine, Adeodatus, and Alypius had been preparing for their baptism ever since their names had been handed in at the cathedral at the beginning of Lent, and on the night before Easter, which in 387 came on 25th April, they were baptized by St. Ambrose himself. Soon afterwards Augustine decided to return to Africa and to become there a lay monk in his native town of Tagaste. In this decision he was joined by his friends Alypius and Evodius. Some time during the summer, when the small group of travellers were waiting at Ostia for the ship that was to take them to Africa, Monica became ill of a fever and died after nine days. While ill, she

had with her son the remarkable conversation recorded in the *Confessions*, in which she said:

> "My hope for the world is now fulfilled. There was but one reason why I wished to remain a little longer in this life. I wanted to see you a Catholic Christian before I died. My God has abundantly satisfied my desire, inasmuch as I see you now, in contempt of the happiness of this world, become His servant. What am I doing here?" [1]

The death of Monica caused, however, a change in plan. Instead of going on to Africa, Augustine now returned to Rome, and for the first time was able to become acquainted with the Christians of the Eternal City, doubtless attending services, studying the Bible more intensely, and, above all, as always, spending his time in writing, for Augustine's pen was rarely out of his hand for long. He now composed the great work *On Free Will*; the short work *On the Quantity of the Soul*, and a polemical work *On the Morals of the Catholic Church and of the Manichaeans*, in which begins his long-sustained attack upon his former faith. In this period Augustine learned with interest of a recent unsuccessful attempt on the part of the Manichaeans in Rome to establish a monastic community, for he had decided that some sort of monasticism was the right way of life henceforth for himself.

II

Late in 388, Augustine with Adeodatus, Alypius and Evodius, finally returned to Carthage and thence

---

[1] *Confessions* 9.10.26.

to Tagaste, where he established, in a property formerly that of his father, a lay monastery that continued there for three years before it was transferred to Hippo. In addition to these four, the small group was later augmented by Possidius, afterwards his first biographer. Navigius, his brother, however, married and had a family. Nebridius, on his part, had the responsibility of a mother's care, and died not many years later. The community was, of course, composed solely of laymen. The life they led was a sort of semi-monasticism marking a midpoint, both in time and type, between the philosophical community at Cassiciacum and the full monasticism afterwards practised at Hippo. The regime consisted of manual labour, moderate asceticism with community of possessions, and especially study of the truths of the Catholic faith.

Works ascribed to this period include the commentary *Genesis against the Manichaeans*, devoted to an explanation of the first three chapters of Genesis; a revision of the book *On the Morals of the Catholics and Manichaeans*; the sixth book *On Music*, five books of which had been begun at Milan; *On the Teacher*, a short dialogue with Adeodatus, who died not very long after the return to Tagaste; and *On the True Religion*, the fifth work against the Manichaeans.

Though Augustine's fame as a Christian scholar was growing, he was now careful not to take orders or to visit a place where there was a vacant see. Bishops in those days were usually chosen by the people of the diocese, and there was certainly real danger that, had Augustine appeared anywhere where a bishop had died, the populace might have

seized on the opportunity to elect him their bishop. Thus, when in 391 a minor official at the port town of Hippo Regius, in Punic called Ubbone, near the site of the modern Bône, invited Augustine to visit Hippo to discuss with him the question of entering a monastery, it must have seemed safe enough, for Hippo then had a bishop named Valerius. Valerius, however, was an old man, and though kindly and devout, not very efficient, because, a Greek by birth, he could speak Punic not at all, and could preach in Latin only with difficulty. His church was not strong, and greatly needed the care of a more vigorous bishop. This Valerius himself knew well, and he happened to ask his people for the assistance of a priest just at the moment when Augustine was visiting the town. The people responded quickly by seizing upon Augustine, who was standing in the church, and though Augustine began to weep, Bishop Valerius at once ordained him.

Augustine was at first dismayed and pleaded inadequate knowledge, not only of much that he would need to know, but particularly of the Scriptures, and asked for time to prepare, yet he appears to have begun his priestly duties at Hippo with the end of the Lenten season of 391. In the church at Hippo much needed to be done. The population of the town contained pagans, heretics, and Jews, and the schismatic Donatists in the town were strong. Soon Augustine began to preach. This, though nowadays a normal function for a priest, was in Africa an innovation, since at this time preaching was there regarded as the exclusive province of the bishop. Valerius, as a Greek, was well aware that in the eastern church priests did preach ; and he permitted

Augustine to do the preaching that he himself, owing to his weakness in Latin, could not properly do. As a result of Augustine's successful example, priests began to preach in other dioceses of Africa, even in the presence of their bishops. Moreover, Augustine gradually took over more and more of the work of the diocese, so that it is not too much to say that he was actually a bishop in all but name for four or five years. Thus, as early as 392, we find him writing on terms of equality to Bishop Aurelius of Carthage.[1]

The monastery at Tagaste was now transferred to a garden at Hippo, where former associates at Tagaste were joined by some new men. Of ten whose names are known, all became bishops: Alypius of Tagaste, Evodius of Uzala, Possidius of Calama, Severus of Milevis, Profuturus, who died soon after consecration, of Cirta, where he was succeeded by Fortunatus, Urbanus of Sicca Veneria; Leporius of Carthage; and Novatus of Sitifis. Six of these became bishops before Augustine himself received consecration as coadjutor to Valerius of Hippo. In reality, this monastery proved to be a theological seminary, sending out to the African Church men of ability and insight who caused the Church greatly to flourish. Credit for the success of the monastery belongs, of course, to its founder and leader.

As the Manichaeans were strongly entrenched in Hippo, the erstwhile Manichaean auditor, now a Christian priest, undertook a vigorous campaign against that sect. He addressed to his friend Honoratus, who was still a Manichaean, a work called *On the Value of Believing* and also wrote *On the Two*

[1] *Epist.* 22.

INTRODUCTION

Souls against the Manichaeans. Living in the city was
a prominent Manichaean priest named Fortunatus,
whom a group of Christians, both Catholic and
Donatist, asked Augustine to challenge to a debate.
Reluctant at first to cross swords with so vigorous a
master of dialectic as Augustine, Fortunatus finally
agreed to accept the challenge. The debate was
held in the Baths of Sozius on 28th and 29th of
August, 392. The proceedings were recorded by
stenographers, and are extant as the *Contra
Fortunatum Manichaeum.* In the end Fortunatus,
here confronted with an opponent equally well
informed, was made to admit that he did not know
how to answer Augustine's attack and would have
to consult his superiors. He even agreed to consider
the Catholic position if they could not answer, but
he left Hippo shortly afterwards and never returned.
Out of this dispute came, though written later, the
thirty-three books *Against Faustus the Manichaean.*
A second debate was later held with another Manichaean, Felix, who in 404 came to Hippo to preach,
and once more a record was kept, the *Proceedings
with Felix the Manichaean.* The result was a
disavowal of the Manichaean faith by Felix. Henceforth, Manichaeism was all but dead, though as late
as 421 there was a recrudescence of the movement
in Carthage, that Augustine helped to suppress.

An unusual honour came to Augustine in the
autumn of 393 when he was asked, though only a
priest, to lecture on the creed before a church council
held at Hippo. The lecture is extant in the work
On Faith and the Creed.

Augustine now began his attack upon the
Donatists, who were, as we have stated, powerful

INTRODUCTION

in Hippo. This sect[1] was schismatic, rather than heretical, at least at first, and had originated nearly a century earlier in the claim made by some that those priests who in time of persecution had handed over the sacred books to the persecutors could not perform valid rites, and thus could not hand on to their successors the true Apostolic tradition. The Donatists themselves suffered naturally from schism, breaking up into several offshoots such as the Maximinianists, the Rogatists, and others; but perhaps the worst feature of the sect, and certainly the one that most aroused Augustine's antagonism, was their encouragement, if nothing more, of armed bands of fanatics called Circumcellions, often led by Donatist priests, who used violence in support of their party. Once, for example, a group of Circumcellions, permitted or even encouraged by the Donatist bishop of Calama, one Crispinus, ambushed a party of Catholics, including the Catholic bishop Possidius, robbed them of their animals and possessions, and set fire to a house in which Possidius had taken refuge.

The first work against the Donatists was an unusual composition, the *Psalm against the Donatist Party*, written in the form of an *abecedarius*, and intended to be chanted by the people. A second in the series, now lost, was the *Book Against the Epistle of the Heretic Donatus*, while a third, begun but not finished, was a literal explanation of Genesis, the so-called *De Genesi ad litteram liber imperfectus*. For the past

[1] See G. G. Willis, *Saint Augustine and the Donatist Controversy* (London, 1950), and W. H. C. Frend, *The Donatist Church: A Movement of Protest in Roman North Africa* (Oxford, 1952).

seven years Augustine had been constantly composing answers to queries from many sources, which he now gathered together in a collection of eighty-three such writings (*De Diversis Quaestionibus LXXXIII*).

Bishop Valerius had now grown so old and feeble that he asked permission of the Bishop of Carthage to have Augustine as coadjutor of Hippo. This permission was granted, Augustine being consecrated by Primate Megalius of Numidia either late in 395 or early in 396. The death of Valerius after about a year made Augustine bishop of the diocese in his own right.

The burdens of this episcopate were great. There were the normal administrative responsibilities attached to any bishopric; and the problems of this local diocese, larger [1] than most—it included Fussala,[2] forty miles from Hippo—consumed much time. There was a large church, probably the cathedral, called the Basilica of Peace;[3] and another large church, the Basilica Leontiana, which at this time may have been controlled by Donatists. The Church of the Eight Martyrs was built under Augustine's leadership, and there was the shrine of St. Theognis, the shrine of St. Stephen, the *memoria* of the Twenty Martyrs and others. Besides the cloistered monastery that had

---

[1] Diocesan organization in Africa at this time differed from that now current in that bishops were often consecrated for quite small places. The technical term used for bishop in this period was often *sacerdos* (priest). See H. Pope, *Saint Augustine of Hippo* (Westminster, 1949), p. 39.

[2] Later, in 423, Augustine attempted to erect Fussala as a separate diocese, but the man selected as first bishop proved an unfortunate choice, and the town continued to be subject to Hippo.

[3] On the church buildings in Africa, see Pope, *op. cit.* 66–77.

been transferred from Tagaste at the beginning of Augustine's residence at Hippo, there was soon established in the episcopal residence a second group of priests, who, living a life only semi-monastic, served the city and countryside as pastors. Not long afterwards Augustine introduced a third, still different, type of community after the cenobitic pattern found in certain communities near Milan and Rome. Of this new type there were two communities which at first accepted men from all walks of life, and were less devoted to scholarly pursuits than the others, but they soon developed also into seminaries for the priesthood.

The fame of the Bishop of Hippo was so great, however, that many persons, both in the church and out, sought him out for his advice and counsel. Though Augustine did not neglect the affairs of his own episcopate, he was increasingly called upon to exert a larger influence upon the whole of the African church, travelling many miles to other cities, attending many a council. We know of such attendance in 397, 401, 403, 411, and 416. Then, too, the task of preparing sermons was an enormous burden, for Augustine preached daily, often more than once.[1] How did one in such a position find time for even a single work of scholarship? Yet this man continued throughout his life to be one of the most prolific writers ever known, and his output after reaching the episcopacy far exceeded that which preceded it.

[1] See Thomas C. Lawler's translation of twenty-three of the *Sermons for Christmas and Epiphany, Ancient Christian Writers*, No. 15 (Westminster, 1952). On the sermons of St. Augustine, of which nearly nine hundred authentic examples have survived, besides several hundred that are spurious, see Pope, *op. cit.* 139–94.

INTRODUCTION

If Augustine ever had a vacation it was only when sickness temporarily halted the tremendous drive of a constitution never strong.[1]

An attempt to arrange a conference with Proculeianus, the Donatist Bishop of Hippo, failed; but while on a visit to Cirta to consecrate Profuturus as its bishop, Augustine succeeded in meeting the Donatist bishop of Tubursicum, one Fortunius, though without positive results.

The first important book written by Augustine after becoming bishop was one (*De Diversis Quaestionibus ad Simplicianum*) in which in 397 he discussed various doctrinal problems presented to him by his old friend Simplicianus, who had been so instrumental in his conversion and had now succeeded St. Ambrose as Bishop of Milan. Yet even more important than these were the beginnings of two great works, *On Christian Doctrine* and the famous *Confessions*; though also begun in 397, the latter was not finished until four years later. The purpose of *On Christian Doctrine*, to give assistance in the understanding of Scripture, was remarkable indeed for an author who only five or six years previously had maintained that he did not know the Scriptures sufficiently well to serve as priest. Augustine had obviously been constant in his study of the Bible, despite distractions.

The *Confessions*, in thirteen books, of which the first nine are spiritual autobiography, are at once the best known and the most widely read of all Augustine's works. They are often quoted today,

[1] On Augustine in sickness and in health, see B. Legewie, " Die körperliche Konstitution und die Krankheiten Augustins " (*Miscell. Agostiniana* 2.5–21).

especially the famous line from the opening chapter:
"Thou hast made us for Thyself, and our heart is
restless until it finds rest in Thee." [1] Addressed
directly to God, the *Confessions*, despite their
autobiographical character, are in no sense an
apology for Augustine's own life, but a demonstration
of the effect of divine grace upon him, a cardinal
doctrine in Augustine's theology. Augustine appears
in these pages, not as the saint he is now recognized to
have been, but as the sinner he knew himself to be,
saved by God's grace, not only from the consequence
of those sins, but even from the sins themselves.
Yet, modest as was the aim of the writer, the literary
quality of the work entitles it to a place among the
masterpieces, sacred or profane, of all time, as was
frankly recognized in Augustine's day, and even, it
would seem, by the author himself. The *Confessions*
bring the story of Augustine's life down to the year of
his mother's death, 387, though the book was probably
completed about 400. For his remaining three
decades, perhaps his most productive period, certainly the period in which he reached maturity of
thought, we have nothing comparable.

The closing years of the fourth century were
marked by the beginnings of the correspondence,[2]

---

[1] *Confessions* 1.1.

[2] Separately edited by J. Schmidt as *SS. Eusebii Hieronymi
et Aurelii Augustini Epistulae Mutuae* (*Florilegium Patristicum*,
Vol. 22, Bonn, 1930), the letters also appear in the edition of
St. Augustine's letters in *Corpus Scriptorum Ecclesiasticorum
Latinorum*, Vols. 33, 34, 44 and 57, where they are numbered
in chronological order as 28, 39, 40, 67, 68, 71, 72, 73, 75, 81,
82, 123, 166, 167, 172, 195, 202. Eight are by Augustine, nine
by Jerome. Nos. 28 and 67 are included in J. H. Baxter's *Select
Letters of Saint Augustine* (Loeb Classical Library, 1930). All

soon to develop into a controversy, with St. Jerome, an older contemporary. At this time the fame of Jerome was already well established by his vast linguistic and philological capacity, which no one, certainly not Augustine, was able to rival, and few in any day have been able to equal. Though Jerome was never to rise above the rank of presbyter, he was under the impression, whatever the truth of the matter, that he had just missed election to the papacy in 384. He then had retired to the east and settled in a monastery in Bethlehem, where the remainder of his life was devoted to the task, gigantic for one man, of preparing a new Latin translation of the Old and New Testaments. Jerome had access to copies of all the biblical literature in Hebrew, Greek and Latin, and was competent to handle them efficiently. Yet his character lacked humility, and he had little patience with lesser men who ventured to take issue with him. Moreover, he possessed a fine command of the language of vituperation.

The correspondence was begun with an unfortunate letter of Augustine, which, written about 395, did not reach Jerome as soon as was expected, even allowing for slow methods of communication in those days, It was entrusted to Profuturus, who took it with him as far as Rome and left it there without delivering it, whence it came by accident into the hands of others who furnished Jerome with a garbled account of the contents. While Augustine expressed appreciation

---

seventeen also appear among the letters of St. Jerome in *Corpus Scriptorum Ecclesiasticorum Latinorum*, Vols. 54, 55, 56—see also Vol. 58, p. *cl*. On this correspondence see G. Simard, " La querelle de deux saints, Saint Jérôme et Saint Augustin " (*Revue de l'Université d'Ottawa*, 12.15–38).

of Jerome's genius and recommended that Jerome should continue to follow in his revised translation of the Bible text the method already used in his edition of Job which Augustine knew, proper attention should be paid, he said, to the Septuagint. This was a point on which Jerome, of all persons, needed no instruction. Here Augustine naïvely remarks:

> " I should be incredibly surprised if anything is found at this date in the Hebrew manuscripts that has escaped so many translators possessing expert knowledge of that language. . . . I am more concerned about the later translators [following the time of the Septuagint who] have also left many points that have remained to be unearthed and brought to light after so long. For if these points are obscure, then it is quite credible that you too may go astray in them; if they are clear, it is incredible that they could have gone astray in them."

Annotations should be carefully added so as to justify any new renderings. Thus far, the novice was giving advice to the expert. The letter went on, however, to criticize Jerome's interpretation of Galatians 2.11–14.[1] Jerome had suggested that St. Paul was guilty of falsehood (*a perniciosa simulatione*) in condemning St. Peter's attitude towards Jewish customs, and this suggestion, so Augustine feared, would cause ordinary readers to suppose that, if one biblical character was capable of falsehood, another, or perhaps any other, might be subject to the same suspicion.

Despite the effort made in the closing lines to

[1] See J. H. Baxter's note on this letter in his edition of the letters (Loeb Classical Library), pp. 60 f.

soften the sting of the criticism, the letter, even when read, was bound to antagonize Jerome. Learning of it, as he did, only at second hand, and in such a way as to make him suspect that Augustine had sent an attack upon him to Rome, he was even more provoked. The addressee nevertheless did not reply to the criticisms in the short note which he wrote to Augustine in 396–7. Thereupon Augustine wrote again and repeated the criticism of Jerome's view of the passage in Galatians, to which he added some adverse remarks on Jerome's work which was then called the *Epitaphium*, now the *De Viris Illustribus*. The effect may be imagined. Further letters were sent to Bethlehem, including a denial that Augustine had written a book against Jerome and sent it to Rome; but Jerome was by this time openly hostile and wrote a sharp retort, in which he advised Augustine to mind his own business, ending with a veiled threat. The unfortunate controversy continued for some years, Augustine always maintaining his composure but persisting in his position. Yet, in 415–16, Jerome was able to see that further controversy was likely to prove a scandal in the Church, and wrote to Augustine a letter full of forbearance and understanding. Henceforth, there was no further controversy between the two.

About the time when the *Confessions* was completed in 400 or 401, Augustine began writing another important work, *On the Trinity*, in fifteen books, but this was not completed for sixteen years.[1] Its

[1] For a discussion of this work and its significance for the study of Augustine's mature mind, see Vernon J. Bourke, *Augustine's Quest of Wisdom* (Milwaukee, 1944), 201–23, and the works cited there.

composition was interrupted by the theft of the unfinished manuscript of some of the earlier books. These were then surreptitiously issued in a form not satisfactory to Augustine.

In 400 also appeared the short work, *The First Catechetical Instruction*,[1] four books, *On the Agreement of the Evangelists*, and one book, *On the Work of the Monks*, all of value to the parish priest. To the same period belong two other works of polemical nature. The first, *Against Faustus the Manichaean*, is in thirty-three books, containing a rejoinder, item by item, to a fictitious dialogue attacking Christianity and defending Manichaeism, the work of Faustus. Donatism was dealt with in the first of two books, *Against the Letters of Petilianus*, an answer to a scurrilous attack on Christianity addressed to the Donatist clergy, of which Augustine had then obtained only a part. Augustine's work naturally came to the notice of Petilianus, who replied, alleging falsely that Augustine had actually been a priest of the Manichaean sect, that he had been condemned in a Manichaean trial some years before, and that there had been irregularities in his consecration as Bishop of Hippo. This provoked a second book, *Against the Letters of Petilianus*, in 401–2, and a year later still a third.

In the next years Augustine's attention was directed to the difficulties of the Donatist church,[2] which were causing it to split, though it claimed to be

---

[1] See J. P. Christopher, *S. Aurelii Augustini Hipponiensis episcopi de catechizandis rudibus liber unus*, tr. with introduction and commentary (Washington, 1926), and the same scholar's later translation in *Ancient Christian Writers*, No. 2 (Westminster, 1946).

[2] See above, p. xxviii, n. 1.

the one true church, into schismatic bodies, one led by Primianus, Donatist primate of Carthage after 392, and another led by Maximianus. A certain Cresconius, a grammarian of the neighbourhood of Carthage, had about 401 written an open *Letter to Augustine* in which he attempted to defend Petilianus and the Donatist church. Augustine's reply fills the four books *Against Cresconius the Grammarian of the Party of Donatus*, written about 405–6. The first three attempt to rebut Donatist claims on the basis of Cresconius' own position, namely, that of a scholar trained in the liberal arts, while the second refutation in the fourth book deals with the history of the schism.

Up to this point Augustine appears to have believed that it might be possible, or at least that an attempt should be made, to come to some sort of amicable agreement with the Donatists that would end the schism without resort to an appeal to the civil power, but the Donatist bishops, never confident of their ability to best Augustine in argument, were wary of getting into any conference in which their party might come off worst. In 404, however, the ninth Council of Carthage, composed of Catholic bishops, requested the intervention of the Emperor Honorius, and he responded with an edict dated 12th February, 405, in which the Donatists were at last condemned by the Roman state. Heretofore they had been religious schismatics or mild heretics, now they were outlaws.

For the most part Augustine's ministry had been up to now directed primarily against the Manichaeists and the Donatists, but now for a time he was to be concerned with opposition from the pagans, who belonged as a rule in this period to the rural areas. When, in 399, laws had been enacted against pagan

idolatry and temples had been closed, some were re-dedicated to Christian use, among them the temple of the Virgo Caelestis at Carthage. Augustine had preached a sermon to the Catholics at Carthage in which he warned them not to resort to violence like the Donatist Circumcellions. In 407 the Roman Government enacted new laws further restricting the worship of the pagan gods and the use of pagan temples in Africa. The civil authorities were commanded to enforce these laws, and the bishops were directed to report local infractions of the laws. In 408 pagans made a violent attack upon the Christians at Calama, and the Bishop Possidius for a second time barely escaped with his life, having taken refuge in a secret hiding-place so close to his pursuers that he was able to overhear their conversation. Moreover, several Christians were killed and much property was damaged or destroyed. Augustine went to Calama to see conditions there for himself. Though he actually met with the leaders of the pagan party, he concluded that the only recourse the Christians now had was to allow the civil authorities to deprive the pagans of the means of continuing this attack, though he did not favour executing or imprisoning the culprits or removing their means of support.

It would appear that Augustine had, in view of the growing unpopularity of the Donatists, begun to look for aid to the civil authorities in combating the schism.[1] To the years 407–10 belongs a well-known letter (No. 93) addressed to Vincentius, the Rogatist

[1] On the whole subject of Augustine's attitude toward the use of force in religious controversies see Pope, *op. cit.* 299–361 (see p. xxix).

bishop who had long been in schism from the parent Donatist church of Parmenianus. Vincentius had complained to Augustine about his use of the secular power. In this long letter Augustine admits that the Rogatists were rather better than most of the other Donatists and that had all the Donatists been of this party, the use of the civil power to subdue them might not have been necessary. Moreover, though Augustine himself had been inclined not to use it, the decision among his brother bishops had been against him in this matter, and in order to preserve harmony among the bishops, he had acceded to their views. As a result, many simple Donatists had been compelled to leave their church and become Catholics. Indeed, the entire Donatist population of Hippo had done so.

The Donatists were not convinced by this line of reasoning, and renewed the violence of the Circumcellions. Near Hippo in 409 there had been an attack by Circumcellions, who threw lime and vinegar in the eyes of the priests, set fire to Christian homes and destroyed properties. The Edict of Toleration of the year 409 did not lessen the boldness of the Donatists, but rather set them on fire, with the result that this edict was cancelled in August, 410, and Honorius ordered the Donatist bishops to attend a meeting with the Catholics under the presidency of the tribune, Marcellinus. This was held in June, 411.

The Bishop of Hippo was one of the seven Catholic spokesmen at this conference and doubtless assumed the leading role. When the Donatist leaders blamed the Catholics for having appealed to the Emperor in a religious matter, they were at once confronted with

a notarized copy of the request for a conference that the Donatists had sent to the Emperor in 406. The Donatists had appealed when it seemed to be to their advantage.

A second error by the Donatists was to demand that a long letter written by them in reply to the Catholic request for the conference be read in full. When this was done, it afforded Augustine an opportunity to discuss the doctrinal and historical issues so introduced, though the Donatists had not wished such a discussion. The Catholic speakers were thus able to cite both Catholic and Donatist writers to prove that the followers of Caecilian, whose consecration as bishop had originated the schism, were not *traditores* but historically and doctrinally the heirs of the original teaching of the Apostolic Church.

After this demonstration Marcellinus drew up his decision, taking care to point out to the Donatists that he was not serving in a judicial capacity but as a sort of chairman of a fact-finding commission. On 26th June he published the proceedings of the conference, concluding that the Donatists were subject to the laws against heretics, and must hence-forth submit to the Edict of Union. An imperial edict against them was issued in the following January.

Henceforth, Donatism had apparently lost its power, though for a time the menace of the Circum-cellions remained, and in September, 413, the Donatists were able to trump up charges of a political nature which resulted in the execution of Marcellinus himself. Here and there Donatism continued to exist for a time. Emeritus returned to his diocese of Caesarea, but his churches were taken from him, and

xl

for a time he had to hide outside the city, though later when he returned he was not molested. In 418 while on a visit to Caesarea, Augustine met him in the streets, and invited him to the cathedral; but despite his hearing Augustine preach twice in that city and his being urged to make his peace with the church, he was never converted.

The suppression of this schism, largely through Augustine's efforts, solved one problem for him. It had occupied most of his attention for the past several years and had largely prevented him from writing other than anti-Donatist polemical works. This controversy contributed little to doctrinal clarification, as the point at issue was schism, rather than heresy.

Yet though Donatism was now vanquished [1] and henceforth needed no great attention, there arose at about the same time a new and serious danger to the peace of the African church in the heresy of Pelagianism. Its founder was a monk named Pelagius, possibly born in Britain, who became well and favourably known in Rome and Sicily in the years 408–11. With a follower named Caelestius he came to Africa in 410, where, though he visited Carthage, he failed to make Augustine's acquaintance. The feature of Pelagius' doctrine that ran counter to theocentric Christian teaching and caused him to be recognized as a heresiarch was his doctrine of free will. According to him, man is naturally capable of willing to do good. Salvation is achieved by man's own desire without the help of divine grace.

---

[1] Gaudentius, the Donatist bishop of Thamugadi, managed as late as 420 to revive Donatism, and drew forth two books by Augustine against him.

The fall of Adam made no change in the status of the human race, and consequently there is no absolute need for baptism. God's grace makes virtuous life easier, but is not necessary to salvation. Redemption by Christ is merely a sign of man's adoption by God. This teaching was recognized at once by the African bishops as unorthodox, and Caelestius was excommunicated by a Council of Carthage in 411. Pelagius himself escaped excommunication at the same time only because he had already departed for Palestine.

Augustine became involved in this affair because in order to prove the orthodoxy of his own views Pelagius had taken from Augustine's treatise *On Free Will* certain passages which, out of context and interpreted by Pelagius, were used to corroborate his views. Such a misinterpretation of Augustine's teaching naturally brought forth a new book from his pen, *On the Merits of Sinners and Forgiveness and on the Baptism of Infants*. In this he states the Catholic teaching on the fall of man and the part played by baptism in restoring the soul, even the soul of a child, and categorically asserts the truth of the doctrine of original sin in face of the Pelagian doctrine of the sinlessness of children. Since Marcellinus, to whom the work was addressed, had difficulty in understanding certain passages, which implied that, though no man is without sin, there might be through divine grace a sinless man, Augustine wrote a new work in three books *On the Spirit and the Letter*, in which he distinguishes between exterior grace (the letter of the law) and interior grace (the spirit of the law).

At this time, as a result of the sack of Rome by the Goths in 410, a number of wealthy and noble

refugees, including a number of women of high rank and wealth, had migrated to Africa. Some of these were amateur theologians, and were in correspondence with Pelagians in the east, if not with Pelagius himself. Augustine, learning of this, saw the need of a fundamental treatise against Pelagius, and produced one in 415 with the title, *On Nature and Grace against Pelagius*.

Similar considerations may have led Augustine to begin *The City of God* soon afterwards, but it will be better to postpone the discussion of this work until a later section.

After the composition of *The City of God* was begun, Augustine acquired a new pupil, the young Spanish priest Paulus Orosius, a pious and intelligent young man. When he had been with Augustine for about a year, the latter sent him to study with St. Jerome, and with him, two important letters (nos. 166–7), really small treatises, one *On the Origin of the Human Soul* and the other *On an Opinion of Saint James*, both part of the anti-Pelagian polemic. Arrived in the east, Orosius himself set about writing a work against Pelagianism for the use of the eastern bishops at the Council of Diospolis. Actually that council all but absolved Pelagius of any heresy. Orosius was soon back in the west and set about writing what he doubtless intended, with the rash confidence of youth, to be a companion piece for *The City of God*. This was his ambitious but rather feeble work, the *Seven Books of Histories against the Pagans*, a summary of universal history completed in too short a time and with too little genius to be of great value.

Yet Pelagianism was still a serious threat. Two

councils in 416 considered this heresy. One in
Carthage, with sixty-nine bishops, of whom Augustine
was not one, reaffirmed the condemnation of 411
and sent to Pope Innocent I a letter exposing the
errors of Pelagius. The other, a provincial council
at Milevis, at which Augustine was one of sixty-one
bishops, also addressed a similar condemnation of
Pelagius to the pope. Later in the same year a
new letter was drawn up, probably written by
Augustine, as it was signed by him and his four
friends, Bishops Aurelius, Alypius, Evodius, and
Possidius. Pope Innocent confirmed the condemnation in February, 417, but this did not end
the anti-Pelagian controversy. Augustine wrote to
Bishop John of Jerusalem, asking for a copy of the
proceedings of the Council of Diospolis that had all
but exculpated Pelagius, and when these proceedings
finally arrived, they occasioned a new work, the
Letter to Aurelius about the Deeds of Pelagius, in which
Augustine reviewed the work of the unfortunate
council. Pelagius had been able to deceive Bishop
John, whose friend he was, by disavowing that part
of his teaching associated with Caelestius and
renouncing the errors condemned at the Carthaginian
Council of 411. At this moment Pope Innocent died.
His successor, Zosimus, who had received a *Libellus
Fidei* from Pelagius and was able to hear from his
own lips Caelestius's defence in Rome, gave the
Carthaginian bishops two months in which to repeat
their charges. The document in which they did this
is no longer extant. On Sunday, 23rd September,
417, Augustine preached at Carthage an anti-Pelagian
sermon in which he announced the papal condemnation of the heresy. It was in this sermon that he

made the remarkable statement, " The case is ended ; would that the error were as speedily ended." This has given rise to the saying popularly attributed to Augustine : " Rome has spoken ; the case is ended."

Pope Zosimus, however, appears not to have changed his position in regard to Caelestius, and the case was not in fact ended. Thereupon, a plenary council of Africa drew up nine canons embodying their judgement on the existence of original sin, the necessity of divine grace, and the question of the sinlessness of man. About this time the Emperor Honorius decreed that Pelagianism was an impious doctrine and banished its two chief adherents from Rome, whereupon the pope also condemned them in a letter to all bishops and in a special letter to the African hierarchy. Now the case was really ended. Even so, Augustine admitted to the people of Carthage that he hardly ever preached a sermon in which he did not affirm the Catholic position that men could be saved only by divine grace, that this grace came not as a reward for their own merits but as God's free gift. Finally, since many in Africa were still confused on the point, he wrote a further work against Pelagius and Caelestius, *On the Grace of Christ and on Original Sin*, addressed to the noble friends Albina, Pinianus and Melania, who were refugees from Rome.

In 420 one more work in the anti-Pelagian polemic was composed, six books *Against Julian, Defender of the Pelagian Heresy*. Though these books contained a detailed refutation of Julian's heresy, that energetic antagonist replied in eight books, which, though written some years before, did not reach Augustine until 428. The old man, now seventy-four years of

age, began still another reply, which was left unfinished when he died.

In the same period we find Augustine engaged in a short polemic against a minor heresy started by Priscillian, a Spanish bishop of the preceding century. Orosius had prepared an outline of the Priscillianist heresy (his *Commonitory on the Error of the Priscillianists*) and Augustine produced for Orosius his *Against the Priscillianists and Followers of Origen* in the same year (415). Priscillian's views appear to have included a denial of the full distinction of the three persons of the Trinity and an affirmation of the Manichaean doctrine of the dualism of good and evil.

Despite the great amount of writing which he completed about the year 415 on the Pelagian heresy, in this same period Augustine found time to continue his study of the Bible, preparing many of the famous *Enarrations on the Psalms*. These were not formal commentaries on the Psalter but either sermons actually delivered (119 of these) or expository notes forming the basis for sermons probably not delivered (eighty-six of these). When we remember that the bulk of the *Enarrations* surpasses that of the twenty-two books of *The City of God*, we must marvel at the amount of labour involved. He also found time to write 124 *Tractates on The Gospel of John*, in bulk about a fourth as large as the *Enarrations*. A shorter work of the same period and type was *On John's Epistle to the Parthians*.

An important event of the summer of 418 was Augustine's visit to Caesarea in Mauretania with several other bishops to transact business at the command of Pope Zosimus. While there Augustine witnessed a barbarous event known as the *caterva*, in

which each year the inhabitants of Caesarea engaged. For a number of days the populace, divided into two parties, would pelt each other with stones, endeavouring to kill as many as possible. To combat this unchristian activity, Augustine used his most effective arm, a sermon, in which he not only roused the populace to great applause but also brought them to tears. Eight years later he was able to report that no *caterva* had been held at Caesarea since the delivery of that sermon.

About this time a series of natural calamities roused in many persons a dread that these were portents forecasting the end of the world. In order to calm the souls of such persons Augustine wrote a letter (No. 199) in which he reviewed the biblical teaching on the end of the world and the second coming of Christ, and sent it to Bishop Hesychius of Salonas in Africa, who had asked help in this subject.

To these late years belongs a short but very popular work known by the unrevealing title of *The Manual (Enchiridion)*, an exposition of Augustine's view on the theological basis of Christian piety.

As the long life of the Bishop of Hippo drew to a close, he demonstrated that, aged as he was, he could still learn from the experience of others. In the summer of 426 the Bishop of Milevis died. He had before his death privately told his priests of his choice as successor, but his failure to make the choice public led, after his death, to a misunderstanding among the people. In order to avoid a similar occurrence in his own case, Augustine determined to name his own successor publicly, which he did on 26th September, A.D. 426, four years before his death. The scene was the Basilica of Peace in Hippo, and

the venerable bishop was joined by Bishops Religianus and Martinianus, accompanied by the priests Saturninus, Leporius, Barnabas, Fortunatianus, Rusticus, Lazarus, and Eraclius. The scene is recorded in an account now preserved as *Epistle* 213. The bishop reminded his flock how he came to Hippo as a young man and had grown old in the service of the diocese. He spoke of the difficulties at Milevis and his wish to obviate any such difficulty at Hippo. He therefore named as his successor the priest Eraclius, still a young man, not long ordained, and asked also that Eraclius should be joined with him at once in bearing some of the burdens of the episcopate, so that the hope that Augustine had cherished at the beginning of his episcopate of having some time free for study might now in life be granted him. The people shouted their assent to both proposals and gave thanks to God and Christ.

Yet if the old bishop now thought that he would at last have more leisure, he was mistaken. Soon he became involved in settling a controversy among the monks of Hadrumetum, who had found there a copy of *Epistle* 194 addressed to that Sixtus who afterwards became Pope Sixtus III. Some of these monks did not understand the Augustinian teaching on grace and predestination, and soon the monastery was divided into two hostile camps. To settle these differences the bishop now composed still another work, *On Grace and Freedom of Choice*, and characteristically, not long after, still another, *On Punishment and Grace*. These works form part of the literature of what in modern times has been called the Semipelagian controversy.

By 427 Augustine was engaged in a task planned

at least fifteen years earlier. He believed that there was need for a revision of his works in a special treatise, " so that men will see that I am not one of those people who try to defend everything they have written." [1] This work now fills two books of *Retractations*,[2] in which he lists all his works, apart from letters [3] and sermons.[4] The number comes to two hundred and thirty-two books, discussed approximately in the order of composition. The letters and sermons were to have been treated in a third book, but this was never written.

The closing years of Augustine were overshadowed by the breakdown of Roman rule in Africa. For many years Boniface, the Count of Africa, had been first the civil administrator and then the military commander. Following the death of his first wife, who had been a Catholic, Boniface went to Spain, where he married an Arian wife, the daughter of a Vandal noble. He also was reported to be maintaining concubines, a sin sharply rebuked by Augustine. Along with the moral deterioration of the ruler, a disintegration of his military power took place. This caused the Empress Placidia, ruling as regent for her son Valentinian, to recall him, but Boniface ignored the command, and to gain support invited the Vandals in Spain to send him aid. When, in May, 429, Genseric arrived in Africa with his horde of Vandals, they proved to have come not to help Boniface but to conquer in their own interest.

---

[1] *Epistle* 143.

[2] The Latin title contains, of course, no suggestion of the English word *retraction*.

[3] On the letters of St. Augustine, see Pope, *op. cit.* 195–227.

[4] On the sermons, see Pope, *op. cit.* 139–94 (see p. xxix).

Their progress across North Africa was characterized by the kind of destruction that has since been known as vandalism. Soon Count Darius, sent from Italy, succeeded in making peace between Boniface and the Empress and in stopping for a time the advance of the Vandals, but early in 430 Boniface, once more the Roman commander, fought his erstwhile friends the Vandals and lost. He took refuge within the fortifications of Hippo. This led to a long siege of the city beginning in May.

Despite the troubles of the times, Augustine had serenely continued his normal life in Hippo. In 427 he had composed the *Mirror of Scripture*, a compendium of texts from the Bible for the use of those unable to read the whole. In the same year came another request, this time from a Carthaginian deacon with the characteristically African name of Quodvultdeus, asking for a brief treatise on all the heresies with a simple refutation for each. With his usual zeal for writing, Augustine in the next year sent him a *Book on Heresies*, listing eighty-eight, but of these only three, Manichaeism, Donatism, and Pelagianism, are described from first-hand experience. His last complete work was a single book now preserved as two, *On Predestination of the Saints* and *On the Gift of Perseverance*. These were written in response to letters (Nos. 225–6) from Prosper and Hilary of Gaul, who reported to Augustine that among the clergy of southern Gaul there were those who, in the estimation of the correspondents, retained traces of Pelagianism, that is, the views now called Semipelagianism.

Augustine made one last attempt to debate with an opponent of orthodox Christianity, this time an

Arian bishop named Maximinus who had come to
Africa with an army of Goths sent to subdue Boniface.
This debate was to be on the Trinity, the principal
subject of disagreement between the Arians and the
Catholics. Maximinus consumed the first day in
quoting long passages of Scripture, then departed
for Carthage, where he reported that he had
vanquished Augustine in debate. Aged as he was,
Augustine could not allow an opponent to have the
last word, so he wrote out an account of the discussion
(*Conference with the Arian bishop Maximinus*), and
then wrote a separate refutation (*Against Maximinus
the Heretic*).

Despite the risk of remaining in Africa, the Bishop
of Hippo believed strongly that his place was with
his people, not in refuge far from them. Bishop
Honoratus of Thiaba, whose diocese in western
Africa was more exposed to the Vandals than
Augustine's, sent him a letter asking whether he
might leave his see before the advancing invaders.
In his reply Augustine took no dogmatic position
but stated his view that the clergy should not desert
their churches and people merely to preserve their
lives. He held to this principle when not long after
he had to make the same decision himself. During
the siege he remained with his church, and was host
to several other bishops, and though frail, kept the
use of his faculties to the end. He prayed constantly
for the deliverance of his people, but if this was not in
accordance with divine will, he asked God to give them
strength to bear up, or to take him out of this world.

In August he was struck down by a fever and
confined to his bed. On the wall facing the bed was
hung a copy of the penitential psalms, which he

recited with tears. For the last ten days he spent his entire time alone and in prayer, seen only by the physician and by those who brought food. In this state he was visited by a man who came to him asking to be cured of illness. Augustine's mind was still active. He pointed out that if he had any such power, he would use it to cure himself. Yet when the man persisted, Augustine did lay hands on him, and it is reported that he was cured.

Death came on the 28th of August, A.D. 430, in the presence of Possidius who had been his friend and a fellow bishop for many years and who afterwards wrote the first biography. As Possidius says, he made no will, because God's poor man had nothing to bequeath.

The populace not long after left the city, and the Vandals a little later burned it, leaving only the cathedral and the library of Augustine untouched. His first place of burial is unknown, but in the next century the remains are said to have been taken to Sardinia, whence in the eighth century they were once more removed to Pavia by Luitprand, the Lombard king. The remains are now exhibited under the high altar of the Church of San Pietro in Ciel d'Oro at Pavia.

The destructive forces let loose in North Africa shortly before Augustine's death and the conquest of the region by Islam two centuries later put an end to the flourishing Christian communities that Augustine did so much to strengthen. Though the results of his pastoral labours were thus soon erased, the fortunate preservation of his library at Hippo during the time of troubles, and above all—except for a few unimportant works now lost, some of them

in Augustine's lifetime—of the corpus of his own writings in it, and their subsequent transmission to later times, have given him an influence throughout the rest of Christendom that has never ceased. Of all the fathers of the African church, he has had most to do with the development of mediaeval and modern thought. Indeed, it has been said that the primary achievement of *The City of God* has been to show that temporal administration must be carried on under moral law.[1]

No portrait of our saint which was taken from life has survived. There is, however, a fresco now preserved below the chapel called " Sancta Sanctorum " in the Lateran Palace at Rome,[2] which depicts some saint not named. It has been thought that the elegiac distich inscribed beneath the fresco best applies to Augustine :

Diversi diversa patres sed hic omnia dixit
Romano eloquio mystica [s]sensa tonans.

" Various doctrines are expounded by various fathers, but all of them by this one, who eloquently in Latin thundered forth the hidden meanings."

[1] A reviewer in *The Times Literary Supplement* for 17th September, 1954 (pp. xxxii–xxxiv) heads his discussion of Reinhold Niebuhr's latest book, *Christian Realism and Political Problems*, with " The Two Cities," and informs us that Niebuhr examines Augustine's " doctrine very closely and his criticism of the Augustinian conception of love deserves careful study." Burleigh had already pointed out that Niebuhr's earlier work, *The Nature and Destiny of Man*, shows close correspondence in tone and function with *The City of God*.

[2] J. Wilpert, *Römische Mosaiken und Wandmalereien der kirchlichen Bauten* (Freiburg i. Br., 1916) 1.149 ff.; 2, pl. 140; *Miscellanea Agostiniana* (1931) 2.1–3.

What is certain is that, since the portrait has been estimated to belong to the sixth century, or possibly even to the fifth, this is certainly the oldest portrait of our saint, if it be he, though it is not likely to have been taken from life.

III

In the foregoing sections we have sketched the life of Saint Augustine in detail because we wished to show that *The City of God* is in no sense a special creation of its author's genius, but is rather a characteristic part of his achievement, product of his learning, his faith and his attitude, and that it came into being in precisely the same way and for the same purpose as his other works.   He was a man ever ready to prepare, however busy he might be, not only for his flock but also for sheep outside the fold, all sorts of monographs desired by acquaintances to help them solve the problems of their thought; and this work makes no exception to the rule.

Composed in the thirteen years from 413 to 426, it is the flower of the mature thought of Augustine, who was about fifty-nine years old when he began it and seventy-two when the arduous task was finally completed.   The hours he could devote to it were those few that could be snatched from his busy days as bishop.   To him came no grant in aid from a great foundation to provide the leisure that is now thought requisite to scholarly creation.   If he had help at all from others, it was but the stenographic assistance of his secretaries.   The greatly extended period of composition, the publication of the work in parts as it progressed, and the pressure of many other literary interests crowding in upon the author are enough to

liv

explain the frequent repetitions, long digressions and promises of future treatment never quite fulfilled.

Let no one expect here a summary book by book of the argument. Those who cannot spare the time to read the whole will find a summary in Rickaby's outline,[1] or a briefer one in the mediaeval chapter headings retained in the translation.

Nor have we any intention of attempting here an essay on the thought or even the significance of *The City of God*. We are content to refer our readers to the bibliography appended, which cites many such available in print. Rather our purpose is to provide the reader with material for the criticism of the work that cannot be obtained from its own pages.

Most critics have praised the work, but there are a few dissentient voices. One [2] regrets that the book would exercise but little influence on the spirit of the pagan world. Another admits that the variety of subjects introduced makes pleasant reading, but maintains that the book asks useless questions and adduces reasons which would satisfy only those already convinced. A third would have it that it is a confused mass of excellent material, but that the gold is still in ingots. To Figgis [3] the two cities are vague and ill-defined in thought and imagination, and the whole book is sketchy and incomplete. Gibbon [4] complains, as Gibbon is fond of doing, that

[1] J. Rickaby, *St. Augustine's City of God : A View of its Contents* (New York, 1925).

[2] These complaints are noted in Welldon's introduction (l.xii f.).

[3] J. N. Figgis, *The Political Aspects of St. Augustine's City of God* (London, 1921), pp. 38 f.

[4] *Decline and Fall of the Roman Empire*, Ch. 28.

the author's learning is too frequently borrowed and his reasoning too often his own, but surely it is the business of the scholar both to borrow from others and to apply his own reasoning powers. Even Gibbon would admit that the whole work claims the merit of a magnificent design, vigorously and not unskilfully executed. To Burleigh [1] the work is often tedious, and who will deny it? Most careful readers would admit that these criticisms are well directed, yet they fail to do justice to the brilliance frequently apparent. The merits of the book far outweigh its defects. Its influence upon the men of its own day was doubtless great, but far less than that upon succeeding generations. It has become a classic, and is still read today, though less than formerly. The crisis of our times is not unlike that in which Augustine wrote, and this should add to its interest for us.

However great the genius of an author, the question of his sources is relevant. In this connection it has been pointed out [2] that the concept of an ideal society is at least as old as the Pythagoreans, but we have our doubts whether Augustine knew more about that sect than we, and are confident that he drew small stimulation, if any, from so tenuous a source. Philosopher as he was, he naturally knew of Plato's great *Republic*; he quotes from it, and, in fact, praises its author more than once, though he probably had read the work only in some Latin version. *The Republic* and *The City of God*, to be sure, have some points of likeness. Moreover, Plato actually uses

---

[1] John H. S. Burleigh, *The City of God: A Study of St. Augustine's Philosophy* (London, 1949), p. 29; see also p. 101.
[2] Vernon J. Bourke, *Augustine's Quest of Wisdom* (Milwaukee, 1945), p. 183.

the concept of " city of God," though not the phrase.[1]
Yet despite the fact that there are these likenesses
between the two works, it is hardly true to say,
without qualification, as a major scholar [2] of our time
has said, that Augustine took Plato's *Republic* and
Christianized it into his *City of God*. A small amount
of reflection on the differences between the two works
will show that these are crucial. The point of view
is different, the technique, the solution to the problem.
The Republic is the greatest and best known of all
treatments of the " ideal commonwealth " preserved
in ancient literature. In any discussion of utopias [3]
The City of God would find a place, but it is not a
typical example of the genre. It does not represent
Augustine's dream of what an ideal society would be,
were it possible to banish all evils from this world in
some perfect constitution. It offers, in fact, no
model form of government. For Augustine the City
of God is no unattainable ideal, but a living reality
created by God Himself, which exists now as an alien
in this terrestrial life, but will later triumph and
endure forever.

We also find the concept of the City of God in
Stoicism.[4] Indeed, the phrase " dear city of Zeus "
occurs in Marcus Aurelius' *Meditations* (4.23).

[1] *Republic* 592 B; *Laws* 713 A and 713 E.

[2] Werner Jaeger, *Paedeia* (New York, 1943), 2.77.

[3] To make a full list would be an endless task, but the first
extant example in European literature is probably the story
of the isle of the Phaeacians in Homer's *Odyssey*, Books 6–8.
Cloud Cuckoo Town in Aristophanes' *Birds* treats the theme
satirically. The greatest modern example of the genre is
More's *Utopia*.

[4] Clement of Alexandria, *Strom.* 4.26.172.2 f.; also Cicero,
De Leg. 1.23; Seneca, *De otio* 4.1.

Augustine was not ignorant of the basic tenets of Stoicism. In the writings of the eclectic philosopher, Posidonius of Apamea, on whose capacious shoulders the scholars of our day are wont to place all sorts of burdens, there was, it is said, a crude description of the city of the world contrasted with the residence of God; and it is certain that Augustine knew of Posidonius. The idea may also have been derived from either Plotinus or Porphyry, both well known to Augustine, for he often cites them in *The City of God*. Another possible source that has been suggested is the work of the Donatist Tyconius,[1] who wrote a now lost commentary on the Apocalypse, in which he contrasted the *civitas Diaboli* with the *civitas Dei*. Here once again we have a source with which Augustine was doubtless well acquainted, for he devotes a section of *On Christian Doctrine* (3.30–7) to a refutation of Tyconius. These examples serve principally to show that the concept of a city of God was current in the philosophical circles of Augustine's day.

The idea is also biblical. The Old Testament has many references to the city of Jerusalem where it may be interpreted as a figure of the celestial society.[2] The Kingdom of Heaven appears often in the Gospels, and though the idea here is not quite the same, Augustine may have been influenced by it. Of Christian writers St. Paul was first to use the figure. In Acts 23.1 he says: " I have been a citizen in all good conscience up to this day," though the flavour

---

[1] T. Hahn, " Tyconius-Studien " (*Stud. z. Gesch. d. Theol. u. d. Kirche* 6.2 [Leipzig, 1900]), pp. 25, 29.

[2] Psalms 87.3, also 46.4, 48.1. See also Hebrews 11.10, 16; 12.22; 13.14; Revelation 3.12; 21.2.

of the phrase is lost in the English versions which
have instead " I have lived."[1] The same verb
appears in the same sense in Philippians 1.27, where
it is again weakly translated in the versions. See
also the same epistle (3.20-1): " But our commonwealth is in heaven, and from it we await a Saviour,
the Lord Jesus Christ, who will change our lowly
body to be like His glorious body, by the power which
enables Him even to subject all things to Himself."
In Ephesians 2.19-21 he says again: " So then you
are no longer strangers and sojourners, but you are
fellow citizens with the saints and members of the
household of God, built upon the foundation of the
apostles and prophets, Christ Jesus Himself being the
chief cornerstone, in whom the whole structure is
joined together and grows into a holy temple in the
Lord." The thought that Christians are strangers
and sojourners on earth appears also in 1 Peter 2.11.
If source be needed for the Augustinian conception,
here is source sufficient.

The immediate circumstances that produced *The
City of God* are also important, and in this connection
we get much illumination from certain letters of the
year 412. *Epistle* 132, addressed to Volusianus, a
Roman official in North Africa, begins the series.

---

[1] Wherever possible we follow the reading of the Revised
Standard Version (New Testament, 1946; Old Testament,
1952), departing from it whenever, as here, it seems not to
bring out the meaning fully, or when Augustine appears to
have had before him a different reading. For the Old Testament Apocrypha, which is not found in many Protestant
Bibles, we cite the Authorized Version of 1611 as revised in
1894. The numbering in both Protestant and Catholic Bibles
is almost always the same, but there are a few differences,
principally in the Psalms, in which case we cite the former.

Volusianus was no Christian, but had a Christian
mother. In this initial letter the bishop urges upon
the pagan the reading of the Scriptures, particularly
the writings of the apostles, which would lead to the
prophets. If special problems are encountered in
this reading, Volusianus is characteristically urged
by the bishop to write for help in their elucidation, for
"the Lord helping me, I may perhaps be more able
to serve you in this way than by personally conversing
with you on such subjects." Volusianus took him at
his word, and in *Epistle* 135 writes to Augustine about
his perplexities with regard to the doctrine of the
Incarnation. His problem is this: how could the
ruler of the universe enter into the womb of the
Virgin and limit Himself by accepting the form of
man?

Augustine doubtless replied to this question in
a letter not now extant, which was shown to
Marcellinus, the Christian official to whom *The City
of God* was afterwards dedicated. Marcellinus then
wrote to Augustine *Epistle* 136, in which he points
out that whatever letters are sent to Volusianus will
be shown to others, and will thus have wider effect.
He adds that not only does the question propounded
by Volusianus bother him, but others as well.
One of these, concerning God's attitude towards
sacrifices, need not here concern us. Marcellinus
continues:

> "Another objection he stated was that the
> Christian doctrine and preaching were in no way
> consistent with the duties and rights of citizens;
> because, to quote an instance frequently alleged,
> among its precepts we find, ' Repay no one evil

for evil,' [1] and ' If anyone strikes you on the right cheek turn to him the other also; and if anyone would sue you and take away your coat, let him have your cloak as well; and if anyone forces you to go one mile, go with him two miles '; [2] all which he affirms to be contrary to the duties and rights of citizens. For who would submit to have anything taken from him by an enemy, or forbear from retaliating the evils of war upon an invader who ravaged a Roman province? The other precepts, as Your Eminence understands, are open to similar objections. Volusianus thinks that all these difficulties may be added to the question formerly stated, especially because it is manifest (though he is silent on this point) that very great calamities have befallen the commonwealth under the government of emperors observing, for the most part, the Christian religion. Wherefore, . . . it is important that all these difficulties be met by a full, thorough, and luminous reply. . . ."

Here was placed squarely before the bishop a problem that not only troubled the minds of Volusianus and his friends, but still troubles those of our own day. *The City of God* has a message for our times.

In the very long *Epistle* 137 Augustine replies to Volusianus, first discussing the problem of the Incarnation and ending with an admirable summary of the history of the Christian Church from its founding down to his own day.

---

[1] Romans 12.17.   [2] Matthew 5.39–41.

" Amid alternations of adversity and prosperity . . . [the successors to the Apostles] . . . watchfully practise patience and self-control; and when the world's day is drawing to its close, and the approaching consummation is heralded by the calamities which exhaust its energies,[1] they, seeing in this the fulfillment of prophecy, only expect with increased confidence the everlasting blessedness of the heavenly city. Moreover, amid all these changes, the unbelief of the pagan nations continues to rage against the Church of Christ. She gains the victory by patient endurance, and by the maintenance of unshaken faith in face of the cruelties of her adversaries."

A little further on the letter turns to

" the two commandments on which Christ says that all the law and the prophets hang: ' You shall love the Lord your God with all your heart, and with all your soul, and with all your mind, and you shall love your neighbour as yourself.' [2] All philosophy is here: physics, ethics, logic.[3] . . . Here also is security for the welfare and renown of a commonwealth; for no state is perfectly established and preserved otherwise than on the foundation and by the bond of faith and of firm concord, when the highest and truest common good, namely, God, is loved by all, and men love each other in Him without dissimulation, because they love one another for His

[1] On the eschatological problem in Augustine's day, see above, p. xlvii.

[2] Matthew 22.37-9.

[3] The three divisions of a philosophical system.

sake from whom they cannot disguise the real character of their love. . . . For I am aware that Your Excellency has to encounter the most determined opposition from certain persons, who think, or would have others think, that Christian doctrine is incompatible with the welfare of the commonwealth, because they wish to see the commonwealth established not by the steadfast practice of virtue but by granting immunity to vice. . . . Moreover, His mercy and grace, published to men by Christ, who is Himself man, and imparted to man by the same Christ, who is also God and the Son of God, never fail those who live by faith in Him and piously worship Him, in adversity patiently and bravely bearing the trials of this life, in prosperity using with self-control and with compassion for others the good things of this life, destined to receive, for faithfulness in both conditions, an eternal recompense in that divine and heavenly city in which there shall be no longer calamity to be painfully endured, nor inordinate desire to be with laborious care controlled, where our only work shall be to preserve, without any difficulty and with perfect liberty, our love to God and to our neighbour."

The final letter in the series (*Epistle* 138), addressed to Marcellinus, is equally long. It begins with a discussion of the supposed change in God's commandments with regard to the sacrifices, the point brought up by Marcellinus, but soon arrives at a more relevant point, the belief held by some pagans that the Christian doctrine of rendering to no man evil for evil was inconsistent with the duties and rights of

citizens. The saint points out that even in Roman history there are to be found examples of clemency which won praise from pagans, e.g., Cicero's praise of Caesar because he was wont to forget nothing but the wrongs done him,[1] but, though such virtues elicit approval from Augustine's pagan contemporaries, when similar virtues are imputed to Christians, they are accounted as vices.

> " If the Christian religion condemned wars of every kind, the command given in the Gospel [2] to soldiers asking counsel as to salvation be to cast away their arms, and withdraw themselves wholly from military service; whereas the word spoken to such was, ' Rob no one by violence or by false accusation, and be content with your wages.' "

Were Christianity treated as it deserves, it would establish, consecrate, strengthen and enlarge the commonwealth.

> " For what is a republic but a commonwealth? Therefore its interests are common to all; they are the interests of the state. Now what is a state but a multitude of men bound together by some bond of concord? In a pagan writer [3] is found: ' What was a scattered and unsettled multitude had by concord become in a short time a state.' "

These remarks will be met with again in *The City of God*.

He then goes on to point out that the true purpose

---

[1] Cicero, *Pro Ligario* 12.   [2] Luke 3.14.
[3] Sallust, *Cat.* 6.2.

of the commandment that had become a stumbling
block to these pagans was, not that evil might be
advanced, but that the wicked man might be overcome with kindness. He directs attention to the
interpretation of the commandment indicated by
statements in the Scriptures themselves. The Lord
Himself, when He was smitten on the face,[1] did not,
" if we look only to the words," [2] obey His own
precept, for He did not present the other cheek to
His persecutors. Likewise, the Apostle Paul, when
smitten on the face, said, " God shall strike you, you
white-washed wall! Are you sitting to judge me
according to the law, and yet contrary to the law
you order me to be struck? " [3] In other words, the
commandment must be interpreted not literally
but spiritually—it is a commandment establishing
the virtue of patience, not a military order that must
be explicitly obeyed.

Soon Augustine comes to one of his characteristic
teachings, that material welfare is to be despised and
spiritual welfare to be sought. In a passage of great
power he says :

" But the perverse and froward hearts of men
think human affairs are prosperous when men
are concerned about magnificent mansions, and
indifferent to the ruin of souls; when mighty
theatres are built up, and the foundations of
virtue are undermined; when the madness of
extravagance is highly esteemed, and works of
mercy are scorned; when, out of the wealth

[1] John 18.23.
[2] A good example of Augustine's principle of interpretation
of Scripture by the spirit, not the letter.
[3] Acts 23.3-5.

and affluence of rich men, luxurious provision is made for actors, and the poor are grudged the necessaries of life; when that God who, by the public declarations of His doctrine, protests against public vice, is blasphemed by impious communities, which demand gods of such character that even those theatrical representations which bring disgrace to both body and soul are fitly performed in honour of them."

The pagans have complained that many calamities have befallen the empire under Christian emperors; but even greater calamities have occurred in the reigns of other emperors not Christians. The beginning of the fall of the Roman Republic can be identified by the testimony of pagan witnesses as coincident with the breakdown of morality.[1] Yet

" in the most opulent and illustrious Empire of Rome,[2] God has shown how great is the influence of even civil virtues without true religion, in order that it might be understood that, when this is added to such virtues, men are made citizens of another commonwealth, of which the king is truth, the law is love, and the duration is eternity."

Here in these quotations, which have been transcribed at length because they strikingly show the thinking of Augustine as he was about to begin the composition of *The City of God*, we find the very obvious seeds from which the great work emerged. It was begun to provide an answer to the problem of the pagan group which centred round Volusianus. Though this

---

[1] Sallust, *Cat.* 11; Juvenal 6.277–95.

[2] This really represents Augustine's opinion of the empire.

correspondence has usually been mentioned by previous writers, the letters in it have not perhaps received their just due as important aids to the study of Augustine's purpose in writing his masterpiece.

The concept of the two cities also appears in other works of Augustine. The earliest reference in the surviving treatises occurs in the work *On Free Will*, 1.15, where the distinction is made between the two kinds of men, the lovers of things eternal and the lovers of things temporal. This work is dated as early as 388. In *On the True Religion* 27, written about 390, the same distinction again appears, though in neither case does the word *civitas* occur:

> " The whole human race, from Adam to the end of this world, is so administered under the laws of divine providence that it appears to be divided into two kinds, in one of which is the mob of the wicked, the type of earthly man, . . . in the other a succession of people devoted to the One God."

Also, in the *First Catechetical Instruction* we find the following passages contained in the model address designed to be given to the catechumens:

> " Thus there are two cities, one of the wicked, the other of the just, which endure from the beginning of the human race even to the end of time, which are now intermingled in body, but separated in will, and which, moreover, are to be separated in body also on the day of judgement. . . . We have already spoken a little before of these two cities running on indistinguishably from the beginning of the

human race to the end of the world through the changing ages, and destined to be separated at the last judgement." [1]

This work has been variously dated between 400 and 405, but in any case antedates the beginning of the writing of *The City of God* by eight years or more.

In his later commentary on Genesis [2] appears a passage contemporaneous with the early years of work on *The City of God*, in which he contrasts the two loves, the first holy, social, concerned with the common welfare for the sake of the heavenly society; submissive to God; quiet, peaceful; preferring truth to the praises of those in error; friendly, desiring for others what it wishes for itself; ruling its neighbour for the good of its neighbour; that is, the love of the good angels, while the second love is, on the other hand, foul, selfish, concerned for domination; rivalling God; is restless, troublesome, greedy for praise however it may be obtained, envious, striving for the subjugation of its neighbour for its own advantage, and this love belongs to the bad angels. These two loves

" also separate the two cities founded among the race of men, under the wonderful and

[1] J. P. Christopher, *De Catechizandis Rudibus* 19.31, 21.37, in *Ancient Christian Writers*, No. 2 (Westminster, 1947), pp. 61, 67, 126 f.

[2] *De Genesi ad litteram* 12.15, 20. Though the twelve books of this work were begun about 401, this passage near the end cannot have been written until about 414 or 415. Bourke (p. 250) unduly emphasizes the fact that this promise was not fulfilled for many years. *The City of God* was, to be sure, not completed until 426, but Augustine certainly began to fulfil the promise almost immediately.

ineffable Providence of God, administering and ordering all things which have been created; the first city is that of the just, the second that of the wicked, and though they are now, during the course of time, intermingled, they shall be divided at the last judgement; the first being joined by the good angels under its king, shall attain eternal life; the second, in union with the bad angels under its king, shall be sent into eternal fire. Perhaps we shall treat, God willing, of these two cities more fully in another place."

As Bourke has brilliantly pointed out,[1] the doctrine of the two loves is not something new in Augustine's thought, but the logical result of his metaphysics, which places man between the two contrasting levels, that is, between God above and the corporeal world below. Man's supreme happiness lies in the concentration of his gaze upon God, and his supreme misery in aversion from the mind of God. Thus in the first case we have the heavenly city, and in the second the terrestrial.

In another work written during the long period of composition of *The City of God* Augustine twice alludes to the two cities, but in passing only. We read in *The Manual*, the date of which lies between 420 and 423, as follows:

> " Thus, the heavenly Jerusalem, our mother, the City of God, will not be robbed of her citizens, but will perhaps reign over a greater number." [2]

[1] *Augustine's Quest for Wisdom*, p. 250.
[2] L. A. Arand, *Enchiridion 29, Ancient Christian Writers*, No. 3 (Westminster, 1947), p. 37.

And again:

> " But after the resurrection, when the general
> judgement has been held and concluded, there
> will remain two cities, each with its own
> boundaries—the one Christ's, the other, the
> devil's; the one, embracing the good, the other,
> the bad; and both consisting of angels and
> men." [1]

The idea of God's city is also employed, though not
always in precisely the same sense as in *The City of
God*, in several of the *Enarrations to the Psalms*.[2]

We are now ready to consider the statement, at
first sight surprisingly brief, in view of the bulk of
The City of God, made by its author in his famous
Retractations concerning the circumstances surround-
ing its composition: [3]

> " At the time [4] when Rome was taken with
> much slaughter by an invasion of the Goths under
> the leadership of King Alaric, the worshippers
> of the many false gods, to whom we commonly
> give the name of pagans, attempting to attribute

[1] *Enchiridion* 111, *ibid*. pp. 104, 144, note 364.

[2] See those on Psalms 62, 65 and 137 (Vulgate: 61, 64 and
136).

[3] For the complete text of the passage, see pp. 2–7. It
should be admitted that as the *Retractations* progress, the
author finds less and less to say about each work.

[4] The three-day attack began on 24th August, A.D. 410.
As Augustine tells us in the opening chapters, it was remarkable
for the respect shown to Christian shrines and asylums. That
the attacking forces were Christians is never mentioned in *The
City of God*, perhaps because they were Arians. In *Sermon*
105, however, quoted below, Augustine makes the point that
Alaric's Goths did not sacrifice to the pagan gods, but even
so, he will not call them Christians.

this invasion to the Christian religion, began more sharply and more bitterly than usual [1] to blaspheme the true God. Burning [2] with the zeal of God's house, I decided to write, against their blasphemies and errors, the books on *The City of God*."

As not only this passage but the opening chapters of the work itself show, the sack of Rome by Alaric certainly had a prime bearing on the project. This capture of the Eternal City by a foreign [3] army for the first time in eight centuries profoundly shocked not only those whose presence in Rome at the time caused them personal anguish but also those who, though safe for the moment in distant lands, could see terrifying possibilities in store. This disaster

[1] From the time of Nero, if not earlier, the Christians had been the favourite scapegoats for the Romans when disaster struck. This is made clear by Tertullian (*Apol.* 20; *Ad Nat.* 1.9; *Ad Scap.* 3); by the opening passages of Cyprian's *Ad Demetrianum* and of Arnobius's *The Case Against the Pagans*, *Ancient Christian Writers*, No. 7 (Westminster, 1949, 1.268); and by Lactantius (*Div. Inst.* 5.4.3). The greater outcry is with reference to previous complaints in Augustine's day, not greater than in time of persecution, which Augustine knew only by report. In addition, the pagan cults had now been disestablished by Christian emperors (on which see Burleigh's remarks, pp. 21–4).

[2] Burning with zeal for the cause of Christ, not shocked into inactivity, Augustine never seems conscious that he is living at the end of an era, and he belongs to classical antiquity, rather than to mediaeval times. One can see this most clearly when he is compared with a much lesser figure, that of Sulpicius Severus, his Gallic contemporary.

[3] The last capture by foreigners, in which the Capitol was not taken, occurred in 390 B.C., or according to another chronology, in 386 B.C. We pass over capture by Roman armies during the civil wars of the first century B.C. and the next.

was, of course, neither the first that the empire had experienced nor yet the most destructive and fatal to the empire's capacity to endure, but the symbolic importance of the ancient city, though it was no longer the capital of the government, was so huge that, when Rome fell, in spite of its recent decline in prestige, it must have seemed to many that the world itself had fallen.

The pagans have left us no account of their sensations. Their historian Zosimus, who finished his six books on the decline of Rome no earlier than A.D. 425, stops short of the siege and sack of the Eternal City. Rutilius Namatianus, prefect of the City in 414, is equally silent in the poem that he wrote two years afterwards (416). That their grief may have been too great for words is perhaps suggested by a remark of Macedonius, the imperial vicar of Africa, who, in a letter [1] acknowledging receipt of the first four books of *The City of God*, tells Augustine that he regrets the necessity of referring once more to a painful topic.

Augustine's initial reaction [2] to the news may perhaps be guessed from the sermon *On the Capture of Rome*,[3] but certainly not from anything in *The*

[1] *Epistle* 154.

[2] Bourke, *op. cit.* p. 248, perhaps overemphasizes the force of the military disaster upon Augustine : " Shocked by the news of the Sack of Rome . . . Augustine began *The City of God*." So also F. van der Meer, *Augustinus der Seelsorger*, tr. from Dutch by N. Greitemann (Cologne, 1951), 196.

[3] *De Urbis Excidio*, in Migne, *Patr. lat.* 40.715–24. It would appear from Schanz-Hosius-Krüger, *Geschichte der römischen Litteratur*, 4 Teil (Munich, 1920), pp. 459 f., that Dom Morin did not consider this sermon to be by Augustine, but it is referred to repeatedly by van der Meer (*op. cit.*) with no misgivings as to its genuineness.

City of God itself. There is, however, another sermon [1] on Luke 11.5, " Which of you who has a friend will go to him at midnight," etc. After speaking of God's mingling bitternesses with the felicities of earth and quoting Job 1.21,[2] he makes allusion to Rome :

> " The city which has given us birth according to the flesh still abides, God be thanked. O that it may receive a spiritual birth, and together with us pass over unto eternity ! . . . The holy city, the faithful city, the city on earth a sojourner, has its foundation in heaven. . . . Why are you alarmed because the kingdoms of the earth are perishing ? "

He then points out that if the kingdoms of the earth perish, this was foretold to them, and they should have been expecting to perish.

> " Let us not then faint, my brethren : an end there will be to all earthly kingdoms. If that end be now, God knows. Perhaps it is not yet, and, we through some infirmity, or mercifulness, or misery, are wishing that it may not be yet. Nevertheless, will it not therefore some day be ? Fix your hope in God, desire the things eternal, wait for the things eternal."

As for Rome,

> " . . . have we not had many brethren there ? Have we not still ? Does not a large portion of

---

[1] *Sermon* 105, Migne, *Patr. lat.* 38.618–25 = No. 55 in the sermons as translated in *A Select Library of Nicene and Post-Nicene Fathers* 6.430–5.

[2] His reading here follows the Septuagint, but also agrees with the Vulgate, of which we are not sure that he had a copy.

the pilgrim city Jerusalem live there?[1] Has it
not there endured temporal afflictions? But it
has not lost the things eternal. What can I say,
then, when I speak of Rome, but that that is
false, which they say of our Christ, that He is
Rome's destroyer, and that the gods of wood and
stone were her defenders? . . . See to what
sort of guardians learned men have entrusted
Rome, to those ' who have eyes, and see not.'
Or if they were able to preserve Rome, why did
they first perish themselves?[2] They say:
' Rome perished at the same time.' Nevertheless, they perished. . . . Alexandria once
lost such gods as these. Constantinople some
time since, ever since it was made a grand city,
for it was made so by a Christian emperor, lost
its false gods; and yet it has increased, and still
increases, and remains. And remain it will, as
long as God pleases. . . . And that which
they say is not true, that immediately on losing
her gods Rome has been taken and ruined. It
is not true at all; their images were overthrown
before, and even so were the Goths with
Rhadagaisus conquered. Remember, my brethren, remember; it is no long time since,[3] but a
few years; call it to mind. When all the images
in the city of Rome had been overthrown,
Rhadagaisus, king of the Goths, came with a
large army, much more numerous than that of

---

[1] *Sermon* 296.6, quoted by P. DeLabriolle, *Hist. de la Litt.
Lat. Chrét.* (Paris, 2nd ed., 1924), p. 522, alludes to the presence
in Rome of the bodies of Saints Peter, Paul and Laurence.

[2] Sentiments repeated with telling effect in *The City of God*.

[3] In A.D. 406. The allusion to Alaric places this sermon
after the sack in 410.

Alaric was. Rhadagaisus was a pagan. He sacrificed to Jupiter every day. Everywhere it was announced that Rhadagaisus did not cease from sacrificing. . . . But God making proof that neither temporal deliverance, nor the preservation of these earthly kingdoms, consists in these sacrifices, Rhadagaisus, by the Lord's help, was marvellously overthrown. Afterwards came other Goths who did not sacrifice;[1] they came, who though they were not Catholics in the Christian faith, were yet hostile and opposed to idols, and they took Rome. They conquered those who put their trust in idols, who were still seeking after the idols they had lost, and desiring still to sacrifice to the lost gods. And among them too were some of our brethren, and these were afflicted also; but they had learned to say, ' I will bless the Lord at all times.' They were involved in the afflictions of their earthly kingdom; but they did not lose the kingdom of heaven; yes, they were made the better for obtaining it through the exercise of tribulations."

Surely this sermon shows no sign of despair.

The shock, however great, had no such effect upon Augustine as it had upon Jerome, whose letters[2] of the period are full of his grief at learning of the recent disaster. Of several striking passages we cite but one:

" I have long wished to attack the prophecies of Ezekiel and to make good the promises which

[1] Alaric and his Arian Christian Goths.
[2] See Jerome's *Epistle* 123 to Ageruchia (*ca.* 409); *Epistle* 127 to Principia (412); *Epistle* 128 to Gaudentius (413). The quoted passage is from *Epistle* 125 to Marcellinus and his wife Anapsychia (412).

I have so often given to anxious readers. When, however, I began to dictate, I was so confounded by the havoc wrought in the west and above all by the sack of Rome that, as the common saying has it, I forgot even my own name. Long did I remain silent, knowing that it was a time to weep."

If Augustine had been in the same plight he had recovered from these emotions by the time, some three years or more after the disaster, when he began his famous work. His mood is calm. He is in full command of logic. Nothing has been lost of the power of his polemic. He is even able to see good aspects of those terrible days on Tiber's banks, and, above all, he is able to be, as always, a master in didactic. Yet the work does, all the same, belong to a time of crisis.

In the passage from the *Retractations* cited above, the author goes on to provide his usual résumé of the argument of *The City of God*, which is printed in full at the beginning of the translation.[1] There is now available a letter addressed to Augustine's friend, the priest Firmus, which was first printed by Dom Lambot as recently as 1939.[2] Unfortunately, it bears no date, and the only internal evidence it contains shows only that it was written after the completion of *The City of God*. Its chief value, therefore, is in what it says about the outline of the work, and in this respect it merely confirms the testimony of the *Retractations*.

Firmus has requested a copy of *The City of God*,

[1] See pp. 2–7.
[2] Cyrille Lambot, " Lettre inédite de S. Augustin relative au *De civitate Dei* " (*Revue Bénédictine*, 51 [1939], 109–21).

and Augustine has sent him one which he himself
has re-read, but it apparently is not yet bound, for
directions are given how it might be bound. Since
the twenty-two books would be cumbersome if all
were bound together, the suggestion is made that
Firmus may wish to bind the work in two volumes,
and, if so, then he should put the first ten books in
one, the other twelve in the second, as the subject
matter in the ten consists of a refutation of the pagans,
and that of the twelve is a demonstration of the
Christian religion, though as Augustine has also said
in the *Retractations*, each of these topics appears also
on occasion in the part devoted principally to the
other.

Firmus might, however, wish to have more than
two volumes, of which the first should have Books
I–V, the second Books VI–X, the third, Books XI–
XIV, the fourth, Books XV–XVIII, and the fifth,
Books XIX–XXII. Thus the first volume would
contain the argument against those who contend that
the worship of the pagan gods is of profit for happiness
in the present life; the second, the argument against
the view that worship of the pagan gods would obtain
happiness in the life to come; the third, the origin
of the city of God; the fourth, its progress or
development (*procursus* or *excursus*), and the fifth, its
appointed ends.

Firmus is encouraged to permit those in Carthage
who may not already have a copy to make copies
from his. Augustine thinks that the work may now
be profitable in instructing those already Christians
and in converting those readers who are not, and
promises to be continually interested in Firmus'
progress, urging upon him the thought that repeated

reading will increase his understanding. He also sends along an epitome (*breviculus*) which will show the subject matter of the twenty-two books, and inquires how Firmus had obtained a copy of Augustine's early work *On the Academics*.

Augustine frequently inserts, as joints between the parts, short résumés of what he believes he has accomplished. Such articulations appear in Book II, Chapter 2; in Book III, Chapter 1; in Book IV, Chapters 1–2; while Book VI has a special preface. In the initial chapters of Books XI, XVIII and XIX he also takes a backward look.

The City of God is addressed in its preface to the author's good friend and fellow Christian, Marcellinus, who had been sent by the Emperor Honorius to Africa about 410 in order to compose the differences between the Catholics and Donatists and had presided over the famous conference at Carthage in the next year.[1] In the corpus of Augustine's extant correspondence he is the author of *Epistle* 136, which we have already discussed,[2] and the addressee of *Epistles* 128, 129, 130, 138, 139 and 140 from Augustine, and of *Epistle* 165 from Jerome. To him also was dedicated the work *On the Merits and Forgiveness of Sinners and on the Baptism of Infants*, which was written in 412, but in September, 413, he was executed on a trumped-up charge amounting to judicial murder, a crime discussed by Augustine in *Epistle* 151.

On the rate of progress made in composing the parts of *The City of God* certain statements can be made, though we are without complete information. The presence of Marcellinus' name in both the Preface and the initial chapter to Book II makes it

[1] See above, p. xxxix.   [2] See above, p. xli f.

certain that both were written before Marcellinus' death in September A.D. 413. The Preface cannot therefore have been composed after the last page of Book XXII, as we might suppose from consideration of modern practice. Since Marcellinus is not mentioned thereafter, it is probable that not much more than these two books, or at most the first three, were written before his death.

In *Epistle* 169, addressed to Evodius, which is generally dated in 415 and must have been written rather late in whatever year it was composed, there appears near the beginning the following passage :

". . . I have now finished several of those [books] which had been commenced by me this year before Easter, near the beginning of Lent. For, to the three [1] books on *The City of God*, in opposition to its enemies, the worshippers of demons, I have added two others, and in these five books I think enough has been said to answer those who maintain that the gods must be worshipped in order to secure prosperity in this present life, and who are hostile to the Christian name because they think that we defeat their hope of prosperity. In the sequel I must, as I promised in the first book,[2] answer those who think that the worship of their gods is the only way to obtain that life after death with a view to obtain which we are Christians."

---

[1] In *Epistle* 154 we learn that Augustine has sent four books to Macedonius. This letter comes between letters written in 413 or 414 and in 414. It may well be that the Benedictines erred in placing it so early.

[2] Book I, Ch. 36, the final chapter.

Thus we see that three books had been completed before the beginning of Lent in 415, if the traditional date of *Epistle* 169 is correct.

In the preface to Orosius' *Historiarum adversus paganos libri VII*, which was written in 417, Orosius shows knowledge only of Book XI of *The City of God*, yet in *Epistle* 184A, probably to be dated in the preceding year, allusion is made to thirteen books of the unfinished work, which are to be carried by Firmus to the monks Peter and Abraham.

There is, in Book XVIII, Chapter 54, the final chapter, an interesting passage of chronological importance. In the preceding chapter Augustine has alluded to the ridiculous pagan charge that St. Peter had by magical enchantments arranged that the worship of Christ should endure for precisely 365 years. At the beginning of this chapter Augustine says that these 365 years were completed " a few years ago " (*ante aliquot annos*), and he then goes on to compute the day on which the end of the period occurred as follows.

He accepts as the date of the beginning of the period, not the birth of Christ, nor the beginning of the ministry, nor even the crucifixion, but, in order to make the point as strong as possible, he adopts the latest of all alternatives, namely, the Day of Pentecost, the fiftieth day after the Crucifixion, which, with Tertullian,[1] he dates on the eighth day before the Kalends of April[2] in the year when the

---

[1] Tertullian, *Adversus Iudaeos* 8. Eusebius (*Chron.* 370) places it in the nineteenth, not the fifteenth, year of Tiberius' reign.

[2] See also *De Trinitate* 4.5; *De Diversis Quaestionibus LXXXIII* 56.

Gemini were consuls, that is, as Lactantius tells us,[1] in the fifteenth year of the reign of Tiberius (14–37). This places the Crucifixion on 25th March, A.D. 29, and Pentecost on the Ides of May, or the fifteenth, in the same year. From Pentecost onwards, a period of 365 years would have been completed in A.D. 394, but Augustine says also that by counting the consuls, the 365 years are found to be completed in the consulship of Honorius and Eutychianus, who are known to have been consuls in A.D. 398. Whatever may be the true date of this fanciful period, it is clear that Augustine believed that it would have ended, not in 394, but in A.D. 398, for he says that Mallius Theodorus was consul in the next year. He was consul with his colleague Eutropius in A.D. 399. Enough has been said to show that Augustine's chronology is out of order.

He goes on to prove that the pagan claim must be false, for, if it were true, when the 365 years were completed, the reign of Christ must have ended, yet in the year 399, the next after the period was completed, abundant proof that Christ was still being worshipped could be cited, e.g.:

> " Meanwhile, as we know, in the most famous and most eminent city of Carthage in Africa, Gaudentius and Jovius, officials [*comites*] of the Emperor Honorius, on the fourteenth day before the Kalends of April [i.e., 19th March], overthrew the temples and smashed the images of the false gods. Who does not see how much the worship of Christ has increased in the almost

[1] Lactantius, *Div. Inst.* 4.10, puts it on the following day.

> thirty years [*per triginta ferme annos*] from that
> date to the present? "

If the word " ferme " in this last sentence is given
but slight force, the eighteenth book of *The City of
God* was being completed—the passage is in the final
chapter—in the year 429. Father Pope (p. 377)
appears to favour this view, yet he suggests that this
passage may have been an interpolation added in
429 during a re-reading or revision of the work.

The traditional date of completion is 426; it was
determined, apparently, by the original Benedictine
editors, who based their conclusions on evidence
unknown to us. There is in the final Book XXII,
Chapter 8, an allusion to the period of two years
(*biennium*) which had elapsed since the establishment
at Hippo of the *memoria* of St. Stephen. Usually
the date for this establishment is given as 424, but
we strongly suspect that it was arrived at by counting
back two years from the assumed date of completion
of the work in 426, and thus we cannot accept the
remark about the *biennium* as proof that Book XXII
was being written in 426. We are inclined, however,
to think that this year really did mark the end of the
arduous task, for it seems almost incredible that four
books could have been dictated in the last year of
the saint's life, especially in view of the condition of
his health and the disturbed conditions of the times.

By a happy circumstance these pages are receiving
their final scrutiny as we celebrate the 1600th
birthday of Augustine, who was born on the Ides of
November, A.D. 354.

GEORGE E. McCRACKEN

Drake University,
Des Moines, Iowa.

BIBLIOGRAPHICAL NOTE

THE most complete edition of the Latin text of St. Augustine's works will be found in J. P. Migne's *Patrologiae Cursus Completus : Series Latina* (Paris, 1844–64), Vols. 32–47, a reprint of the celebrated edition issued by the Benedictines of St. Maur (Paris, 1679–1700). Critical editions of a large number of the works have appeared also in the *Corpus Scriptorum Ecclesiasticorum Latinorum*, published by the Vienna Academy, in particular in Vols. 12, 25, 28, 33, 34, 36, 39–44, 51–3, 57, 58 and 60.

Extensive collections of the works in English translations first appeared in the so-called " Oxford edition," issued under the general direction of Dr. E. B. Pusey, as *A Library of Fathers of the Holy Catholic Church anterior to the Division of the East and West ; translated by Members of the English Church* (Oxford and London, 1840–57), in which Vol. 1 contains Pusey's translation of the *Confessions* ; Vols. 16 and 20, R. G. MacMullen's translation of " Sermons on Selected Lessons of the New Testament " ; Vols. 21, 25, 30, 32, 37 and 39, translations by J. Tweed, T. Scratton, H. M. Wilkins and, probably, Charles Marriott, of the *Enarrations to the Psalms* ; Vol. 22, translations of seventeen short treatises, eleven of them by C. L. Cornish, six by H. Browne ; and Vols. 26 and 29, Browne's translations of the *Homilies on the Gospel According to St. John and his First Epistle*.

A more complete edition was somewhat later

prepared by British scholars under the editorship of Marcus Dods and printed as the *Library of Nicene and Post-Nicene Fathers* in fifteen volumes (Edinburgh, 1871–76). This was reprinted under the general editorship of Philip Schaff, and augmented by supplementary material from the pens of certain American scholars, as *A Select Library of the Nicene and Post-Nicene Fathers of the Christian Church* (Buffalo, 1886–88), the volumes containing works of Augustine comprising the first eight of the series. Included in this work is all of the Oxford edition except that Pusey's translation of the *Confessions* was replaced by another, done by J. G. Pilkington; Browne's translation of the homilies on the Fourth Gospel by a new one by John Gibb and James Innes; and three of Cornish's translations by the work of J. F. Shaw and S. D. F. Salmond, while a fourth was omitted.

New material includes J. G. Cunningham's version of many, but not all, of the *Epistles* ; Marcus Dods' version of *The City of God* ; A. W. Haddan's translation of *On the Holy Trinity* ; J. F. Shaw's version of *On Christian Doctrine* ; seven anti-Manichaean treatises translated by Richard Stothert and A. H. Newman; three anti-Donatist treatises translated by J. R. King; thirteen anti-Pelagian writings translated by Peter Holmes and Robert E. Wallis; a translation of the harmony of the Gospels by Salmond; and a translation of the *Soliloquies* by C. C. Starbuck.

The two volumes of the *Basic Writings of Saint Augustine*, edited by Whitney J. Oates (New York, 1948), contain complete texts of the *Confessions*, *Soliloquies*, and of eleven shorter works, as well as

parts of *The City of God* and of *On the Trinity*, all taken from Schaff's edition except two shorter works by G. C. Leckie.

In the series *Ancient Christian Writers*, edited by Johannes Quasten and Joseph C. Plumpe (Westminster, 1947 ff.), the following works of Augustine appear in new translation with introduction and commentary : No. 2, *The First Catechetical Instruction*, by J. P. Christopher (1947); No. 3, *Faith, Hope, and Charity* [the Enchiridion], by L. A. Arand (1947); No. 5, *The Lord's Sermon on the Mount*, by John J. Jepson (1948); No. 9, *The Greatness of the Soul* and *The Teacher*, by J. M. Colleran (1950); No. 12, *Against the Academics*, by John J. O'Meara (1950); and No. 15, *Sermons for Christmas and Epiphany*, by T. C. Lawler (1952).

The *Library of Christian Classics*, edited by John Baillie, John T. McNeill and Henry P. Van Dusen, has in Vol. 6 (1953) translations by John H. S. Burleigh of the *Soliloquies, The Teacher, On Free Will, Of True Religion, The Usefulness of Belief, The Nature of the Good, Faith and the Creed*, and of the first book of *To Simplician—On Various Questions*. Vol. 7 (1955) of the same series has complete translations by Albert Cook Outler of the *Confessions* and *Enchiridion*, while Vol. 8 (1955) has John Burnaby's translation of *The Trinity* (in part), *The Spirit and the Letter*, and *Ten Homilies on the First Epistle General of St. John*.

The series *Fathers of the Church*, edited by Ludwig Schopp, R. J. Deferrari and other Catholic scholars, contains in ten volumes which have already appeared (exclusive of the three-volume translation of *The City of God*, cited below) translations of many works

of Augustine, including the *Confessions*, translated by Vernon J. Bourke, and the *Epistles*, by W. Parsons.

Of Latin editions of the *De Civitate Dei* the following still have importance:

(*a*) B. Dombart, in the *Bibliotheca Teubneriana* (Leipzig, 1st ed., 1853; 2nd ed., 1877; 3rd ed., 1905–8; 4th ed., 1928–29). The fourth edition, which was revised by A. Kalb, has been used as the basis for this translation. The text of the work is sound; whenever we have departed from it, that fact has been noted in the apparatus. We have made some changes in punctuation to conform to English usage.

(*b*) Emanuel Hoffmann, in the *Corpus Scriptorum Ecclesiasticorum Latinorum*, Vol. 30, Parts 1–2 (Vienna, 1899–1900).

(*c*) Carl Weyman (Munich, 1924).

(*d*) J. E. C. Welldon, *Society for Promoting Christian Knowledge* (London, 1924). This is the only modern edition with an extensive commentary.

Other English translations of *The City of God* began with that of " J. H." that is, J. Healey, first printed in 1610 with a reprint of an older commentary by J. L. Vives; revised and reprinted in 1620. In 1903 F. W. Bussell reprinted Healey's version in *The Temple Classics*, but reduced the number of books to eighteen, re-arranged some of the chapters so as to produce a version in which the description of the City of God would be, in his view, in consecutive form, and also attempted to separate authentic work of Augustine from what he thought " later accretions supplied by monkish followers." Healey's vigorous

translation (not Bussell's version) was again reprinted
in 1945 in the *Everyman Library* (London and New
York), with an introduction (written in 1930) by Sir
Ernest Barker (Vol. 1, pp. vi–xxxvi).

Marcus Dods' translation first appeared in the
Library of Nicene and Post-Nicene Fathers (Edinburgh,
1872). Dr. Dods was assisted by J. J. Smith (Books
V–VIII) and George Wilson (Books IV, XVII, XVIII).
This was reprinted in Schaff's American edition
(Buffalo, 1886), Vol. 2, pp. 1–511 ; again reprinted in
The Hafner Library of Classics (New York, 1948);
once more reprinted, with a short introduction by
Thomas Merton, in *The Modern Library* (New York,
1950); and it forms the basis for the partial reprint
in Oates' *Basic Writings of Saint Augustine* (New York,
1948), which contains all of Books I, V, VIII, XI–
XXII, parts of Books II, IV, VI, VII, IX and X, but
none of Book III.

Another translation has appeared in the series
Fathers of the Church (New York, 1950–54), the work
of D. B. Zema, G. G. Walsh, G. Monahan and D. J.
Honan. The volumes are doubly numbered as Vols.
6–8 of the " Writings of Saint Augustine " = Vols. 8,
14 and 24 of the whole series *Fathers of the Church.*
In the first volume appears a foreword by Étienne
Gilson (pp. vi–xcviii).

SELECT BIBLIOGRAPHY ON SAINT AUGUSTINE

Abercrombie, Nigel. *Saint Augustine and French
Classical Thought* (Oxford, 1938).

Alfaric, P. *L'évolution intellectuale de s. Augustin*
(Paris, 1918).

Angus, S. *The Sources of the First Ten Books of
Augustine's City of God* (Princeton, 1906).

Bardy, G.   *Saint Augustin : l'homme et l'oeuvre* (Paris, 6th ed., 1946).

Battenhouse, Roy, ed.   *A Companion to the Study of St. Augustine* (New York, 1954).

Bourke, Vernon J.   " The Political Philosophy of Saint Augustine " (*Proc. American Cath. Philos. Assoc.* 7 [1931], 45–55).

Bourke, Vernon J.   *Augustine's Quest of Wisdom* (Milwaukee, 1947).

Boyer, Charles.   *Christianisme et néo-platonisme dans la formation de Saint Augustin* (Paris, 1920).

Burleigh, John H. S.   *The City of God : A Study of St. Augustine's Philosophy* (London, 1949).

Butti, C.   *La mente di S. Agostino nella Città di Dio* (Firenze, 1930).

D'Arcy, M. C., and others, *A Monument to Saint Augustine* (London, 1930 ; reprinted 1945).

Figgis, J. N.   *The Political Aspects of St. Augustine's City of God* (London, 1921).

Foran, E. A.   *The Augustinians* (London, 1938).

Gilson, Étienne.   *Introduction à l'étude de s. Augustin* (Paris, 1931, 3rd ed., 1949).

Hermelink, H.   " Die civitas terrena bei Augustin " (*Festgabe für A. von Harnack* [Tübingen, 1921], 302–24).

Lesaar, Heinrich Hubert.   *Saint Augustine*, tr. by T. Pope Arkell (London, 1931).

Marrou, H. I.   *Saint Augustin et la fin de la culture antique* in *Bibliothèque de l'École Française de Rome et d'Athènes*, fasc. 145, 145bis (Paris, 1938).

O'Meara, J. J.   *The Young Augustine : the Growth of St. Augustine's Mind up to his Conversion* (London, 1954).

BIBLIOGRAPHICAL NOTE

Papini, Giovanni. *Sant'Agostino* (Firenze, 1930), tr. by L. P. Agnetti (New York, 1930).

Pope, Hugh. *Saint Augustine of Hippo : Essays dealing with his Life and Times and Some Features of his Work* (London, 1937 ; reprinted Westminster, 1949). These lectures were delivered in 1930.

Rickaby, J. *St. Augustine's City of God : A View of its Contents* (New York, 1925).

Schilling, O. *Die Staats- und Soziallehre des hl. Augustinus* (Freiburg i. Br., 1910).

Scholz, Heinrich. *Glaube und Unglaube in der Weltgeschichte : ein Kommentar zu Augustins De Civitate Dei* (Leipzig, 1911).

NOTE

For discussion of the text used in this volume see p. lxxxvi ; for our practice in translating scriptural quotations, see p. lix.

SAINT AUGUSTINE

THE CITY OF GOD AGAINST THE PAGANS

S. AURELII AUGUSTINI

DE CIVITATE DEI CONTRA PAGANOS

RETRACTATIONUM
Libri II Cap. LXIX

Interea Roma Gothorum inruptione agentium sub rege Alarico atque impetu magnae cladis eversa est, cuius eversionem deorum falsorum multorumque cultores, quos usitato nomine paganos vocamus, in Christianam religionem referre conantes solito acerbius et amarius Deum verum blasphemare coeperunt. Unde ego exardescens zelo domus Dei adversus eorum blasphemias vel errores libros *de civitate Dei* scribere institui. Quod opus per aliquot annos me tenuit eo quod alia multa intercurrebant quae differe non oporteret, et me prius ad solvendum occupabant. Hoc autem *de civitate Dei* grande opus tandem viginti duobus libris est terminatum.

Quorum quinque primi eos refellunt qui res humanas ita prosperari volunt ut ad hoc multorum deorum cultum quos pagani colere consuerunt, neces-

SAINT AURELIUS AUGUSTINE

THE CITY OF GOD AGAINST THE PAGANS

RETRACTATIONS

Book II, Chapter 69

In the meantime Rome had been swept by an invasion of the Goths under the leadership of King Alaric and the impact of a great disaster; and the worshippers of the many false gods, to whom we commonly give the name of pagans, attempting to attribute this visitation to the Christian religion, began more sharply and more bitterly than usual to blaspheme the true God. Burning with the zeal of God's house, I decided to write against their blasphemies and errors the books on *The City of God*. This work engaged me for some years because many other matters intervened that I could not conscientiously postpone, and kept me busy completing them first. At last, however, this huge work on *The City of God* was brought to a conclusion in twenty-two books.

The first five books refute those whose interest in the welfare of mankind is bound up with the belief that this depends on the worship of the many gods whom the pagans were wont to worship, and who

sarium esse arbitrentur, et quia prohibetur, mala ista exoriri atque abundare contendunt. Sequentes autem quinque adversus eos loquuntur qui fatentur haec mala nec defuisse umquam nec defutura mortalibus, et ea nunc magna, nunc parva, locis temporibus personisque variari, sed deorum multorum cultum quo eis sacrificatur propter vitam post mortem futuram esse utilem disputant. His ergo decem libris duae istae vanae opiniones Christianae religioni adversariae refelluntur.

Sed ne quisquam nos aliena tantum redarguisse, non autem nostra asseruisse reprehenderet, id agit pars altera operis huius quae libris duodecim continetur, quamquam ubi opus est et in prioribus decem quae nostra sunt asseramus et in duodecim posterioribus redarguamus adversa.

Duodecim ergo librorum sequentium primi quattuor continent exortum duarum civitatum, quarum est una Dei, altera huius mundi; secundi quattuor excursum earum sive procursum; tertii vero, qui et postremi, debitos fines. Ita omnes viginti et duo libri, cum sint de utraque civitate conscripti, titulum tamen a meliore acceperunt ut *de civitate Dei* potius vocarentur.

In quorum decimo libro non debuit pro miraculo poni in Abrahae sacrificio flammam caelitus factam inter divisas victimas cucurrisse, quoniam hoc illi in visione monstratum est. In septimo decimo libro quod dictum est de Samuele: *Non erat de filiis Aaron*,

---

[1] Book Ten, Chapter 8.
[2] Book Seventeen, Chapter 5.

maintain that the misfortunes in question owe their existence and magnitude to the prohibition of that worship. The next five books, again, are an answer to such as, though they admit that mortal men were never in the past spared such misfortunes nor will be in the future, and that ill fortune is sometimes greater, sometimes less as it affects different regions, eras or individuals, yet maintain that the worship of many gods, in which sacrifices are made to them, is advantageous because of the life that will be ours after death. In these ten books, then, are refuted those two false notions that are contrary to the Christian religion.

But lest someone reply that we have only argued against the opinions of others but have not stated our own, this is attended to in the second part of this work, which comprises twelve books. When need arises, however, our own position is also stated in the first ten books, and opposing views are also refuted in the twelve later books.

Of these twelve succeeding books, the first four contain the origin of the two cities, the one of God, the other of this world; the second four, their course or progress; the third and last four, their appointed ends. And so all twenty-two books, though they dealt with both cities, yet took their title from the better, with the result that they were called by preference *The City of God*.

In the tenth book [1] it should not have been accounted a miracle when, in the sacrifice of Abraham, a flame was divinely sent from heaven to run between the divided victims, since this was shown to him in a vision. In the seventeenth book [2] what is said about Samuel, " He was not of the sons of Aaron," should

5

dicendum potius fuit: Non erat filius sacerdotis. Filios quippe sacerdotum defunctis sacerdotibus succedere magis legitimi moris fuit. Nam in filiis Aaron reperitur pater Samuelis, sed sacerdos non fuit, nec ita in filiis ut eum ipse genuerit Aaron, sed sicut omnes illius populi dicuntur filii Israel.

Hoc opus sic incipit: *Gloriosissimam civitatem Dei* etc.

rather have been put: " He was not the son of a priest." It was, of course, more legal custom for sons of priests to succeed priests; for the father of Samuel appears among the sons of Aaron, but he was not a priest, nor was he among the sons in the sense that Aaron himself begat him, but in the same sense in which all who belong to the people Israel are called sons of Israel.

This work begins with the words: " Most glorious is and will be the City of God," etc.

BOOK I

LIBER I

Praefatio

De suscepti operis consilio et argumento.

Gloriosissimam civitatem Dei sive in hoc temporum
cursu, cum inter impios peregrinatur ex fide vivens,
sive in illa stabilitate sedis aeternae quam nunc ex-
pectat per patientiam, *quoadusque iustitia convertatur
in iudicium,* deinceps adeptura per excellentiam victoria ultima et pace perfecta, hoc opere instituto et
mea ad te promissione debito defendere adversus eos
qui conditori eius deos suos praeferunt, fili carissime
Marcelline, suscepi, magnum opus et arduum, sed
Deus adiutor noster est.

Nam scio quibus viribus opus sit ut persuadeatur
superbis quanta sit virtus humilitatis, qua fit ut omnia
terrena cacumina temporali mobilitate nutantia non
humano usurpata fastu, sed divina gratia donata
celsitudo transcendat. Rex enim et conditor civitatis huius de qua loqui instituimus, in scriptura
populi sui sententiam divinae legis aperuit, qua dictum est: *Deus superbis resistit, humilibus autem dat
gratiam.* Hoc vero, quod Dei est, superbae quoque

---

[1] Psalms 94.15.   [2] James 4.6.

BOOK I

Preface

On the design and plan of the undertaking.

Most glorious is and will be the City of God, both in this fleeting age of ours, wherein she lives by faith, a stranger among infidels, and in the days when she shall be established in her eternal home. Now she waits for it with patience, " until righteousness returns to judgement ";[1] then she shall possess it with preëminence in final victory and perfect peace. In this work, on which I embark in payment of my promise to you, O dearest son Marcellinus, it is my purpose to defend the City of God against those who esteem their own gods above her Founder. The work is great and difficult, but God is my helper.

Well do I know the powers needed to persuade the proud how great is the virtue of humility, that lofty quality by which our city is raised above all earthly heights that are rocked by ever-streaming time, not raised by the devices of human arrogance but by the endowment of grace divine. For the King and Founder of this City, which is the subject of my discourse, has revealed in the scripture of his people a statement of divine law, which I quote: " God resists the proud but gives grace to the humble." [2] Indeed, it is this distinction, which belongs to God, that the

animae spiritus inflatus adfectat amatque sibi in laudibus dici:

> Parcere subiectis et debellare superbos.[1]

Unde etiam de terrena civitate, quae cum dominari adpetit, etsi populi serviant, ipsa ei dominandi libido dominatur, non est praetereundem silentio quidquid dicere suscepti huius operis ratio postulat et facultas datur.

I

De adversariis nominis Christi, quibus in vastatione urbis propter Christum barbari pepercerunt.

Ex hac namque existunt inimici adversus quos defendenda est Dei civitas, quorum tamen multi correcto impietatis errore cives in ea fiunt satis idonei; multi vero in eam tantis exardescunt ignibus odiorum tamque manifestis beneficiis redemptoris eius ingrati sunt ut hodie contra eam linguas non moverent nisi ferrum hostile fugientes in sacratis eius locis vitam de qua superbiunt invenirent. An non etiam illi Romani Christi nomini infesti sunt quibus propter Christum barbari pepercerunt? Testantur hoc martyrum loca et basilicae apostolorum, quae in illa vastatione Urbis ad se confugientes suos alienosque receperunt.

Huc usque cruentus saeviebat inimicus, ibi accipiebat limitem trucidatoris furor, illo ducebantur a miserantibus hostibus, quibus etiam extra ipsa loca

---

[1] Virgil, *Aeneid* 6.853.

inflated fancy of a proud spirit assumes when it
chooses to be praised in the following terms:

> To spare the fallen and subdue the proud.[1]

This is why I cannot, in so far as the plan of my undertaking demands and my own ability permits, pass
over in silence that earthly city which, when it seeks
for mastery, though the nations are its slaves, has as
its own master that very lust for mastery.

I

On the adversaries of Christ's name, spared by the barbarians at the sack of Rome because of Christ.

FOR it is from this earthly city that the enemies
spring against whom the City of God must be defended. Many of them, when the error of irreligion
is corrected, become her fully qualified citizens, but
many, on the other hand, so blaze with fiery hatred
against her and are so ungrateful for the obvious
favours received from her Redeemer that they could
not stir a tongue against her today, were it not that
they take refuge from hostile swords on her consecrated ground and so find means to live their life
of pride. Are not even those Romans whom the
barbarians spared for Christ's sake hostile to the name
of Christ? The graves of the martyrs and the
basilicas of the apostles bear witness to this, which,
when the city was sacked, sheltered those who fled
for refuge—their own people and strangers too.

Thus far and no farther raged the bloody enemy;
there the murderous fury found its limit; thither the
merciful among the enemy led those they had spared

pepercerant, ne in eos incurrerent qui similem misericordiam non habebant. Qui tamen etiam ipsi alibi
truces atque hostili more saevientes posteaquam ad
loca illa veniebant ubi fuerat interdictum quod alibi
belli iure licuisset, tota feriendi refrenabatur inmanitas et captivandi cupiditas frangebatur.

Sic evaserunt multi qui nunc Christianis temporibus
detrahunt et mala quae illa civitas pertulit Christo
inputant; bona vero quae in eos ut viverent propter
Christi honorem facta sunt non inputant Christo
nostro, sed fato suo, cum potius deberent, si quid
recti saperent, illa quae ab hostibus aspera et dura
perpessi sunt, illi providentiae divinae tribuere quae
solet corruptos hominum mores bellis emendare
atque conterere itemque vitam mortalium iustam
atque laudabilem talibus adflictionibus exercere
probatamque vel in meliora transferre vel in his
adhuc terris propter usus alios detinere.

Illud vero, quod eis vel ubicumque propter Christi
nomen vel in locis Christi nomini dicatissimis et
amplissimis ac pro largiore misericordia ad capaci-
tatem multitudinis electis praeter bellorum morem
truculenti barbari pepercerunt, hoc tribuere temporibus Christianis, hinc Deo agere gratias, hinc ad
eius nomen veraciter currere, ut effugiant poenas
ignis aeterni, quod nomen multi eorum mendaciter
usurparunt, ut effugerent poenas praesentis exitii.

14

even outside those bounds, lest they fall foul of others who had no such mercy. Moreover, once the very men who elsewhere were bloodthirsty and raged in hostile wise, had reached the area where acts that the laws of war would have permitted elsewhere were banned, all the cruelty with which they smote was curbed and the avarice with which they took men prisoner was shattered.

Thus many escaped who now reproach the Christian era and lay at Christ's door the miseries which that city suffered; but the kindness that they received, whereby life was granted them out of reverence for Christ, that they impute, not to our Christ, but to their Fate. Rather ought they, if they had any sound wisdom, to attribute the harsh and cruel things that they suffered at their enemies' hands to that divine providence which is wont to employ wars for the castigation or humiliation of morally corrupt characters, as well as to provide a trial by such affliction for righteous and praiseworthy men, and after they have been approved, either to translate them to a better world or to keep them longer on this earth for further services.

Moreover, they ought to attribute it to the Christianity of our times that the fierce barbarians, contrary to the usages of war, spared them either without regard to place for the name of Christ, or in such places as were especially dedicated to the name of Christ—large areas selected to contain a great throng that mercy might be spread wider. They ought, therefore, to give thanks to God, and they ought, therefore, in order to escape the penalty of eternal fire, to flee truthfully to his name, a name that many of them untruthfully made use of to escape the pains

Nam quos vides petulanter et procaciter insultare servis Christi, sunt in eis plurimi qui illum interitum clademque non evasissent, nisi servos Christi se esse finxissent. Et nunc ingrata superbia atque impiissima insania eius nomini resistunt corde perverso, ut sempiternis tenebris puniantur, ad quod nomen ore vel subdolo confugerunt, ut temporali luce fruerentur.

II

Quod nulla umquam bella ita gesta sint, ut victores propter deos eorum, quos vicerunt, parcerent victis.

Tot bella gesta conscripta sunt vel ante conditam Romam vel ab eius exortu et imperio; legant et proferant sic ab alienigenis aliquam captam esse civitatem, ut hostes qui ceperant parcerent eis quos ad deorum suorum templa confugisse compererant, aut aliquem ducem barbarorum praecepisse ut inrupto oppido nullus feriretur qui in illo vel illo templo fuisset inventus. Nonne vidit Aeneas Priamum per aras

Sanguine foedantem quos ipse sacraverat ignes?

Nonne Diomedes et Ulixes

       caesis summae custodibus arcis
Corripuere sacram effigiem manibusque cruentis
Virgineas ausi divae contingere vittas?

---

[1] Virgil, *Aeneid* 2.502.   [2] *Ibid.* 166–8.

of momentary death. For among those whom you now see impudently and boldly insulting Christ's servants are not a few who would scarcely have escaped that deadly massacre, had they not masqueraded as Christ's servants. And now, in thankless pride and most wicked madness, they perversely oppose, that they may suffer punishment in eternal darkness, that name to which they fled, if only with lying lips, that they might enjoy a light that is temporary.

II

In no previous wars have the victors spared the vanquished for the sake of their gods.

LET them read the countless descriptions of wars fought before Rome was founded or carried on after her rise and expansion of power, and let them cite any city captured by foreign troops in which the conquerors spared those they found seeking refuge in the temples of their gods, or any barbarian commander who gave direction that when a town was entered, none should be struck down who was found in this or that temple. Did not Aeneas see Priam before the altars

Staining with his blood the fires himself had consecrated? [1]

Did not Diomedes and Ulysses

slay the keepers of the topmost citadel,
Snatch up the sacred image, and make bold
With bloody hands to touch the fillets
Of the virgin goddess? [2]

Nec tamen quod sequitur verum est:

> Ex illo fluere ac retro sublapsa referri
> Spes Danaum.

Postea quippe vicerunt, postea Troiam ferro ignibusque delerunt, postea confugientem ad aras Priamum obtruncaverunt. Nec ideo Troia periit quia Minervam perdidit. Quid enim prius ipsa Minerva perdiderat, ut periret? an forte custodes suos? Hoc sane verum est; illis quippe interemptis potuit auferri. Neque enim homines a simulacro, sed simulacrum ab hominibus servabatur. Quo modo ergo colebatur, ut patriam custodiret et cives, quae suos non valuit custodire custodes?

III

Quam inprudenter Romani deos penates, qui Troiam custodire non potuerant, sibi crediderint profuturos.

Ecce qualibus diis Urbem Romani servandam se commisisse gaudebant! O nimium miserabilem errorem! Et nobis suscensent, cùm de diis eorum talia dicimus; nec suscensent auctoribus suis, quos ut ediscerent mercedem dederunt doctoresque ipsos insuper et salario publico et honoribus dignissimos habuerunt. Nempe apud Vergilium, quem propterea parvuli legunt ut videlicet poeta magnus omniumque praeclarissimus atque optimus teneris

---

[1] Virgil, *Aeneid* 166 f.

Nor again is what follows true:

> Henceforth the Danaän hopes ran out
> And backward sliding drew away.[1]

For after this they conquered; after this they destroyed Troy with fire and sword; after this they cut down Priam fleeing to the altars. Nor did Troy perish because it lost Minerva. For what had Minerva herself lost first, that she should perish? Perhaps her guards? Just that, of course, for when they were slain, then she could be kidnapped. For it was not the men who were protected by the image but the image by the men. How then was she worshipped that she might guard the land and folk, she who was not strong enough to guard her own guards?

III

How unwisely the Romans believed it would help them when they trusted themselves to household gods who could not protect Troy.

SEE the sort of gods to whom the Romans were pleased to have entrusted the protection of the city! It is too pitiful a blunder! Yet they are vexed with us when we say such things about their gods, instead of being vexed with their own writers. Indeed, they paid a fee to be taught their works and held the very teachers well worthy of a stipend from the state to boot, as well as of marks of honour. Without question Virgil has—and they read him in their early years precisely in order, yes, in order that when their tender minds have been soaked in the great poet,

ebibitus animis non facile oblivione possit aboleri, secundum illud Horatii:

> Quo semel est inbuta recens servabit odorem
> Testa diu—

apud hunc ergo Vergilium nempe Iuno inducitur infesta Troianis Aeolo ventorum regi adversus eos inritando dicere:

> Gens inimica mihi Tyrrhenum navigat aequor
> Ilium in Italiam portans victosque penates.

Itane istis penatibus victis Romam, ne vinceretur, prudenter commendare debuerunt? Sed haec Iuno dicebat velut irata mulier, quid loqueretur ignorans. Quid Aeneas ipse, pius totiens appellatus, nonne ita narrat:

> Panthus Othryades, arcis Phoebique sacerdos,
> Sacra manu victosque deos parvumque nepotem
> Ipse trahit cursuque amens ad limina tendit?

Nonne deos ipsos, quos victos non dubitat dicere, sibi potius quam se illis perhibet commendatos, cum ei dicitur:

> Sacra suosque tibi commendat Troia penates?

Si igitur Vergilius tales deos et victos dicit et, ut vel victi quoquo modo evaderent, homini commen-

---

[1] Horace, *Epistles* 1.2.69 f.
[2] Virgil, *Aeneid* 1.67 f.
[3] *Ibid*. 2.319–21.   [4] *Ibid*. 293.

surpassing all in fame, it may not be easy for him to
vanish from their memory. To quote Horace:

> With what the cask when new is steeped,
> Of that the scent will long be kept—[1]

well, this Virgil of theirs has a scene in which beyond
a doubt Juno, who is hostile to the Trojans, is made to
say, as she eggs on Aeolus, king of the winds, against
them:

> A race hateful to me now sails the Tuscan sea,
> Bearing Ilium to Italy, and the conquered gods.[2]

Can it have been wise thus to entrust Rome, lest
she be conquered, to those same conquered household gods? But Juno, it may be, spoke, angry woman
that she was, without heeding what she said! How
about Aeneas himself, so often called the dutiful?
Doesn't he tell this tale?

> Panthus, Othrys' son, priest of the citadel
> And of Phoebus, bearing in his arm the holy objects
> And the vanquished gods, trailing his little grand-
>   son after,
> Comes running witless to my threshold.[3]

These gods whom he does not hesitate to call vanquished—he represents them, doesn't he? as entrusted
to himself rather than himself to them, when he is
told:

> Troy entrusts to you her holy things and household
>   gods.[4]

If consequently, Virgil says that the gods were of
this sort and vanquished, and entrusted to a man so
that, vanquished or not, they might somehow escape,

datos, quae dementia est existimare his tutoribus
Romam sapienter fuisse commissam et nisi eos
amisisset non potuisse vastari? Immo vero victos
deos tamquam praesides ac defensores colere, quid
est aliud quam tenere non numina bona, sed nomina [1]
mala? Quanto enim sapientius creditur, non Romam
ad istam cladem non fuisse venturam, nisi prius illi
perissent, sed illos potius olim fuisse perituros, nisi
eos quantum potuisset Roma servasset! Nam quis
non, cum adverterit, videat quanta sit vanitate
praesumptum non posse vinci sub defensoribus victis
et ideo perisse quia custodes perdidit deos, cum vel
sola esse potuerit causa pereundi custodes habere
voluisse perituros? Non itaque, cum de diis victis
illa conscriberentur atque canerentur, poetas libebat
mentiri, sed cordatos homines cogebat veritas con-
fiteri.

Verum ista oportunius alio loco diligenter copiose-
que tractanda sunt; nunc, quod institueram de ingratis hominibus dicere, parumper expediam ut
possum, qui ea mala, quae pro suorum morum per-
versitate merito patiuntur, blasphemantes Christo
inputant; quod autem illis etiam talibus propter
Christum parcitur, nec dignantur adtendere et eas
linguas adversus eius nomen dementia sacrilegae
perversitatis exercent quibus linguis usurpaverunt
mendaciter ipsum nomen, ut viverent, vel quas linguas in locis ei sacratis metuendo presserunt, ut illic

[1] numina, omina, omnia, demonia *various MSS.*

---

[1] See below 3.2 ff.

what madness it is to think that it was an intelligent
act to entrust Rome to such guardians as these, and
to think that she could never have been laid waste if
she had not lost them! On the contrary, to worship
conquered gods as protectors and defenders, what is
this but to have in hand, not good deities, but bad
securities? How much wiser then to believe, not
that Rome would never have come to that slaughter,
had they not perished first, but that they would have
perished long since, had Rome not preserved them as
long as she could! For who does not see, when he
thinks about it, how foolish is the supposition that
she could not be conquered while protected by
defenders who were conquered and that she perished
because she lost her guardian gods, when it might be
cause enough of destruction in itself to have chosen
guardians who would be destroyed? Thus the poets,
when they composed their verses and sang about
conquered gods, did not invent fictions to please themselves; rather they were as thinking men compelled
by truth to make confessions.

But another place will be more suitable for a careful
and full discussion of this topic.[1] At the present
juncture, I shall briefly try, as best I can, to say what
I had set about to say about these ingrates who
blasphemously attribute to Christ the evils that they
rightly suffer by reason of the perversity of their
character. The fact, however, that even such men
are spared, thanks to Christ, they deign not to notice,
and in the madness of their blasphemous perversity
they employ against his name those very tongues
with which they took his name untruthfully to save
their lives, or else those very tongues that in the
shrines dedicated to him they restrained in terror, so

tuti atque muniti, ubi propter eum inlaesi ab hostibus
fuerant, inde in eum maledictis hostilibus prosilirent.

IV

*De asylo Iunonis in Troia, quod neminem liberavit a
Graecis, et basilicis apostolorum, quae omnes ad
se confugientes a barbaris defenderunt.*

IPSA, ut dixi, Troia, mater populi Romani, sacratis
locis deorum suorum munire non potuit cives suos ab
ignibus ferroque Graecorum, eosdem ipsos deos
colentium; quin etiam

                    Iunonis asylo
Custodes lecti, Phoenix et dirus Ulixes,
Praedam adservabant; huc undique Troia gaza
Incensis erepta adytis mensaeque deorum
Crateresque auro solidi captivaque vestis
Congeritur. Pueri et pavidae longo ordine matres
Stant circum.

Electus est videlicet locus tantae deae sacratus, non
unde captivos non liceret educere, sed ubi captivos
liberet includere. Compara nunc asylum illud non
cuiuslibet dei gregalis vel de turba plebis, sed Iovis
ipsius sororis et coniugis et reginae omnium deorum
cum memoriis nostrorum apostolorum. Illuc incensis
templis et diis erepta spolia portabantur, non donanda

---

[1] Virgil, *Aeneid* 2.761–7.

that, safe and fortified in their retreat, where, thanks to him, they had been untouched by the foe, they might sally forth from it against him with hostile objurgations.

On the asylum of Juno in Troy, which freed no one from the Greeks, and the basilicas of the apostles, which protected all who fled to them from the barbarians.

TROY herself, the mother of the Roman people, was, as I said, quite unable to afford, in the areas consecrated to her gods, any protection for her own citizens from the fire and steel of the Greeks, who themselves worshipped those same gods. Nay, even

> in the sanctuary of Juno
> Phoenix and dread Ulysses, chosen guards, were
> Watching over the booty.   Here from all sides
> The Trojan treasure, torn from blazing shrines,
> And tables of the gods, bowls of solid gold, and
> Plundered raiment, are gathered up.   Boys and
> Trembling matrons in long line stand about.[1]

The place consecrated to so great a goddess was chosen, obviously, not as a place whence none might lawfully be led captive, but as a place where captives might at will be penned.   Compare now that asylum, not an asylum of any undistinguished or plebeian god, but the asylum of the sister and wife of Jupiter himself and of the queen of all the gods, with the memorial shrines of our apostles.   To the former, spoils snatched from the burning temples and the

25

victis, sed dividenda victoribus; huc autem et quod
alibi ad ea loca pertinere compertum est cum honore
et obsequio religiosissimo reportatum est. Ibi
amissa, hic servata libertas; ibi clausa, hic interdicta
captivitas; ibi possidendi a dominantibus hostibus
premebantur, huc liberandi a miserantibus ducebantur; postremo illud Iunonis templum sibi elegerat
avaritia et superbia levium Graeculorum, istas Christi
basilicas misericordia et humilitas etiam inmanium
barbarorum. Nisi forte Graeci quidem in illa sua
victoria templis deorum communium pepercerunt
atque illo confugientes miseros victosque Troianos
ferire vel captivare non ausi sunt, sed Vergilius
poetarum more illa mentitus est. Immo vero morem
hostium civitates evertentium ille descripsit.

V

De generali consuetudine hostium victas civitates evertentium quid Cato senserit.

Quem morem etiam Cato, sicut scribit Sallustius,
nobilitatae veritatis historicus, sententia sua, quam de
coniuratis in senatu habuit, commemorare non
praetermittit: " Rapi virgines pueros, divelli liberos
a parentum complexu, matres familiarum pati quae
victoribus conlibuisset, fana atque domos spoliari,
caedem incendia fieri, postremo armis cadaveribus

---

[1] The manuscripts of Augustine attribute the statement to
Cato, but Sallust places the sentiment in the mouth of Caesar.

[2] Sallust was a favourite historian of Augustine.

gods were carried, not to be given to the vanquished but to be divided among the victors. To the latter, on the other hand, were carried back with the most reverent respect and consideration even such belongings as were discovered elsewhere to be owned by them. There liberty was lost, here preserved; there captivity was jailed, here barred out. There men were forced in for slavery by despotic foes; hither men were led for freedom by the compassionate. Finally, that temple of Juno was selected by the greed and pride of those polished Greeklings; these basilicas of Christ, by the mercy and humility of still untamed barbarians. Can it be that the Greeks in that victory of theirs did spare the temples of the gods they worshipped in common with the Trojans, and did not dare to slaughter or enslave the unhappy vanquished Trojans who took refuge there? Did Virgil, rather, after the fashion of poets, make it all up? Not so. He drew a picture true to life of the wrecking of a great city by invaders.

V

What Cato said about the universal custom of an enemy in sacking a city.

Cato [1] too, as Sallust,[2] a historian famous for his veracity, writes, did not neglect to insert such a record from life in the opinion that he delivered in the Senate regarding the conspirators: "Virgins, boys, are violated, children torn from the embrace of their parents; mothers of families gratify the whims of the victors; shrines and residences are robbed; slaughter and burning are rife; in short, no place is

27

cruore atque luctu omnia compleri." Hic si fana
tacuisset, deorum sedibus solere hostes parcere
putaremus. Et haec non ab alienigenis hostibus, sed
a Catilina et sociis eius, nobilissimis senatoribus et
Romanis civibus, Romana templa metuebant. Sed hi
videlicet perditi et patriae parricidae.

VI

*Quod ne Romani quidem ita ullas ceperint civitates,
ut in templis earum parcerent victis.*

Quid ergo per multas gentes, quae inter se bella
gesserunt et nusquam victis in deorum suorum
sedibus pepercerunt, noster sermo discurrat? Romanos ipsos videamus, ipsos, inquam, recolamus respicia-
musque Romanos, de quorum praecipua laude dictum
est:

Parcere subiectis et debellare superbos,

et quod accepta iniuria ignoscere quam persequi male-
bant: quando tot tantasque urbes, ut late domina-
rentur, expugnatas captasque everterunt, legatur
nobis quae templa excipere solebant, ut ad ea quisquis
confugisset liberaretur. An illi faciebant et scriptores earundem rerum gestarum ista reticebant? Ita
vero, qui ea quae laudarent maxime requirebant,
ista praeclarissima secundum ipsos pietatis indicia
praeterirent?

---

[1] Sallust, *Catilinarian Conspiracy* 51.9.
[2] Virgil, *Aeneid* 6.853.

free from arms, the dead, gore, and lamentation." [1]
Had he been silent here about the shrines, we might
have thought that enemies usually spared the seats
of the gods. Yet the Roman temple feared such
treatment, not from a foe of alien race, but from
Catiline and his fellows, most noble senators and
Roman citizens. But these, to be sure, were scoun-
drels and murderers of their fatherland.

VI

*Not even the Romans, when they took cities, spared
the conquered in the temples.*

WHY, then, must I run through all the many nations
that waged war and never spared the vanquished
when found in the divine sanctuaries? Let us
examine the Romans themselves—let us, I say, consider and reflect upon these very Romans who are
especially renowned in that they are said

To spare the fallen and subdue the proud,[2]

and in that they preferred to forgive an injury rather
than to avenge it. When, in their expansion of
power, they overthrew many great cities, is there ever
any reference to temples that they were accustomed
to set apart so that anyone who fled to them won his
freedom? Or though they had the practice, did
their historians say nothing about it? Would they
really have been so neglectful, when their great quest
was for items to praise, as to pass over such magnificent proofs of religious feeling according to their
standards?

Egregius Romani nominis Marcus Marcellus, qui Syracusas urbem ornatissimam cepit, refertur eam prius flevisse ruituram et ante eius sanguinem suas illi lacrimas effudisse. Gessit et curam pudicitiae etiam in hoste servandae. Nam priusquam oppidum victor iussisset invadi, constituit edicto, ne quis corpus liberum violaret. Eversa est tamen civitas more bellorum, nec uspiam legitur ab imperatore tam casto atque clementi fuisse praeceptum ut quisquis ad illud vel illud templum fugisset haberetur inlaesus. Quod utique nullo modo praeteriretur, quando nec eius fletus nec quod edixerat pro pudicitia minime violanda potuit taceri.

Fabius, Tarentinae urbis eversor, a simulacrorum depraedatione se abstinuisse laudatur. Nam cum ei scriba suggessisset quid de signis deorum, quae multa capta fuerant, fieri iuberet, continentiam suam etiam iocando condivit. Quaesivit enim cuius modi essent, et cum ei non solum multa grandia, verum etiam renuntiarentur armata: " Relinquamus," inquit, " Tarentinis deos iratos." Cum igitur nec illius fletum nec huius risum, nec illius castam misericordiam nec huius facetam continentiam Romanarum rerum gestarum scriptores tacere potuerint: quando praetermitteretur, si aliquibus hominibus in honorem cuiuspiam deorum suorum sic pepercissent, ut in quoquam templo caedem vel captivitatem fieri prohiberent?

---

[1] Marcellus took Syracuse in 212 B.C. (Livy 25.24). The story is referred to again in 3.14.

[2] Q. Fabius Maximus Cunctator took Tarentum in 209 B.C. (Livy 27.15 f.; Plutarch, *Fabius* 21 f.).

A distinguished Roman, Marcus Marcellus, who took Syracuse, a most splendid city, is reported to have wept in advance of its downfall, and before he shed its blood, to have shed over it his tears.[1] He took care also to preserve chastity even in an enemy. For before the victor gave orders to enter the city, he issued a directive that no free person should be violated. Nevertheless, the city was sacked according to the practices of war, and nowhere is it read that a general so pure and merciful gave a command that any one who had fled to this temple or that should be given sanctuary. This, if it had occurred, would by no means be passed over in silence, seeing that neither his weeping nor his directive against violation of chastity could be hidden.

Fabius, the conqueror of the city of Tarentum, is praised for having refrained from making booty of the images.[2] When his secretary had brought up the question of what he wanted done with the statues of the gods, many of which had been captured, he even spiced his restraint with a witticism. He asked what sort they were, and when it was reported that there were many of large size and even some armed, he said, " Let us leave their angry gods to the Tarentines ! " Since the Roman historical writers were not able to suppress either the weeping of Marcellus or the laughter of Fabius, either the former's merciful provision for chastity or the latter's witty restraint, what room is there to believe that it would not be mentioned, if ever the Romans had spared a number of people in deference to any one of their gods, by forbidding either slaughter or enslavement in no matter what temple ?

31

VII

Quod in eversione Urbis, quae aspere gesta sunt, de consuetudine acciderint belli; quae vero clementer, de potentia provenerint nominis Christi.

QUIDQUID ergo vastationis trucidationis depraedationis concremationis adflictionis in ista recentissima Romana clade commissum est, fecit hoc consuetudo bellorum; quod autem novo more factum est, quod inusitata rerum facie inmanitas barbara tam mitis apparuit, ut amplissimae basilicae implendae populo cui parceretur eligerentur et decernerentur, ubi nemo feriretur, unde nemo raperetur, quo liberandi multi a miserantibus hostibus ducerentur, unde captivandi ulli nec a crudelibus hostibus abducerentur, hoc Christi nomini, hoc Christiano tempori tribuendum quisquis non videt, caecus, quisquis videt nec laudat, ingratus, quisquis laudanti reluctatur, insanus est. Absit ut prudens quisquam hoc feritati inputet barbarorum. Truculentissimas et saevissimas mentes ille terruit, ille frenavit, ille mirabiliter temperavit qui per prophetam tanto ante dixit: *Visitabo in virga iniquitates eorum et in flagellis peccata eorum; misericordiam autem meam non dispergam ab eis.*

32

VII

*The cruelties in the sack of Rome were in accord with
the customs of war; the acts of compassion were
manifestations of the power of Christ's name.*

ACCORDINGLY, whatever destruction, slaughter,
plundering, burning, misery, occurred in that recent
calamity at Rome, was occasioned by the customary
procedures of war. On the other hand, what set a
new precedent, the aspect, novel in history and so
gentle, that barbarian cruelty displayed, in that
basilicas of the most generous capacity were selected
and set apart by decree to be occupied as asylums of
mercy for the people, where no one should be smitten,
whence no one should be ravished, whither many
should be conducted by compassionate soldiers for
release from bondage, and where none should be
taken captive even by ruthless foes—he who does not
see that this accrues to the credit of Christ's name,
and to the credit of a Christian era, is blind; he who
sees, but does not applaud, is churlish; he who
would suppress such applause, is mad. God forbid
that any man of sound judgement should attribute
this behaviour to the savagery of barbarians. Their
hearts are ferocious in the highest degree, relentless
in the highest degree; he it was that dismayed, he
that bridled, he that miraculously softened their
hearts—he who so long ago declared through the
prophet: " I will visit their transgressions with the
rod, and their sins with stripes. Nevertheless,
my lovingkindness will I not take utterly from
them." [1]

[1] Psalms 89.32 f.

33

VIII

De commodis atque incommodis, quae bonis ac malis plerumque communia sunt.

DICET aliquis: " Cur ergo ista divina misericordia etiam ad impios ingratosque pervenit? " Cur putamus, nisi quia eam ille praebuit, qui cotidie *facit oriri solem suum super bonos et malos et pluit super iustos et iniustos?* Quamvis enim quidam eorum ista cogitantes paenitendo ab impietate se corrigant, quidam vero, sicut apostolus dicit, *divitias bonitatis et longanimitatis Dei* contemnentes *secundum duritiam cordis sui et cor inpaenitens* thesaurizent *sibi iram in die irae et revelationis iusti iudicii Dei, qui reddet unicuique secundum opera eius,* tamen patientia Dei ad paenitentiam invitat malos, sicut flagellum Dei ad patientiam erudit bonos; itemque misericordia Dei fovendos amplectitur bonos, sicut severitas Dei puniendos corripit malos. Placuit quippe divinae providentiae praeparare in posterum bona iustis quibus non fruentur iniusti, et mala impiis quibus non excruciabuntur boni; ista vero temporalia bona et mala utrisque voluit esse communia, ut nec bona cupidius adpetantur quae mali quoque habere cernuntur, nec mala turpiter evitentur quibus et boni plerumque adficiuntur.

Interest autem plurimum qualis sit usus vel earum

---

[1] Matthew 5.45. [2] Romans 2.4–6.

VIII

*On the advantages and disadvantages which often
afflict the good and evil alike.*

SOMEONE will say: " Why, then, did this lovingkindness reach even to the wicked and ungrateful? "
What do we suppose, except that it was a gift of
him who daily " makes his sun to rise on the good and
on the evil and sends his rain upon the just and upon
the unjust "? [1] For although some individuals
among them reflecting on this, repent of their irreligion and reform their ways, others, on the other hand,
despising, as the Apostle says, " the riches of God's
goodness and his forbearance by reason of their
hardness of heart and their impenitent heart "
treasure up " for themselves wrath against the day of
wrath and of revelation of the righteous judgement
of God, who will repay each man according to his
works." [2] Yet the patience of God invites the
wicked to repentance, as the scourge of God instructs
the good in patience. So, too, the mercy of God
embraces the good to cherish them, just as the
severity of God lays hold on the wicked to punish
them. The divine providence, to be sure, has seen
fit to hold in reserve for the righteous some good
things that will not be enjoyed by the unrighteous,
and for the irreligious, excruciating pains that the
good will not suffer. The good things, however, and
the evil things of this world are by his will common to
both, that he may restrain us from too eager pursuit
of goods such as we see enjoyed also by the wicked,
and from cowardly avoidance of evils such as good men
too as a rule experience.

It is also very important how we take what befalls

35

rerum quae prosperae, vel earum quae dicuntur adversae. Nam bonus temporalibus nec bonis extollitur nec malis frangitur; malus autem ideo huiusce modi infelicitate punitur, quia felicitate corrumpitur. Ostendit tamen Deus saepe etiam in his distribuendis evidentius operationem suam. Nam si nunc omne peccatum manifesta plecteret poena, nihil ultimo iudicio servari putaretur; rursus si nullum nunc peccatum puniret aperta divinitas, nulla esse divina providentia crederetur. Similiter in rebus secundis, si non eas Deus quibusdam petentibus evidentissima largitate concederet, non ad eum ista pertinere diceremus; itemque si omnibus eas petentibus daret, non nisi propter talia praemia serviendum illi esse arbitraremur, nec pios nos faceret talis servitus, sed potius cupidos et avaros.

Haec cum ita sint, quicumque boni et mali pariter adflicti sunt, non ideo ipsi distincti non sunt quia distinctum non est quod utrique perpessi sunt. Manet enim dissimilitudo passorum etiam in similitudine passionum, et licet sub eodem tormento non est idem virtus et vitium. Nam sicut sub uno igne aurum rutilat palea fumat, et sub eadem tribula stipulae comminuuntur frumenta purgantur, nec ideo cum oleo amurca confunditur quia eodem preli pondere exprimitur, ita una eademque vis inruens

us, whether our fortunes be of the sort called happy
or such as are termed the contrary. For the good
man is neither elated by the gains of this world nor
crushed by its losses, whereas the wicked man is
punished by this kind of misfortune for the very
reason that he lets his good fortune spoil him. Yet
even in apportioning these things, God often shows
quite clearly his interposition. For though, if obvious
punishment should now be visited for every sin, it
would be thought that nothing is reserved for the
last judgement, yet on the other hand, if no sin were
now plainly punished by divine action, men would
believe that there is no such thing as divine providence. In the same way, in the case of prosperity,
if God did not grant it with clearest proof of his
bounty to some individuals who pray for it, we should
say that he had no interest in such things, and likewise, were he to grant it to everyone who prayed, we
should conclude that except for such rewards we have
no obligation to serve him, and service of that kind
would prove us not religious but greedy and covetous.

Though this is so, in any case where good and bad
are equally afflicted, they are not themselves without
difference just because there is no difference in the
thing that they both suffer. For unlikeness in the
sufferers is still found even with likeness in their
sufferings, and though the instrument of suffering
may be the same for virtue as for vice, yet they are not
the same thing. Exposed to the same fire gold grows
red but chaff smokes, and under the same threshing-
sledge the straw is broken to pieces but the grain
separated, nor is the oil of olives intermixed with the
mash because it is extracted by weight of the same
press. Just so one and the same force assailing the

bonos probat purificat eliquat, malos damnat vastat exterminat. Unde in eadem adflictione mali Deum detestantur atque blasphemant, boni autem precantur et laudant. Tantum interest, non qualia, sed qualis quisque patiatur. Nam pari motu exagitatum et exhalat horribiliter caenum et suaviter fragrat unguentum.

IX

De causis correptionum, propter quas et boni et mali pariter flagellantur.

QUID igitur in illa rerum vastitate Christiani passi sunt quod non eis magis fideliter ista considerantibus ad provectum valeret?

Primum quod ipsa peccata, quibus Deus indignatus implevit tantis calamitatibus mundum, humiliter cogitantes, quamvis longe absint a facinerosis [1] flagitiosis atque impiis, tamen non usque adeo se a delictis deputant alienos ut nec temporalia pro eis mala perpeti se iudicent dignos. Excepto enim quod unusquisque quamlibet laudabiliter vivens cedit in quibusdam carnali concupiscentiae, etsi non ad facinorum inmanitatem et gurgitem flagitiorum atque impietatis abominationem, ad aliqua tamen peccata vel rara vel tanto crebriora, quanto minora—hoc ergo excepto quis tandem facile reperitur, qui eosdem ipsos, propter quorum horrendam superbiam

---

[1] *Perhaps* facinoribus *should be read.*

good tries, purifies and purges them clean, but condemns, ruins and destroys the wicked. Hence comes it that in the same affliction the wicked curse and blaspheme God, while the good are praying and praising him. So important is it, not what the suffering is like, but what the individual who suffers is like. For stirred by a like motion, filth emits a horrid stink, but ointment has a sweet smell.

IX

Why both good and evil persons are equally afflicted.

WHAT, then, did Christians suffer in that historic disaster that would not contribute to their development, let them but reflect on it faithfully?

First, though when they humbly consider those sins, because of which God in his wrath has filled the world with such great calamities, they are far removed from the state of criminals who are outrageous and irreligious, nevertheless they do not regard themselves as so exempt from all faults that they do not consider themselves worthy even of temporal punishment for their errors. Leaving it out of account that every single one of us, no matter how praiseworthy his life, yet in some cases yields to carnal desire, short albeit of falling into atrocious crimes or into the sink of profligacy or into the abomination of irreligion, but still so far as to commit a good many sins—infrequent sins, it may be, or the more frequent they are, the less serious they would have to be—leaving this out of account, where in the world can you readily produce a Christian who treats as they should be treated those very people on account of whose revolting arrogance

luxuriamque et avaritiam atque execrabiles iniquitates et impietates Deus, sicut minando praedixit,
conterit terras, sic habeat ut habendi sunt? Sic cum
eis vivat ut cum talibus est vivendum?

Plerumque enim ab eis docendis ac monendis,
aliquando etiam obiurgandis et corripiendis male
dissimulatur, vel cum laboris piget, vel cum os eorum
verecundamur offendere, vel cum inimicitias devita-
mus, ne impediant et noceant in istis temporalibus
rebus, sive quas adipisci adhuc adpetit nostra cupiditas, sive quas amittere formidat infirmitas, ita ut,
quamvis bonis malorum vita displiceat et ideo cum eis
non incidant in illam damnationem quae post hanc
vitam talibus praeparatur, tamen, quia propterea
peccatis eorum damnabilibus parcunt, dum eos in suis
licet levibus et venialibus metuunt, iure cum eis
temporaliter flagellantur, quamvis in aeternum
minime puniantur, iure istam vitam, quando divinitus
adfliguntur cum eis, amaram sentiunt, cuius amando
dulcedinem peccantibus eis amari esse noluerunt.

Nam si propterea quisque obiurgandis et corripiendis male agentibus parcit quia opportunius
tempus inquirit vel eisdem ipsis metuit ne deteriores
ex hoc efficiantur, vel ad bonam vitam et piam
erudiendos impediant alios infirmos et premant atque
avertant a fide, non videtur esse cupiditatis occasio,
sed consilium caritatis.

and luxury, their greed and detestable iniquities, their sins against religion, God, precisely as he prophetically threatened, now shatters land after land? Or one whose life among them is what among such men it should be?

For, as a rule, we hypocritically fail in our duty of instructing them and warning them, or even on some occasions of denouncing and rebuking them, either when we weary of the effort or when we are too courteous to affront their dignity or when we fight shy of feuds that might obstruct or impair our success in the present world, whether it be that an eager heart so covets some gain, or a faint heart boggles at some loss. Therefore, although the good do not accept the life of the wicked and therefore do not incur with them the condemnation that is prepared for such men when this life is ended, nevertheless, this indulgence toward their damnable sins, motivated by fear, justifies, despite the light and venial character of their own sins, their chastisement with the wicked in this life, though they by no means receive eternal punishment. It is only right that they should taste bitterness in this life, when they feel the scourge of God in company with the pagans, for it was through love of its sweets that they would not be bitter to them in their sins.

Note that if anyone abstains from denouncing or rebuking evildoers because he seeks a more favourable occasion or fears for the sinners themselves, lest the result be to make them worse, or lest they hinder others who are weak and should be guided to a good and pious life, using pressure to turn them from the faith, this is not regarded as the pleading of self-indulgence but as the prompting of Christian love.

Illud est culpabile, quod hi, qui dissimiliter vivunt
et a malorum factis abhorrent, parcunt tamen peccatis
alienis, quae dedocere aut obiurgare deberent, dum
eorum offensiones cavent, ne sibi noceant in his rebus,
quibus licite boni atque innocenter utuntur, sed
cupidius quam oportebat eos qui in hoc mundo pere-
grinantur et spem supernae patriae prae se gerunt.
Non solum quippe infirmiores, vitam ducentes
coniugalem, filios habentes vel habere quaerentes,
domos ac familias possidentes (quos apostolus in
ecclesiis adloquitur docens et monens quem ad
modum vivere debeant et uxores cum maritis et
mariti cum uxoribus, et filii cum parentibus et
parentes cum filiis, et servi cum dominis et domini
cum servis), multa temporalia, multa terrena libenter
adipiscuntur et moleste amittunt, propter quae non
audent offendere homines quorum sibi vita con-
taminatissima et consceleratissima displicet; verum
etiam hi, qui superiorem vitae gradum tenent nec
coniugalibus vinculis inretiti sunt et victu parvo ac
tegimento utuntur, plerumque, suae famae ac saluti
dum insidias atque impetus malorum timent, ab
eorum reprehensione sese abstinent, et quamvis non
in tantum eos metuant ut ad similia perpetranda
quibuslibet eorum terroribus atque inprobitatibus
cedant, ea ipsa tamen, quae cum eis non perpetrant,
nolunt plerumque corripere, cum fortasse possint
aliquos corripiendo corrigere, ne, si non potuerint,

The point that is open to censure is that those who
live differently and are shocked by the deeds of the
wicked, are nevertheless indulgent toward the sins of
others instead of teaching them better or denouncing
them, as they ought—and do so to avoid offending
such men—who might injure them in matters that are
not forbidden or harmful for good men to enjoy in
themselves, were it not that the desire for them
exceeds what is proper for those who in this world are
but sojourners and cherish the hope of a heavenly
country. Not only, to be sure, do the weaker, who
are married, who have children or hope to have them,
possess houses and servants—whom the Apostle
addresses in the churches, teaching them and ad-
monishing them how they are to live together, wives
with husbands and husbands with wives, children with
parents and parents with children, servants with
masters and masters with children—not only do
these rejoice to acquire many temporal and many
earthly goods, and grieve when they lose them, so
that on their account they dare not give offence to
men whose way of life, polluted and criminal as it is in
the highest degree, they condemn, but even such as
occupy a higher level in life, are not enmeshed in the
bonds of matrimony and are modest in food and
raiment, often refrain from reproving the wicked for
fear of losing reputation or security through the plots
or violence of the wicked. So, although they are not
carried so far by fear as to consent to commit sins of
that kind, no matter what menaces or base tricks are
used, yet they are not willing to rebuke crimes that
they will not join in perpetrating, though their
rebukes might well produce reform in a good many
cases. They fear to jeopardize or lose, in case of

sua salus ac fama in periculum exitiumque perveniat,
nec ea consideratione qua suam famam ac salutem
vident esse necessariam utilitati erudiendorum hominum, sed ea potius infirmitate qua delectat lingua
blandiens et humanus dies, et reformidatur vulgi
iudicium et carnis excruciatio vel peremptio, hoc est
propter quaedam cupiditatis vincula, non propter
officia caritatis.

Non mihi itaque videtur haec parva esse causa
quare cum malis flagellentur et boni, quando Deo
placet perditos mores etiam temporalium poenarum
adflictione punire. Flagellantur enim simul, non
quia simul agunt malam vitam, sed quia simul amant
temporalem vitam, non quidem aequaliter, sed tamen
simul, quam boni contemnere deberent, ut illi correpti
atque correcti consequerentur aeternam, ad quam
consequendam si nollent esse socii, ferrentur et dili-
gerentur inimici, quia donec vivunt semper incertum
est utrum voluntatem sint in melius mutaturi.

Qua in re non utique parem, sed longe graviorem
habent causam, quibus per prophetam dicitur:
Ille quidem in suo peccato morietur,[1] *sanguinem autem eius
de manu speculatoris requiram.* Ad hoc enim speculatores, hoc est populorum praepositi, constituti sunt in
ecclesiis, ut non parcant obiurgando peccata. Nec

[1] *Ezechiel 33.6 (Vulgate) reads:* ille quidem in iniquitate
sua captus est, sanguinem autem (etc.), *which harmonizes with
AV and RSV.*

---

[1] Ezekiel 33.6. Augustine's quotation of the first clause
differs from other versions which have : " He is taken in his
iniquity," etc. Augustine usually follows the Septuagint, or
Greek version, but that agrees with the Vulgate here.

[2] By using the Latin word *speculatores,* instead of the loan
word *episcopi,* cognate of the Greek word ἐπίσκοποι, Augustine

failure, their own safety and reputation, and this not on the ground that they see their own safety and reputation as indispensable instruments whereby men may receive instruction, but rather because of the weakness that is pleased by a flattering tongue and the favour of men and is in terror of the verdict of the mob and of the torture or death of the flesh; that is, they serve certain bonds of selfishness, not the ties of love.

This seems to me to be, therefore, no small reason why the good are afflicted with the wicked, when God is pleased to punish profligate characters by corporal penalties. For they are punished together, not because they lead a wicked life together but because they love this present life—not, to be sure, equally, but nevertheless together. This life the good ought to deem of no value, so that the wicked, when rebuked and reformed, might gain the life eternal; but if they are unwilling to be allies of the good in pursuit of that gain, let them be tolerated and loved as enemies, since as long as they live, it will always remain uncertain whether they will not change their minds for the better.

In this they have a much more serious cause for fear to whom through the prophet it is said: "He shall die in his sin but his blood will I require from the watchman's hand." [1] This is indeed the reason why watchmen, [2] that is, those placed over the people, have been established in the churches, namely, that they may not be sparing in denouncing sins.

is attempting to impress upon his reader the etymology of the word bishop. The alternative renderings, *sacerdotes*, *antistites* and *pontifices*, would not have made the meaning clear.

45

ideo tamen ab huius modi culpa penitus alienus est,
qui, licet praepositus non sit, in eis tamen, quibus
vitae huius necessitate coniungitur, multa monenda
vel arguenda novit et neglegit, devitans eorum offensiones propter illa quibus in hac vita non indebitis
utitur, sed plus quam debuit delectatur.

Deinde habent aliam causam boni, quare temporalibus affligantur malis, qualem habuit Iob: ut
sibi ipse humanus animus sit probatus et cognitus,
quanta virtute pietatis gratis Deum diligat.

X

Quod sanctis in amissione rerum temporalium nihil
pereat.

QUIBUS recte consideratis atque perspectis adtende
utrum aliquid mali acciderit fidelibus et piis quod eis
non in bonum verteretur, nisi forte putandum est
apostolicam illam vacare sententiam, ubi ait: *Scimus
quia diligentibus Deum omnia cooperatur in bonum.*

Amiserunt omnia quae habebant. Numquid fidem?
numquid pietatem? numquid interioris hominis
bona, qui est ante Deum dives? Hae sunt opes
Christianorum, quibus opulentus dicebat apostolus:
*Est autem quaestus magnus pietas cum sufficientia.
Nihil enim intulimus in hunc mundum, sed nec auferre*

---

[1] Romans 8.28.

Yet that does not wholly exempt from guilt of this
sort the man who, though he be not set over the
people, yet observes in those with whom he is joined
by the requirements of daily life many faults that
merit admonition or reproof, but ignores them, being
chary of giving offence because he loves the kind of
thing I mentioned, a thing which it is not wrong to
use in this life, but which it is wrong to have loved
so much.

Then the good are afflicted with temporal ills for
another reason, the same as in Job's case, namely, in
order that a man's heart may be tested in itself and
that it may be known how solid the religion is whereby it loves God without reward.

<h1 style="text-align:center">X</h1>

*That the saints lose nothing when they are deprived of
temporal goods.*

Now that these points have been accurately considered and scrutinized, let the reader give thought
to the question whether any evil has befallen the
faithful and religious that was not turned to their
profit—unless we are to suppose that there is nothing
in the pronouncement of the Apostle when he says,
" For we know that all things work together for good
to them that love God." [1]

They lost everything they had. Their faith?
Their piety? The goods of the inner man, who is
rich in the sight of God? Here is the wealth of the
Christians, the wealth of the Apostle when he said:
" Godliness with enough for oneself is great gain.
For we brought nothing into this world, nor on the

*aliquid possumus. Habentes autem victum et tegumentum
his contenti sumus. Nam qui volunt divites fieri, incidunt
in temptationem et laqueum et desideria multa stulta* [1] *et
noxia, quae mergunt homines in interitum et perditionem.
Radix enim est omnium malorum avaritia, quam quidam
adpetentes a fide pererraverunt et inseruerunt se doloribus
multis.*

Quibus ergo terrenae divitiae in illa vastatione
perierunt, si eas sic habebant quem ad modum ab isto
foris paupere, intus divite audierant, id est, si mundo
utebantur tamquam non utentes, potuerunt dicere,
quod ille graviter temptatus et minime superatus:
*Nudus exivi de utero matris meae, nudus revertar in
terram. Dominus dedit, Dominus abstulit, sicut Domino
placuit, ita factum est ; sit nomen Domini benedictum ;* ut
bonus servus magnas facultates haberet ipsam sui
Domini voluntatem, cui pedisequus mente ditesceret,
nec contristaretur eis rebus vivens relictus quas cito
fuerat moriens relicturus.

Illi autem infirmiores, qui terrenis his bonis, quamvis ea non praeponerent Christo, aliquantula tamen
cupiditate cohaerebant, quantum haec amando
peccaverint, perdendo senserunt. Tantum quippe
doluerunt quantum se doloribus inseruerant, sicut
apostolum dixisse supra commemoravi. Oportebat
enim ut eis adderetur etiam experimentorum discip-
lina a quibus tam diu fuerat neglecta verborum.

[1] *Omitted by codex Corbeiensis (saec. vii), codex Monacensis
(saec. x) and many editors.*

---

[1] 1 Timothy 6.6–10.   [2] Job 1.21.

other hand can we take anything out. But if we have food and raiment, we are content with these. For they that wish to become rich, fall into temptation and a trap and into many foolish and hurtful lusts, which sink men down to destruction and perdition. For greed of gain is the root of all evils; some who have pursued gain have strayed from the faith and thrust themselves among many pangs." [1]

They whose worldly riches were lost in the sack, if they had possessed their riches in the manner of which they had heard in the words of this Apostle who was poor without but rich within; that is to say, if they had made use of the world as if not using it, they could have said what was said by Job, sorely tried and never a whit conquered: "Naked came I out of my mother's womb, naked I shall return into the earth. The Lord gave, the Lord has taken away; as it pleased the Lord, so has it come to pass. Blessed be the name of the Lord." [2] Thus, as a good servant, he counted as great abundance the will of his Lord itself, in attendance on which his soul should grow rich, and he was not grief-stricken at losing in his lifetime the sort of thing that he was bound to lose before long when he died.

But those weaker souls who, though they did not prefer these earthly goods to Christ, yet clung to them with ever so little desire, discovered when they lost them how much they had sinned in loving them. For their grief was great or small to the extent that, in the words of the Apostle mentioned above, they had thrust themselves among many pangs. For it was proper that those who had long disregarded the schooling of words should receive in addition the schooling of experience. When the Apostle says:

49

Nam cum dixit apostolus: *Qui volunt divites fieri,*
incidunt in temptationem et cetera, profecto in divitiis
cupiditatem reprehendit, non facultatem, quoniam
praecepit alibi dicens: *Praecipe divitibus huius mundi*
non superbe sapere neque sperare in incerto divitiarum, sed
in Deo vivo, qui praestat nobis omnia abundanter ad
fruendum ; bene faciant, divites sint in operibus bonis,
facile tribuant, communicent, thesaurizent sibi funda-
mentum bonum in futurum, ut adprehendant veram
vitam.

Haec qui de suis divitiis faciebant, magnis sunt
lucris levia damna solati plusque laetati ex his quae
facile tribuendo tutius servaverunt quam contristati
ex his quae timide retinendo facilius amiserunt.
Hoc enim potuit in terra perire quod piguit inde
transferre. Nam qui receperunt consilium Domini
sui dicentis: *Nolite vobis condere thesauros in terra, ubi*
tinea et rubigo exterminant et ubi fures effodiunt et
furantur ; sed thesaurizate vobis thesaurum in caelo, quo
fur non accedit neque tinea corrumpit ; ubi enim est
thesaurus tuus, illic erit et cor tuum, tribulationis tempore probaverunt quam recte sapuerint non contem-
nendo veracissimum praeceptorem et thesauri sui
fidelissimum invictissimumque custodem. Nam si
multi gavisi sunt ibi se habuisse divitias suas, quo
contigit ut hostis non accederet, quanto certius et

---

[1] 1 Timothy 6.9.

[2] *Ibid.* 17–19.

[3] The meaning is that by giving charity to the poor, funds
are transferred to the other world. Riches not given away
could not be so transferred. See the passage of Scripture
immediately quoted.

[4] Matthew 6.19–21.

" They that wish to become rich fall into temptation," [1] and so on, he surely is rebuking in the case of riches, not the possession, but the desire for them, since, speaking elsewhere, he lays down the rule: " Instruct those who are wealthy in this world not to be proud-minded nor to trust in the uncertainty of riches, but in the living God who bestows on us all things in abundance for us to enjoy. Let them do good, let them be rich in good works, ready to distribute, given to sharing, as they lay up for themselves a sound basis for the future, in order to possess the true life." [2]

Those who did this with their riches were consoled for light losses by great gains, and were more gladdened by those possessions which by ready distribution they had preserved the more securely, than they were saddened by those that they had lost the more easily by cautiously holding them back. For anything that could be destroyed on earth was something that they had shirked transferring elsewhere.[3] They received from their Lord this word of wisdom, " Lay not up for yourselves treasures upon earth, where moth and rust destroy, and where thieves break through and steal; but lay up for yourselves treasures in heaven, a place to which no thief makes his way and in which no moth does any damage; for where your treasure is, there will your heart be also." [4] They have found by test in time of tribulation how wise they were not to despise that truest teacher, that most faithful and unconquered guardian of their treasure. For if many rejoiced that they kept their treasure where, as it chanced, the enemy did not come, how much more certainly and more securely were those able to rejoice

securius gaudere potuerunt qui monitu Dei sui illuc migraverunt quo accedere omnino non posset!

Unde Paulinus noster, Nolensis episcopus, ex opulentissimo divite voluntate pauperrimus et copiosissime sanctus, quando et ipsam Nolam barbari vastaverunt, cum ab eis teneretur, sic in corde suo, ut ab eo postea cognovimus, precabatur: "Domine, non excrucier propter aurum et argentum; ubi enim sint omnia mea, tu scis." Ibi enim habebat omnia sua ubi eum condere et thesaurizare ille monstraverat qui haec mala mundo ventura praedixerat. Ac per hoc qui Domino suo monenti oboedierant, ubi et quo modo thesaurizare deberent, nec ipsas terrenas divitias barbaris incursantibus amiserunt. Quos autem non oboedisse paenituit, quid de talibus rebus faciendum esset, si non praecedente sapientia, certe consequente experientia didicerunt.

At enim quidam boni etiam Christiani tormentis excruciati sunt, ut bona sua hostibus proderent. Illi vero nec prodere nec perdere potuerunt bonum quo ipsi boni erant. Si autem torqueri quam mammona iniquitatis prodere maluerunt, boni non erant. Admonendi autem fuerant, qui tanta patiebantur pro auro quanta essent sustinenda pro Christo, ut eum potius diligere discerent qui pro se passos aeterna

52

who by the advice of their God had migrated to a region whither the enemy could not possibly come!

Thus, my friend Paulinus,[1] Bishop of Nola, who voluntarily gave up his great wealth and became exceedingly poor, yet abundantly holy, when the barbarians sacked even Nola itself and he was in their hands, used to pray in his heart, as I afterwards learned from him, " Lord, let me not be tormented for gold and silver, for thou knowest where all my possessions are." He kept all his possessions where he had been taught to store and treasure them by him who had foretold that these evils would come to the world. Consequently, those who had obeyed their Lord when he counselled them where and how they should lay up treasure, did not lose even their earthly treasures in the invasion of barbarians. Those, moreover, who were sorry that they had not obeyed, have learned, if not by wisdom in advance, at least by subsequent experience, what they should have done with such possessions.

Some good men, to be sure, even Christian men, have been put to torture to make them reveal their property to the enemy. But they could neither betray nor lose that good by which they were themselves good. If, moreover, they preferred to be tortured rather than to forsake the mammon of unrighteousness, they were not good. These who endured as much suffering for gold, as they ought to have borne for Christ, should have been warned to learn rather to love him who enriches with eternal happiness all who

[1] Paulinus (d. A.D. 431) gave all his great wealth to the poor. He became Bishop of Nola in Campania, probably in A.D. 409.

felicitate ditaret, non aurum et argentum, pro quo pati miserrimum fuit, seu mentiendo occultaretur, seu verum dicendo proderetur.

Namque inter tormenta nemo Christum confitendo amisit, nemo aurum nisi negando servavit. Quocirca utiliora erant fortasse tormenta quae bonum incorruptibile amandum docebant quam illa bona, quae sine ullo utili fructu dominos sui amore torquebant.

Sed quidam etiam non habentes quod proderent, dum non creduntur, torti sunt. Et hi forte habere cupiebant nec sancta voluntate pauperes erant; quibus demonstrandum fuit non facultates, sed ipsas cupiditates talibus dignas esse cruciatibus. Si vero vitae melioris proposito reconditum aurum argentumque non habebant, nescio quidem utrum cuiquam talium acciderit ut dum habere creditur torqueretur; verum tamen etiamsi accidit, profecto, qui inter illa tormenta paupertatem sanctam confitebatur, Christum confitebatur. Quapropter etsi non meruit ab hostibus credi, non potuit tamen sanctae paupertatis confessor sine caelesti mercede torqueri.

Multos, inquiunt, etiam Christianos fames diuturna vastavit. Hoc quoque in usus suos boni fideles pie tolerando verterunt. Quos enim fames necavit, malis vitae huius, sicut corporis morbus, eripuit; quos autem non necavit, docuit parcius vivere, docuit productius ieiunare.

suffer on his behalf—not to love gold and silver for which in either case it was the height of wretchedness to suffer, whether they lied and kept them concealed or told the truth and surrendered them.

For during the torture no man lost Christ by confessing; no one preserved wealth except by denying. For this reason it may be that the tortures which taught them that the good to be held dear is a good that cannot decay were more profitable than those goods of theirs, which without any profitable service at all, brought torture upon their owners through love of them.

Certain others there were who, even though they had nothing to surrender, were tortured because they were not believed. Yet these too perhaps had some desire to possess wealth and were not poor by a holy act of will. These had to be shown that not merely the possession of wealth but the very desire for it was worthy of such tortures. Even if they had no hidden gold and silver through hope of a better life—I do not know whether it happened to any such that he was tortured in the belief that he did possess—but even if this did happen, surely he who under those tortures confessed holy poverty, confessed Christ. For this reason, even if he did not succeed in convincing the enemy, the confessor of this holy poverty could not have been tormented without a heavenly reward.

Many, they say, even Christians, were laid low by the long famine. This also the good and faithful turned to good purposes by piously bearing it. For those whom the famine slew, it snatched from the evils of this life, as sickness does from bodily ailments. Those whom it did not, were taught to live more scantily, were taught to fast more extensively.

XI

De fine temporalis vitae sive longioris sive brevioris.

SED enim multi etiam Christiani interfecti sunt, multi multarum mortium foeda varietate consumpti. Hoc si aegre ferendum est, omnibus qui in hanc vitam procreati sunt, utique commune est. Hoc scio, neminem fuisse mortuum qui non fuerat aliquando moriturus. Finis autem vitae tam longam quam brevem vitam hoc idem facit. Neque enim aliud melius et aliud deterius, aut aliud maius et aliud brevius est, quod iam pariter non est. Quid autem interest, quo mortis genere vita ista finiatur, quando ille cui finitur iterum mori non cogitur? Cum autem unicuique mortalium sub cotidianis vitae huius casibus innumerabiles mortes quodam modo comminentur, quamdiu incertum est quaenam earum ventura sit, quaero utrum satius sit unam perpeti moriendo an omnes timere vivendo. Nec ignoro quam citius eligatur diu vivere sub timore tot mortium quam semel moriendo nullam deinceps formidare. Sed aliud est quod carnis sensus infirmiter pavidus refugit, aliud quod mentis ratio diligenter enucleata convincit.

Mala mors putanda non est quam bona vita prae-cesserit. Neque enim facit malam mortem, nisi quod sequitur mortem. Non itaque multum curandum est eis qui necessario morituri sunt, quid accidat ut moriantur, sed moriendo quo ire cogantur. Cum igitur Christiani noverint longe meliorem fuisse reli-

XI

Whether it matters how long this present life endures.

But in fact many Christians were slain and many were wasted in horrible and manifold forms of death. If this is hard to bear, it is, at any rate, common to all who have been born into this life. This I know, that no one has ever died who was not destined to die some time. The end of life is the same event when it affects a long life as when a short one. For there is no distinction of better or worse, no distinction of longer or shorter in reference to something that uniformly does not now exist. And what difference does the kind of death which ends this life make inasmuch as the man whose life ends is not compelled to die a second death? When, moreover, in the daily vicissitudes of this life each mortal is in a way threatened by innumerable deaths, so long as it is uncertain which of them will really come, I ask whether it is better to suffer one and die or to fear all and live? I am not unaware how much sooner a man would choose to live long under the menace of so many deaths rather than by dying once to fear none of them henceforth, but it is one menace that the apprehension of the flesh weakly seeks to escape and quite another that the carefully analysed calculation of the mind pins down.

That death should not be thought an evil which follows a good life, nor is death in fact made evil except by what follows death. Accordingly, those who are necessarily bound to die, need not care greatly by what accident they die, but must care where they are forced to go when they die. Since, then, Christians are aware how far better was the

giosi pauperis mortem inter lingentium canum linguas quam impii divitis in purpura et bysso, horrenda illa genera mortium quid mortuis obfuerunt qui bene vixerunt?

XII

De sepultura humanorum corporum, quae Christianis etiamsi fuerit negata nil adimit.

AT enim in tanta strage cadaverum nec sepeliri potuerunt. Neque istuc pia fides nimium reformidat, tenens praedictum nec absumentes bestias resurrecturis corporibus obfuturas, quorum capillus capitis non peribit. Nullo modo diceret veritas: *Nolite timere eos qui corpus occidunt, animam autem non possunt occidere,* si quicquam obesset futurae vitae, quidquid inimici de corporibus occisorum facere voluissent.

Nisi forte quispiam sic absurdus est ut contendat eos qui corpus occidunt non debere timeri ante mortem, ne corpus occidant, et timeri debere post mortem, ne corpus occisum sepeliri non sinant. Falsum est ergo quod ait Christus [1]: *Qui corpus occidunt, et postea non habent quid faciant,* si habent tanta quae de cadaveribus faciant. Absit ut falsum sit quod veritas dixit. Dictum est enim aliquid eos facere cum occidunt, quia in corpore sensus est occidendo; postea vero nihil habere quod faciant, quia nullus sensus est in corpore occiso.

[1] Christus, *though generally omitted in the MSS., seems to be needed and has been actually added in corrections to the important codices CAK.*

---

[1] Luke 16.19–31.   [2] Matthew 10.28.
                [3] Luke 12.4.

death of the poor and pious man while the dogs licked his sores than that of the wicked rich man, clothed in purple and fine linen, what harm did those terrible deaths do to the dead who had lived well? [1]

XII

On the burial of men's bodies and that Christians lose nothing even if burial be denied.

WHAT about the fact that when so many were slaughtered the corpses could not even be buried? This does not overmuch dismay a religious faith, holding to the promise that not even devouring beasts will be prejudicial to bodies that are to rise again, for not a hair of their head will perish. In no wise could Truth say: " Fear not men who kill the body but are not able to kill the soul," [2] if anything that the enemy had chosen to do with the bodies of the slain could be prejudicial to a future life.

Perhaps, however, someone is so foolish as to maintain that those who kill the body ought not to inspire fear before death that they will kill the body, and yet ought to inspire fear that after death they will not permit the body when slain to be buried? If so, then what Christ says is false: " Those who slay the body and after that can do no more," [3] if they can indeed do to us as much as they do to our bodies. Far be it from us to think that what Truth has said is false! For it is said that they do something to us when they kill us, because there is sensation in the body when they kill it, but after that they have nothing they can do because there is no sensation in a body once slain.

SAINT AUGUSTINE

Muita itaque corpora Christianorum terra non texit, sed nullum eorum quisquam a caelo et terra separavit, quam totam implet praesentia sui qui novit unde resuscitet quod creavit. Dicitur quidem in psalmo : *Posuerunt mortalia servorum tuorum escam volatilibus caeli, carnes sanctorum tuorum bestiis terrae ; effuderunt sanguinem eorum sicut aquam in circuitu Hierusalem, et non erat qui sepeliret*, sed magis ad exaggerandam crudelitatem eorum qui ista fecerunt, non ad eorum infelicitatem qui ista perpessi sunt. Quamvis enim haec in conspectu hominum dura et dira videantur, sed *pretiosa in conspectu Domini mors sanctorum eius.*

Proinde ista omnia, id est [1] curatio funeris, conditio sepulturae, pompa exequiarum, magis sunt vivorum solacia quam subsidia mortuorum. Si aliquid prodest impio sepultura pretiosa, oberit pio vilis aut nulla. Praeclaras exequias in conspectu hominum exhibuit purpurato illi diviti turba famulorum, sed multo clariores in conspectu Domini ulceroso illi pauperi ministerium praebuit angelorum, qui eum non extulerunt in marmoreum tumulum, sed in Abrahae gremium sustulerunt.

Rident haec illi, contra quos defendendam suscepimus civitatem Dei. Verum tamen sepulturae curam etiam eorum philosophi contempserunt. Et saepe universi exercitus, dum pro terrena patria morerentur, ubi postea iacerent vel quibus bestiis esca

---

[1] id est *omitted by many MSS.*

---

[1] Psalms 79.2 f.   [2] *Ibid.* 115.16.

Accordingly, though there are many bodies of Christians that earth has not covered, yet no one has separated any of them from heaven and earth which is wholly filled by the presence of him who knows whence he shall restore to life what he has created. Indeed, it is said in the Psalm : "The dead bodies of thy servants have they given to be meat unto the fowls of the heaven, the flesh of thy saints unto the beasts of the earth. Their blood have they shed like water round Jerusalem ; and there was none to bury them." [1] But the intent was to enlarge on the cruelty of those who did this, rather than on the misery of those who suffered it. For though in the eyes of men such a lot seems harsh and dreadful, yet " precious in the sight of the Lord is the death of his saints." [2]

Therefore, all such offices, that is, the care taken with funerals, the embalming for burial, the procession of the mourners, are more for the comfort of the survivors than to assist the dead. If a costly burial does any good to a wicked man, then a good man will be harmed by a cheap one or by none at all. A funeral, gorgeous in the sight of men, was given that purple-clad rich man by his crowd of servants, but much more glorious, in the sight of the Lord, was the one granted that poor man with his sores, at the hands of the angels who carried him, not to a marble tomb, but to the bosom of Abraham.

The men against whom I have undertaken to defend the City of God laugh at these things, but for all that their philosophers too have scorned to concern themselves about burial. And often whole armies, dying for the soil of their native land, cared not where afterwards they were to lie or to what beasts they fell

fierent, non curarunt, licuitque de hac re poetis
plausibiliter dicere:

>Caelo tegitur, qui non habet urnam.

Quanto minus debent de corporibus insepultis insultare Christianis, quibus et ipsius carnis membrorum-
que omnium reformatio non solum ex terra, verum
etiam ex aliorum elementorum secretissimo sinu, quo
dilapsa cadavera recesserunt, in temporis puncto
reddenda et redintegranda promittitur.

XIII

Quae sit ratio sanctorum corpora sepeliendi.

Nec ideo tamen contemnenda et abicienda sunt
corpora defunctorum maximeque iustorum atque
fidelium, quibus tamquam organis et vasis ad omnia
bona opera sancte usus est Spiritus. Si enim
paterna vestis et anulus, ac si quid huius modi, tanto
carius est posteris, quanto erga parentes maior ad-
fectus, nullo modo ipsa spernenda sunt corpora, quae
utique multo familiarius atque coniunctius quam
quaelibet indumenta gestamus. Haec enim non
ad ornamentum vel adiutorium, quod adhibetur
extrinsecus, sed ad ipsam naturam hominis pertinent. Unde et antiquorum iustorum funera offi-
ciosa pietate curata sunt et exequiae celebratae et
sepultura provisa, ipsique cum viverent de sepeliendis
vel etiam transferendis suis corporibus filiis manda-

---

[1] Lucan, *Pharsalia* 7.819.

as food, and of this matter the poets had licence to
say with general approval:

His covering is the sky who has no urn.[1]

How much less ought they to make unburied bodies a
theme of taunts against the Christians, who have
been promised that there shall be a transformation
restoring the flesh itself and all parts of the body, not
only from the earth but even from the most hidden
embrace of other elements to which the bodies, as they
decomposed, have departed; in a moment of time
they are to be brought back and made whole again.

XIII

Reasons for burying the bodies of the saints.

On the other hand, the bodies of the dead should
not on this account be despised and cast away,
particularly not those of the righteous and faithful of
which the Spirit has made sanctified use as instruments and vessels for all good works. For if a
parent's garment or ring, or any object of this kind,
be dear to his children in proportion to the love they
bore him, their actual bodies should not be despised
in any way, bodies that we certainly wear much more
intimately and closely than we wear any garments
whatever. For they are no ornament or subsidiary
attached to us externally but a natural component of
man's being. It was for this reason that the righteous
of old received the tribute of solemn religious rites,
funeral processions and provision for burial; and they
themselves while yet living gave their sons directions
concerning the burial and even the conveyance of

verunt, et Tobis sepeliendo mortuos Deum prome-
ruisse teste angelo commendatur. Ipse quoque
Dominus die tertio resurrecturus religiosae mulieris
bonum opus praedicat praedicandumque commendat,
quod unguentum pretiosum super membra eius
effuderit atque hoc ad eum sepeliendum fecerit. Et
laudabiliter commemorantur in evangelio qui corpus
eius de cruce acceptum diligenter atque honorifice
tegendum sepeliendumque curarunt.

Verum istae auctoritates non hoc admonent, quod
insit ullus cadaveribus sensus, sed ad Dei provi-
dentiam, cui placent etiam talia pietatis officia,
corpora quoque mortuorum pertinere significant
propter fidem resurrectionis astruendam. Ubi et
illud salubriter discitur, quanta possit esse remunera-
tio pro elemosynis, quas viventibus et sentientibus
exhibemus, si neque hoc apud Deum perit quod
exanimis hominum membris officii diligentiaeque
persolvitur. Sunt quidem et alia quae sancti patriarchae de corporibus suis vel condendis vel transferendis prophetico spiritu dicta intellegi voluerunt;
non autem hic locus est ut ea pertractemus, cum
sufficiant ista quae diximus.

Sed si ea quae sustentandis viventibus sunt neces-
saria, sicut victus et amictus, quamvis cum gravi
adflictione desint, non frangunt in bonis perferendi
tolerandique virtutem nec eradicant ex animo pietatem, sed exercitatam faciunt fecundiorem, quanto
magis, cum desunt ea quae curandis funeribus con-

---

[1] Tobit 2.9; 12.12.   [2] Matthew 26.7–13.
[3] John 19.38–41.

their bodies, and Tobit, according to the angel's testimony, is commended and is said to have won God's favour by burying the dead.[1] The Lord himself too, though he was to rise again on the third day, praises and commends to our praise, the good work of a pious woman in that she poured a precious ointment over his limbs and did this for his burial.[2] And in the Gospel there is mention with praise of those who took charge of his body when it was received from the cross and saw that it was tenderly and reverently wrapped and buried.[3]

Nevertheless, the maxim to be drawn from these authoritative instances is not that there is some sensation in corpses; they mean that God's providence, since he is pleased with such offices of piety, also embraces the bodies of the dead in order to buttress our faith in the resurrection. In this there is another wholesome lesson for us, namely to note how great must be the reward for the alms we bestow on the living and sentient, if even the attentions and services paid to the lifeless bodies of men are not forgotten by God. There are indeed other cases as well, where the holy patriarchs in speaking of the laying away or transporting of their bodies intended their words to be taken as prophetically inspired. This, however, is not the place for protracted discussion, since what we have said is enough.

But if the lack of things necessary for the sustaining of the living, such as food and clothing, although it cause serious suffering, does not overcome in good men the strength of their patience and endurance or eradicate godliness from the soul, but rather renders it more fruitful by exercise, how much less does the lack of customary rites in the holding of funerals and

dendisque corporibus defunctorum adhiberi solent,
non efficiunt miseros in occultis piorum sedibus iam
quietos! Ac per hoc quando ista cadaveribus
Christianorum in illa magnae Urbis vel etiam aliorum
oppidorum vastatione defuerunt, nec vivorum culpa
est, qui non potuerunt ista praebere, nec poena
mortuorum, qui non possunt ista sentire.

XIV

De captivitate sanctorum, quibus numquam divina solacia defuerunt.

SED multi, inquiunt, Christiani etiam captivi ducti
sunt. Hoc sane miserrimum est, si aliquo duci
potuerunt ubi Deum suum non invenerunt. Sunt in
scripturis sanctis huius etiam cladis magna solacia.
Fuerunt in captivitate tres pueri, fuit Daniel, fuerunt
alii prophetae; nec Deus defuit consolator. Sic ergo
non deseruit fideles suos sub dominatione gentis, licet
barbarae, tamen humanae, qui prophetam non
deseruit nec in visceribus beluae. Haec quoque illi,
cum quibus agimus, malunt inridere quam credere,
qui tamen suis litteris credunt Arionem Methym-
naeum, nobilissimum citharistam, cum esset deiectus
e navi, exceptum delphini dorso et ad terras esse
pervectum. Verum illud nostrum de Iona propheta
incredibilius est. Plane incredibilius quia mirabilius, et mirabilius quia potentius.

---

[1] Daniel 4. [2] *Ibid.* 1.6. [3] Jonah 2.1.
[4] Herodotus 1.23.

the laying away of the bodies of the dead make miserable those who are already at rest in the hidden abodes of the godly! Consequently, when such rites were wanting in the case of Christian corpses in that sack of the Great City, or of other towns as well, no blame attaches to the living, who were unable to pay that tribute, nor any punishment to the dead, who cannot feel the loss.

XIV

On the captivity of the saints, who never lacked divine comforts.

BUT many Christians, they say, were also led into captivity. This, of course, is great misery, if they could have been led anywhere where they did not find their God. There are in the Holy Scriptures many consolations for this kind of calamity too. The three young men were in captivity.[1] Daniel was in captivity.[2] Other prophets were in captivity, and God did not fail them as comforter. So, also, he has not deserted his faithful under the domination of a nation which, though barbarous, is yet human, as he did not desert the prophet in the belly of the monster.[3] Our opponents again prefer to ridicule rather than to believe these facts, yet they believe the story that appears in their own literature,[4] how Arion of Methymna, a most famous lyre player, when he was cast out of a ship, was received on a dolphin's back and borne to land. But that story of ours about the prophet Jonah is more incredible, more incredible evidently because more miraculous, and more miraculous because it displays greater power.

67

SAINT AUGUSTINE

XV

De Regulo, in quo captivitatis ob religionem etiam sponte tolerandae extat exemplum, quod tamen illi deos colenti prodesse non potuit.

HABENT tamen isti de captivitate religionis causa etiam sponte toleranda et in suis praeclaris viris nobilissimum exemplum. Marcus Regulus, imperator populi Romani, captivus apud Carthaginienses fuit. Qui cum sibi mallent a Romanis suos reddi quam eorum tenere captivos, ad hoc impetrandum etiam istum praecipue Regulum cum legatis suis Romam miserunt, prius iuratione constrictum, si quod volebant minime peregisset, rediturum esse Carthaginem. Perrexit ille atque in senatu contraria persuasit, quoniam non arbitrabatur utile esse Romanae rei publicae mutare captivos. Nec post hanc persuasionem a suis ad hostes redire compulsus est, sed quia iuraverat, id sponte complevit. At illi eum excogitatis atque horrendis cruciatibus necaverunt. Inclusum quippe angusto ligno, ubi stare cogeretur, clavisque acutissimis undique confixo, ut se in nullam eius partem sine poenis atrocissimis inclinaret, etiam vigilando peremerunt. Merito certe laudant virtutem tam magna infelicitate maiorem.

Et per deos ille iuraverat, quorum cultu prohibito has generi humano clades isti opinantur infligi. Qui

---

¹ The heroism of M. Atilius Regulus, consul in 267 and 256 B.C., captured the imagination, not only of the Romans (see Horace, *Odes* 3.5), but of the early Christian writers as well (see index for other references).

XV

On Regulus, an example of the necessity of enduring, even by choice, captivity for religion's sake, which nevertheless could have done him no good as a worshipper of gods.

YET they have among their famous men a most noble example of even voluntary endurance of captivity because of religious scruple. Marcus Regulus,[1] a general of the Roman people, was a captive among the Carthaginians. They, being more desirous of securing the return of their own soldiers by the Romans than of keeping Roman soldiers prisoners, to obtain this sent this Regulus in chief place with their own ambassadors to Rome, having previously bound him with an oath, that if he did not succeed in obtaining what they wanted, he would return to Carthage. He went in and in the Senate advised the contrary course, since he did not think it to the advantage of the Roman republic to exchange captives. After giving this advice he was not forced by his own people to return to the enemy, but because he had taken the oath, he fulfilled it voluntarily. But the Carthaginians put him to death with ingenious and dreadful tortures. They shut him up in a narrow box, in which he was forced to stand. It was studded with the sharpest nails on all sides, so that he could lean on it nowhere without sharp pain. Thus they killed him by keeping him awake. Rightly do they praise a fortitude superior to such a great misfortune.

And the gods he swore by were those who are now supposed to be inflicting these present calamities upon the human race because their worship has been

ergo propterea colebantur ut istam vitam prosperam redderent, si verum iuranti has inrogari poenas seu voluerunt seu permiserunt, quid periuro gravius irati facere potuerunt?

Sed cur non ratiocinationem meam potius ad utrumque concludam? Deos certe ille sic coluit ut propter iuris iurandi fidem nec maneret in patria, nec inde quolibet ire, sed ad suos acerrimos inimicos redire minime dubitaret. Hoc si huic vitae utile existimabat, cuius tam horrendum exitum meruit, procul dubio fallebatur. Suo quippe docuit exemplo nihil deos ad istam temporalem felicitatem suis prodesse cultoribus, quando quidem ille eorum deditus cultui et victus et captivus abductus et, quia noluit aliter quam per eos iuraverat facere, novo ac prius inaudito nimiumque horribili supplicii genere cruciatus extinctus est.

Si autem deorum cultus post hanc vitam velut mercedem reddit felicitatem, cur calumniantur temporibus Christianis, ideo dicentes Urbi accidisse illam calamitatem quia deos suos colere destitit, cum potuerit etiam illos diligentissime colens tam infelix fieri, quam ille Regulus fuit? Nisi forte contra clarissimam veritatem tanta quisquam dementia mirae caecitatis obnititur ut contendere audeat universam civitatem deos colentem infelicem esse non posse, unum vero hominem posse, quod videlicet potentia deorum suorum multos potius sit idonea

forbidden. Now the object of worshipping these gods was to induce them to make this life prosperous; but if they willed or even permitted such a punishment to be inflicted on one who swore by them, and kept his oath, what worse penalty could they inflict in anger on one who perjured himself?

Why may I not sum up my argument in the form of a dilemma? Regulus certainly so worshipped his gods that on account of an oath he neither remained in his own country, nor went to some other country, but without the least hesitation returned to his bitterest enemies. If he thought this advantageous for this life, he most certainly was mistaken, for he gained a most dreadful death. Indeed, by his example, he taught that the gods bring no happiness to their worshippers with respect to this life, since he, devoted to their worship, was both conquered and led captive, and because he was unwilling to do otherwise than what he had sworn by them to do, he was tortured and put to death by a new, unheard-of and most horrible kind of punishment.

If, on the other hand, the worship of the gods brings as its reward happiness after this life, why then is the Christian era slandered? Why say that this disaster has befallen the City because it has ceased to worship its gods, when, though it worshipped them never so diligently, it might yet have been as unfortunate as that Regulus was? Yet perhaps someone will be so wonderfully blinded by his madness as to contend, in the face of the clearest truth, that the whole city, worshipping the gods, cannot be unfortunate, yet one man can be, because, you must know, the power of their gods is better suited to preserve the many than

conservare quam singulos, cum multitudo constet ex singulis.

Si autem dicunt M. Regulum etiam in illa captivitate illisque cruciatibus corporis animi virtute beatum esse potuisse, virtus potius vera quaeratur, qua beata esse possit et civitas. Neque enim aliunde beata civitas, aliunde homo, cum aliud civitas non sit quam concors hominum multitudo. Quam ob rem nondum interim disputo, qualis in Regulo virtus fuerit; sufficit nunc, quod isto nobilissimo exemplo coguntur fateri non propter corporis bona vel earum rerum quae extrinsecus homini accidunt, colendos deos, quando quidem ille carere his omnibus maluit quam deos per quos iuravit offendere.

Sed quid faciamus hominibus, qui gloriantur se talem habuisse civem, qualem timent habere civitatem? Quod si non timent, tale ergo aliquid, quale accidit Regulo, etiam civitati tam diligenter quam ille deos colenti accidere potuisse fateantur et Christianis temporibus non calumnientur. Verum quia de illis Christianis orta quaestio est, qui etiam captivati sunt, hoc intueantur et taceant, qui saluberrimae religioni hinc inpudenter atque inprudenter inludunt, quia, si diis eorum probro non fuit, quod adtentissimus cultor illorum, dum eis iuris iurandi fidem servaret, patria caruit, cum aliam non haberet, captivusque

individuals, though a multitude is made up of individuals.

If, however, they say that Regulus even as a prisoner and while undergoing those bodily tortures may have been happy in the quality or virtue of his mind, then let that true quality or virtue be sought for by which a city also can be blessed. For the happiness of a city and the happiness of an individual human being have no different sources, since a city is nothing more than a single-minded multiplicity of individual men. I do not, meanwhile, dispute the quality of virtue that Regulus exhibited; at the moment I am satisfied with the admission, forced from them by that sublime example, that the gods should be worshipped for other reasons than to acquire bodily benefits or such goods as fall externally to men, in view of the fact that he preferred to forgo everything of the sort rather than to offend the gods by whom he had sworn.

What can we do with men who take pride in the fact that they had such a citizen, yet fear to have such a city? If they do not fear this, let them acknowledge that the sort of thing that happened to Regulus can happen to a city, even to a city that worships the gods as devotedly as he did, and let them not cast aspersions on the Christian era. But since our discussion started with the Christians who were also made prisoners, let those who shamelessly and foolishly mock our most wholesome religion on their account, keep this in mind and hold their peace, namely, that if it was not a reproach to their gods that one who worshipped them most studiously, keeping inviolate the oath he had sworn by them, was deprived of his own country with no other to replace

apud hostes per longam mortem supplicio novae crudelitatis occisus est, multo minus nomen criminandum
est Christianum in captivitate sacratorum suorum, qui
supernam patriam veraci fide expectantes etiam in
suis sedibus peregrinos se esse noverunt.

XVI

*An stupris, quae etiam sacrarum forte virginum est passa
captivitas, contaminari potuerit virtus animi sine
voluntatis assensu.*

MAGNUM sane crimen se putant obicere Christianis,
cum eorum exaggerantes captivitatem addunt etiam
stupra commissa, non solum in aliena matrimonia
virginesque nupturas, sed etiam in quasdam sancti-
moniales. Hic vero non fides, non pietas, non ipsa
virtus, quae castitas dicitur, sed nostra potius disputatio inter pudorem atque rationem quibusdam
coartatur angustiis. Nec tantum hic curamus alienis
responsionem reddere, quantum ipsis nostris consolationem.

Sit igitur in primis positum atque firmatum virtutem, qua recte vivitur, ab animi sede membris corporis imperare sanctumque corpus usu fieri sanctae
voluntatis, qua inconcussa ac stabili permanente,
quidquid alius de corpore vel in corpore fecerit quod
sine peccato proprio non valeat evitari praeter culpam
74

it, and in captivity among enemies suffered a lingering death by cruel torture of a novel kind, much less ought the Christian name to be charged with the captivity of its devoted adherents, who, awaiting a heavenly country with sound confidence, recognize that they are but aliens in their own dwelling-places.

XVI

Whether the violation of captured virgins, even those con-secrated, defiled their virtuous character, though their will did not consent.

They think that they can saddle the Christians with a charge that is serious indeed when they enlarge on their treatment as prisoners by bringing in the violations not only of married women and maidens expecting to marry but even of certain consecrated virgins. But here we find ourselves forced by certain difficulties into a strait between modesty and logic, not that our faith or religion or the virtue called chas-tity is itself in any strait, but rather the course of our argument. Nor are we here concerned so much to deliver a reply to those not of our kind as to bring comfort to our own people themselves.

In the first place, then, let the principle be stated and affirmed that the virtue whereby a good life is lived controls the members of the body from its seat in the mind and that the body becomes holy through the exercise of a holy will, and while such a will remains unshaken and steadfast, no matter what anyone else does with the body or in the body that a person has no power to avoid without sin on his own part, no blame attaches to the one who suffers it. But

esse patientis. Sed quia non solum quod ad dolorem, verum etiam quod ad libidinem pertinet, in corpore alieno perpetrari potest, quidquid tale factum fuerit, etsi retentam constantissimo animo pudicitiam non excutit, tamen pudorem incutit, ne credatur factum cum mentis etiam voluntate, quod fieri fortasse sine carnis aliqua voluptate non potuit.

XVII

De morte voluntaria ob metum poenae sive dedecoris.

Ac per hoc et quae se occiderunt ne quicquam huius modi paterentur, quis humanus affectus eis nolit ignosci? et quae se occidere noluerunt, ne suo facinore alienum flagitium devitarent, quisquis eis hoc crimini dederit, ipse crimen insipientiae non cavebit.

Nam utique si non licet privata potestate hominem occidere vel nocentem, cuius occidendi licentiam lex nulla concedit, profecto etiam qui se ipsum occidit homicida est, et tanto fit nocentior, cum se occiderit, quanto innocentior in ea causa fuit, qua se occidendum putavit. Nam si Iudae factum merito detestamur eumque veritas iudicat, cum se laqueo suspendit, sceleratae illius traditionis auxisse potius quam expiasse commissum, quoniam Dei misericordiam desperando exitiabiliter paenitens nullum sibi salubris paenitentiae locum reliquit, quanto magis a sua nece se abstinere debet, qui tali supplicio quod in se puniat non habet!

since it is not only the occasion of pain, but also the occasion of lust that can be inflicted on another's body by force, in the latter case, though shamefastness, to which a superlatively steadfast mind holds fast, is not thrust out, yet shame is thrust in, shame for fear that the mind too may be thought to have consented to an act that could perhaps not have taken place without some carnal pleasure.

XVII

On suicide caused by fear of punishment or disgrace.

CONSEQUENTLY, if some of these women took their lives in preference to suffering such a fate, who so lacks human sympathy as to refuse to pardon them? And as for those who refused to take their lives lest in avoiding outrage by another they should commit a sin of their own, anyone who makes that a charge against them, will not himself escape the charge of witlessness.

For if it is not right on individual authority to slay even a guilty man for whose killing no law has granted permission, certainly a suicide is also a homicide, and he is guilty, when he kills himself, in proportion to his innocence of the deed for which he thought he ought to die. If we rightly execrate Judas' deed, and truth pronounces that when he hanged himself, he increased rather than expiated the crime of that accursed betrayal, since by despairing of God's mercy, though he was at death repentant, he left himself no place for a saving repentance, how much more should the man who has no guilt in him to be punished by such means refrain from killing himself!

Iudas enim cum se occidit, sceleratum hominem
occidit, et tamen non solum Christi, verum etiam suae
mortis reus finivit hanc vitam, quia licet propter suum
scelus alio suo scelere occisus est.   Cur autem homo,
qui mali nihil fecit, sibi malefaciat et se ipsum inter-
ficiendo hominem interficiat innocentem, ne alium
patiatur nocentem, atque in se perpetret peccatum
proprium, ne in eo perpetretur alienum?

XVIII

De aliena violentia et libidine, quam in oppresso corpore
mens invita perpetitur.

AT enim, ne vel aliena polluat libido, metuitur.
Non polluet, si aliena erit; si autem polluet, aliena
non erit.   Sed cum pudicitia virtus sit animi comitem-
que habeat fortitudinem, qua potius quaelibet mala
tolerare quam malo consentire decernit, nullus autem
magnanimus et pudicus in potestate habeat, quid de
sua carne fiat, sed tantum quid adnuat mente vel
renuat, quis eadem sana mente putaverit perdere se
pudicitiam, si forte in adprehensa et oppressa carne
sua exerceatur et expleatur libido non sua?

Si enim hoc modo pudicitia perit, profecto pudicitia virtus animi non erit, nec pertinebit ad ea bona
quibus bene vivitur, sed in bonis corporis numerabitur,
qualia sunt vires pulchritudo sana valetudo ac si quid
78

When Judas killed himself, he killed an accursed man, and he ended his life guilty not only of Christ's death but also of his own, because, though he was killed to atone for his crime, the killing itself was another crime of his. Why, then, should a man who has done no evil do evil to himself, and in doing away with himself do away with an innocent man so as not to suffer from the crime of another, and perpetrate upon himself a sin of his own, so that another's may not be perpetrated on him?

XVIII

Violence from others and sexual pleasure experienced by an unwilling mind in the subjected body.

But there is a fear that even another's lust may pollute. It will not pollute if it be another's; if it pollutes, it will not be another's. But since purity is a virtue of the mind and has as its companion a strength of mind that chooses to endure any evils whatever rather than consent to evil, and since no one, however magnanimous and shamefast, has it always in his power to decide what shall be done with his flesh, having power only to decide what he will in his mind accept or refuse, who, if that same mind is sane, will hold that he loses his shamefastness if by chance his flesh is seized and held down and a lust not his own is put in play and sated on it?

If purity can in this way be destroyed, certainly purity is no virtue of the mind nor does it belong to the good things of the good life, but it should be counted among the goods of the body, such as strength, beauty, sound health and any other similar

huius modi est; quae bona, etiamsi minuantur, bonam iustamque vitam omnino non minuunt. Quod si tale aliquid est pudicitia, ut quid pro illa, ne amittatur, etiam cum periculo corporis laboratur?

Si autem animi bonum est, etiam oppresso corpore non amittitur. Quin etiam sanctae continentiae bonum cum inmunditiae carnalium concupiscentiarum non cedit, et ipsum corpus sanctificatur, et ideo, cum eis non cedere inconcussa intentione persistit, nec de ipso corpore perit sanctitas, quia eo sancte utendi perseverat voluntas et, quantum est in ipso, etiam facultas.

Neque enim eo corpus sanctum est, quod eius membra sunt integra, aut eo, quod nullo contrectantur adtactu, cum possint diversis casibus etiam vulnerata vim perpeti, et medici aliquando saluti opitulantes haec ibi faciant, quae horret aspectus. Obstetrix virginis cuiusdam integritatem manu velut explorans sive malevolentia sive inscitia sive casu, dum inspicit, perdidit. Non opinor quemquam tam stulte sapere ut huic perisse aliquid existimet etiam de ipsius corporis sanctitate, quamvis membri illius integritate iam perdita. Quocirca proposito animi permanente, per quod etiam corpus sanctificari meruit, nec ipsi corpori aufert sanctitatem violentia libidinis alienae, quam servat perseverantia continentiae suae.

An vero si aliqua femina, mente corrupta violatoque proposito quod Deo voverat, pergat vitianda ad deceptorem suum, ad hoc eam pergentem sanctam vel

quality, good things which even if lessened, do not lessen at all the good and just life. If purity is one of these, to what end are pains taken to prevent its loss, even at the expense of the body?

If, however, purity is a possession of the soul, neither is it lost when the body is violated. And, what is more, the virtue of holy continence, when it does not yield to the uncleanness of carnal desires, hallows the body itself as well and therefore, when it remains steadfast and unbroken in intent not to yield to desire, the holy quality of the very body is not destroyed, because the will to employ it in a holy manner endures, and, as far as in it lies, the capacity also.

The holiness of the body lies not in the integrity of its parts nor in the fact that they are not violated by contact, for in various accidents they are liable to suffer violence even by wounds, and sometimes physicians, ministering to the health of the body, perform operations there which are gruesome to see. A midwife, as she investigated the maidenhead of a certain virgin, destroyed it either by ill intent or clumsiness or accident during examination. I do not imagine that anyone is so stupid that he thinks that any of the holiness of her body itself has perished, though that one member of the body be no longer intact. And so, as long as the mind's resolve remains constant, whereby the body too made good its claim to be holy, the violence of another's lust does not deprive even the body of its holiness, which is preserved by the steadfastness of one's own control.

Well, then, if some woman of depraved mind, breaking the pledge that she had vowed to God, is on the way to her seducer to be violated, do we say that she, on her way, is holy even of body, when the

corpore dicimus, ea sanctitate animi per quam corpus sanctificabatur amissa atque destructa? Absit hic error et hinc potius admoneamur ita non amitti corporis sanctitatem manente animi sanctitate etiam corpore oppresso, sicut amittitur et corporis sanctitas violata animi sanctitate etiam corpore intacto.

Quam ob rem non habet quod in se morte spontanea puniat femina sine ulla sua consensione violenter oppressa et alieno conpressa peccato; quanto minus antequam hoc fiat! Ne admittatur homicidium certum, cum ipsum flagitium, quamvis alienum, adhuc pendet incertum.

XIX

De Lucretia, quae se ob inlatum sibi stuprum peremit.

An forte huic perspicuae rationi, qua dicimus corpore oppresso nequaquam proposito castitatis ulla in malum consensione mutato illius tantum esse flagitium, qui opprimens concubuerit, non illius, quae oppressa concumbenti nulla voluntate consenserit, contradicere audebunt hi, contra quos feminarum Christianarum in captivitate oppressarum non tantum mentes, verum etiam corpora sancta defendimus?

Lucretiam certe, matronam nobilem veteremque Romanam, pudicitiae magnis efferunt laudibus. Huius corpore cum violenter oppresso Tarquinii regis

---

[1] Livv 1.58.

holiness of her mind, by which the body was kept holy, is already lost and destroyed? Let there be no such mistake, and let us draw from this case the conclusion that holiness of the body is not lost while holiness of the soul remains, even though the body is forced to yield, just as holiness of the body is lost when holiness of the soul is violated, even though the body remain intact.

For this reason, a woman who has been subjected by force and violated by another's sin without any consent on her part, has no fault in herself to be punished by voluntary death. How much less has she any before the event! Let there be no incurring the sure guilt of murder when the outrage itself, though not hers, is still poised, undecided.

XIX

On Lucretia, who committed suicide because she was violated.

Our reasoning is clear in support of the statement that when a body is forced to yield though the pledge of chastity remains no whit vitiated by any consent to evil, the crime belongs only to the man who lay with her perforce and not to the woman who, though forced, consented by no act of will to his lying with her. Can it be that those against whom we are defending as holy, not only the minds, but also the bodies of such Christian women as were forced when prisoners, will be so bold as to maintain the contrary?

They certainly exalt with high praise the purity of Lucretia, that noble matron of ancient Rome.[1] When the son of King Tarquin violently forced her and lust-

filius libidinose potitus esset, illa scelus improbissimi
iuvenis marito Collatino et propinquo Bruto, viris
clarissimis et fortissimis, indicavit eosque ad vindictam
constrinxit. Deinde foedi in se commissi aegra
atque inpatiens se peremit. Quid dicemus? Adultera haec an casta iudicanda est? Quis in hac
controversia laborandum putaverit? Egregie quidam ex hoc veraciterque declamans ait: " Mirabile
dictu, duo fuerunt, et adulterium unus admisit."
Splendide atque verissime. Intuens enim in duorum
corporum commixtione unius inquinatissimam cupiditatem, alterius castissimam voluntatem, et non quid
coniunctione membrorum, sed quid animorum diversitate ageretur adtendens: " Duo," inquit, " fuerunt,
et adulterium unus admisit."

Sed quid est hoc, quod in eam gravius vindicatur,
quae adulterium non admisit? Nam ille patria cum
patre pulsus est, haec summo est mactata supplicio.
Si non est illa inpudicitia qua invita opprimitur, non
est haec iustitia qua casta punitur. Vos appello,
leges iudicesque Romani. Nempe post perpetrata
facinora nec quemquam scelestum indemnatum inpune voluistis occidi. Si ergo ad vestrum iudicium
quisquam deferret hoc crimen vobisque probaretur
non solum indemnatam, verum etiam castam et
innocentem, interfectam esse mulierem, nonne eum,
qui id fecisset, severitate congrua plecteretis?

Hoc fecit illa Lucretia; illa, illa sic praedicata
Lucretia innocentem, castam, vim perpessam Lucre-

---

[1] The declaimer is unknown.

fully possessed her body, she made known the crime
of this utterly wicked young man to her husband
Collatinus and her kinsman Brutus, men of highest
position and courage, and bound them by an oath to
take revenge. Then sick at heart and unable to bear
the shame put upon her, she took her life. What
shall we say about her? Must she be judged an
adulteress or chaste? Who can think it necessary to
ponder over the answer? A certain declaimer
develops this theme admirably and accurately: " A
wonderful tale! There were two and only one committed adultery."[1] Very striking and very true!
For he, taking into consideration in this intermingling
of two bodies the utterly foul passion on one side and
the utterly chaste will of the other, and paying attention, not to the union of the bodies, but to the variance
in the souls, says: " There were two and only one
committed adultery."

But what of the fact that she, who did not commit
adultery, is more severely punished? He was
banished from his fatherland with his father; she
suffered the supreme penalty. If there is no im-
purity in her being ravished not consenting, there is
no justice in her being punished not unchaste. I
appeal to you, ye laws and judges of Rome! We
know that, when crimes had been perpetrated, you
forbade any execution even of the guilty without
trial. If, therefore, anyone should bring this charge
to your tribunal, and it should be shown you that a
woman, not only uncondemned, but even chaste and
innocent, had been put to death, would you not punish
the one who had done this with fitting severity?

Lucretia did this, that Lucretia so famous; when
Lucretia was innocent and chaste and had suffered

tiam insuper interemit. Proferte sententiam. Quod
si propterea non potestis, quia non adstat quam
punire possitis, cur interfectricem innocentis et
castae tanta praedicatione laudatis? Quam certe
apud infernos iudices etiam tales, quales poetarum
vestrorum carminibus cantitantur, nulla ratione
defenditis, constitutam scilicet inter illos,

> qui sibi letum
> Insontes peperere manu lucemque perosi
> Proiecere animas;

cui ad superna redire cupienti

> Fas obstat, tristisque palus inamabilis undae
> Adligat.

An forte ideo ibi non est quia non insontem, sed male
sibi consciam, se peremit? Quid si enim (quod ipsa
tantummodo nosse poterat) quamvis iuveni violenter
inruenti etiam sua libidine inlecta consentit idque in
se puniens ita doluit ut morte putaret expiandum?

Quamquam ne sic quidem se occidere debuit, si
fructuosam posset apud deos falsos agere paenitentiam. Verum tamen si forte ita est falsumque est
illud, quod duo fuerunt et adulterium unus admisit,
sed potius ambo adulterium commiserunt, unus
manifesta invasione, altera latente consensione:
non se occidit insontem, et ideo potest a litteratis eius
defensoribus dici non esse apud inferos inter illos,
" qui sibi letum insontes peperere manu." Sed ita
haec causa ex utroque latere coartatur ut, si ex-

---

[1] Virgil, *Aeneid* 6.434–6.   [2] *Ibid.* 438 f.

violence, Lucretia added death over and above. Pronounce sentence. But if you cannot, because she is not in attendance before you to be punished, why do you praise with such eloquence the murderess of an innocent and chaste woman? You certainly cannot defend her at all before those judges of the lower world of whom your poets are continually harping, for she is, of course, numbered among those

> who guiltless
> Laid fatal hands upon themselves and, loathing
> The light of day, dispatched their souls.[1]

If she wants to return to the realms of life

> Fate bars the way; the dismal swamp's
> Unfriendly pools emprison them.[2]

Perhaps, however, she is not there because she slew herself, not innocently, but conscious of her guilt? What if—but she herself alone could know—she was seduced by her own lust and, though the youth violently attacked her, consented, and in punishing that act of hers was so remorseful that death seemed to be due expiation?

Even so, she should not have killed herself if it was possible to engage in penance that would gain her credit with her false gods. If this is the case and the story that there were two and only one committed adultery is false, and both committed adultery instead, one in open attack and the other secretly consenting, then she did not kill herself innocently, and therefore the learned defenders can say she is not in the lower world among those " who guiltless laid fatal hands upon themselves." But then the case is reduced to a dilemma: if the murder is less heinous,

87

tenuatur homicidium, adulterium confirmetur; si
purgatur adulterium, homicidium cumuletur; nec
omnino invenitur exitus, ubi dicitur: " Si adulterata,
cur laudata; si pudica, cur occisa? "

Nobis tamen in hoc tam nobili feminae huius exemplo ad istos refutandos, qui Christianis feminis in
captivitate compressis alieni ab omni cogitatione
sanctitatis insultant, sufficit quod in praeclaris eius
laudibus dictum est: " Duo fuerunt et adulterium
unus admisit."

Talis enim ab eis Lucretia magis credita est, quae
se nullo adulterino potuerit maculare consensu.
Quod ergo se ipsam, quoniam adulterum pertulit,
etiam non adultera occidit, non est pudicitiae caritas,
sed pudoris infirmitas. Puduit enim eam turpitudinis
alienae in se commissae, etiamsi non secum, et Romana mulier, laudis avida nimium, verita est ne
putaretur, quod violenter est passa cum viveret,
libenter passa si viveret. Unde ad oculos hominum
testem mentis suae illam poenam adhibendam putavit, quibus conscientiam demonstrare non potuit.
Sociam quippe facti se credi erubuit si, quod alius in
ea fecerat turpiter, ferret ipsa patienter.

Non hoc fecerunt feminae Christianae, quae passae
similia vivunt tamen nec in se ultae sunt crimen
alienum, ne aliorum sceleribus adderent sua, si,

then the adultery is confirmed; if the adultery is extenuated, the charge of murder is aggravated; and there is no escape from the dilemma, when you say: " If she was made an adulteress, why has she been praised; if she was chaste, why was she slain ? "

Nevertheless, in appealing to the example set by this noble lady, to refute those who, far removed from any conception of holiness, exult over Christian women who were violated while prisoners, it is sufficient for us that her distinguished eulogies included the tribute: " There were two and only one committed adultery."

For they held rather the belief that Lucretia was not one who could have soiled herself with any spot of adulterous consent. In that case her killing herself, because, though she was not an adulteress, yet she endured the act of an adulterer, proves, not her love of chastity, but her irresolute shame. For she was ashamed of another's foul crime committed on her person, even though not committed with her, and being a Roman lady, too greedy of praise, she feared that if she remained alive, she would be thought to have enjoyed suffering the violence that she had suffered while alive. For this reason she thought that she must present evidence before men's eyes to show what was in her heart—the evidence of that self-punishment, since she could not exhibit her conscience to them. In fact, she blushed at the possibility of being believed to be an accomplice of the deed if she were to bear passively the shame that another had actively inflicted upon her.

This is not what the Christian women who had the same experience and still survive did. They did not avenge a crime not their own upon themselves, but feared to add crimes of their own to those of others,

quoniam hostes in eis concupiscendo stupra commiserant, illae in se ipsis homicidia erubescendo committerent. Habent quippe intus gloriam castitatis, testimonium conscientiae; habent autem coram oculis Dei sui nec requirunt amplius, ubi quid recte faciant non habent amplius, ne devient ab auctoritate legis divinae, cum male devitant offensionem suspicionis humanae.

XX

Nullam esse auctoritatem quae Christianis in qualibet causa ius voluntariae necis tribuat.

NEQUE enim frustra in sanctis canonicis libris nusquam nobis divinitus praeceptum permissumve reperiri potest, ut vel ipsius adipiscendae inmortalitatis vel ullius cavendi carendive mali causa nobismet ipsis necem inferamus. Nam et prohibitos nos esse intellegendum est, ubi lex ait: *Non occides*, praesertim quia non addidit: " proximum tuum ", sicut falsum testimonium cum vetaret: *Falsum*, inquit, *testimonium non dices adversus proximum tuum.* Nec ideo tamen si adversus se ipsum quisquam falsum testimonium dixerit, ab hoc crimine se putaverit alienum, quoniam regulam diligendi proximum a semet ipso dilector accepit, quando quidem scriptum est: *Diliges proximum tuum tamquam te ipsum.*

Porro si falsi testimonii non minus reus est qui de se ipso falsum fatetur quam si adversus proximum hoc

---

[1] Exodus 20.13. [2] Exodus 20.16.
[3] Matthew 22.39.

which they would have done, if, because foes lusting had committed rape upon them, they blushing had committed murder upon themselves. For indeed they have within themselves the glory of chastity, the witness of their conscience. They have it also in the presence of their God and need nothing more. In this case there is nothing more for them to do and do right, if they would not deviate from the authority of God's law while doing wrong to obviate the scandal of man's suspicion.

XX

That there is no authority that allows Christians in any case the right to die of their own will.

NOT for nothing is it that in the holy canonical books no divinely inspired order or permission can be found authorizing us to inflict death upon ourselves, neither in order to acquire immortality nor in order to avert or divert some evil. For we must certainly understand the commandment as forbidding this when it says: " Thou shalt not kill," [1] particularly since it does not add " thy neighbour," as it does when it forbids false witnessing. It says: " Thou shalt not bear false witness against thy neighbour." [2] No one should, however, think that he is free from this charge if he has borne false witness only against himself, for he who loves his neighbour has received a rule of love based on himself, since indeed Scripture says: " Thou shalt love thy neighbour as thyself." [3]

If, moreover, a man is not less guilty of false witness who bears false witness against himself than if he were to do so against his neighbour, though in the

91

faceret, cum in eo praecepto, quo falsum testimonium prohibetur, adversus proximum prohibeatur possitque non recte intellegentibus videri non esse prohibitum ut adversus se ipsum quisque falsus testis adsistat, quanto magis intellegendum est non licere homini se ipsum occidere, cum in eo, quod scriptum est: *Non occides,* nihilo deinde addito nullus, nec ipse utique, cui praecipitur, intellegatur exceptus!

Unde quidam hoc praeceptum etiam in bestias ac pecora conantur extendere, ut ex hoc nullum etiam illorum liceat occidere. Cur non ergo et herbas et quidquid humo radicitus alitur ac figitur? Nam et hoc genus rerum, quamvis non sentiat, dicitur vivere ac per hoc potest et mori, proinde etiam, cum vis adhibetur, occidi. Unde et apostolus, cum de huius modi seminibus loqueretur: *Tu,* inquit, *quod seminas non vivificatur, nisi moriatur*; et in psalmo scriptum est: *Occidit vites eorum in grandine.* Num igitur ob hoc, cum audimus, *Non occides,* virgultum vellere nefas ducimus et Manichaeorum errori insanissime adquiescimus?

His igitur deliramentis remotis cum legimus, *Non occides,* si propterea non accipimus hoc dictum de frutectis esse, quia nullus eis sensus est, nec de inrationalibus animantibus, volatilibus natatilibus, ambulatilibus reptilibus, quia nulla nobis ratione sociantur, quam non eis datum est nobiscum habere communem (unde iustissima ordinatione creatoris et vita et mors eorum nostris usibus subditur), restat ut

---

[1] 1 Corinthians 15.36.
[2] Psalms 78.47.
[3] See also Augustine, *On the Heresies* 46; *On the Manichaeans* 54.

commandment that prohibits false witness the prohibition specifies only false witness against a neighbour, and those who do not rightly understand might
get the notion that no individual is forbidden to take
the stand as a false witness against himself, how much
the more should we understand that a man may not
kill himself, since in the commandment, " Thou shall
not kill," there is no more added to this, and hence no
one is understood to be excepted, certainly not the
very man to whom the order is addressed !

On this basis some try to extend this commandment
even to wild and domestic animals and maintain that
it is wrong to kill any of them.   Why not then extend
it also to plants and to anything fixed and fed by
roots in the earth ?   For things of this kind, though
they have no feeling, are said to live, and therefore
can also die, and hence, when violence is exercised, be
slain.   Thus the Apostle, when he speaks of seeds of
this sort, says : " That which thou sowest is not
quickened except it die," [1] and we find in a psalm,
" He killed their vines with hail." [2]   Do we from this
conclude, when we hear " Thou shalt not kill," that it
is wrong to pull up a shrub ?   Are we so completely
deranged that we assent to the Manichaean error ? [3]

Hence, putting aside these ravings, if when we
read, " Thou shalt not kill," we do not understand
this phrase to apply to bushes, because they have no
sensation, nor to the unreasoning animals that fly,
swim, walk or crawl, because they are not partners
with us in the faculty of reason, the privilege not
being given them to share it in common with us—
and therefore by the altogether righteous ordinance
of the Creator both their life and death are a matter
subordinate to our needs—the remaining possibility

de homine intellegamus, quod dictum est, *Non occides*, nec alterum ergo nec te. Neque enim qui se occidit aliud quam hominem occidit.

XXI

De interfectionibus hominum quae ab homicidii crimine excipiuntur.

QUASDAM vero exceptiones eadem ipsa divina fecit auctoritas, ut non liceat hominem occidi. Sed his exceptis, quos Deus occidi iubet sive data lege sive ad personam pro tempore expressa iussione, (non autem ipse occidit, qui ministerium debet iubenti, sicut adminiculum gladius utenti; et ideo nequaquam contra hoc praeceptum fecerunt, quo dictum est. *Non occides,* qui Deo auctore bella gesserunt aut personam gerentes publicae potestatis secundum eius leges, hoc est, iustissimae rationis imperium, sceleratos morte punierunt; et Abraham non solum non est culpatus crudelitatis crimine, verum etiam laudatus est nomine pietatis, quod voluit filium nequaquam scelerate, sed oboedienter occidere; et merito quaeritur utrum pro iussu Dei sit habendum, quod Iephte filiam, quae patri occurrit, occidit, cum id se vovisset immolaturum Deo quod ei redeunti de proelio victori primitus occurrisset; nec Samson

---

[1] Judges 11.29–40.

is to understand this commandment, " Thou shalt not kill," as meaning man alone, that is, " neither another nor thyself," for in fact he who kills himself kills what is no other than a man.

XXI

What cases of homicide are excepted from the charge of murder?

THIS very same divine law, to be sure, made certain exceptions to the rule that it is not lawful to kill a human being. The exceptions include only such persons as God commands to be put to death, either by an enacted law or by special decree applicable to a single person at the given time—but note that the man who is bound to this service under orders, as a sword is bound to be the tool of him who employs it, is not himself the slayer, and consequently there is no breach of this commandment, which says, " Thou shalt not kill," in the case of those who by God's authorization have waged wars, or, who, representing in their person the power of the state, have put criminals to death in accordance with God's law, being vested, that is, with the imperial prerogative of altogether righteous reason. Abraham too not only was not blamed for cruelty, but was even praised for piety, because he resolved to slay his son, not with criminal motives but in obedience to God. And it is properly a question whether we should regard it as equivalent to a command of God when Jephthah slew his daughter who ran to meet him after he had vowed to sacrifice to God the first victim that met him as he returned victorious from battle.[1] Nor is Samson

95

aliter excusatur, quod se ipsum cum hostibus ruina
domus oppressit, nisi quia Spiritus latenter hoc
iusserat, qui per illum miracula faciebat)—his igitur
exceptis, quos vel lex iusta generaliter vel ipse fons
iustitiae Deus specialiter occidi iubet, quisquis
hominem vel se ipsum vel quemlibet occiderit, homicidii crimine innectitur.

XXII

An umquam possit mors voluntaria ad magnitudinem animi pertinere.

ET quicumque hoc in se ipsis perpetraverunt, animi
magnitudine fortasse mirandi, non sapientiae sanitate
laudandi sunt. Quamquam si rationem diligentius
consulas, ne ipsa quidem animi magnitudo recte
nominabitur ubi quisque non valendo tolerare vel
quaeque aspera vel aliena peccata se ipse interemerit.
Magis enim mens infirma deprehenditur quae ferre
non potest vel duram sui corporis servitutem vel
stultam vulgi opinionem, maiorque animus merito
dicendus est qui vitam aerumnosam magis potest ferre
quam fugere et humanum iudicium maximeque
vulgare, quod plerumque caligine erroris involvitur,
prae conscientiae luce ac puritate contemnere.

Quam ob rem si magno animo fieri putandum est,
cum sibi homo ingerit mortem, ille potius Theombrotus in hac animi magnitudine reperitur, quem
ferunt lecto Platonis libro, ubi de inmortalitate

---

[1] Judges 16.28–30.
[2] Cicero, *Tusculan Disputations* 1.34.84, tells the same story
of Cleombrotus, an Ambraciot Academic philosopher.

acquitted of guilt on any other plea, inasmuch as he crushed himself by the collapse of the house along with his enemies, than the plea that the Spirit who through him had been working miracles,[1] had secretly ordered this. With these exceptions then, those slain either by application of a just law or by command of God, the very fount of justice, whoever kills a human being, either himself or no matter who, falls within the meshes of the charge of murder.

XXII

Whether suicide is ever a sign of greatness of mind.

THOSE who have laid violent hands upon themselves are perhaps to be admired for the greatness of their souls, but not to be praised for the soundness of their wisdom. If, however, you take reason more carefully into account, you will not really call it greatness of soul which brings anyone to suicide because he or she lacks strength to bear whatever hardships or sins of others may occur. For the mind is rather detected in weakness, if it cannot bear whether it be the harsh enslavement of its own body, or the stupid opinion of the mob; and a mind might better be called greater that can endure instead of fleeing from a distressful life, and that can in the light of pure conscience despise the judgement of men, especially that of the mob, which as a rule is wrapped in a fog of error.

Therefore, if suicide can be thought to be a great-souled act, this quality of greatness of soul was possessed by that Theombrotus [2] of whom they say that, when he had read Plato's book containing a dis-

animae disputavit, se praecipitem dedisse de muro
atque ita ex hac vita emigrasse ad eam quam credidit
esse meliorem. Nihil enim urguebat aut calamitatis
aut criminis seu verum seu falsum, quod non valendo
ferre se auferret; sed ad capessendam mortem atque
ad[1] huius vitae suavia vincla rumpenda sola adfuit
animi magnitudo. Quod tamen magne potius factum
esse quam bene testis ei esse potuit Plato ipse quem
legerat, qui profecto id praecipue potissimumque
fecisset vel etiam praecepisset, nisi ea mente qua
inmortalitatem animae vidit, nequaquam faciendum,
quin etiam prohibendum esse iudicasset.

At enim multi se interemerunt, ne in manus hostium pervenirent. Non modo quaerimus utrum sit
factum, sed utrum fuerit faciendum. Sana quippe
ratio etiam exemplis anteponenda est, cui quidem et
exempla concordant, sed illa quae tanto digniora sunt
imitatione quanto excellentiora pietate. Non fecerunt patriarchae, non prophetae, non apostoli, quia
et ipse Dominus Christus, quando eos, si persecu-
tionem paterentur, fugere admonuit de civitate in
civitatem, potuit admonere ut sibi manus inferrent,
ne in manus persequentium pervenirent. Porro si
hoc ille non iussit aut monuit ut eo modo sui ex hac
vita emigrarent, quibus migrantibus mansiones
aeternas praeparaturum esse se promisit, quaelibet

---

[1] Ad *omitted by many MSS.*

---

[1] Plato's *Phaedo.*   [2] Matthew 10.5–15.

cussion of the immortality of the soul,[1] he hurled himself headlong from a wall and so departed from this life to that which he thought a better. He was not urged to this act by any calamity of fortune or accusation, false or true, that he had not strength to bear and so made away with himself. Nay, his sole motive for seeking death and breaking the sweet bonds of this life was his greatness of soul. Nevertheless, this Plato himself whom he had read could have borne witness that he acted greatly rather than well, for assuredly Plato would have made this act the first step and the most important step he took himself, and might well have pronounced in favour of it too, had he not, with that intellect by which he saw the soul's immortality, reached the conclusion that suicide should not be committed, nay more, should be forbidden.

Yet in fact many have killed themselves to prevent falling into the hands of the enemy. We are not now asking whether this was done but whether it should have been done. Sound reasoning, naturally, is to be preferred even to precedents, but there are precedents for that matter not discordant with reason—such, be it noted, as are precedents the more worthy of imitation as they are more outstanding in piety. No case of suicide occurred among patriarchs, among prophets, among apostles, seeing that the Lord Christ himself, when he advised them, if they suffered persecution, to flee from city to city,[2] might then have advised them to lay hands upon themselves to avoid falling into the hands of their persecutors. Furthermore, granted that he gave no command or advice to His disciples to employ this means of departing from life, though he promised that he would prepare everlasting mansions for them when they de-

exempla proponant gentes quae ignorant Deum,
manifestum est hoc non licere colentibus unum verum
Deum.

XXIII

*Quale exemplum sit Catonis, qui se victoriam Caesaris
non ferens interemit.*

Sed tamen etiam illi praeter Lucretiam, de qua
supra satis quod videbatur diximus, non facile re-
periunt de cuius auctoritate praescribant, nisi illum
Catonem qui se Uticae occidit; non quia solus id
fecit, sed quia vir doctus et probus habebatur, ut
merito putetur etiam recte fieri potuisse vel posse
quod fecit.

De cuius facto quid potissimum dicam, nisi quod
amici eius etiam docti quidam viri, qui hoc fieri prudentius dissuadebant, inbecillioris quam fortioris
animi facinus esse censuerunt, quo demonstraretur
non honestas turpia praecavens, sed infirmitas adversa
non sustinens? Hoc et ipse Cato in suo carissimo
filio iudicavit. Nam si turpe erat sub victoria
Caesaris vivere, cur auctor huius turpitudinis filio fuit,
quem de Caesaris benignitate omnia sperare praecepit? Cur non et illum secum coegit ad mortem?
Nam si eum filium, qui contra imperium in hostem
pugnaverat, etiam victorem laudabiliter Torquatus
occidit, cur victus victo filio pepercit Cato, qui non

---

[1] Dio Cassius 43.10–13; Plutarch, *Cato the Younger* 65–70.
[2] T. Manlius Torquatus, consul in the Latin War (340 b.c.),
put his victorious son to death for disobedience (Livy 7.7;
Aulus Gellius 9.13; Cicero, *On Ends* 2.32.105).

parted, then, no matter what precedents are brought
forward by heathen that know not God, it is obvious
that suicide is unlawful for those who worship the
one true God.

XXIII

What are we to think of the precedent set by Cato,
who, unable to bear Caesar's victory, slew himself?

BESIDES Lucretia, of whom we sufficiently stated
our opinion earlier, even our opponents do not easily
find another precedent whose authority may serve as a
warrant apart from the great Cato who killed himself
at Utica.   He is their warrant, not because he is the
only suicide, but because he passed as a learned and
good man, so that there would be justification for the
view that what he did might have been rightly done
and may still be rightly done.

Of this act of his, what can I say but that some of
his friends, also learned men, who even more wisely
argued against such a course, declared their opinion
that it springs from a feeble rather than a strong mind,
being an act that exhibits not self-respect guarding
against dishonour, but weakness unable to bear adversity? Cato himself reached the same verdict in the
case of his beloved son.   For if it was a disgrace to live
after Caesar's victory, why did he recommend this disgrace to his son whom he instructed to put hope only in
Caesar's clemency? [1]   Why did he not compel him
too to share death with himself?   If Torquatus [2]
gained praise for slaying his son who, contrary to
orders, had fought the enemy and won, why did
vanquished Cato spare his vanquished son when he did

pepercit sibi? An turpius erat contra imperium esse
victorem, quam contra decus ferre victorem?

Nullo modo igitur Cato turpe esse iudicavit sub
victore Caesare vivere; alioquin ab hac turpitudine
paterno ferro filium liberaret. Quid ergo, nisi quod
filium quantum amavit, cui parci a Caesare et speravit
et voluit, tantum gloriae ipsius Caesaris, ne ab illo
etiam sibi parceretur, ut ipse Caesar dixisse fertur,
invidit, ut aliquid nos mitius dicamus, erubuit?

XXIV

Quod in ea virtute, qua Regulus Catone praestantior fuit, multo magis emineant Christiani.

NOLUNT autem isti, contra quos agimus, ut sanctum
virum Iob, qui tam horrenda mala in sua carne perpeti
maluit quam inlata sibi morte omnibus carere cruciatibus, vel alios sanctos ex litteris nostris summa auctoritate celsissimis fideque dignissimis, qui captivitatem
dominationemque hostium ferre quam sibi necem inferre maluerunt, Catoni praeferamus; sed ex litteris
eorum eundem illum Marco Catoni Marcum Regulum
praeferam. Cato enim numquam Caesarem vicerat,
cui victus dedignatus est subici et, ne subiceretur, a se
ipso elegit occidi.

---

[1] Plutarch, *Cato the Younger* 72; *Julius Caesar* 54.
[2] See above, ch. 15.

not spare himself? Was it more a disgrace to be victorious contrary to orders than to submit to a victor contrary to propriety?

Cato, therefore, in no wise judged it a disgrace to live under Caesar's victorious rule, for otherwise a father's sword would have freed his son from this disgrace. What can we conclude but that his love for his son, who, he hoped and resolved, would be spared by Caesar, was equalled by the feeling with which he begrudged Caesar the glory of pardoning himself, to use the phrase attributed to Caesar,[1] or to put it more gently in our own terms, by his discomfiture for fear that Caesar should have the glory of pardoning him.

XXIV

The virtue for which Regulus was more distinguished than Cato, reaches much greater heights in the Christians.

OUR opponents, furthermore, do not want us to prefer to Cato that saintly man Job, who chose rather to suffer dreadful evils in his flesh than by self-inflicted death to be rid of all these pains, or the other holy men of whom it is recorded in our books—and they are most lofty in their supreme authority and most trustworthy—that they chose rather to bear capture and enslavement by the enemy than to take their own lives. On the contrary, I shall prefer to Marcus Cato an example taken from their books, that same Marcus Regulus.[2] For Cato never had defeated Caesar, but, when he was defeated by him, disdained to be subject to him, and to avoid being subject, chose suicide instead.

Regulus autem Poenos iam vicerat imperioque
Romano Romanus imperator non ex civibus dolendam,
sed ex hostibus laudandam victoriam reportaverat;
ab eis tamen postea victus maluit eos ferre serviendo
quam eis se auferre moriendo. Proinde servavit et
sub Carthaginiensium dominatione patientiam et in
Romanorum dilectione constantiam, nec victum
auferens corpus ab hostibus nec invictum animum a
civibus. Nec quod se occidere noluit, vitae huius
amore fecit. Hoc probavit, cum causa promissi iuris-
que iurandi ad eosdem hostes, quos gravius in senatu
verbis quam in bello armis offenderat, sine ulla
dubitatione remeavit.

Tantus itaque vitae huius contemptor, cum saevientibus hostibus per quaslibet poenas eam finire quam
se ipse perimere maluit, magnum scelus esse, si se
homo interimat, procul dubio iudicavit. Inter omnes
suos laudabiles et virtutis insignibus inlustres viros
non proferunt Romani meliorem, quem neque felicitas
corruperit, nam in tanta victoria mansit pauperrimus,
nec infelicitas fregerit, nam ad tanta exitia revertit
intrepidus.

Porro si fortissimi et praeclarissimi viri terrenae
patriae defensores deorumque licet falsorum, non
tamen fallaces cultores, sed veracissimi etiam iura-
tores, qui hostes victos more ac iure belli ferire
potuerunt, hi ab hostibus victi se ipsos ferire noluerunt

Regulus, however, had already defeated the Carthaginians, and as Roman commander with a Roman commission had won a victory—not a deplorable victory over citizens, but a laudable victory over foes. Yet afterwards, being defeated by them, he preferred to take what came as their slave rather than to take his life and escape them. Henceforth he maintained his patience under the slavery imposed by the Carthaginians and his constancy in loyalty to the Romans, depriving neither the enemy of his conquered body nor the citizens of his unconquered spirit. Nor was his refusal to resort to suicide motivated by love of this life, as he demonstrated when, to keep his promise and his oath, he returned with no hesitation to those same enemies whom he had in the Senate more grievously provoked by his words than in the war by his arms.

Therefore, though he set so little store on life, yet in choosing to end his life among fierce enemies by any tortures they might devise rather than by doing away with himself, there can be no doubt that he gave it as his judgement that suicide is a great crime. Among all their men deserving of praise and distinguished by notable virtues, the Romans offer none better than Regulus. Neither did good fortune spoil him, for, though so great a victor, he remained a very poor man, nor did evil fortune crush him, for he went back to that terrible fate unmoved.

But if the bravest and most famous men, defenders of an earthly fatherland and of gods—false gods, to be sure, yet they were not false worshippers and were even most genuine keepers of their oath—if these men could after the custom and rule of war smite the vanquished enemy, yet when vanquished

et, cum mortem minime formidarent, victores tamen
dominos ferre quam eam sibi inferre maluerunt,
quanto magis Christiani, verum Deum colentes et
supernae patriae suspirantes, ab hoc facinore tem-
perabunt, si eos divina dispositio vel probandos vel
emendandos ad tempus hostibus subiugaverit, quos in
illa humilitate non deserit qui propter eos tam
humiliter altissimus venit, praesertim quos nullius
militaris potestatis vel talis militiae iura constringunt
ipsum hostem ferire superatum. Quis ergo tam
malus error obrepit, ut homo se occidat, vel quia in
eum peccavit, vel ne in eum peccet inimicus, cum vel
peccatorem vel peccaturum ipsum occidere non
audeat inimicum ?

XXV

Quod peccatum non per peccatum debeat declinari.

At enim timendum est et cavendum, ne libidini
hostili [1] subditum corpus inlecebrosissima voluptate
animum adliciat consentire peccato. Proinde, inquiunt, non iam propter alienum, sed propter suum
peccatum, antequam hoc quisque committat, se debet
occidere.

Nullo modo quidem hoc faciet animus, ut consentiat
libidini carnis suae aliena libidine concitatae, qui Deo
potius eiusque sapientiae quam corpori eiusque concupiscentiae subiectus est. Verum tamen si detestabile
facinus et damnabile scelus est etiam se ipsum hominem occidere, sicut veritas manifesta proclamat, quis

[1] *Added in many MSS.*

by the enemy were unwilling to smite themselves;
if, though they had no fear of death, they preferred to
endure enslavement rather than inflict it by their own
hand, how much more will Christians, who worship a
true God and aspire to a heavenly fatherland, refrain
from this crime, supposing Divine Providence for a
season to subject them to enemies, either that they
may be tried or that they may be corrected! For in
this humbling experience they are not deserted by
him, the Most High, who came so humbly for their
sakes, and above all they are bound by no loyalty to
military authority or duty of such service to slay
even a conquered enemy. What stealthy error, then,
is as serious as this, to suppose that a man may kill
himself because a foe has sinned or may sin against
him, though he dare not kill even an enemy who has
sinned or may sin against him?

XXV

That a sin should not be avoided by a sin.

BUT we should fear and take precautions lest the
body, when it is subdued to the enemy's lust, may
entice the soul through a most insidious pleasure to
consent to the sin. Hence it follows, they say, that
the individual ought to kill himself, no longer urging
another's sin as the ground, but the individual's own
not yet committed sin.

The mind that is subject rather to God and his
wisdom than to the body and its concupiscence will in
fact never do such a thing as to consent to the desire
aroused in its own flesh by another's lust. But in
any case, if for a man to kill himself is also a detestable
crime and a damnable sin, as the truth clearly pro-

ita desipiat, ut dicat : " Iam nunc peccemus, ne postea forte peccemus ; iam nunc perpetremus homicidium, ne postea forte incidamus in adulterium " ?

Nonne si tantum dominatur iniquitas, ut non innocentia sed peccata potius eligantur, satius est incertum de futuro adulterium quam certum de praesenti homicidium ? Nonne satius est flagitium committere, quod paenitendo sanetur, quam tale facinus, ubi locus salubris paenitentiae non relinquitur ?

Haec dixi propter eos vel eas, quae non alieni, sed proprii peccati devitandi causa, ne sub alterius libidine etiam excitatae suae forte consentiant, vim sibi, qua moriantur, inferendam putant. Ceterum absit a mente Christiana, quae Deo suo fidit in eoque spe posita eius adiutorio nititur, absit, inquam, ut mens talis quibuslibet carnis voluptatibus ad consensum turpitudinis cedat. Quod si illa concupiscentialis inoboedientia quae adhuc in membris moribundis habitat, praeter nostrae voluntatis legem quasi lege sua movetur, quanto magis absque culpa est in corpore non consentientis, si absque culpa est in corpore dormientis !

XXVI

De his, quae fieri non licent, cum a sanctis facta noscuntur, qua ratione facta credenda sint.

SED quaedam, inquiunt, sanctae feminae tempore persecutionis, ut insectatores suae pudicitiae devi-

claims, who is so mad as to say, " Let us sin now at once, lest we chance to sin later; let us now at once commit murder lest we chance to fall into adultery later "?

If wickedness is so powerful over us that we have in our choice no innocent acts but only sins, is it not better to elect an uncertain adultery in the future rather than a certain homicide in the present? Is it not better to commit a crime that repentance may heal than be guilty of an act whereby no place is left for salutary penance?

I have said this on behalf of those men or women who think they ought to do mortal violence to themselves in order to avoid, not another's sin, but a sin of their own. They are afraid, if they are subjected to another's lust, that their own will be awakened and they consent to it. But far be it from the heart of a Christian trusting in God and with hope in him relying on his aid—far be it, I say, from such a heart, induced by any pleasures at all, to yield a shameful consent. But if that lustful disobedience, which still dwells in our mortal members, acts by its own law apart from any law of our willing, how much more is there no fault where the body of one who does not consent is involved, if there is none where the body of one asleep is concerned!

XXVI

What explanation we should adopt to account for the saints' doing certain things that they are known to have done which it is not lawful to do.

But, they say, in time of persecution certain saintly women, to avoid the pursuers of their chastity, cast

tarent, in rapturum atque necaturum se fluvium proiecerunt eoque modo defunctae sunt earumque martyria in catholica ecclesia veneratione celeberrima frequentantur.

De his nihil temere audeo judicare. Utrum enim ecclesiae aliquibus fide dignis testificationibus, ut earum memoriam sic honoret, divina persuaserit auctoritas, nescio; et fieri potest ut ita sit. Quid si enim hoc fecerunt, non humanitus deceptae, sed divinitus iussae, nec errantes, sed oboedientes? sicut de Samsone aliud nobis fas non est credere. Cum autem Deus iubet seque iubere sine ullis ambagibus intimat, quis oboedientiam in crimen vocet? quis obsequium pietatis accuset?

Sed non ideo sine scelere facit, quisquis Deo filium immolare decreverit, quia hoc Abraham etiam laud-abiliter fecit. Nam et miles cum oboediens potestati, sub qualibet legitime constitutus est, hominem occidit, nulla civitatis suae lege reus est homicidii, immo, nisi fecerit, reus est imperii deserti atque contempti; quod si sua sponte atque auctoritate fecisset, crimen effusi humani sanguinis incidisset. Itaque unde punitur si fecit iniussus, inde punietur nisi fecerit iussus.

Quod si ita est iubente imperatore, quanto magis iubente creatore! Qui ergo audit non licere se occi-

themselves into a river that would ravish and drown them, and in that way they died and their memorial shrines are frequented by great numbers who venerate them as martyrs in the Catholic Church.

With regard to these women I dare not give any rash judgement. I do not know whether the divine authority has counselled the church by some trustworthy testimonies to honour their memory in this, and it may be so. For what if the women acted as they did, not by human misconception, but by divine command, and they did not go astray in their act, but were obedient? Compare the case of Samson, where it would be sin to hold any other view. When God, moreover, gives a command and makes it clear without ambiguity that he gives it, who can summon obedience to judgement? Who can draw up a brief against religious deference to God?

But a decision by any random person to sacrifice his son to God, is not without sin, just because Abraham did it and even won praise. For the soldier, who, obedient to some power under which he has been commissioned according to law, has slain a man, is not guilty of homicide under the terms of any law of his state; on the contrary, if he does not slay him, he is then guilty of dereliction and contempt of authority, whereas, had he done this of his own accord and on his own authority, he would have become liable to the charge of shedding human blood. Accordingly, the deed that is punished, if he does it without orders, is the same as that for which he will be punished, if he does not do it when ordered.

Well, if this is so when a general gives an order, how much more is it so when the Creator gives the order! Let anyone, therefore, who is told that he

dere, faciat, si iussit cuius non licet iussa contemnere; tantummodo videat utrum divina iussio nullo nutet incerto. Nos per aurem conscientiam convenimus, occultorum nobis iudicium non usurpamus. Nemo *scit quid agatur in homine nisi spiritus hominis, qui in ipso est.*

Hoc dicimus, hoc asserimus, hoc modis omnibus adprobamus, neminem spontaneam mortem sibi inferre debere velut fugiendo molestias temporales, ne incidat in perpetuas; neminem propter aliena peccata, ne hoc ipso incipiat habere gravissimum proprium, quem non polluebat alienum; neminem propter sua peccata praeterita, propter quae magis hac vita opus est, ut possint paenitendo sanari; neminem velut desiderio vitae melioris, quae post mortem speratur, quia reos suae mortis melior post mortem vita non suscipit.

XXVII

An propter declinationem peccati mors spontanea adpetenda sit.

RESTAT una causa, de qua dicere coeperam, qua utile putatur ut se quisque interficiat, scilicet ne in peccatum inruat vel blandiente voluptate vel dolore saeviente. Quam causam si voluerimus admittere, eo usque progressa perveniet ut hortandi sint homines

---

[1] 1 Corinthians 2.11.

has no right to kill himself, do the deed if he is so ordered by him whose orders must not be slighted. There is just one proviso: he must be sure that his divine command is not made precarious by any doubt. It is through the ear that we take note of men's thoughts; we do not arrogate to ourselves any right to judge such as are kept secret. No one "knows what goes on in a man except the spirit of the man that is in him." [1]

This we say, this we declare, this we by all means endorse: that no man ought to inflict on himself a voluntary death, thinking to escape temporary ills, lest he find himself among ills that are unending; that no one ought to do so because of another's sins, lest by the very act he bring into being a sin that is his own, when he would not have been polluted by another's; that no one ought to do so on account of any past sins, inasmuch as he needs this life the more to make possible their healing by repentance; that no one ought to do so thinking to satisfy his hunger for the better life for which we hope after death, inasmuch as the better life after death does not accept those who are guilty of their own death.

XXVII

Whether one should commit suicide to avoid sinning.

THERE remains one reason for thinking suicide profitable that I had started to discuss, namely, to prevent being impelled to sin whether by the seduction of pleasure or by cruel suffering. Once we consent to the acceptance of this reason, it will not stop until it has brought us to think that men ought to be

tunc se potius interimere, cum lavacro sanctae re-
generationis abluti universorum remissionem acceperint peccatorum. Tunc enim tempus est cavendi
omnia futura peccata, cum sunt omnia deleta praeterita. Quod si morte spontanea recte fit, cur non
tunc potissimum fit? Cur baptizatus sibi quisque
parcit? Cur liberatum caput tot rursus vitae huius
periculis inserit, cum sit facillimae potestatis inlata
sibi nece omnia devitare scriptumque sit: *Qui amat
periculum, incidet in illud?* Cur ergo amantur tot et
tanta pericula vel certe, etiamsi non amantur, sus-
cipiuntur, cum manet in hac vita cui abscedere
licitum est?

An vero tam insulsa perversitas cor evertit et a
consideratione veritatis avertit, ut, si se quisque interimere debet, ne unius captivantis dominatu conruat
in peccatum, vivendum sibi existimet, ut ipsum per-
ferat mundum per omnes horas temptationibus
plenum, et talibus qualis sub uno domino formidatur,
et innumerabilibus ceteris sine quibus haec vita non
ducitur? Quid igitur causae est cur in eis exhorta-
tionibus tempora consumamus quibus baptizatos ad-
loquendo studemus accendere sive ad virginalem
integritatem sive ad continentiam vidualem sive ad
ipsam tori coniugalis fidem, cum habeamus meliora et
ab omnibus peccandi periculis remota compendia, ut,
quibuscumque post remissionem recentissimam peccatorum adripiendam mortem sibique ingerendam per-

exhorted rather to kill themselves at the moment when, being washed in the baptism of holy regeneration, they have received the remission of all their sins. For the time to avoid all future sins is when all past sins have been blotted out. If this is a thing to be rightly achieved by a voluntary death, why is not that the best time for it? Why does the individual, once baptized, spare himself? Why does he thrust a head once freed back into the dangers of this life when he has the power so easily to avoid them all by suicide, and it is written, " He who loveth danger shall fall into it." [1] Why are so many and so great dangers preferred, or if not preferred, accepted, as they are, when he who might legitimately withdraw from this life, remains?

Is anyone, however, so preverted in his folly or so diverted from examination of the truth as to think that, granted that a man ought to take his life to prevent falling into sin when he has one master whose prisoner he is, yet he ought to keep on living though he must bear the burden of worldly life itself, which teems with temptations from one hour to another, not only such as resemble the one that alarms those who have one master, but countless others from which there is no exemption in this life? What reason is there for us to waste time on those exhortations of which the object is to rouse the baptized to keep themselves inviolate as virgins, or continent as widows, or faithful as partners in the conjugal bed itself, when we dispose of better ways, short cuts that avoid all risks of any sin, namely, to persuade whatsoever persons we can at the earliest moment after remission of sins to clutch death quickly and inflict it

[1] Ecclesiasticus 3.26.

suadere potuerimus, eos ad Dominum saniores
purioresque mittamus?

Porro si quisquis hoc adgrediendum et suadendum
putat, non dico desipit, sed insanit, qua tandem fronte
homini dicit: " Interfice te, ne parvis tuis peccatis
adicias gravius, dum vivis sub domino barbaris moribus inpudico," qui non potest nisi sceleratissime
dicere: " Interfice te peccatis tuis omnibus absolutis,
ne rursus talia vel etiam peiora committas, dum vivis
in mundo tot inpuris voluptatibus inlecebroso, tot
nefandis crudelitatibus furioso, tot erroribus et
terroribus inimico "? Hoc quia nefas est dicere,
nefas est profecto se occidere. Nam si hoc sponte
faciendi ulla causa iusta esse posset, procul dubio
iustior quam ista non esset. Quia vero nec ista est,
ergo nulla est.

XXVIII

Quo iudicio Dei in corpora continentium libido hostilis
peccare permissa sit.

Non itaque vobis, o fideles Christi, sit taedio vita
vestra, si ludibrio fuit hostibus castitas vestra.
Habetis magnam veramque consolationem, si fidam
conscientiam retinetis non vos consensisse peccatis
eorum qui in vos peccare permissi sunt. Quod
si forte, cur permissi sint, quaeritis, alta quidem
est providentia creatoris mundi atque rectoris,

---

[1] Women enslaved by barbarians had not even the security
provided in civilized society by social custom or good manners.

on themselves, and so dispatch them to the Lord whole and pure?

Well, then, granted that anyone who thinks it right to take that course and advocate it is—foolish? No! but mad—then how on earth does anyone say to a human being, " Do away with yourself so as not to add to your petty sins one more serious, living as you do in slavery to a shameless master who has the manners of a savage," [1] when he cannot say without utter wickedness, ' Do away with yourself now that all your sins have been washed away, lest you commit the like again or even worse, living, as you do, in a world so alluring with its unclean pleasures, so insane with its abominable cruelties, so hostile with its errors and its terrors " ? As it is wicked to say this, so it is wicked, surely, to kill oneself. For if there could be any legitimate reason for committing suicide, there could be none more legitimate than this, I am sure. But since not even this one is legitimate, therefore there is none such.

XXVIII

By what judgement of God the enemy was permitted to sin against the bodies of the continent.

LET not your life, therefore, ye who are of the faith of Christ, make you weary, since your chastity was made the sport of your enemies. You have a great and true comfort if you can with an honest conscience remember that you did not consent to the sins of those who were permitted to sin against you. Should you ask why they were permitted to do this, profound indeed is the prudence of the Creator and Ruler of the

et inscrutabilia sunt iudicia eius et investigabiles viae eius.

Verum tamen interrogate fideliter animas vestras, ne forte de isto integritatis et continentiae vel pudicitiae bono vos inflatius extulistis et humanis laudibus delectatae in hoc etiam aliquibus invidistis. Non accuso quod nescio, nec audio quod vobis interrogata vestra corda respondent. Tamen si ita esse responderint, nolite admirari hoc vos amisisse, unde hominibus placere gestistis, illud vobis remansisse, quod ostendi hominibus non potest. Si peccantibus non consensistis, divinae gratiae, ne amitteretur, divinum accessit auxilium; humanae gloriae, ne amaretur, humanum successit opprobrium. In utroque consolamini, pusillanimes, illinc probatae hinc castigatae, illinc iustificatae hinc emendatae.

Quarum vero corda interrogata respondent numquam se de bono virginitatis vel viduitatis vel coniugalis pudicitiae superbisse, sed humilibus consentiendo de dono Dei cum tremore exultasse, nec invidisse cuiquam paris excellentiam sanctitatis et castitatis, sed humana laude postposita, quae tanto maior deferri solet quanto est bonum rarius quod exigit laudem, optasse potius ut amplior earum numerus esset, quam ut ipsae in paucitate amplius eminerent.

Nec istae, quae tales sunt, si earum quoque aliquas barbarica libido compressit, permissum hoc esse

world, and " unsearchable are his judgements, and his ways past finding out." [1]

Nevertheless, faithfully question your souls to see whether perhaps you were too much puffed up with pride in your possession of maidenhood and continence or chastity, and whether, flattered by human praise, you have even begrudged others this possession in some cases. I do not accuse where I do not know, and I do not hear what answer your hearts make when questioned. But if their answer should be yes, be not astonished that you have lost that for which you longed to be praised by men, but have retained that which cannot be exhibited to men. If you gave no consent to the sinners, divine grace was fortified by divine assistance to prevent the loss of it, and human glory was mortified by human calumny to prevent the love of it. In respect to both, faint-hearted ones, take comfort ; your virtue is approved, your fault reproved, your virtue is vindicated, your fault eradicated.

But what of those whose hearts when questioned answer that they have never been arrogant in their possession of virginity or widowhood or married chastity, but casting their lot with the lowly, rejoiced with trembling at God's gift, and never begrudged anyone equal excellence in sanctity and chastity? Nay, but subordinating human praise, which is commonly awarded in greater measure the rarer the virtue that excites it, they have chosen rather the growth of their numbers than the growth of their own eminence by being few.

Let not such women, though savage lust outraged some of them too, argue that this was permitted ; let

[1] Romans 11.33.

causentur, nec ideo Deum credant ista neglegere, quia
permittit quod nemo inpune committit. Quaedam
enim veluti pondera malarum cupiditatum et per
occultum praesens divinum iudicium relaxantur et
manifesto ultimo reservantur.

Fortassis autem istae, quae bene sibi sunt consciae
non se ex isto castitatis bono cor inflatum extulisse, et
tamen vim hostilem in carne perpessae sunt, habebant
aliquid latentis infirmitatis, quae posset in superbiae
fastum, si hanc humilitatem in vastatione illa evasissent, extolli. Sicut ergo quidam morte rapti sunt,
ne malitia mutaret intellectum eorum, ita quiddam
ab istis vi raptum est, ne prosperitas mutaret modes-
tiam earum. Utrisque igitur, quae de carne sua,
quod turpem nullius esset perpessa contactum, vel
iam superbiebant vel superbire, si nec hostium
violentia contrectata esset, forsitan poterant, non
ablata est castitas, sed humilitas persuasa; illarum
tumori succursum est inmanenti, istarum occursum est
inminenti.

Quamquam et illud non sit tacendum, quod quibusdam, quae ista perpessae sunt, potuit videri continentiae bonum in bonis corporalibus deputandum
et tunc manere, si nullius libidine corpus adtrectare-
tur; non autem esse positum in solo adiuto divinitus
robore voluntatis ut sit sanctum et corpus et spiritus;

---

[1] An allusion, probably, to Wisdom of Solomon 4.11 : He
was caught away, lest wickedness should change his understanding.

them not suppose, because a sin is permitted that
never goes unpunished when committed, that consequently God is unmindful in such cases. For there
are certain, so to speak, heavy burdens belonging to
guilty lusts that are at the same time remitted by the
present unseen judgement of God and stored up for a
last judgement visible to all.

Moreover, perhaps those women whose consciences
are clear that they never let their hearts soar in
swollen pride because of that boon of chastity, yet
nevertheless endured violation of their flesh by the
foe, possessed some hidden ailment which might have
swollen to the point of disdainful arrogance, had they
escaped this humbling experience amid the catastrophe. So, as some people were removed by death to
prevent wickedness from changing their understanding,[1] so, too, certain of these women were violated to
prevent good fortune from changing their modesty.
Neither of them then, neither those who took pride
in their flesh that it had never known the touch of
shame, nor those who perhaps might have taken
pride, had it not been roughly handled by the enemy,
suffered, not diminution of chastity, but argument for
humility. The former were treated for a tumour
already swollen; the latter for a tumour all ready to
swell.

We should not, however, fail to point out that to
some of the sufferers it may have appeared that
continence is to be counted as a good among bodily
goods and that it is present just so long as the body
has not been subject to anyone's lustful tampering.
They may not have understood that the sanctity of
both body and spirit depend on strength of will alone
divinely assisted and that it is one of those goods that

nec tale bonum esse quod invito animo non possit auferri; qui error eis fortasse sublatus est. Cum enim cogitant qua conscientia Deo servierint, et fide inconcussa non de illo sentiunt quod ita sibi servientes eumque invocantes deserere ullo modo potuerit, quantumque illi castitas placeat dubitare non possunt, vident esse consequens nequaquam illum fuisse permissurum ut haec acciderent sanctis suis, si eo modo perire posset sanctitas, quam contulit eis et diligit in eis.

XXIX

Quid familia Christi respondere debeat infidelibus, cum exprobrant quod eam a furore hostium non liberaverit Christus.

HABET itaque omnis familia summi et veri Dei consolationem suam, non fallacem nec in spe rerum nutantium vel labentium constitutam, vitamque etiam ipsam temporalem minime paenitendam, in qua eruditur ad aeternam, bonisque terrenis tamquam peregrina utitur nec capitur, malis autem aut probatur aut emendatur. Illi vero, qui probitati eius insultant eique dicunt, cum forte in aliqua temporalia mala devenerit: *Ubi est Deus tuus?* ipsi dicant, ubi sint dii eorum, cum talia patiuntur, pro quibus evitandis eos vel colunt vel colendos esse contendunt.

---

[1] Psalms 42.3.

cannot be taken away, as long as the mind refuses consent. From this mistaken notion they are probably now freed. When they reflect how conscientiously they served God and when with faith unshaken they do not hold that he can ever fail those who serve him and call upon him, and when they may not doubt the great value that he sets on chastity, they see that it follows from these premisses that he could never have allowed these misfortunes to happen to his saints if that saintliness could thereby be undone which he granted to them and which he rejoices to see in them.

XXIX

What the servants of Christ should say to infidels, when they cast the reproach that Christ did not free them from the enemy's rage.

THE whole family of the highest and true God, accordingly, has now its proper message of comfort, free from fallacy and based on no expectation of things subject to shock or lapse. It has a life in this world that even so is nothing to regret, since it is a school from which we graduate to life eternal, employing earthly goods like aliens, without capitulation to them, and finding in earthly ills either trial or correction. Those who vent their spite on the rectitude of God's family, say, when by chance it falls among the ills of this world, " Where is thy God ? " [1] —let them say themselves where their own gods are when those things befall them to avoid which they either worship their gods or maintain that they should be worshipped.

Nam ista respondet: Deus meus ubique praesens, ubique totus, nusquam inclusus, qui possit adesse secretus, abesse non motus; ille cum me adversis rebus exagitat, aut merita examinat aut peccata castigat mercedemque mihi aeternam pro toleratis pie malis temporalibus servat; vos autem qui estis cum quibus loqui dignum sit, saltem de diis vestris, quanto minus de Deo meo, qui *terribilis est super omnes deos, quoniam omnes* [1] *dii gentium daemonia, Dominus autem caelos fecit*?

XXX

Quam pudendis prosperitatibus affluere velint, qui de Christianis temporibus conqueruntur.

Sɪ Nasica ille Scipio vester quondam pontifex viveret, quem sub terrore belli Punici in suscipiendis Phrygiis sacris, cum vir optimus quaereretur, universus senatus elegit, cuius os fortasse non auderetis aspicere, ipse vos ab hac inpudentia cohiberet. Cur enim adflicti rebus adversis de temporibus querimini Christianis, nisi quia vestram luxuriam cupitis habere securam et perditissimis moribus remota omni molestiarum asperitate diffluere? Neque enim propterea cupitis habere pacem et omni genere copiarum abundare, ut his bonis honeste utamini, hoc est

[1] *Some MSS. omit* omnes.

---

[1] Psalms 96.4.
[2] In 204 B.C. when the statue of the Phrygian goddess Cybele was imported to Rome (Livy 29.14).

For the family of God replies: " Our God is everywhere present, wholly everywhere, nowhere confined. He can be present in secret, be absent without moving. When he exposes me to adversity, he is either testing my deserts or chastising my sins; he has in store for me an eternal reward in return for any misfortunes of this life, that have been borne in accordance with religious duty. But who are you that we should deign to speak to you, in any case about your gods, and how much less about our God, who ' is to be feared above all gods, for all the gods of the nations are demons but the Lord made the heavens ' ? " [1]

XXX

Those who complain of the Christian era really wish to prosper in shameful luxury.

WERE your famous Scipio Nasica,[2] once your pontiff, still living—who was unanimously chosen by the Senate when the best man was required, and appointed to take up the sacred objects from Phrygia during the panic of the Carthaginian war, a man whom perhaps you would hardly dare to look in the face—even he would hold you back from impudence like this. Why, when afflicted by adversities, do you complain against the Christian era unless because you wish to maintain your luxury untroubled and to abandon yourselves to the most damnable practices with no harsh touch of vexing problems ? For your desire for peace and abundant wealth of every sort does not spring from any intention of enjoying these boons in a respectable way, that is, decently, soberly,

modeste sobrie, temperanter pie, sed ut infinita
varietas voluptatum insanis effusionibus exquiratur,
secundisque rebus ea mala oriantur in moribus quae
saevientibus peiora sunt hostibus.

At ille Scipio pontifex maximus vester, ille iudicio
totius senatus vir optimus, istam vobis metuens calamitatem nolebat aemulam tunc imperii Romani
Carthaginem dirui et decernenti ut dirueretur contra-
dicebat Catoni, timens infirmis animis hostem securi-
tatem et tamquam pupillis civibus idoneum tutorem
necessarium videns esse terrorem

Nec eum sententia fefellit; re ipsa probatum est
quam verum diceret. Deleta quippe Carthagine
magno scilicet terrore Romanae rei publicae depulso
et extincto tanta de rebus prosperis orta mala continuo subsecuta sunt ut corrupta diruptaque concordia prius saevis cruentisque seditionibus, deinde
mox malarum conexione causarum bellis etiam civilibus tantae strages ederentur, tantus sanguis effun-
deretur, tanta cupiditate proscriptionum ac rapi-
narum ferveret inmanitas, ut Romani illi, qui vita
integriore mala metuebant ab hostibus, perdita integritate vitae crudeliora paterentur a civibus; eaque
ipsa libido dominandi, quae inter alia vitia generis
humani meracior inerat universo populo Romano,
postea quam in paucis potentioribus vicit, obtritos
fatigatosque ceteros etiam iugo servitutis oppressit.

---

[1] " Age cannot wither her, nor custom stale her infinite
variety "—Shakespeare, *Ant. and Cleop.* 2.2.243.

[2] There is confusion here between father and son. It was
P. Cornelius Scipio Nasica Corculum who answered Cato's
Carthago delenda est with a negative. See Livy, Summary of
Book 48, end, and Plutarch, *Cato Major* 27.

temperately, devoutly. Rather you would use them
to procure an infinite variety [1] in your unwholesome
dissipations; you would engender in times of
prosperity a moral plague of ills worse than raging
enemies.

That Scipio, your chief pontiff, the best man of all
in the judgement of the whole Senate, because he
feared that calamity, refused to agree to the destruction of Rome's rival for empire, Carthage, and said
the opposite of Cato, who advised its destruction.[2]
For he feared security as the enemy of unstable minds
and saw that fear was indispensable to the citizens to
serve, as it were, as guardian of their immaturity.

In this opinion he was not mistaken, for the outcome showed how truly he spoke. Of course, once
Carthage was destroyed, which meant that the great
bugbear of the Roman republic had been beaten off
and annihilated, these mighty evils sprang up as a
sequel to prosperity. First, harmony was crumpled
and breached in the fierce and bloody strife of parties.
Next, there followed, by a chain of evil causes, civil
wars, which brought such great massacres, so much
bloodshed, such effervescence of cruelty induced
by the craving for proscriptions and plunder, that
those Romans who, when life had more integrity,
feared the evils enemies might bring, now when that
integrity of living went by the board, suffered greater
cruelties from fellow citizens. Finally, that passion
for rule which among the other vices of mankind was
found more concentrated in the Roman people one
and all, when it had won victory in the case of a
few more dominating men, subjected the others,
worn out and tired, to the yoke of slavery.

SAINT AUGUSTINE

XXXI

Quibus vitiorum gradibus aucta sit in Romanis cupido regnandi.

NAM quando illa quiesceret in superbissimis mentibus, donec continuatis honoribus ad potestatem regiam perveniret? Honorum porro continuandorum facultas non esset, nisi ambitio praevaleret. Minime autem praevaleret ambitio, nisi in populo avaritia luxuriaque corrupto. Avarus vero luxuriosusque populus secundis rebus effectus est, quas Nasica ille providentissime cavendas esse censebat, quando civitatem hostium maximam fortissimam opulentissimam nolebat auferri, ut timore libido premeretur, libido pressa non luxuriaretur luxuriaque cohibita nec avaritia grassaretur; quibus vitiis obseratis civitati utilis virtus floreret et cresceret eique virtuti libertas congrua permaneret.

Hinc etiam erat et ex hac providentissima patriae caritate veniebat, quod idem ipse vester pontifex maximus, a senatu illius temporis (quod saepe dicendum est) electus sine ulla sententiarum discrepantia vir optimus, caveam theatri senatum construere molientem ab hac dispositione et cupiditate compescuit persuasitque oratione gravissima, ne Graecam luxuriam virilibus patriae moribus paterentur obrepere et ad virtutem labefactandam enervandamque Romanam peregrinae consentire nequitiae, tantum-

---

[1] Augustine has again confused the father with the son: in 155 B.C. P. Cornelius Scipio Nasica Corculum in his second consulship persuaded the Senate to pull down the cavea of the first stone theatre when it was partly erected. See Livy 48, fr. 48   Valerius Maximus 2.42; Appian 1.28.

XXXI

On what stepping-stones of vice the passion for rule increased among the Romans.

FOR at what point could that lust for power come to rest in the haughtiest spirits until by a series of offices held they reached despotic power? Again there would be no provision for such offices held in series if ambition were not prevalent, while ambition could not be prevalent except in a society corrupted by avarice and luxury. Moreover, a society is made greedy and luxury-loving by prosperity, the thing that Nasica with the greatest prudence voted to avoid when he refused to let a very large, strong and rich city of the enemy be destroyed. He intended that lust for power should be repressed by fear, that thus repressed, lust should not live luxuriously, and that, luxury prevented, avarice should not run riot. These vices being barred, virtue would flourish and increase to the advantage of the state, and liberty proportionate to that virtue would endure.

Hence it was, and from such extremely prudent love of country it came that your very own chief pontiff, chosen without a dissenting vote by the Senate of his day as the best man, a point worth repeating, when the Senate was setting about the construction of banked seats for a theatre, restrained them so as no longer to be so disposed or to desire it.[1] In a most impressive address he persuaded them not to allow the luxury of the Greeks to overrun the manly practices of the fatherland, and not by favouring foreign frivolity to allow Roman manhood to be

que auctoritate valuit ut verbis eius commota senatoria providentia etiam subsellia, quibus ad horam
congestis in ludorum spectaculo iam uti civitas
coeperat, deinceps prohiberet adponi.

Quanto studio iste ab urbe Roma ludos ipsos scaenicos abstulisset, si auctoritati eorum quos deos putabat resistere auderet, quos esse noxios daemones non
intellegebat aut, si intellegebat, placandos etiam ipse
potius quam contemnendos existimabat! Nondum
enim fuerat declarata gentibus superna doctrina, quae
fide cor mundans ad caelestia vel supercaelestia
capessenda humili pietate humanum mutaret affectum et a dominatu superborum daemonum liberaret.

XXXII

De scaenicorum institutione ludorum.

VERUM tamen scitote, qui ista nescitis et qui vos
scire dissimulatis, advertite, qui adversus liberatorem
a talibus dominis murmuratis: ludi scaenici, spectacula turpitudinum et licentia vanitatum, non hominum vitiis, sed deorum vestrorum iussis Romae instituti sunt. Tolerabilius divinos honores deferretis illi
Scipioni quam deos huius modi coleretis. Neque
enim erant illi dii suo pontifice meliores. Ecce
adtendite, si mens tam diu potatis erroribus ebria vos
aliquid sanum cogitare permittit! Dii propter

---

[1] Perhaps a reference to Colossians 3.2 : Set your minds on
things that are above, not on things that are on earth.

undermined and sapped. His prestige was so great
that, moved by his words, the Senate wisely thenceforth
prohibited the setting up of even those temporary
benches which the citizenry had begun to use at the
games.

How zealously would such a man as that have
banished from the city of Rome those stage performances themselves, had he dared to oppose the
authority of those he believed to be gods! He did
not understand that they are foul demons or, if he
did understand, even he held that they should be
appeased rather than despised. For not yet had that
heavenly teaching been revealed to the gentiles [1]
which should purify their hearts by faith and shift
their human affections in humble piety to the pursuit
of celestial or supercelestial things, and free them
from slavery to arrogant demons.

XXXII

On the establishment of stage plays.

Know, then, all ye who are ignorant of this, and ye
who pretend to be ignorant, take note while you
murmur against the One who sets men free from
such masters: the stage performances, exhibitions
of shameful acts and a licence for folly were established at Rome not by men's vices but at the command of your gods. It would be more bearable if you
rendered divine honours to that Scipio instead of
worshipping gods like this. Actually those gods were
no better than their high priest. Listen, give ear,
now, if your minds, intoxicated as they are with
errors so long quaffed, allow you to have a sober

sedandam corporum pestilentiam ludos sibi scaenicos
exhiberi iubebant, pontifex autem propter animorum
cavendam pestilentiam ipsam scaenam constitui
prohibebat. Si aliqua luce mentis animum corpori
praeponitis, eligite quem colatis! Neque enim et
illa corporum pestilentia ideo conquievit quia populo
bellicoso et solis antea ludis circensibus adsueto ludorum scaenicorum delicata subintravit insania; sed
astutia spirituum nefandorum praevidens illam
pestilentiam iam fine debito cessaturam aliam longe
graviorem, qua plurimum gaudet, ex hac occasione
non corporibus, sed moribus curavit inmittere, quae
animos miserorum tantis obcaecavit tenebris, tanta
deformitate foedavit, ut etiam modo (quod incredibile
forsitan erit, si a nostris posteris audietur) Romana
urbe vastata, quos pestilentia ista possedit atque inde
fugientes Carthaginem pervenire potuerunt, in
theatris cotidie certatim pro histrionibus insanirent.

XXXIII

De vitiis Romanorum, quos patriae non correxit
eversio.

O MENTES amentes! Quis est hic tantus non error,
sed furor, ut exitium vestrum, sicut audivimus, plan-
gentibus orientalibus populis et maximis civitatibus in
132

thought. The gods, in order to put an end to physical pestilence, commanded stage plays to be exhibited in their honour; to ward off a pestilence affecting the mind, on the other hand, the high priest forbade the stage itself to be constructed. If by any light of reason you prefer the mind to the body, choose whom you will worship. That bodily pestilence did not subside because a warlike people, hitherto accustomed only to the games of the circus, had been infected by such a dainty frenzy for stage plays. No, it was the craft of profane spirits, foreseeing that the pestilence had run its appointed course and would soon cease, that took the opportunity to infect, not their corporal but their moral nature with another, far more serious, plague, in which that craft has the greatest delight. This so blinded the minds of the poor unfortunates with thick darkness, so polluted them with a foul deformity, that even now—this will quite possibly be incredible to our descendants—when the city of Rome was sacked, those who were so possessed by this disease and were able to reach Carthage, after fleeing thence, were daily in the theatres, indulging the craze of partisan support for favourite actors.

XXXIII

That the vices of the Romans were not corrected by the fall of their homeland.

O minds out of their minds! How great an error, or rather what insanity was this! When, as we have heard, the nations of the east and the largest states in the uttermost parts of the earth were bewailing

remotissimis terris publicum luctum maeroremque
ducentibus vos theatra quaereretis intraretis implere-
tis et multo insaniora quam fuerant antea faceretis?

Hanc animorum labem ac pestem, hanc probitatis
et honestatis eversionem vobis Scipio ille metuebat,
quando construi theatra prohibebat, quando rebus
prosperis vos facile corrumpi atque everti posse
cernebat, quando vos securos esse ab hostili terrore
nolebat. Neque enim censebat ille felicem esse rem
publicam stantibus moenibus, ruentibus moribus.
Sed in vobis plus valuit quod daemones impii se-
duxerunt quam quod homines providi praecaverunt.
Hinc est quod mala quae facitis vobis inputari non
vultis, mala vero quae patimini Christiani stempori-
bus inputatis. Neque enim in vestra securitate
pacatam rem publicam, sed luxuriam quaeritis in-
punitam, qui depravati rebus prosperis nec corrigi
potuistis adversis. Volebat vos ille Scipio terreri ab
hoste, ne in luxuriam flueretis; nec contriti ab hoste
luxuriam repressistis, perdidistis utilitatem calamitatis, et miserrimi facti estis et pessimi permansistis.

XXXIV

De clementia Dei, quae Urbis excidium temperavit.

Et tamen quod vivitis Dei est, qui vobis parcendo
admonet ut corrigamini paenitendo, qui vobis etiam

your destruction with public lamentation and mourn-ing, it was theatres that you sought, entered, packed and far outdid your previous lunatic behaviour.

It was this pestilential ruin, this overthrow of honesty and decency that our Scipio feared for you when he forbade the construction of theatres, when he foresaw that you could easily be corrupted and subverted by prosperity, when he would not have you untroubled by the menace of a foe. In fact, he did not count a republic happy whose walls stand while its moral fabric crumbles. But in your history the seduction of sacrilegious demons outweighed any precautions taken by human foresight. This is the reason why you are unwilling to be charged with the evil that you do, why in truth you make the evils that you suffer a charge against the Christian era. In fact, the kind of security you seek is not concerned with national serenity but luxurious impunity; you deteriorated in times of prosperity, and the time of adversity could not reform you. Scipio wanted you to be so fearful of some enemy that you could not dissipate yourselves in luxury; now even crushed by the enemy, you have not brought your luxury within bounds. You have failed to get the good of your calamity and have become utterly wretched without ceasing to be utterly vile.

XXXIV

On God's mercy in moderating the City's destruction.

NEVERTHELESS, the fact that you still live is God's doing, who in sparing you gives you notice to correct your ways by repentance. Ungrateful as you are, it

ingratis praestitit ut vel sub nomine servorum eius
vel in locis martyrum eius hostiles manus evaderetis.
Romulus et Remus asylum constituisse perhibentur,
quo quisquis confugeret ab omni noxa liber esset,
augere quaerentes creandae multitudinem civitatis.
Mirandum in honorem Christi processit exemplum.
Hoc constituerunt eversores Urbis, quod constituerant
antea conditores.   Quid autem magnum, si hoc fecerunt illi ut civium suorum numerus suppleretur, quod
fecerunt isti ut suorum hostium numerositas ser-
varetur?

XXXV

De latentibus inter impios ecclesiae filiis et de falsis
intra ecclesiam Christianis.

HAEC et alia, si qua uberius et commodius potuerit,
respondeat inimicis suis redempta familia domini
Christi et peregrina civitas regis Christi.

Meminerit sane in ipsis inimicis latere cives
futuros, ne infructuosum vel apud ipsos putet, quod,
donec perveniat ad confessos, portat infensos; sicut
ex illorum numero etiam Dei civitas habet secum,
quamdiu peregrinatur in mundo, conexos communione sacramentorum, nec secum futuros in
aeterna sorte sanctorum, qui partim in occulto, partim

---

[1] Livy 1.8.   The asylum was in the lower ground between
the two peaks of the Capitoline Hill.

is He who has granted you to escape the enemy's
hands either by taking the name of His servants
or in the sanctuaries of the martyrs. Romulus and
Remus, seeking a means of increasing the population
of the city they were founding, are alleged to have
established an asylum where any man might seek
refuge and be free from guilt,[1] an admirable precedent that in due course was followed in the respect
shown to Christ's name. The destroyers of the city
have set up the very thing that its founders had set
up before. Furthermore, how can we regard their
doing so as a great thing, who did it to supplement
the number of their own citizens, when these did the
same in order to preserve the great numbers of their
own enemies?

XXXV

*On sons of the Church, hidden among the wicked,
and on false Christians within the Church.*

THESE and other answers, if any fuller and fitter
arguments can be found, let the redeemed family of
the Lord Christ and the pilgrim city of Christ the
King deliver to their enemies.

Let the city by all means remember that among the
very enemy lurk some who will become citizens. Let
her not assume even in their case that no harvest can
be reaped while we bear their enmity until such time
as they profess Christianity. Likewise among those
now professing, the City of God has in her company
during her pilgrimage in the world, joined to her by
sharing the sacraments, some who will not be with her
to share eternally in the lot of the saints. Some
secretly and some openly there are who even in com-

in aperto sunt, qui etiam cum ipsis inimicis adversus
Deum, cuius sacramentum gerunt, murmurare non
dubitant, modo cum illis theatra, modo ecclesias
nobiscum replen es.

De correctione autem quorundam etiam talium
multo minus est desperandum, si apud apertissimos
adversarios praedestinati amici latitant, adhuc ignoti
etiam sibi. Perplexae quippe sunt istae duae civitates in hoc saeculo invicemque permixtae, donec
ultimo iudicio dirimantur; de quarum exortu et pro-
cursu et debitis finibus quod dicendum arbitror,
quantum divinitus adiuvabor, expediam propter
gloriam civitatis Dei, quae alienis a contrario com-
paratis clarius eminebit.

XXXVI

De quibus causis sequenti disputatione sit disserendum.

Sed adhuc mihi quaedam dicenda sunt adversus eos,
qui Romanae rei publicae clades in religionem
nostram referunt, qua diis suis sacrificare prohibentur.
Commemoranda sunt enim quae et quanta occurrere
poterunt vel satis esse videbuntur mala, quae illa
civitas pertulit vel ad eius imperium provinciae per-
tinentes, antequam eorum sacrificia prohibita fuis-
sent; quae omnia procul dubio nobis tribuerent, si
iam vel illis clareret nostra religio, vel ita eos a sacris
sacrilegis prohiberet.

pany with our enemies do not hesitate to murmur against God under whose standards they serve, at one time with our enemies crowding the theatres, at another the churches with us.

There is less reason to despair about the reclamation even of some of these, if among our most openly avowed opponents lie hidden, unknown as yet even to themselves, those who are predestined to become our friends.   True it is that those two cities are entangled in the present age and mutually intermingled till the final judgement, when they will be detached from one another.   The origin and progress and appointed ends of these two cities is a theme on which I shall expound what I think needs to be said, in so far as I am divinely aided, in order to glorify the City of God.   Its excellence will be thrown into greater relief by contrast when it is compared in detail with the other.

XXXVI

On the subjects to be discussed in the sequel.

There are still, however, some things that I must say in answer to those who blame our religion for the disasters of the Roman republic, because it forbids sacrificing to their gods.   I must list in detail, for instance, as many misfortunes and as great as may suggest themselves, or as shall seem sufficient, that the commonwealth of Rome or the provinces under its rule had to bear before their sacrifices were prohibited.   Without doubt they would attribute all these disasters to us, if our religion had already shed its light upon them and had forbidden them the sacrilegious sacrifices.

Deinde monstrandum est, quos eorum mores et quam ob causam Deus verus ad augendum imperium adiuvare dignatus est, in cuius potestate sunt regna omnia, quamque nihil eos adiuverint hi, quos deos putant, et potius quantum decipiendo et fallendo nocuerint. Postremo adversus eos dicetur, qui manifestissimis documentis confutati atque convicti conantur asserere non propter vitae praesentis utilitatem sed propter eam, quae post mortem futura est, colendos deos.

Quae, nisi fallor, quaestio multo erit operosior et subtiliore disputatione dignior, ut et contra philosophos in ea disseratur, non quoslibet, sed qui apud illos excellentissima gloria clari sunt et nobiscum multa sentiunt, et de animae immortalitate et quod Deus verus mundum condiderit et de providentia eius, qua universum quod condidit regit. Sed quoniam et ipsi in illis quae contra nos sentiunt, refellendi sunt, deesse huic officio non debemus, ut refutatis impiis contradictionibus pro viribus quas Deus inpertiet, asseramus civitatem Dei veramque pietatem et Dei cultum, in quo uno veraciter sempiterna beatitudo promittitur.

Hic itaque modus sit huius voluminis, ut deinceps disposita ab alio sumamus exordio.

Next I must show what their moral standards were and for what reason the true God, in whose power all kingdoms are, deigned to grant them assistance in expanding their empire, and how far from helping them were those whom they rate as gods and how much harm they did instead with their trickery and deceit. Finally, I shall reply to those who, though refuted and convicted by the clearest evidence, attempt to declare that the gods should be worshipped, not for advantages to be enjoyed in this present life, but for those in the life to come after death.

This, if I am not mistaken, will be a much more difficult matter for discussion and more deserving of closer-knit argumentation, inasmuch as in this case I shall not only be discussing the subject with philosophers—not just any philosophers, but with such as are most renowned among the pagans and agree with us on many points—but shall also take as subjects of discussion the immortality of the soul, the proof that the world was created by the true God, and the providence of God whereby he rules the universe that he has established. But since they too require to be refuted on those points on which they disagree, I am bound to answer the call of duty in order that, first refuting contrary opinions of the wicked to the best of such ability as God imparts, I may then speak in support of the City of God and of true religion and worship of God, in which alone is found a truthful promise of everlasting bliss.

Here accordingly let this book end, that we may make a fresh start in disposing of succeeding topics.

BOOK II

LIBER II

I

De modo qui necessitati disputationis adhibendus est.

Sɪ rationi perspicuae veritatis infirmus humanae consuetudinis sensus non auderet obsistere, sed doctrinae salubri languorem suum tamquam medicinae subderet, donec divino adiutorio fide pietatis inpetrante sanaretur, non multo sermone opus esset ad convincendum quemlibet vanae opinationis errorem his qui recte sentiunt et sensa verbis sufficientibus explicant. Nunc vero quoniam ille est maior et taetrior insipientium morbus animorum, quo inrationabiles motus suos, etiam post rationem plene redditam, quanta homini ab homine debetur, sive nimia caecitate, qua nec aperta cernuntur, sive obstinatissima pervicacia, qua et ea quae cernuntur non feruntur, tamquam ipsam rationem veritatemque defendunt, fit necessitas copiosius dicendi plerumque res claras, velut eas non spectantibus intuendas, sed quodam modo tangendas palpantibus et coniventibus offeramus.

Et tamen quis disceptandi finis erit et loquendi

BOOK II

I

On the limits to be used in refutation.

IF the infirmity of sense usually found in man did not make bold to resist the clear reasoning of truth, but yielded its lethargy to wholesome doctrine as to medicine until with God's help it obtained healing by the intercession of religious faith, those who have right ideas and who express them effectively in words would need no long discourse to refute no matter what error of futile conjecture. As things are, however, foolish minds are affected by this distemper in a severer and more loathsome form, so that, even after the account has been paid in full and every debt of reason that one human being owes to another has been satisfied, they defend their own unaccountable vagaries as if they were the very accounting of truth, either because they are too blind even to see what is obvious, or because they are utterly obstinate in a stubborn refusal to accept the truth though they see it. Hence we are forced, as often as not, to give eloquence more play though the matter is plain enough. It is as if we had, not so much to present such matters for the inspection of men who fix their eyes on them, as for the examination by feeling of men who keep their eyes closed and use their fingers.

Yet what end will there be to our discourse and

modus, si respondendum esse respondentibus semper existimemus? Nam qui vel non possunt intellegere quod dicitur, vel tam duri sunt adversitate mentis, ut, etiamsi intellexerint, non oboediant, respondent, ut scriptum est, et loquuntur iniquitatem atque infatigabiliter vani sunt. Quorum dicta contraria si totiens velimus refellere, quotiens obnixa fronte statuerint non cogitare quid dicant, dum quocumque modo nostris disputationibus contradicant, quam sit infinitum et aerumnosum et infructuosum vides. Quam ob rem nec te ipsum, mi fili Marcelline, nec alios quibus hic labor noster in Christi caritate utiliter ac liberaliter servit, tales meorum scriptorum velim iudices qui responsionem semper desiderent, cum his quae leguntur audierint aliquid contradici, ne fiant similes earum muliercularum, quas commemorat apostolus *semper discentes et numquam ad veritatis scientiam pervenientes.*

II

De his quae primo volumine expedita sunt.

Superiore itaque libro, cum de civitate Dei dicere instituissem, unde hoc universum opus illo adiuvante in manus sumptum est, occurrit mihi resistendum esse primitus eis, qui haec bella, quibus mundus iste conteritur, maximeque Romanae urbis recentem a barbaris vastationem Christianae religioni tribuunt, qua prohibentur nefandis sacrificiis servire daemonibus,

---

[1] Psalms 94.4.   [2] 2 Timothy 3.7.

what limit to our discussion if we imagine that we must answer those who always answer in return? For those who either cannot understand what is said or are so hardened by a perverse heart that, even if they were to understand, they would not act accordingly, keep answering back, and, as it is written, " speak wickedness "[1] and are indefatigably futile. If we were bound to refute their objections every time they make their bull-headed resolve not to consider the meaning of their words as long as they deny our arguments, no matter how, you see how endless and wearisome and unprofitable it would be. Therefore, my dear Marcellinus, I should not want either you or any others of those for whose useful and cheerful service this labour of mine is for the love of Christ undertaken, to be such judges of my works as to desire always an answer to every statement heard that goes counter to what is read in my works, for they should not become like those weak women whom the Apostle mentions, " always learning, and never able to come to the knowledge of the truth."[2]

II

Summary of the discussion in Book One.

In the preceding book, accordingly, since it was my intent to treat of the City of God, and this led to my taking in hand with his help the whole project, I felt that I must first withstand those who attribute these wars now afflicting the world, and particularly the recent sack of the City of Rome by the barbarians, to the Christian religion, by reason of which they are restrained from doing service by abominable

cum potius hoc deberent tribuere Christo, quod propter eius nomen contra institutum moremque bellorum eis, quo confugerent, religiosa et amplissima loca barbari libera praebuerunt, atque in multis famulatum deditum Christo non solum verum, sed etiam timore confictum sic honoraverunt, ut quod in eos belli iure fieri licuisset inlicitum sibi esse iudicarent.

Inde incidit quaestio, cur haec divina beneficia et ad impios ingratosque pervenerint, et cur illa itidem dura, quae hostiliter facta sunt, pios cum impiis pariter adflixerint? Quam quaestionem per multa diffusam (in omnibus enim cotidianis vel Dei muneribus vel hominum cladibus, quorum utraque bene ac male viventibus permixte atque indiscrete saepe accidunt, solet multos movere) ut pro suscepti operis necessitate dissolverem, aliquantum inmoratus sum maxime ad consolandas sanctas feminas et pie castas, in quibus ab hoste aliquid perpetratum est quod intulit verecundiae dolorem, etsi non abstulit pudicitiae firmitatem, ne paeniteat eas vitae quas non est unde possit paenitere nequitiae.

Deinde pauca dixi in eos qui Christianos adversis illis rebus adfectos et praecipue pudorem humiliatarum feminarum quamvis castarum atque sanctarum protervitate inpudentissima exagitant, cum sint

rites to demons. What they should rather attribute to Christ is this, namely that for his name's sake, in spite of the established rules of warfare, the barbarians set apart as sanctuaries precincts sacred to religion and of the widest area, and in many instances showed such respect, not only for genuine membership in the household of Christ but even for false claims inspired by fear, that they condemned as illicit for themselves acts that by the laws of war would have been permitted them in dealing with those to whom I refer.

Here we were met by the question why these divine benefits were extended even to the wicked and thankless, and why those hardships of war likewise afflicted the just equally with the unjust. This question has many implications, for in all our daily adventures, whether we experience God's bounty or human disasters, in either case those who live a good or a bad life are often jointly and indiscriminately affected; and many are disturbed by this fact. As the plan of my projected work required me to answer it, I dwelt on it at some length, and chiefly to bring consolation to the holy and religiously chaste women who were criminally attacked by an enemy in such a way as to grieve their modesty, although they lost nothing of their unshaken chastity. I would not have them sorry to be alive, when there is nothing in their lives to make them sorry for sin.

Next I dealt briefly with such as in the utter shamelessness of their presumption belabour the point that Christians were not exempt in those days of adversity, and twit us above all on the outrage to modesty suffered by women who were indeed humiliated—chaste and holy though they remain.

nequissimi et inreverentissimi, longe ab eis ipsis Romanis degeneres, quorum praeclara multa laudantur et litterarum memoria celebrantur, immo illorum gloriae vehementer adversi. Romam quippe partam veterum auctamque laboribus foediorem stantem fecerant quam ruentem, quando quidem in ruina eius lapides et ligna, in istorum autem vita omnia non murorum, sed morum munimenta atque ornamenta ceciderunt, cum funestioribus eorum corda cupiditatibus quam ignibus tecta illius urbis arderent.

Quibus dictis primum terminavi librum. Deinceps itaque dicere institui quae mala civitas illa perpessa sit ab origine sua sive apud se ipsam sive in provinciis sibi iam subditis, quae omnia Christianae religioni tribuerent, si iam tunc evangelica doctrina adversus falsos et fallaces deos eorum testificatione liberrima personaret.

III

De assumenda historia, qua ostendatur quae mala acciderint Romanis, cum deos colerent, antequam religio Christiana obcresceret.

MEMENTO autem me ista commemorantem adhuc contra inperitos agere, ex quorum inperitia illud quoque ortum est vulgare proverbium : Pluvia defit, causa Christiani sunt. Nam qui eorum studiis

Well may they scoff, utter scamps and railers as they
are, far from truebred sons of those very Romans
even, who have to their credit many glorious feats
for which they are honoured in the book of history.
Nay, they are headlong foes to the renown of their
ancestors. Truly they had made the name of Rome,
that Rome that was conceived and nourished by the
pains of their elders, sink lower while she stood than
ever it sank when she fell, forasmuch as in her fall
were overturned but stones and timbers, while in
their way of living were overturned all the ramparts
and splendours, not of mural, but of moral strength.
Deadlier were the lusts that raged in their hearts
than the flames that raged in their city's edifices.

When I had covered these points, I ended my first
book. The next item on my programme accordingly
is to recount what misfortunes the aforesaid city has
endured from its beginning, whether in the capital
itself or in its provinces after their subjection, all of
which would be attributed to the Christian religion,
if the teaching of the gospel in opposition to their
false and deceitful gods had in those early days
resounded on the lips of witnesses quite free to bear
their witness.

III

*That history must be consulted, in order to show what
calamities the Romans suffered when they worshipped
their gods before Christianity overgrew them.*

BEAR in mind, moreover, that in recalling those
times I am stating a case for men still uninformed,
whose ignorance has given rise to the common saying :
" There's not enough rain ; the Christians are respon-

liberalibus instituti amant historiam, facillime ista
noverunt; sed ut nobis ineruditorum turbas infestis-
simas reddant, se nosse dissimulant atque hoc apud
vulgus confirmare nituntur, clades, quibus per certa
intervalla locorum et temporum genus humanum
oportet adfligi, causa accidere nominis Christiani,
quod contra deos suos ingenti fama et praeclarissima
celebritate per cuncta diffunditur.

Recolant ergo nobiscum, antequam Christus venisset in carne, antequam eius nomen ea cui frustra
invident gloria populis innotesceret, quibus calamitatibus res Romanae multipliciter varieque contritae
sint, et in his defendant, si possunt, deos suos, si
propterea coluntur, ne ista mala patiantur cultores
eorum; quorum si quid nunc passi fuerint, nobis
inputanda esse contendunt. Cur enim ea quae
dicturus sum permiserunt accidere cultoribus suis,
antequam eos declaratum Christi nomen offenderet
eorumque sacrificia prohiberet?

IV

Quod cultores deorum nulla umquam a diis suis
praecepta probitatis acceperint et in sacris eorum
turpia quaeque celebraverint.

PRIMO ipsos mores ne pessimos haberent, quare dii
eorum curare noluerunt? Deus enim verus eos, a
quibus non colebatur, merito neglexit; dii autem illi,

sible." For those among the pagans who have been
trained in liberal studies, to whom history is an old
friend, readily recognize the facts, but to rouse the
greatest hostility among the unlearned masses, they
pretend not to recognize them, and they strive to
strengthen the mob in their belief that disasters,
which are fated to afflict at fixed intervals of place or
time the whole human race, occur because of the name
of Christian, which in opposition to their gods is now
spreading with great publicity and most glorious
popularity to every region.

Let them rehearse with us, then, the manifold and
varied calamities that crushed the Roman state before
Christ had come in the flesh, before his name was
revealed to the nations with the glory that they
vainly envy. Let them, if they can, defend their
gods in these cases, if they are worshipped that they
may keep worshippers from suffering these evils.
If they have suffered such evil in our day, they maintain that we are to blame. Why then did the gods
permit those disasters of which I shall now speak, to
fall on their worshippers before the publishing of
Christ's name gave offence and before the prohibition
of sacrifice to them ?

IV

*That the worshippers of the gods never got any moral
teachings from them, and in their rites enacted all
kinds of shameful things.*

FIRST, why were their gods unwilling to see that
they were free from the worst of immoral practices ?
The true God, to be sure, had good reason to dis-
regard those who did not worship him. Why did

a quorum cultu se prohiberi homines ingratissimi conqueruntur, cultores suos ad bene vivendum quare nullis legibus adiuverunt? Utique dignum erat ut, quo modo isti illorum sacra, ita illi istorum facta curarent.

Sed respondetur, quod voluntate propria quisque malus est. Quis hoc negaverit? Verum tamen pertinebat ad consultores deos vitae bonae praecepta non occultare populis cultoribus suis, sed clara praedicatione praebere, per vates etiam convenire atque arguere peccantes, palam minari poenas male agentibus, praemia recte viventibus polliceri. Quid umquam tale in deorum illorum templis prompta et eminenti voce concrepuit?

Veniebamus etiam nos aliquando adulescentes ad spectacula ludibriaque sacrilegiorum, spectabamus arrepticios, audiebamus symphoniacos, ludis turpissimis, qui diis deabusque exhibebantur, oblectabamur, Caelesti virgini et Berecynthiae matri omnium, ante cuius lecticam die sollemni lavationis eius talia per publicum cantitabantur a nequissimis scaenicis qualia, non dico matrem deorum, sed matrem qualiumcumque senatorum vel quorumlibet honestorum virorum, immo vero qualia nec matrem ipsorum scaenicorum deceret audire. Habet enim quiddam erga parentes humana verecundia, quod

---

[1] An African divinity particularly worshipped at Carthage; see Tertullian, *Apology* 24; Augustine, *Enarr. in Psalm.* 62.7; 14.98.

[2] Cybele, the Mother of the Gods, a Phrygian goddess brought to Rome during the Second Punic War.

those gods, however, whose worship those ungrateful characters complain is forbidden them, not lay down laws to aid their worshippers in leading a good life? It would certainly seem proper that their concern for the gods' rites should have been matched by the gods' concern for their behaviour.

But someone replies that it is by his own will that every bad man is bad. Who would deny this? Nevertheless, it was incumbent on the gods who were men's advisers, not to hide from the nations who worshipped them the maxims of right living, but to set them forth in well-defined statements. They should have employed the mouths of prophets also to address and convince sinners, to warn evildoers publicly of coming punishment, and to promise rewards to those who live a righteous life. What message of this sort ever pealed forth in the temples of those gods with ready and resounding eloquence?

I myself too in my youth sometimes went along to spectacles and games of their irreligious ceremonies. I would watch the dervishes, would listen to the musicians, would take delight in the shameful shows that were put on in honour of gods and goddesses, of the virgin Caelestis [1] and the Berecynthian mother of all,[2] before whose couch on the anniversary of her washing were chanted publicly by the vilest players such tales as—I do not say the mother of gods, but the mothers of senators, no matter what they are like, or of honourable men, no matter who, or better, such things as were not fit for the mother of the very players to hear. For there is something in human reverence for parents that not even vileness personified can destroy. Accordingly, the players themselves would have been ashamed to rehearse at home

nec ipsa nequitia possit auferre. Illam proinde turpitudinem obscenorum dictorum atque factorum scaenicos ipsos domi suae proludendi causa coram matribus suis agere puderet, quam per publicum agebant coram deum matre spectante atque audiente utriusque sexus frequentissima multitudine. Quae si inlecta curiositate adesse potuit circumfusa, saltem offensa castitate debuit abire confusa.

Quae sunt sacrilegia, si illa sunt sacra? aut quae inquinatio, si illa lavatio? Et haec fercula appellabantur, quasi celebraretur convivium quo velut suis epulis inmunda daemonia pascerentur. Quis enim non sentiat cuius modi spiritus talibus obscenitatibus delectentur, nisi vel nesciens utrum omnino sint ulli inmundi spiritus deorum nomine decipientes, vel talem agens vitam in qua istos potius quam Deum verum et optet propitios et formidet iratos?

V

De obscenitatibus quibus mater deum a cultoribus suis honorabatur.

Nequaquam istos, qui flagitiosissimae consuetudinis vitiis oblectari magis quam obluctari student, sed illum ipsum Nasicam Scipionem, qui vir optimus a senatu electus est, cuius manibus eiusdem daemonis simulacrum susceptum est in Urbemque pervectum, habere de hac re iudicem vellem. Diceret nobis, utrum matrem suam tam optime de re publica vellet mereri ut ei divini honores decernerentur; sicut et

---

[1] An untranslatable pun : the " services " are " servings " ; a *ferculum* is either a litter or a plate of food, and the word *lectisternia* corresponds to both senses.

in their mothers' presence the villainy of those same obscene words and deeds that they publicly performed in the presence of the mother of the gods, while a huge assembly of both sexes lent their eyes and ears. Though this throng might have been there so abundant on all sides, inveigled only by curiosity, it should at least have departed in confusion at the shock to modesty.

What are profane, if these are sacred, rites? Or what is pollution, if this is ablution? And the rites were termed " servings " [1] as if some banquet were being celebrated at which foul demons fed on viands peculiar to them. For who could fail to discern what sort of spirits take delight in such lewd acts except either a man who professes ignorance whether any foul spirits exist at all to cheat men with the name of gods, or one who leads such a life that he hopes to win their favour and fears to incur their anger rather than that of the true God?

V

On the obscenities practised in honour of the mother of the gods by her worshippers.

On this point I should choose as arbiter, certainly not those who eagerly seek pleasure in the vices of a most profligate custom rather than take measures against it, but that Scipio Nasica who was chosen " best man " by the Senate and took into his hands the image of that demon and carried it into the city. Let him tell us whether he would want his mother to be so highly deserving in the eyes of the state that divine honours should be awarded to her—as we know

Graecos et Romanos aliasque gentes constat quibusdam decrevisse mortalibus, quorum erga se beneficia
magni penderant, eosque inmortales factos atque in
deorum numerum receptos esse crediderant. Profecto ille tantam felicitatem suae matri, si fieri
posset, optaret.

Porro si ab illo deinde quaereremus, utrum inter
eius divinos honores vellet illa turpia celebrari:
nonne se malle clamaret, ut sua mater sine ullo
sensu mortua iaceret, quam ad hoc dea viveret ut
illa libenter audiret? Absit, ut senator populi
Romani ea mente praeditus qua theatrum aedificari
in urbe fortium virorum prohibuit, sic vellet coli
matrem suam ut talibus dea sacris propitiaretur
qualibus matrona verbis offenderetur. Nec ullo
modo crederet verecundiam laudabilis feminae ita in
contrarium divinitate mutari ut honoribus eam
talibus advocarent cultores sui qualibus conviciis in
quempiam iaculatis, cum inter homines viveret, nisi
aures clauderet seseque subtraheret, erubescerent
pro illa et propinqui et maritus et liberi.

Proinde talis mater deum, qualem habere matrem
puderet quemlibet etiam pessimum virum, Romanas
occupatura mentes quaesivit optimum virum, non
quem monendo et adiuvando faceret, sed quem
fallendo deciperet, ei similis de qua scriptum est:
Mulier autem virorum pretiosas animas captat, ut ille
magnae indolis animus hoc velut divino testimonio

---

[1] Proverbs 6.26.

that the Greeks and the Romans and other nations have voted such honours to certain mortals because they set great value on their services and had adopted the view that they were now made immortal and admitted to the roster of the gods. Certainly he would choose such happiness for his mother, if it were possible.

If we should then put a further question and ask whether he would want such shameful exhibitions among her divine honours, would he not cry out that he preferred to see his mother lying there dead and feeling nothing, rather than see her live on as a goddess for the purpose of relishing such obscenities? God forbid that a Roman senator so serious of purpose that he forbade a theatre to be built in a city of brave men, should want his mother to be honoured as a goddess with such services that as a matron the words would scandalize her. He would hardly believe that the virtuous modesty of a woman of so praiseworthy a character could be so completely reversed by the process of deification that her worshippers would seek her favour in such terms that, if she had while alive among men heard them employed against someone as terms of abuse without stopping her ears and withdrawing, her relatives and husband and children would have blushed for her.

And so, this mother of the gods, such a character that even the worst of men would be ashamed to have her as a mother, in order to win the hearts of the Romans, sought out the best man not to do him good by advice and aid, but to deceive him, like her of whom it is written, " A woman, moreover, sets her trap for precious souls of men." [1] She intended that this man of high character, by a testimony to his merit

sublimatus et vere se optimum existimans veram
pietatem religionemque non quaereret, sine qua omne
quamvis laudabile ingenium superbia vanescit et
decidit. Quo modo igitur nisi insidiose quaereret
dea illa optimum virum, cum talia quaerat in suis
sacris qualia viri optimi abhorrent suis adhibere
conviviis?

VI

*Deos paganorum numquam bene vivendi sanxisse
doctrinam.*

Hinc est quod de vita et moribus civitatum atque
populorum a quibus colebantur illa numina non
curarunt, ut tam horrendis eos et detestabilibus malis
non in agro et vitibus, non in domo atque pecunia,
non denique in ipso corpore, quod menti subditur,
sed in ipsa mente, in ipso rectore carnis animo, eos
impleri ac pessimos fieri sine ulla sua terribili pro-
hibitione permitterent.

Aut si prohibebant, hoc ostendatur potius, hoc
probetur. Nec nobis nescio quos susurros paucis-
simorum auribus anhelatos et arcana velut religione
traditos iactent, quibus vitae probitas castitasque
discatur; sed demonstrentur vel commemorentur
loca talibus aliquando conventiculis consecrata, non
ubi ludi agerentur obscenis vocibus et motibus histrio-

apparently divine, should be exalted to the point of thinking himself really the best and should not pursue true piety and worship, without which every natural endowment, however praiseworthy, is dimmed by pride and deteriorates. How except by guile could that goddess have asked for the best of men, when in her ceremonials she asks for things that the best men would be shocked to have at their banquets?

VI

That the pagans' gods never laid down any holy doctrine of right living.

It follows that those divinities were not concerned about the life and morals of the cities and nations that worshipped them and consequently, by issuing no formidable prohibition of their own, permitted them to become most evil and to be infected by those dread and abominable evils, which were not plagues of field and vines, nor of house and wealth, nor finally of the body that is subject to the mind, but of the mind itself, of the very spirit that rules the body.

If there was any such prohibition, let it be exhibited, let it be proved. Let them not flaunt against us any doctrines there may have been that were whispered into the ears of a very small group and so transmitted by a kind of mystic cult that should inculcate an honest and chaste life. Let them, on the contrary, show us or recall to our memory sites that were at some time consecrated for the meeting of assemblies, where there were, not plays performed by actors with obscene words and gestures, not the celebration with every licentious indulgence in

num, nec ubi Fugalia celebrarentur effusa omni licentia turpitudinum (et vere Fugalia, sed pudoris et honestatis); sed ubi populi audirent quid dii praeciperent de cohibenda avaritia, ambitione frangenda, luxuria refrenanda, ubi discerent miseri quod discendum Persius increpat dicens:

Discite, o miseri, et causas cognoscite rerum,
Quid sumus et quidnam victuri gignimur, ordo
Quis datus aut metae qua mollis flexus et unde,
Quis modus argenti, quid fas optare, quid asper
Utile nummus habet, patriae carisque propinquis
Quantum largiri deceat, quem te Deus esse
Iussit et humana qua parte locatus es in re.

Dicatur in quibus locis haec docentium deorum solebant praecepta recitari et a cultoribus eorum populis frequenter audiri, sicut nos ostendimus ad hoc ecclesias institutas, quaqua versum religio Christiana diffunditur.

VII

Inutilia esse inventa philosophica sine auctoritate divina, ubi quemque ad vitia pronum magis movet quid dii fecerint quam quid homines disputarint.

AN forte nobis philosophorum scholas disputationesque memorabunt?

---

[1] The *Fugalia*, or *Regifugium*, a festival commemorating the expulsion of the kings from Rome, celebrated on February 24th.
[2] Persius, *Satires* 3.66–72 (Ramsay) inexactly quoted.

shamelessness of the Feast of Flight [1]—a feast of flight indeed, but one that put to flight modesty and good manners—but where there was a message for the people giving the gods' instructions about repressing avarice, crushing ambition, and curbing luxury, where the wretched might learn the lesson that, as Persius dins it in our ears, must be learned:

" Come and learn, O miserable souls, and be instructed in the causes of things: learn what we are, and for what sort of lives we are born; what place was assigned to us at the start; how to round the turning-post gently, and from what point to begin the turn; what limit should be placed on wealth; what prayers may rightfully be offered; what good there is in fresh-minted coin; how much should be spent on country and on kin; what part God has ordered you to play, and at what point of the human commonwealth you have been stationed." [2]

Let them tell us where these precepts of gods who gave instruction were commonly recited and often heard by the nations who worshipped them, just as we point to our churches established for this purpose in any quarter to which the Christian religion spreads.

VII

That the findings of philosophers, lacking divine sanction, as they do, are useless because man is more apt to follow the gods' examples than the arguments of men.

Will they perhaps remind us of the schools of the philosophers and their disputations?

Primo haec non Romana, sed Graeca sunt; aut si propterea iam Romana quia et Graecia facta est Romana provincia, non deorum praecepta sunt, sed hominum inventa qui utcumque conati sunt ingeniis acutissimis praediti ratiocinando vestigare quid in rerum natura latitaret, quid in moribus adpetendum esset atque fugiendum, quid in ipsis ratiocinandi regulis certa conexione traheretur, aut quid non esset consequens vel etiam repugnaret.

Et quidam eorum quaedam magna, quantum divinitus adiuti sunt, invenerunt; quantum autem humanitus impediti sunt, erraverunt, maxime cum eorum superbiae iuste providentia divina resisteret, ut viam pietatis ab humilitate in superna surgentem etiam istorum comparatione monstraret; unde postea nobis erit in Dei veri Domini voluntate disquirendi ac disserendi locus.

Verum tamen si philosophi aliquid invenerunt quod agendae bonae vitae beataeque adipiscendae satis esse possit, quanto iustius talibus divini honores decernerentur! Quanto melius et honestius in Platonis templo libri eius legerentur quam in templis daemonum Galli absciderentur, molles consecrarentur, insani secarentur, et quidquid aliud vel crudele vel turpe, vel turpiter crudele vel crudeliter turpe in sacris talium deorum celebrari solet! Quanto satius erat ad erudiendam iustitia iuventutem publice

---

¹ See Books VIII–XII.
² Priests of Cybele, so named from the River Gallus in Galatia, emasculated themselves.

In the first place, these examples are not Roman in origin but Greek, or if they are now Roman because Greece too has been made a Roman province, yet they are not precepts of gods but findings of men who as best they could, being endowed with keenest intellects, tried to detect by the power of reason what was hidden in the realm of nature, what was desirable or undesirable in the realm of morals, and what—in the field of logic—was entailed by strict deduction and what was not a valid conclusion or was even inconsistent with the premisses.

And some of them, in so far as they were led of God, did make great discoveries; in so far, however, as they were fettered by human limitations, they fell into error, especially when divine providence rightly resisted their pride, that it might show by comparison even with them that the way of piety mounts to higher things from a lowly origin. There will be hereafter springing from this a topic for us to investigate and discuss in the will of God, the true Lord.[1]

But if the philosophers ever discovered a satisfactory method of leading the good life and of reaching a state of blessedness, how much more justly would divine honours be decreed for them! How much better and more decorous that in a temple of Plato his books should be read than that in the temples of the devils the Galli [2] should be mutilated, the effeminate should be consecrated, the madmen should cut themselves, or any other cruel or shameful thing or shamefully cruel or cruelly shameful thing be enacted, such as is customarily celebrated in the sacrifices of such gods! How much more satisfactory as a means to train the young in virtue if there were

recitari leges deorum quam laudari inaniter leges atque instituta maiorum! Omnes enim cultores talium deorum, mox ut eos libido perpulerit ferventi, ut ait Persius, tincta veneno, magis intuentur quid Iuppiter fecerit, quam quid docuerit Plato vel censuerit Cato.

Hinc apud Terentium flagitiosus adulescens spectat tabulam quandam pictam in pariete,

> ubi inerat pictura haec, Iovem
> Quo pacto Danaae misisse aiunt quondam in
> gremium imbrem aureum,

atque ab hac tanta auctoritate adhibet patrocinium turpitudini suae, cum in ea se iactat imitari deum.

> At quem deum!

inquit;

> qui templa caeli summo sonitu concutit.
> Ego homuncio id non facerem? Ego vero illud feci
> ac libens.

VIII

De ludis scaenicis, in quibus dii non offenduntur
editione suarum turpitudinum, sed placantur.

AT enim non traduntur ista sacris deorum, sed fabulis poetarum.

---

[1] Persius, *Satires* 3.37.
[2] Terence, *Eunuchus* 584 f.
[3] *Ibid.* 590 f.

public recitations of the laws of the gods instead of
vain praise of the laws and customs of our forefathers!
For all the worshippers of such gods, when once they
have been driven by lust " imbued " as Persius [1]
says, " with burning poison," would rather contemplate the deeds of Jupiter than the teachings of
Plato or the opinions of Cato.

So the young rake in Terence gazes at a certain
picture painted on a wall

> Where in the painting was the tale
> How into Danaê's lap a golden shower fell
> Dispatched by Jove, men say,[2]

and finds in so great an authority a sponsor for his own
disgraceful act, boasting that, in what he does, he is
copying the god.

> But what a god!

he says,

> The one who smites the temples
> From the lofty height of heaven with his thunder—
> Should I, poor creature that I am, not do
> The same? Indeed, I did it and with pleasure.[3]

VIII

*On the theatrical shows, where the gods are not
offended, but propitiated, by the publication of
their shameful acts.*

SOMEONE will, however, object that these lewd
exhibitions derive not from divine ritual but from the
fictions of poets.

Nolo dicere illa mystica quam ista theatrica esse turpiora; hoc dico, quod negantes convincit historia, eosdem illos ludos, in quibus regnant figmenta poetarum, non per inperitum obsequium sacris deorum suorum intulisse Romanos, sed ipsos deos, ut sibi sollemniter ederentur et honori suo consecrarentur, acerbe imperando et quodam modo extorquendo fecisse; quod in primo libro brevi commemoratione perstrinxi. Nam ingravescente pestilentia ludi scaenici auctoritate pontificum Romae primitus instituti sunt.

Quis igitur in agenda vita non ea sibi potius sectanda arbitretur quae actitantur ludis auctoritate divina institutis, quam ea quae scriptitantur legibus humano consilio promulgatis? Adulterum Iovem si poetae fallaciter prodiderunt, dii utique casti, quia tantum nefas per humanos ludos confictum est, non quia neglectum, irasci ac vindicare debuerunt.

Et haec sunt scaenicorum tolerabiliora ludorum, comoediae scilicet et tragoediae, hoc est fabulae poetarum agendae in spectaculis multa rerum turpitudine, sed nulla saltem, sicut alia multa, verborum obscenitate compositae; quas etiam inter studia, quae honesta ac liberalia vocantur, pueri legere et discere coguntur a senibus.

168

I would not maintain that the rites of those mysteries are more lewd than the theatrical performances. I do maintain—and history refutes anyone who would deny it—that those same games in which the fictions of the poets rule were not introduced by the Romans into the festivals of their gods through ignorant devotion. No, the gods themselves brought it about by sharp commands and by putting men on the rack, as it were, that the shows should be exhibited ceremonially and dedicated to their honour. I touched upon this point briefly in my first book. It was when a pestilence was growing worse that the stage performances were originally established at Rome through the instigation of the pontiffs.

Who, therefore, would not suppose that in the life he led he ought rather to follow the example set in plays inaugurated by divine initiative, rather than the prescription of laws promulgated by human wisdom? If the poets were untrustworthy when they presented Jupiter as an adulterer, in any case chaste gods ought to have shown their anger and avenged themselves for the production on the stage of so great a crime against religion—not for the failure to produce it.

Of these plays the more tolerable are comedies and tragedies, that is, dramas composed by poets for presentation on the stage, which, though the stories contain many disgraceful items, are not, at least, like many other shows, expressed in obscene language. They are even included in the curriculum of what is termed a select and liberal education, and boys are forced by their elders to read and learn them.

IX

Quid Romani veteres de cohibenda poetica licentia
senserint, quam Graeci deorum secuti iudicium
liberam esse voluerunt.

QUID autem hinc senserint Romani veteres, Cicero
testatur in libris, quos de re publica scripsit, ubi
Scipio disputans ait: " Numquam comoediae, nisi
consuetudo vitae pateretur, probare sua theatris
flagitia potuissent." Et Graeci quidem antiquiores
vitiosae suae opinionis quandam convenientiam ser-
varunt, apud quos fuit etiam lege concessum ut quod
vellet comoedia, de quo vellet, nominatim diceret.
Itaque, sicut in eisdem libris loquitur Africanus,
" Quem illa non adtigit, vel potius quem non vexavit,
cui pepercit? Esto, populares homines inprobos, in
re publica seditiosos, Cleonem, Cleophontem, Hyper-
bolum laesit. Patiamur," inquit, " etsi eius modi
cives a censore melius est quam a poeta notari. Sed
Periclen, cum iam suae civitati maxima auctoritate
plurimos annos domi et belli praefuisset, violari
versibus et eos agi in scaena non plus decuit, quam si
Plautus," inquit, " noster voluisset aut Naevius
Publio et Gn. Scipioni aut Caecilius Marco Catoni
maledicere."

Dein paulo post: " Nostrae," inquit, " contra
duodecim tabulae cum perpaucas res capite sanxis-
sent, in his hanc quoque sanciendam putaverunt, si

---

[1] Cicero, *Republic* 4.10 f.
[2] The reference is to Old Comedy, as represented by
Aristophanes.

IX

*What the ancient Romans thought about the poetic
licence to which the Greeks, following the decision
of the gods, chose to accord full liberty.*

THE verdict of the ancient Romans on this point is
attested by Cicero in his work on *The Republic*, where
Scipio, taking part in the discussion, says, " The
comedies could never have won acceptance in the
theatre for their scenes of debauchery, if the manners
of the time had not tolerated the like." [1] The more
ancient Greeks also were in fact true in a way to their
faulty theory, for in their time it was a legal privilege
of comedy to say what it pleased about any one it
pleased, and to name names.[2] Accordingly, as
Africanus says in the same work, " Whom did comedy
not mention? Or rather whom did it not belabour?
Whom did it spare? Granted that it assailed base
demagogues, factious politicians, a Cleon, a Cleophon,
a Hyperbolus.[3] Let us tolerate this," says Africanus,
" although it is better for citizens of that type to be
stigmatized by the censor than by the poets. But for
them to make attacks on Pericles in their verses, and
for these to be produced—who for many years had
with the highest quality of leadership guided his
city in war and peace—was no more proper than if our
own Plautus or Naevius had chosen to revile Publius
or Gnaeus Scipio, or our Caecilius to revile Marcus
Cato."

After a bit he continues: " Though our Twelve
Tables had prescribed the death penalty for very few
crimes, among those so punished was the crime of

[3] Athenian demagogues attacked by Aristophanes in his
plays.

quis occentavisset sive carmen condidisset, quod
infamiam faceret flagitiumve alteri. Praeclare.
Iudiciis enim magistratuum, disceptationibus legi-
timis propositam vitam, non poetarum ingeniis
habere debemus, nec probrum audire nisi ea lege,
ut respondere liceat et iudicio defendere."

Haec ex Ciceronis quarto de re publica libro ad
verbum excerpenda arbitratus sum, nonnullis propter
faciliorem intellectum vel praetermissis vel paululum
commutatis. Multum enim ad rem pertinet quam
molior explicare si potero. Dicit deinde alia et sic
concludit hunc locum ut ostendat veteribus dis-
plicuisse Romanis vel laudari quemquam in scaena
vivum hominem vel vituperari.

Sed, ut dixi, hoc Graeci quamquam inverecundius,
tamen convenientius licere voluerunt, cum viderent
diis suis accepta et grata esse opprobria non tantum
hominum, verum et ipsorum deorum in scaenicis
fabulis, sive a poetis essent illa conficta, sive flagitia
eorum vera commemorarentur et agerentur in theatrís
atque ab eorum cultoribus. Utinam [1] solo risu, ac
non etiam imitatione digna viderentur. Nimis enim
superbum fuit famae parcere principum civitatis et
civium, ubi suae famae parci numina noluerunt.

[1] Cultoribus utinam *Dombart* (*no stop*).

---

[1] The word *occentare* in the Twelve Tables probably refers
to black magic, rather than to libel and slander.

anyone who brought ill repute or disgrace on another by chanting or composing verses aimed at him.[1] An admirable provision that. For the life we lead should be a matter for the decisions of magistrates and the judgements of courts, not for the exercise of poetic gifts; nor should anyone be exposed to vilification without the right to reply and to make defence in court." [2]

These passages have been quoted from the fourth book of Cicero's *Republic*, and I have thought best to quote word for word, though with some phrases omitted or transposed a little, to make the meaning clearer. The extract is certainly apposite to the subject that I am endeavouring to explain if I can. He then goes on to make some other remarks and ends the passage by showing that the ancient Romans did not desire any living man to be either praised or berated on the stage.

But the Greeks, as I said, though less mannerly, were more consistent in permitting this licence, since they saw that such ribald charges were acceptable and pleasing to their gods when directed in dramas not only against men but even against themselves. It matters not whether such themes were poetic fictions or whether actual debauchery on their part was recorded and acted out in the theatres and by their worshippers. Would that they were found worthy only of a laugh and not of imitation! For it would have been too presumptuous to spare the reputation of the leaders of the state and of the citizens when the divinities did not wish their own reputation to be spared.

[2] Cicero, *ibid.*

X

*Qua nocendi arte daemones velint vel falsa de se
crimina vel vera narrari.*

NAM quod adfertur pro defensione, non illa vera in
deos dici, sed falsa atque conficta, id ipsum est
scelestius, si pietatem consulas religionis; si autem
malitiam daemonum cogites, quid astutius ad decipiendum atque callidius? Cum enim probrum iacitur
in principem patriae bonum atque utilem, nonne
tanto est indignius quanto a veritate remotius et a
vita illius alienius? Quae igitur supplicia sufficiunt,
cum deo fit ista tam nefaria, tam insignis iniuria?

Sed maligni spiritus, quos isti deos putant, etiam
flagitia quae non admiserunt, de se dici volunt, dum
tamen humanas mentes his opinionibus velut retibus
induant et ad praedestinatum supplicium secum
trahant, sive homines ista commiserint, quos deos
haberi gaudent qui humanis erroribus gaudent, pro
quibus se etiam colendos mille nocendi fallendique
artibus interponunt; sive etiam non ullorum hominum illa crimina vera sint, quae tamen de numinibus
fingi libenter accipiunt fallacissimi spiritus, ut ad
scelesta ac turpia perpetranda velut ab ipso caelo
traduci in terras satis idonea videatur auctoritas.

Cum igitur Graeci talium numinum servos se esse
sentirent, inter tot et tanta eorum theatrica opprobria

X

*With what crafty malice the demons choose to allow
their crimes, whether real or fictitious, to be enacted.*

As for the defence that is offered, namely, that what
is said of the gods is not true but false and imaginary,
that is even more outrageous if you are concerned for
religious devotion. If, however, you imagine the
possibility of malice on the part of the demons,
what device to deceive could be shrewder or more
clever? When some aspersion is cast on a leader of
the state who is upright and serviceable, is it not the
more discreditable the further it departs from the
truth and the less it is compatible with his life? What
punishments, then, will answer when so wicked and so
notable a wrong is done to a god?

These malign spirits, however, whom they hold to
be gods, choose to be charged with crimes that they
did not commit, so long as they can enmesh men's
minds with such beliefs as with nets and drag them
along with themselves to a predestined punishment.
This is the case whether the crimes were actually
committed by men—by men who are held to be gods
to the joy of those whose joy it is to see men go astray,
and for whom the demons substitute themselves as
objects of worship by a thousand harmful and deceitful tricks—or whether, though no such crimes were
really committed by any men, the utterly deceitful
spirits gladly welcome such inventions about divinities
to the end that sufficient authority may seem to have
been transferred to earth from heaven itself for the
perpetration of such crimes and villainies.

Since, then, the Greeks accounted themselves
servants of such gods, they adopted the view that,

parcendum sibi a poetis nullo modo putaverunt, vel
diis suis etiam sic consimilari adpetentes, vel metuen-
tes ne honestiorem famam ipsi requirendo et eis se
hoc modo praeferendo illos ad iracundiam pro-
vocarent.

XI

De scaenicis apud Graecos in rei publicae administra-
tionem receptis, eo quod placatores deorum iniuste
ab hominibus spernerentur.

Ad hanc convenientiam pertinet, quod etiam
scaenicos actores earundem fabularum non parvo
civitatis honore dignos existimarunt, si quidem, quod
in eo quoque de re publica libro commemoratur, et
Aeschines Atheniensis, vir eloquentissimus, cum
adulescens tragoedias actitavisset, rem publicam
capessivit et Aristodemum, tragicum item actorem,
maximis de rebus pacis ac belli legatum ad Philippum
Athenienses saepe miserunt. Non enim consen-
taneum putabatur, cum easdem artes eosdemque
scaenicos ludos etiam diis suis acceptos viderent,
illos per quos agerentur infamium loco ac numero
deputare. Haec Graeci turpiter quidem, sed sane
diis suis omnino congruenter, qui nec vitam civium
lacerandam linguis poetarum et histrionum sub-
trahere ausi sunt, a quibus cernebant deorum vitam
eisdem ipsis diis volentibus et libentibus carpi,

---

[1] Cic. *Rep.* 4.11.35; the statement about Aeschines' acting
may have been a false charge brought by Demosthenes—see
On the Crown 209, 262; Aulus Gellius, *Attic Nights* 11.9.
[2] See Aulus Gellius, *loc. cit.*

since gods were so often and so shamefully exhibited on the stage, men themselves must not be exempt in any way from abuse by poets, either because they yearned to be one with their gods in this respect too, or because they feared that if they demanded for themselves a more respectable reputation, and so rated themselves higher than the gods, they might provoke them to wrath.

XI

That Greek actors were elected to office, since those who pleased the gods might not properly be rejected by men.

AGAIN this consistency is seen to be at work, in that the Greeks thought actors of these same plays worthy of no small honour from the state. For in that same book of *The Republic* it is mentioned that Aeschines, an Athenian and most eloquent, who as a youth had acted more than once in tragedies, engaged in political life.[1] Aristodemus, likewise a tragic actor, was often sent by the Athenians as their ambassador to Philip to handle matters of the greatest moment in peace and war.[2] For it was considered incongruous, when they saw the dramatic arts and its stage shows accepted even by the gods, to condemn the actors to ignominious status and reckoning. The Greeks, to be sure, in doing so disgraced themselves, but at least they took their cue from their gods. As they had not ventured to exempt the lives of citizens from rending by the sharp tongues of poets and actors, when they observed that the lives of the gods were assailed with the consent and good pleasure of those same gods,

et ipsos homines, per quos ista in theatris agebantur quae numinibus quibus subditi erant grata
esse cognoverant, non solum minime spernendos in
civitate, verum etiam maxime honorandos putarunt.

Quid enim causae reperire possent, cur sacerdotes
honorarent quia per eos victimas diis acceptabiles
offerebant, et scaenicos probrosos haberent per quos
illam voluptatem sive honorem diis exhiberi petentibus et, nisi fieret, irascentibus eorum admonitione
didicerant? cum praesertim Labeo, quem huiusce
modi rerum peritissimum praedicant, numina bona a
numinibus malis ista etiam cultus diversitate dis-
tinguat, ut malos deos propitiari caedibus et tristibus
supplicationibus asserat, bonos autem obsequiis
laetis atque iucundis, qualia sunt, ut ipse ait, ludi
convivia lectisternia. Quod totum quale sit, postea,
si Deus iuverit, diligentius disseremus.

Nunc ad rem praesentem quod adtinet, sive
omnibus omnia tamquam bonis permixte tribuantur
(neque enim esse decet deos malos, cum potius isti,
quia inmundi sunt spiritus, omnes sint mali), sive
certa discretione, sicut Labeoni visum est, illis illa,
istis ista distribuantur obsequia, competentissime
Graeci utrosque honori ducunt, et sacerdotes, per
quos victimae ministrantur, et scaenicos, per quos
ludi exhibentur, ne vel omnibus diis suis, si et ludi
omnibus grati sunt, vel, quod est indignius, his, quos

---

[1] Cornelius Labeo, perhaps of the third century A.D., wrote a
lost book on the Romano-Etruscan religion.

[2] A promise apparently not fulfilled.

so the persons who acted in the dramas that the Greeks had found to be pleasing to the gods, whose thralls they were, seemed to them not only by no means worthy of disfranchisement, but also by all means worthy of public recognition.

What good reason could they find for honouring the priests through whose medium they offered sacrifices acceptable to the gods, while holding reprehensible the actors through whom they presented to the gods such shows, whether for their pleasure or for their honour, as by the instruction of the priests they had been taught to think that the gods desired of them and were angered by failure to perform ? Labeo [1] in particular, a man who is heralded as most expert in matters of this kind, notes that good and evil powers are also distinguished by a difference of worship in that the evil gods are appeased, he assured us, by slaughter and mournful prayers, but the good by a happy and joyful worship—for instance, to quote his own words, shows, banquets, and feasts for the gods. I shall give more attention to an assessment of the whole matter, God helping me, at a later time. [2]

Limiting myself at the moment to our present theme, whether all kinds of sacrifices are to be offered to all gods indiscriminately—for it is in fact improper to speak of bad gods when they are rather all of them bad gods, inasmuch as they are unclean spirits—or, as Labeo thought fit, one kind of observance is offered to some and another to the rest by definite discrimination, the Greeks are quite right to hold in honour both the priests by whom the sacrifices are performed and the players by whom the dramas are enacted. Thus they escape any charge that they wrong all their gods, supposing shows to give pleasure also to all, or,

bonos putant, si ludi ab eis solis amantur, facere convincantur iniuriam.

XII

Quod Romani auferendo libertatem poetis in homines, quam dederunt in deos, melius de se quam de diis suis senserint.

AT Romani, sicut in illa de re publica disputatione Scipio gloriatur, probris et iniuriis poetarum subiectam vitam famamque habere noluerunt, capite etiam sancientes, tale carmen condere si quis auderet. Quod erga se quidem satis honeste constituerunt, sed erga deos suos superbe et inreligiose; quos cum scirent non solum patienter, verum etiam libenter poetarum probris maledictisque lacerari, se potius quam illos huiusce modi iniuriis indignos esse duxerunt seque ab eis etiam lege munierunt, illorum autem ista etiam sacris sollemnitatibus miscuerunt.

Itane tandem, Scipio, laudas hanc poetis Romanis negatam esse licentiam, ut cuiquam opprobrium infligerent Romanorum, cum videas eos nulli deorum pepercisse vestrorum? Itane pluris tibi habenda visa est existimatio curiae vestrae quam Capitolii? immo Romae unius quam caeli totius, ut linguam maledicam in cives tuos exercere poetae etiam lege prohiberentur, et in deos tuos securi tanta convicia

180

and this would be a more serious charge, that they wrong such as they consider to be good, supposing them alone to appreciate shows.

XII

That the Romans in granting poets no licence to attack men as they attacked gods showed greater respect to the men than to the gods.

BUT the Romans, as Scipio boasts in that same discussion about the republic, declined to expose life and reputation to railings and slanders of the poets, even making it a capital offence should anyone venture to write such a poem. With regard to the Romans themselves, this was a very honourable thing to do, but with regard to their gods it was arrogant and impious, for, knowing that the gods not only suffered themselves to be slashed by the railings and objurgations of the poets but even took pleasure in it, adopted the view that they themselves rather than the gods were too good to be insulted in that way, and so even protected themselves by statute, though they made such treatment of the gods even a part of their own sacred celebrations.

How, then, Scipio, do you praise the denial to the Roman poets of this privilege of slandering any Roman when you see that they spared none of your country's gods? Do you think that your Senate House should be more highly regarded than the Capitol? Is Rome alone worth more than the whole heaven, that poets are legally restrained from wagging their slanderous tongues against your fellow citizens but may cheerfully make your gods a target

nullo senatore, nullo censore, nullo principe, nullo
pontifice prohibente iacularentur? Indignum videlicet fuit ut Plautus aut Naevius Publio et Gn.
Scipioni aut Caecilius M. Catoni malediceret, et
dignum fuit ut Terentius vester flagitio Iovis optimi
maximi adulescentium nequitiam concitaret?

XIII

Debuisse intellegere Romanos, quod dii eorum, qui se
turpibus ludis coli expetebant, indigni essent honore
divino.

Sed responderet mihi fortasse, si viveret: Quo
modo nos ista inpunita esse nollemus quae ipsi dii
sacra esse voluerunt, cum ludos scaenicos, ubi talia
celebrantur dictitantur actitantur, et Romanis moribus invexerunt et in[1] suis honoribus dicari exhiberi-
que iusserunt?

Cur non ergo hinc magis ipsi intellecti sunt non esse
dii veri nec omnino digni quibus divinos honores
deferret illa res publica? Quos enim coli minime
deceret minimeque oporteret, si ludos expeterent
agendos conviciis Romanorum, quo modo quaeso
colendi putati sunt, quo modo non detestandi spiritus
intellecti, qui cupiditate fallendi inter suos honores
sua celebrari crimina poposcerunt?

Itemque Romani, quamvis iam superstitione noxia
premerentur ut illos deos colerent quos videbant sibi

---

[1] *Dombart omits* in *with MSS.*

for such great aspersions, with no senator, no censor, no leading citizen, no high priest to say them nay? It was, we must suppose, improper that Plautus or Naevius should say evil of Publius or Gnaeus Scipio, or Caecilius of Marcus Cato, and proper that your Terence should incite a youth to villainy by the lasciviousness of Jupiter, the best and greatest!

XIII

That the Romans should have seen that gods who insisted on being worshipped with shameful shows were worthy of no divine honour.

But perhaps, if he were alive, he would answer, " How could we do other than decide that what the gods willed to be holy should carry no penalty? They introduced these theatrical performances, in which such acts are commemorated, related and acted out, into Roman usage and gave command that they should be dedicated and exhibited among their own honours."

If so, why were they not clearly recognized not to be true gods, in no respect worthy of receiving divine honours from the republic? Those whom it would be most unfitting and immoral to worship if they required the acting of plays in which Romans were vilified—how, pray tell, did they come to be reckoned worthy of worship, how did it come that they were not seen to be execrable spirits, they who, lusting to beguile us, demanded that their own crimes should be displayed among the honours paid them?

And so the Romans, though compelled by a vicious superstition to worship those gods who, they observed,

voluisse scaenicas turpitudines consecrari, suae tamen dignitatis memores ac pudoris actores talium fabularum nequaquam honoraverunt more Graecorum, sed, sicut apud Ciceronem idem Scipio loquitur, " Cum artem ludicram scaenamque totam in probro ducerent, genus id hominum non modo honore civium reliquorum carere, sed etiam tribu moveri notatione censoria voluerunt."

Praeclara sane et Romanis laudibus adnumeranda prudentia; sed vellem se ipsa sequeretur, se imitaretur. Ecce enim recte, quisquis civium Romanorum esse scaenicus elegisset, non solum ei nullus ad honorem dabatur locus, verum etiam censoris nota tribum tenere propriam minime sinebatur. O animum civitatis laudis avidum germaneque Romanum!

Sed respondeatur mihi: qua consentanea ratione homines scaenici ab omni honore repelluntur, et ludi scaenici deorum honoribus admiscentur? Illas theatricas artes diu virtus Romana non noverat quae si ad oblectamentum voluptatis humanae quaererentur, vitio morum inreperent humanorum. Dii eas sibi exhiberi petierunt; quo modo ergo abicitur scaenicus, per quem colitur deus? et theatricae illius turpitudinis qua fronte notatur actor, si adoratur exactor?

184

had chosen to have dedicated to them the filth of the stage, yet were so mindful of their own honour and modesty as by no manner of means to grant civil rights to the actors of these plays, as was the Greek custom. Rather, to quote what that same Scipio says in Cicero's words, " Since they held comedy and all stage shows to be reprehensible, they determined that all men of that class should not only be barred from every right enjoyed by the rest of the citizens, but should even be removed from the censors' lists as members of the tribe." [1]

An excellent provision, of course, and one that must be listed to the credit of the Romans, but I could wish that they had followed up and reproduced such wise provision. For there you have a model! Any Roman citizen who had chosen a career on the stage was not only barred from any post of honour but was even quite estopped by the censors' stigma from keeping his own tribe. What a spirit animated that state, a spirit avid of glory and genuinely Roman!

But I demand an answer: " What is the consistent principle that excludes scenic actors from all right to honour and permits scenic shows to be included among honours paid to gods?" Roman virtue had long been ignorant of those theatrical arts which, if they had been demanded for the titillation of human pleasure, could have insinuated themselves only by a failure of human character. It was the gods who demanded those exhibitions for themselves; how, then, is the player cast out by whose means a god is worshipped? How can you have the face to stigmatize the actor, if you solemnize the exactor of that dramatic filth?

[1] Cicero, *Republic* 4.10.10.

In hac controversia Graeci Romanique concertent.
Graeci putant recte se honorare homines scaenicos,
quia colunt ludorum scaenicorum flagitatores deos;
Romani vero hominibus scaenicis nec plebeiam
tribum, quanto minus senatoriam curiam, dehonestari
sinunt. In hac disceptatione huiusce modi ratio-
cinatio summam quaestionis absolvit. Proponunt
Graeci: Si dii tales colendi sunt, profecto etiam tales
homines honorandi. Adsumunt Romani: Sed nullo
modo tales homines honorandi sunt. Concludunt
Christiani: Nullo modo igitur dii tales colendi sunt.

XIV

*Meliorem fuisse Platonem, qui poetis locum in bene
morata urbe non dederit, quam hos deos, qui se
ludis scaenicis voluerint honorari.*

DEINDE quaerimus, ipsi poetae talium fabularum
compositores, qui duodecim tabularum lege prohibentur famam laedere civium, tam probrosa in deos
convicia iaculantes cur non ut scaenici habeantur
inhonesti. Qua ratione rectum est ut poeticorum
figmentorum et ignominiosorum deorum infamentur
actores, honorentur auctores? An forte Graeco
Platoni potius palma danda est, qui cum ratione
formaret qualis esse civitas debeat, tamquam adversarios veritatis poetas censuit urbe pellendos? Iste
vero et deorum iniurias indigne tulit et fucari corrum-
pique figmentis animos civium noluit.

186

Let the Greeks and Romans fight this out. The Greeks think they are right in honouring the players because they worship the gods who demand the plays; the Romans, however, do not permit the players to besmirch even their plebeian tribe, much less the Senate House. The nub of the matter may be put in the form of a syllogism. The Greeks lay down the major premise: If such gods must be worshipped, certainly such men should also be honoured. The Romans add the minor: But such men should by no means be honoured. The Christians draw the conclusion: Therefore, such gods are by no means to be worshipped.

XIV

That Plato, who excluded poets from his well-regulated state, was better than the gods who chose to be honoured by stage performances.

WE next ask why the poets themselves, who compose such dramatic pieces and are restrained by the law of the Twelve Tables from injuring the reputation of citizens, but cast infamous abuse upon the gods, are not reckoned disreputable like the players. How is it that the actors of these poetical fictions and contemptible gods are defamed, while their authors are honoured? Should we, perhaps, rather, give the palm to Plato, the Greek, who, in framing the ideal state, gave his judgement that poets should be banished from the city as enemies of truth? He in truth could not stomach insults offered to the gods, nor would he suffer the minds of the citizens to be tarnished and depraved by poetic fictions.

Confer nunc Platonis humanitatem a civibus decipiendis poetas urbe pellentem cum deorum divinitate honori suo ludos scaenicos expetente. Ille, ne talia vel scriberentur, etsi non persuasit disputando, tamen suasit levitati lasciviaeque Graecorum; isti, ut talia etiam agerentur, iubendo extorserunt gravitati et modestiae Romanorum. Nec tantum haec agi voluerunt, sed sibi dicari, sibi sacrari, sibi sollemniter exhiberi.

Cui tandem honestius divinos honores decerneret civitas? Utrum Platoni haec turpia et nefanda prohibenti, an daemonibus hac hominum deceptione gaudentibus, quibus ille vera persuadere non potuit? Hunc Platonem Labeo inter semideos commemorandum putavit, sicut Herculem, sicut Romulum. Semideos autem heroibus anteponit; sed utrosque inter numina conlocat. Verum tamen istum, quem appellat semideum, non heroibus tantum, sed etiam diis ipsis praeferendum esse non dubito.

Propinquant autem Romanorum leges disputationibus Platonis, quando ille cuncta poetica figmenta condemnat, isti autem poetis adimunt saltem in homines maledicendi licentiam; ille poetas ab urbis ipsius habitatione, isti saltem actores poeticarum fabularum removent a societate civitatis; et si contra deos ludorum scaenicorum expetitores aliquid auderent, forte undique removerent. Nequaquam igitur leges ad instituendos bonos aut corrigendos

188

Compare now Plato's humanity in banishing poets from the city, to prevent the deception of the citizens, and the godliness of gods that demanded plays in their own honour. Plato, though without success, strove to persuade the light-minded and lascivious Greeks not even to write the plays; the gods, however, commanded and extorted from the grave and chaste Romans even the performance of the plays. Moreover, they chose not only to have them performed, but also to have them dedicated to themselves, consecrated to themselves, exhibited in their solemn rites.

To which, then, would it be more becoming for a city to decree divine honours, to Plato, who forbade these shameful and unspeakable performances, or to the evil spirits, who took pleasure in deceiving thereby men who refused to believe the truth that Plato urged upon them? Labeo held that this Plato should be commemorated among the demigods, like Hercules, like Romulus. Moreover, he ranks demigods above heroes, though he places both among divinities. None the less I do not doubt that this man, whom he calls a demigod, should be ranked not only above the heroes but also above the gods themselves.

The laws of the Romans are close to the dialogues of Plato in that, while Plato rejects all poetic fictions, the Roman laws prohibit any railing by the poets, at least against men. He excludes poets from dwelling in his city; they at least exclude actors of poetic dramas from fellowship with citizens, and if they were courageous enough to challenge the gods who demand the performances, they would perhaps banish them altogether. Hardly, then, could the Romans have received laws for the inculcation of good morals

malos mores a diis suis possent accipere seu sperare
Romani, quos legibus suis vincunt atque convincunt.

Illi enim honori suo deposcunt ludos scaenicos, isti
ab honoribus omnibus repellunt homines scaenicos;
illi celebrari sibi iubent figmentis poeticis opprobria
deorum, isti ab opprobriis hominum deterrent in-
pudentiam poetarum. Semideus autem ille Plato et
talium deorum libidini restitit, et ab indole Romanorum quid perficiendum esset ostendit, qui poetas ipsos
vel pro arbitrio mentientes vel hominibus miseris
quasi deorum facta pessima imitanda proponentes
omnino in civitate bene instituta vivere noluit.

Nos quidem Platonem nec deum nec semideum
perhibemus, nec ulli sancto angelo summi Dei nec
veridico prophetae nec apostolo alicui nec cuilibet
Christi martyri nec cuiquam Christiano homini com-
paramus; cuius nostrae sententiae ratio Deo prospe-
rante suo loco explicabitur. Sed eum tamen, quando
quidem ipsi volunt fuisse semideum, praeferendum
esse censemus, si non Romulo et Herculi (quamvis
istum nec fratrem occidisse, nec aliquod perpetrasse
flagitium quisquam historicorum vel poetarum dixit
aut finxit), certe vel Priapo vel alicui Cynocephalo,
postremo vel Febri, quae Romani numina partim
peregrina receperunt, partim sua propria sacraverunt.

---

[1] Plato, *Republic*, II, 383 C to III, 392 A, would exclude
many passages of the extant Greek poetry because they
represent the gods in disgraceful roles and furnish to the young
improper models for imitation.

[2] A fertility god, originating in the Hellespont region.

[3] The dog-headed Anubis introduced from Egypt.

[4] There were no fewer than three temples to this goddess in

or the restraint of bad from their gods or even have hoped for them, since in their own laws they surpass and convict the gods.

The gods demand plays in their honour; the Romans exclude the players from every honour. The gods order the disgraces of the gods to be enacted in their rites in poetic fictions; the Romans warn shameless poets not to bring disgrace on men. Plato,[1] however, that " half-god," not only took a stand against the wanton desire of such gods, but also held up a standard that the Roman genius should have put into practice, for he would not permit the poets themselves even to reside in a state with a sound constitution, either because poets in their fiction propose a model sanctioned only by themselves, or because they hold up to wretched men the worst possible examples in their stories of the gods.

We, however, call Plato neither a god nor a demigod, and we do not compare him with any holy angel of the supreme God, or with any prophet of truth, or with any apostle, or with any of Christ's martyrs, or even with any human being who is a Christian. The reason for this opinion of ours will, with God's favour, be given in its own place. But since they insist that he was a demigod, we think he should be preferred, if not to Romulus or to Hercules (although no historian has said or poet pretended that Plato slew his brother or was guilty of any other outrage), certainly to Priapus,[2] or to any Cynocephalus,[3] or to Fever,[4] divinities who were in part received by the Romans from foreign lands and in part hallowed as peculiar to themselves.

Rome. See S. B. Platner-Thomas Ashby, *Topographical Dictionary of Ancient Rome* (London, 1929), 206.

Quo modo igitur tanta animi et morum mala bonis praeceptis et legibus vel inminentia prohiberent, vel insita extirpanda curarent dii tales, qui etiam seminanda et augenda flagitia curaverunt, talia vel sua vel quasi sua facta per theatricas celebritates populis innotescere cupientes ut tamquam auctoritate divina sua sponte nequissima libido accenderetur humana, frustra hoc exclamante Cicerone, qui cum de poetis ageret: " Ad quos cum accessit," inquit, " clamor et adprobatio populi quasi cuiusdam magni et sapientis magistri, quas illi obducunt tenebras, quos invehunt metus, quas inflammant cupiditates! "

XV

Quod Romani quosdam sibi deos non ratione, sed adulatione instituerint.

Quae autem illic eligendorum deorum etiam ipsorum falsorum ratio ac non potius adulatio est? quando istum Platonem, quem semideum volunt, tantis disputationibus laborantem, ne animi malis, quae praecipue cavenda sunt, mores corrumperentur humani, nulla sacra aedicula dignum putarunt, et Romulum suum diis multis praetulerunt, quamvis et ipsum semideum potius quam deum velut secretior eorum doctrina commendet. Nam etiam flaminem illi instituerunt, quod sacerdotii genus adeo in Romanis sacris testante apice excelluit, ut tres solos

---

[1] Cicero, *Republic,* 4.9.9.

How could gods such as these prevent by good instruction and legislation the threat of such great vices of the mind and of morals, or get them eradicated once they had taken root? These gods made it their business to plant and foster outrages, inasmuch as they were desirous of spreading among communities the knowledge of such acts through theatrical festivals—acts, whether truly or falsely, said to be theirs. Thus, the basest lust was fanned into flame as having divine sanction on their initiative. All in vain does Cicero raise his voice against this, who says in his discussion of poets, " When the cheers and approval of the people, as if it were some great and good teacher, uphold the poets, what deep shadows they cast, what fears they inspire, what lusts they enkindle! " [1]

XV

That the Romans established certain gods through flattery, not reason.

Moreover, how can their method of selecting gods, false though they are, be termed rational and not rather an exercise of servile flattery? That demigod Plato, as they choose to call him, though in so many dialogues he strove to prevent the corruption of human society by vices of the mind—and they are the kind that we most need to shun—Plato, I say, was not thought to deserve even a tiny shrine, yet they have preferred their own Romulus to many gods, though even so a kind of esoteric doctrine of theirs puts him forward as a demigod rather than as a god. For they even assigned a flamen to him, a kind of priest so distinguished in the Roman religion, as witness the

flamines haberent tribus numinibus institutos, Dialem Iovi, Martialem Marti, Quirinalem Romulo. Nam benevolentia civium velut receptus in caelum Quirinus est postea nominatus. Ac per hoc et Neptuno et Plutoni, fratribus Iovis, et ipsi Saturno, patri eorum, isto Romulus honore praelatus est, ut pro magno sacerdotium quod Iovi tribuerant, hoc etiam huic tribuerent, et Marti tamquam patri eius forsitan propter ipsum.

XVI

Quod, si diis ulla esset cura iustitiae, ab eis Romani accipere debuerint praecepta vivendi potius quam leges ab aliis hominibus mutuari.

Si autem a diis suis Romani vivendi leges accipere potuissent, non aliquot annos post Romam conditam ab Atheniensibus mutuarentur leges Solonis, quas tamen non ut acceperunt tenuerunt,[1] sed meliores et emendatiores facere conati sunt; quamvis Lycurgus Lacedaemoniis leges ex Apollinis auctoritate se instituisse confinxerit, quod prudenter Romani credere noluerunt, propterea non inde acceperunt.

Numa Pompilius, qui Romulo successit in regnum, quasdam leges, quae quidem regendae civitati nequaquam sufficerent, condidisse fertur, qui eis multa etiam sacra constituit; non tamen perhibetur

---

[1] tenuerunt *second hand in one MS.* ; *omitted in others.*

---

[1] Livy 3.31–33 dates the mission in 454 B.C.

[2] Lycurgus was the traditional lawgiver of Sparta, and is said to have obtained the laws, or at least approval for them, from the oracle of Apollo at Delphi.

conical cap, that they had only three flamens assigned to three divinities, the Flamen Dialis to Jupiter, the Flamen Martialis to Mars and the Flamen Quirinalis to Romulus. For after his so-called admittance to heaven, by the grace of his fellow citizens he was afterwards named Quirinus. Furthermore, Romulus was thereby granted greater honour than either Neptune or Pluto, brothers of Jupiter, or even Saturn himself, their father, inasmuch as they assigned to him the same priesthood they had assigned as a great honour to Jupiter—and another to Mars, his reputed father, as well—perhaps indeed because he was his father.

XVI

That had the gods really cared for righteousness, the Romans should have received moral precepts from them, rather than borrow laws from others.

MOREOVER, had the Romans been able to obtain a rule of life from their own gods, they would not have borrowed the laws of Solon from the Athenians some years after the founding of Rome.[1] They did not, nevertheless, keep them as they received them, but tried to improve and correct them. Although Lycurgus [2] pretended that he had drawn up laws for the Lacedaemonians by Apollo's authority, this the Romans wisely refused to believe, and for this reason took nothing from that source.

Numa Pompilius, Romulus' successor on the throne, is said to have established some legislation, which was, however, not sufficient for governing the city. Among his laws many pertained to the religious ordinances, and yet not even these are re-

easdem leges a numinibus accepisse. Mala igitur
animi, mala vitae, mala morum, quae ita magna sunt,
ut his doctissimi eorum viri etiam stantibus urbibus
res publicas perire confirment, dii eorum, ne suis
cultoribus acciderent, minime curarunt; immo vero
ut augerentur, sicut supra disputatum est, omni modo
curarunt.

XVII

De raptu Sabinarum aliisque iniquitatibus, quae
in civitate Romana etiam laudatis viguere temporibus.

An forte populo Romano propterea leges non sunt
a numinibus constitutae, quia, sicut Sallustius ait,
" ius bonumque apud eos non legibus magis quam
natura valebat "?

Ex hoc iure ac bono credo raptas Sabinas. Quid
enim iustius et melius quam filias alienas fraude
spectaculi inductas non a parentibus accipi, sed vi, ut
quisque poterat, auferri? Nam si inique facerent
Sabini negare postulatas, quanto fuit iniquius rapere
non datas! Iustius autem bellum cum ea gente geri
potuit, quae filias suas ad matrimonium conregionali-
bus et confinalibus suis negasset petitas, quam cum
ea, quae repetebat ablatas.

---

[1] Sallust, *Catilinarian Conspiracy* 9.1.

ported to have come from divinities. Spiritual evils, evils of life, evils of conduct, which are so important that through their agency states perish even though the cities themselves still stand, so their most learned men affirm—such evils their gods were not concerned to prevent in the least from afflicting their worshippers. Indeed, as has been maintained above, they took the greatest pains to increase them.

XVII

On the rape of the Sabine women and other iniquities that flourished in the Roman state even in the era of her good fame.

Perhaps the divinities did not establish laws for the Roman people because, as Sallust says, " equity and virtue prevailed among them no more by laws than by nature." [1]

This " equity and virtue," I suppose, produced the rape of the Sabine women! What is more just and virtuous than to take other men's daughters, lured by the trick of presenting a show, without their fathers' consent, and to carry them off by force, as each man was able? For if the Sabines were wrong to refuse their daughters on request, how much more wrong to kidnap them on refusal! Moreover, it would have been a more righteous war, if they had waged war against a people who refused to give their daughters in marriage to those who belonged to the same country and were their neighbours, than it was when they waged war against the same people seeking return of their daughters after abduction.

197

Illud ergo potius fieret; ibi Mars filium suum pugnantem iuvaret ut coniugiorum negatorum armis ulcisceretur iniuriam, et eo modo ad feminas quas voluerat perveniret. Aliquo enim fortasse iure belli iniuste negatas iuste victor auferret; nullo autem iure pacis non datas rapuit et iniustum bellum cum earum parentibus iuste suscensentibus gessit. Hoc sane utilius feliciusque successit, quod, etsi ad memoriam fraudis illius circensium spectaculum mansit, facinoris tamen in illa civitate et imperio non placuit exemplum, faciliusque Romani in hoc erraverunt, ut post illam iniquitatem deum sibi Romulum consecrarent, quam ut in feminis rapiendis factum eius imitandum lege ulla vel more permitterent.

Ex hoc iure ac bono post expulsum cum liberis suis regem Tarquinium, cuius filius Lucretiam stupro violenter oppresserat, Iunius Brutus consul Lucium Tarquinium Collatinum, maritum eiusdem Lucretiae, collegam suum, bonum atque innocentem virum, propter nomen et propinquitatem Tarquiniorum coegit magistratu se abdicare nec vivere in civitate permisit. Quod scelus favente vel patiente populo fecit, a quo populo consulatum idem Collatinus sicut etiam ipse Brutus acceperat.

Ex hoc iure ac bono Marcus Camillus, illius temporis vir egregius, qui Veientes, gravissimos hostes populi Romani, post decennale bellum, quo Romanus

Such a war, then, might better have been made. In that case Mars might have helped his son in a struggle to avenge with arms the wrong done him when alliance in marriage was refused and to attain in this way the women that he had chosen. For perhaps some law of war might have justified a victor in taking away women who had been unjustly refused. But no law of peace gave sanction to his kidnapping women not conceded to him, and waging an unjust war with their parents who were justly enraged against him. In the sequel, to be sure, they gained a better and more fortunate outcome, in that, though the games of the circus remained to commemorate the trick, still the precedent did not find favour in that state and realm. It proved easier for the Romans to make the mistake of deifying Romulus as a god after that breach of justice than to permit by any law or custom the emulation of his feat when he kidnapped women.

By that " equity and virtue " it came about that after the expulsion, with his children, of King Tarquin, whose son had raped Lucretia, the consul Junius Brutus forced Lucius Tarquinius Collatinus, husband of that same Lucretia, his colleague and a good and innocent man, to resign his magistracy, and would not allow him to live in the city, because of the name and blood of the Tarquins that were his. Brutus perpetrated his crime with the good will or sufferance of the people, from whom the aforesaid Collatinus, as well as Brutus himself, had received the consulship.

By that " equity and virtue " it came about that Marcus Camillus, an outstanding man of the time, who after a decade of war, in which the Roman army

exercitus totiens male pugnando graviter adflictus
est, iam ipsa Roma de salute dubitante atque trepi-
dante facillime superavit eorumque urbem opulentissimam cepit, invidia obtrectatorum virtutis suae et
insolentia tribunorum plebis reus factus est tamque
ingratam sensit quam liberaverat civitatem ut de sua
damnatione certissimus in exilium sponte discederet
et decem milia aeris absens etiam damnaretur, mox
iterum a Gallis vindex patriae futurus ingratae.

Multa commemorare iam piget foeda et iniusta,
quibus agitabatur illa civitas, cum potentes plebem
sibi subdere conarentur plebsque illis subdi recusaret,
et utriusque partis defensores magis studiis agerent
amore vincendi, quam aequum et bonum quicquam
cogitarent.

XVIII

*Quae de moribus Romanorum aut metu compressis aut
securitate resolutis Sallustii prodat historia.*

Itaque habebo modum et ipsum Sallustium testem
potius adhibebo, qui cum in laude Romanorum
dixisset, unde nobis iste sermo ortus est: "Ius
bonumque apud eos non legibus magis quam natura
valebat," praedicans illud tempus, quo expulsis
regibus incredibiliter civitas brevi aetatis spatio

because of so many defeats was seriously impaired and at last the city itself was full of misgivings and alarmed for her safety, easily overpowered the people of Veii, Rome's most dreaded enemies, and captured their city with its vast wealth, was, through the envious malice of his detractors and the insolence of the tribunes of the people, put on trial, and when he perceived the ingratitude of the city which he had liberated and that he would be most certainly condemned, went into voluntary exile, and while absent was fined 10,000 *asses*, though he was presently destined to be a second time the deliverer of his ungrateful fatherland from the Gauls.

It would be tedious to recite the many shameful and iniquitous acts with which the peace of that city was shaken in the period when the powerful were attempting to make the populace their subjects and the populace rebelled against subjection, and the champions of both parties were more motivated in their zeal by a contentious spirit than they were animated by any notion of fair play and virtue.

XVIII

What Sallust's history reveals concerning the character of the Romans both under pressure of fear and when relaxed by security.

I SHALL, therefore, limit myself to citing as witness Sallust himself, whose encomium on the Romans— " equity and virtue prevailed among them not more by laws than by nature "—furnished me with a point of departure for this discussion. He was speaking of that period immediately after the expulsion of the kings when the city grew great in an unbelievably

plurimum crevit, idem tamen in primo historiae suae
libro atque ipso eius exordio fatetur etiam tunc, cum
ad consules a regibus esset translata res publica, post
parvum intervallum iniurias validiorum et ob eas
discessionem plebis a patribus aliasque in Urbe
dissensiones fuisse.

Nam cum optimis moribus et maxima concordia
populum Romanum inter secundum et postremum
bellum Carthaginiense commemorasset egisse cau-
samque huius boni non amorem iustitiae, sed stante
Carthagine metum pacis infidae fuisse dixisset (unde
et Nasica ille ad reprimendam nequitiam servandos-
que istos mores optimos, ut metu vitia cohiberentur,
Carthaginem nolebat everti) continuo subiecit idem
Sallustius et ait: " At discordia et avaritia atque
ambitio et cetera secundis rebus oriri sueta mala post
Carthaginis excidium maxime aucta sunt," ut in-
tellegeremus etiam antea et oriri solere et augeri.
Unde subnectens cur hoc dixerit: " Nam iniuriae,"
inquit, " validiorum et ob eas discessio plebis a patribus aliaeque dissensiones domi fuere iam inde a
principio, neque amplius quam regibus exactis, dum
metus a Tarquinio et bellum grave cum Etruria
positum est, aequo et modesto iure agitatum."

Vides quem ad modum etiam illo tempore brevi, ut
regibus exactis, id est eiectis, aliquantum aequo et
modesto iure ageretur, metum dixit fuisse causam,

---

[1] Sallust, *History* fr. 1.11.   [2] *Ibid.*

short time. Yet the same man in the first book of his
history, in the very introduction to it, admits that
only a short time after the government had been
transferred from kings to consuls, acts of oppression
by the powerful took place in the City with resultant
secession of the people from the patricians as well as
other disorders.

For he first remarks that between the second and
the last war with Carthage the Roman people enjoyed
a period of excellent morality and the greatest harmony, and that the cause of this happy state was, not
any love of justice, but fear of a treacherous peace,
as long as Carthage remained standing. (This was,
incidentally, the reason why Nasica opposed the
destruction of Carthage, to repress vice and to preserve the aforesaid high state of morality by restrain-
ing immorality through fear.) The same Sallust
immediately adds: " On the other hand, after the
destruction of Carthage, discord, avarice, ambition,
and other vices commonly arising from prosperity,
particularly increased." [1] Thus he gives us to understand that even before this such vices had been
wont both to arise and to increase. Then he adds
the reason for his statement: " For oppression by the
powerful, with resultant secession of the people from
the patricians and other disorders, had occurred in the
state from the beginning; and the reign of just and
righteous law lasted, after the expulsion of the kings,
only until fear of Tarquin and the serious war with
Etruria were ended." [2]

You see how even in that brief interval after the
kings were expelled, that is, cast out, when justice
and righteous law to some extent reigned, he gives
fear as the reason. The object of their fear was the

quoniam metuebatur bellum, quo rex Tarquinius
regno atque Urbe pulsus Etruscis sociatus contra
Romanos gerebat. Adtende itaque quid deinde
contexat: " Dein," inquit, " servili imperio patres
plebem exercere, de vita atque tergo regio more consulere, agro pellere et ceteris expertibus soli in imperio
agere. Quibus saevitiis et maxime faenore oppressa
plebes cum assiduis bellis tributum et militiam simul
toleraret, armata montem sacrum atque Aventinum
insedit, tumque tribunos plebis et alia iura sibi
paravit. Discordiarum et certaminis utrimque finis
fuit secundum bellum Punicum." Cernis ex quo
tempore, id est parvo intervallo post reges exactos,
quales Romani fuerint, de quibus ait: " Ius bonumque apud eos non legibus magis quam natura
valebat."

Porro si illa tempora talia reperiuntur, quibus pulcherrima atque optima fuisse praedicatur Romana res
publica, quid iam de consequenti aetate dicendum aut
cogitandum arbitramur, cum " paulatim mutata," ut
eiusdem historici verbis utar, " ex pulcherrima atque
optima pessima ac flagitiosissima facta est," post
Carthaginis videlicet, ut commemoravit, excidium ?

Quae tempora ipse Sallustius quem ad modum
breviter recolat et describat, in eius historia legi
potest; quantis malis morum, quae secundis rebus
exorta sunt, usque ad bella civilia demonstret esse
perventum. " Ex quo tempore," ut ait, " maiorum

---

[1] Sallust, *History* fr. 1.11.
[2] Sallust, *Catilinarian Conspiracy* 5.9.

war being waged against the Romans by King Tarquin in alliance with the Etruscans, when he was expelled from kingdom and city. Note the sequel in his text: " From that time on the patricians treated the people as slaves, ordered them executed and flogged as the kings had done, drove them from their land, or behaved like tyrants to the rest who were landless. The common people, crushed by this savage treatment and particularly by high rates of interest, and bearing a double burden of taxation and military service in the constant wars, withdrew under arms to the Sacred Hill and to the Aventine, and at last gained tribunes of the people and other rights for themselves. The end of discord and strife on both sides was reached only with the Second Punic War." [1] You observe what kind of men the Romans were at that time, that is, a short time after the expulsion of the kings, men of whom he says, " Equity and virtue prevailed among them no more by law than by nature."

Furthermore, if the era when the Roman government is declared to have been fairest and best, was like that, what will seem proper to say or imagine when we come to the succeeding age when the city " altering by slow degrees," in the words of the same historian, " from being the fairest and best became the worst and most dissolute "? [2] This was, of course, as he records, after the destruction of Carthage.

How Sallust briefly treats of and describes this era can be read in his history, in which he points out how great were the moral evils that, arising from prosperity, led at last to civil wars. " From then on," he says, " the morals of our ancestors were swept away,

mores non paulatim ut antea, sed torrentis modo praecipitati, adeo iuventus luxu atque avaritia corrupta, ut merito dicatur genitos esse qui neque ipsi habere possent res familiares neque alios pati." Dicit deinde plura Sallustius de Sullae vitiis ceteraque foeditate rei publicae, et alii scriptores in haec consentiunt, quamvis eloquio multum impari.

Cernis tamen, ut opinor, et quisquis adverterit, facillime perspicit, conluvie morum pessimorum quo illa civitas prolapsa fuerit ante nostri superni regis adventum. Haec enim gesta sunt non solum antequam Christus in carne praesens docere coepisset, verum etiam antequam de virgine natus esset.

Cum igitur tot et tanta mala temporum illorum vel tolerabiliora superius, vel post eversam Carthaginem intoleranda et horrenda diis suis imputare non audeant, opiniones humanis mentibus, unde talia vitia silvescerent, astutia maligna inserentibus, cur mala praesentia Christo inputant, qui doctrina saluberrima et falsos ac fallaces deos coli vetat et istas hominum noxias flagitiosasque cupiditates divina auctoritate detestans atque condemnans his malis tabescenti ac labenti mundo ubique familiam suam sensim subtrahit, qua condat aeternam et non plausu vanitatis, sed iudicio veritatis gloriosissimam civitatem?

not by slow degrees, as hitherto, but in a headlong torrent. Indeed, the youth were so corrupted by high living and avarice that it could be truthfully said that sons were born who could neither themselves preserve their property nor let others preserve theirs." [1] Sallust then adds further comment on Sulla's vices and all the other corruption in the republic; other writers say the same, though with far inferior eloquence.

You see, I suppose, and any one who examines the matter closely will easily perceive, into what a slough of utter immorality that city had sunk before the coming of our Heavenly King. These things took place not only before Christ present in the flesh had begun to teach but even before he was born of a virgin.

If, therefore, they do not dare impute to their gods the many great evils of those eras, whether the more bearable evils in earlier days or the unbearable and gruesome evils that ensued after the destruction of Carthage, though it was those gods who implanted in men's minds with malevolent craft the beliefs whence all these vices ran wild, why do they impute to Christ the evils of this present age, who by his most wholesome teaching forbids the worship of the falsified and falsifying gods, and who, abominating and condemning by divine authority those noxious and outrageous lusts of men, slowly withdraws his family from a world everywhere infected with those evils and going to ruin, in order with that family to establish a city everlasting, whose supreme glory depends, not on the plaudits of vanity, but on the verdict of veracity?

[1] Sallust, *History* 1.16.

XIX

De corruptione Romanae rei publicae, priusquam
cultum deorum Christus auferret.

Ecce Romana res publica (quod non ego primus
dico, sed auctores eorum, unde haec mercede didi-
cimus, tanto ante dixerunt ante Christi adventum)
" paulatim mutata ex pulcherrima atque optima
pessima ac flagitiosissima facta est." Ecce ante
Christi adventum, post deletam Carthaginem
" maiorum mores non paulatim, ut antea, sed torrentis
modo praecipitati, adeo iuventus luxu atque avaritia
corrupta est."

Legant nobis contra luxum et avaritiam praecepta
deorum suorum populo Romano data; cui utinam
tantum casta et modesta reticerent, ac non etiam ab
illo probrosa et ignominiosa deposcerent, quibus per
falsam divinitatem perniciosam conciliarent auctoritatem. Legant nostra et per prophetas et per
sanctum evangelium, et per apostolicos actus et per
epistulas tam multa contra avaritiam atque luxuriam
ubique populis ad hoc congregatis quam excellenter,
quam divine non tamquam ex philosophorum con-
certationibus strepere, sed tamquam ex oraculis et
Dei [1] nubibus intonare. Et tamen luxu atque
avaritia saevisque ac turpibus moribus ante adventum
Christi rem publicam pessimam ac flagitiosissimam
factam non inputant diis suis; adflictionem vero

---

[1] *Probably* de *should be read.*

XIX

*On the corruption of the Roman government before
Christ abolished the worship of the gods.*

THERE you see that Roman republic which, " changing by slow degrees from the fairest and best, became the worst and most dissolute " ! These words are not original with me ; they were written by men whose words we learned in school for a fee, who uttered them so long before Christ's coming. There you have it ! Before Christ's coming and after Carthage was destroyed, " the morals of our ancestors were swept away, not by slow degrees, as hitherto, but in a headlong torrent, so greatly were the youth corrupted by high living and avarice."

Let them cite us the commandments forbidding high living and avarice that the Roman people received from their gods. If only they would be content to say nothing to the people about chastity and modesty, and would not actually require of them shameless and indecent performances, for which they gained a fatal sanction by their pretended godhead ! Let them read ours, all those many commandments against avarice and high living, found in the prophets, in the holy Gospel, in the Acts of the Apostles and in the Epistles, which everywhere are read to congregations gathered for this purpose. How loftily, how divinely they strike the ear, not like the buzz of philosophic squabbles, but issuing from shrines or from the clouds in a voice of thunder. And yet they do not impute to their gods the degradation and utter profligacy brought to the state by luxury and avarice, and by the barbarous and filthy morals that prevailed before Christ's coming ; but any affliction

eius, quamcumque isto tempore superbia deliciaeque eorum perpessae fuerint, religioni increpitant Christianae.

Cuius praecepta de iustis probisque moribus si simul audirent atque curarent reges terrae et omnes populi, principes et omnes iudices terrae, iuvenes et virgines, seniores cum iunioribus, aetas omnis capax et uterque sexus, et quos baptista Iohannes adloquitur, exactores ipsi atque milites, et terras vitae praesentis ornaret sua felicitate res publica, et vitae aeternae culmen beatissime regnatura conscenderet. Sed quia iste audit, ille contemnit, pluresque vitiis male blandientibus quam utili virtutum asperitati sunt amiciores, tolerare Christi famuli iubentur, sive sint reges sive principes sive iudices, sive milites sive provinciales, sive divites sive pauperes, sive liberi sive servi, utriuslibet sexus, etiam pessimam, si ita necesse est, flagitiosissimamque rem publicam et in illa angelorum quadam sanctissima atque augustissima curia caelestique re publica, ubi Dei voluntas lex est, clarissimum sibi locum etiam ista tolerantia comparare.

XX

Quali velint felicitate gaudere et quibus moribus vivere, qui tempora Christianae religionis incusant.

VERUM tales cultores et dilectores deorum istorum, quorum etiam imitatores in sceleribus et flagitiis se

that in these days has befallen their arrogance and self-indulgence, that they use continually to cry down the Christian religion.

If the kings of earth and all the nations, the princes and all the judges of the earth, the young men and maidens, aged men and others, all times of life that are capable without regard to sex—if they whom John the Baptist addresses, the very tax collectors and soldiers—were all together to hear and to heed these commandments of the Christian religion about righteousness and honesty of character, then would the republic adorn with its felicity its lands in this life, and mount the pinnacle of life eternal to reign most blessedly. But because one is a listener, another is a scoffer and more are enamoured rather of the evil blandishments of the vices than of the wholesome rigour of the virtues, therefore Christ's servants, whether they be kings or princes or judges, soldiers or provincials, rich or poor, bond or free, without regard to sex, are bidden to suffer the burden of this republic, wicked and most vicious though it be, if so it must be, and also by so suffering to gain a place of highest honour for themselves in that certain most holy and august assembly of angels in the heavenly republic where God's will is law.

XX

On the kind of happiness that the accusers of Christianity wish to enjoy and the moral standards by which they wish to live.

But the worshippers and the lovers of those gods, whom they are even delighted to copy in their evil

esse laetantur, nullo modo curant pessimam ac
flagitiosissimam non [1] esse rem publicam. " Tantum
stet, inquiunt, tantum floreat copiis referta, victoriis
gloriosa, vel, quod est felicius, pace secura sit. Et
quid ad nos? Immo id ad nos magis pertinet, si
divitias quisque augeat semper, quae cotidianis
effusionibus suppetant, per quas sibi etiam infirmiores subdat quisque potentior. Obsequantur
divitibus pauperes causa saturitatis atque ut eorum
patrociniis quieta inertia perfruantur, divites pauperi-
bus ad clientelas et ad ministerium sui fastus abu-
tantur. Populi plaudant, non consultoribus utili-
tatum suarum, sed largitoribus voluptatum. Non
dura iubeantur, non prohibeantur inpura. Reges non
curent quam bonis, sed quam subditis regnent.
Provinciae regibus non tamquam rectoribus morum,
sed tamquam rerum dominatoribus et deliciarum
suarum provisoribus serviant, eosque non sinceriter
honorent, sed [2] serviliter timeant. Quid alienae
vineae potius quam quid suae vitae quisque noceat,
legibus advertatur. Nullus ducatur ad iudicem, nisi
qui alienae rei domui saluti vel cuiquam invito fuerit
inportunus aut noxius.

" Ceterum de suis vel cum suis vel cum quibusque
volentibus faciat quisque quod libet. Abundent
publica scorta vel propter omnes quibus frui placuerit,
vel propter eos maxime qui habere privata non
possunt. Exstruantur amplissimae atque ornatissi-

---

[1] *Dombart wrongly brackets this word.*
[2] *Dombart here wrongly retains* nequiter ac *omitted in many*
MSS.

deeds, are not concerned to prevent the republic from
sinking to the lowest level of wickedness and profligacy. " Only let it stand," they say, " only let it
flourish with abundant resources, glorious in victory
or, and that is better, secure in peace. And how
does it concern us? No, no! it interests us more
that the individual should constantly increase his
wealth to support his daily extravagance, and to
enable the more powerful individual thereby to
make weaker men his subjects. Let the poor court
the rich to fill their bellies and to enjoy under their
patronage an undisturbed idleness; let the rich
misuse the poor as clients and to minister to their
pride. Let the people hail with applause, not those
who have their interests at heart, but those who are
lavish with pleasures. Let no hard task be assigned,
let no foulness be forbidden. Let kings care not
how good their subjects are but how abject. Let
provinces be subservient to kings not as directors of
morals but as lords of their lives and providers of
their pleasures; and let them not honour them in
sincerity but fear them in servility. Let the laws
penalize the damage a man does to his neighbour's
vineyard rather than the damage he does to his own
soul. Let no man be haled into court unless he
harms another's property, household, health, or is a
nuisance or impediment to someone against his
will.

" Otherwise, let each man do what he will with his
own either in the company of his own people or of
anyone else who is willing. Let there be an abundant
supply of public prostitutes, whether for anyone to
use who chooses or for those chiefly who are unable to
keep their own. Let huge and ornate houses be built;

mae domus, opipara convivia frequententur, ubi
cuique libuerit et potuerit, diu noctuque ludatur,
bibatur, vomatur, diffluatur. Saltationes undique
concrepent, theatra inhonestae laetitiae vocibus atque
omni genere sive crudelissimae sive turpissimae
voluptatis exaestuent. Ille sit publicus inimicus, cui
haec felicitas displicet; quisquis eam mutare vel
auferre temptaverit, eum libera multitudo avertat ab
auribus, evertat a sedibus, auferat a viventibus. Illi
habeantur dii veri, qui hanc adipiscendam populis
procuraverint adeptamque servaverint. Colantur ut
voluerint, ludos exposcant quales voluerint, quos cum
suis vel de suis possint habere cultoribus; tantum
efficiant, ut tali felicitati nihil ab hoste, nihil a peste,
nihil ab ulla clade timeatur."

Quis hanc rem publicam sanus, non dicam Romano
imperio, sed domui Sardanapali comparaverit? Qui
quondam rex ita fuit voluptatibus deditus, ut in
sepulcro suo scribi fecerit ea sola se habere mortuum,
quae libido eius, etiam cum viveret, hauriendo
consumpserat. Quem regem si isti haberent sibi in
talibus indulgentem nec in eis cuiquam ulla severitate
adversantem, huic libentius quam Romani veteres
Romulo templum et flaminem consecrarent.

---

[1] According to ancient historians he was the last and most
luxurious of the Assyrian kings who reigned at Nineveh.
Cicero (*Tusculan Disputations* 5.35.101) quotes the inscription.

let lavish banquets be largely attended where for anyone who has the desire and the power there may be by day and by night indulgence in sport, drinking, vomiting, dissipation. Let the noise of dancing everywhere be heard, let the theatres erupt in cries of indecent merriment and with every kind of utterly cruel and utterly degraded pleasure. Let him be regarded as an enemy of the people who frowns on such bliss; whoever would try to change it or do away with it, let the mob unrestrained deny him a hearing, toss him from the seats, remove him from the living. Let those be considered true gods who saw to it that the people should win the occasion of such bliss and preserved it when won. Let them be worshipped as they choose, let them demand whatever games they choose, let them hold them in the company or at the expense of their worshippers. Only let them see to it that such a state of happiness be not endangered by an enemy, by a plague, by any disaster."

What man in his right mind would compare such a republic—I do not say with the Roman empire—but with the palace of Sardanapalus? [1] This king long ago was so devoted to his pleasures that he commanded to be carved on his tomb the statement that he possessed after death only those things that, while he still lived, had gone to feed his lust, as they poured down his gullet. Had these men a king of this type, who was not only self-indulgent in such matters, but in no serious way opposed the indulgence of anyone else in them, they would consecrate a temple and a flamen to him with more alacrity than the ancient Romans showed in the case of Romulus.

XXI

Quae sententia fuerit Ciceronis de Romana re publica.

SED si contemnitur qui Romanam rem publicam pessimam ac flagitiosissimam dixit, nec curant isti quanta morum pessimorum ac flagitiosissimorum labe ac dedecore impleatur, sed tantummodo ut consistat et maneat, audiant eam non, ut Sallustius narrat, pessimam ac flagitiosissimam factam, sed, sicut Cicero disputat, iam tunc prorsus perisse et nullam omnino remansisse rem publicam.

Inducit enim Scipionem, eum ipsum qui Carthaginem extinxerat, de re publica disputantem, quando praesentiebatur ea corruptione, quam describit Sallustius, iam iamque peritura. Eo quippe tempore disputatur, quo iam unus Gracchorum occisus fuit, a quo scribit seditiones graves coepisse Sallustius. Nam mortis eius fit in eisdem libris commemoratio.

Cum autem Scipio in secundi libri fine dixisset, " Ut in fidibus aut tibiis atque cantu ipso ac vocibus concentus est quidam tenendus ex distinctis sonis, quem inmutatum aut discrepantem aures eruditae ferre non possunt, isque concentus ex dissimillimarum vocum moderatione concors tamen efficitur et congruens, sic ex summis et infimis et mediis interiectis ordinibus, ut sonis, moderata ratione civitatem consensu dissimillimorum concinere, et quae harmonia a musicis dicitur in cantu, eam esse in civitate con-

---

[1] Sallust, *History* 1.17.
[2] Tiberius Gracchus, tribune of the people in 133 B.C.

XXI

Cicero's opinion of the Roman government.

If, however, they scorn him who said that the Roman republic was utterly wicked and profligate, and those men care naught how charged it is with the disgrace and decay of utterly wicked and profligate immorality, so long as it holds together and goes on, let them listen, not to Sallust's statement that it became utterly wicked and profligate, but to Cicero's argument that in his time it was utterly extinct and no republic remained at all.

He brings on the stage that Scipio, the very man who had finally destroyed Carthage, discussing the republic at a time when there were already presentiments that it would at any moment perish because of the corruption that Sallust describes.[1] In fact, at the time when this discussion is supposed to have taken place, the death of one of the Gracchi had already taken place,[2] with whom, so Sallust says, began the serious seditions. In fact, his death is recorded in those same books.

At the end of the second book, Scipio says : " As, when lyres or flutes accompany the voices of singers, a kind of harmony should be maintained out of separate sounds, and the trained ear cannot endure any false note or disagreement, and such harmony, concordant and exact, may be produced by the regulation even of voices most unlike, so by combining the highest, lowest and between them the middle class of society, as if they were tones of different pitch, provided they are regulated by due proportion, the state may produce a unison by agreement of elements quite unlike. The agreement that musicians call harmony in singing is

217

cordiam, artissimum atque optimum omni in re
publica vinculum incolumitatis, eamque sine iustitia
nullo pacto esse posse."

Ac deinde cum aliquanto latius et uberius disse-
ruisset, quantum prodesset iustitia civitati quantumque obesset, si afuisset, suscepit deinde Philus, unus
eorum qui disputationi aderant, et poposcit ut haec
ipsa quaestio diligentius tractaretur ac de iustitia
plura dicerentur, propter illud quod iam vulgo
ferebatur, rem publicam regi sine iniuria non posse.

Hanc proinde quaestionem discutiendam et eno-
dandam esse adsensus est Scipio responditque nihil
esse quod adhuc de re publica dictum putaret, quo
possent longius progredi, nisi esset confirmatum non
modo falsum esse illud, sine iniuria non posse, sed
hoc verissimum esse, sine summa iustitia rem publicam regi non posse. Cuius quaestionis explicatio
cum in diem consequentem dilata esset, in tertio libro
magna conflictione res acta est. Suscepit enim
Philus ipse disputationem eorum, qui sentirent sine
iniustitia geri non posse rem publicam, purgans
praecipue, ne hoc ipse sentire crederetur, egitque
sedulo pro iniustitia contra iustitiam, ut hanc esse
utilem rei publicae, illam vero inutilem, veri similibus
rationibus et exemplis velut conaretur ostendere.
Tum Laelius rogantibus omnibus iustitiam defendere
adgressus est adseruitque, quantum potuit, nihil tam

---

[1] The Greek equivalent of this phrase, δεσμὸν σωτήριον is
found in Plato, *Epistle* 8, 354 B. The idea is probably taken
from the " undergirding " of ships (Acts 27.17).

[2] Cicero, *Republic* 2.42.

[3] L. Fabius Philus, a member of the literary coterie that
included Laelius and Scipio Africanus.

known as concord in the body politic. This is the tightest and best rope of safety [1] in every state, and it cannot exist at all without justice." [2]

When Scipio had gone on to discuss somewhat more extensively and in greater detail the benefits of justice to the state and the disadvantages of its absence, then Philus,[3] one of those present at the discussion, interposed and demanded that this question should receive fuller treatment, and that more should be said about justice because of the saying that was then current, " a state cannot be governed without injustice."

Accordingly, Scipio agreed that this question should be discussed and unravelled, remarking that he could find nothing that had yet been said about the state to serve as a basis for further progress if it were not first established, not only that the saying about the necessity of injustice was false, but also that the opposite is superlatively true, namely, that no state can be governed without the utmost justice. The elucidation of this question was postponed until the next day, when—in the third book—the debate was conducted with no little rivalry. For Philus championed the thesis of those who held that the state could not be governed without injustice, though he cleared his skirts at the start lest it be supposed that he held this opinion himself. He zealously took the part of injustice against justice, and made a show of endeavouring to prove by probable pleas and examples that injustice is beneficial to the state, and justice disadvantageous. Then Laelius, at the request of everyone present, proceeded to defend justice and maintained to the best of his ability that nothing is so inimical to the best interests of a state as

inimicum quam iniustitiam civitati nec omnino nisi magna iustitia geri aut stare posse rem publicam.

Qua quaestione, quantum satis visum est, pertractata Scipio ad intermissa revertitur recolitque suam atque commendat brevem rei publicae definitionem, qua dixerat eam esse rem populi. Populum autem non omnem coetum multitudinis, sed coetum iuris consensu et utilitatis communione sociatum esse determinat. Docet deinde quanta sit in disputando definitionis utilitas, atque ex illis suis definitionibus colligit tunc esse rem publicam, id est rem populi, cum bene ac iuste geritur sive ab uno rege sive a paucis optimatibus sive ab universo populo. Cum vero iniustus est rex, quem tyrannum more Graeco appellavit, aut iniusti optimates, quorum consensum dixit esse factionem, aut iniustus ipse populus, cui nomen usitatum non repperit, nisi ut etiam ipsum tyrannum vocaret, non iam vitiosam, sicut pridie fuerat disputatum, sed, sicut ratio ex illis definitionibus conexa docuisset, omnino nullam esse rem publicam, quoniam non esset res populi, cum tyrannus eam factiove capesseret, nec ipse populus iam populus esset, si esset iniustus, quoniam non esset multitudo iuris consensu et utilitatis communione sociata, sicut populus fuerat definitus.

Quando ergo res publica Romana talis erat, qualem illam describit Sallustius, non iam pessima ac flagitiosissima, sicut ipse ait, sed omnino nulla erat secundum

injustice; and that a government cannot be carried on or endure at all without a high degree of justice.

When this point has been treated to the satisfaction of those present, Scipio once more returns to the main theme, and resumes and recommends his own brief definition of a state, in which he had said that a state is the people's estate. He specifies, however, that by a people he means, not every gathering of a throng, but a gathering united in fellowship by a common sense of right and a community of interest. Then he explains the great advantage of definition in debate, and he concludes from those particular definitions that a state, that is, a people's estate, exists when there is good and lawful government whether in the hands of a monarch, or of a few nobles or of the whole people. When, however, the monarch is unlawful—he used the usual Greek term " tyrant " for such a monarch—or the nobles are unlawful—he called their mutual agreement a faction —or the people itself is unlawful—for this he found no current term if he were not to call it too a tyrant— then the state is no longer merely defective, as had been argued the day before, but, as a chain of reasoning from the foregoing definitions would have made plain, does not exist at all. For there was no people's estate, he said, when a tyrant or a party took over the state, nor was the people itself any longer a people, if it was unjust, since in that case it was not a throng united in fellowship by a common sense of right and a community of interest, as specified in the definition.

When, therefore, the Roman republic took on the character described by Sallust, it was no longer utterly wicked and profligate, as he asserts, but did not exist at all according to the foregoing theory—a theory

istam rationem, quam disputatio de re publica inter magnos eius tum principes habita patefecit. Sicut etiam ipse Tullius non Scipionis nec cuiusquam alterius, sed suo sermone loquens in principio quinti libri commemorato prius Enni poetae versu, quo dixerat:

Moribus antiquis res stat Romana virisque,

"quem quidem" ille "versum," inquit, "vel brevitate vel veritate tamquam ex oraculo quodam mihi esse effatus videtur. Nam neque viri, nisi ita morata civitas fuisset, neque mores, nisi hi viri praefuissent, aut fundare aut tam diu tenere potuissent tantam et tam vaste lateque imperantem rem publicam. Itaque ante nostram memoriam et mos ipse patrius praestantes viros adhibebat, et veterem morem ac maiorum instituta retinebant excellentes viri. Nostra vero aetas cum rem publicam sicut picturam accepisset egregiam, sed evanescentem vetustate, non modo eam coloribus isdem quibus fuerat renovare neglexit, sed ne id quidem curavit, ut formam saltem eius et extrema tamquam liniamenta servaret. Quid enim manet ex antiquis moribus, quibus ille dixit rem stare Romanam, quos ita oblivione obsoletos videmus, ut non modo non colantur, sed iam ignorentur? Nam de viris quid dicam? Mores enim ipsi interierunt virorum penuria, cuius tanti mali non modo reddenda ratio nobis, sed etiam tamquam reis capitis quodam modo dicenda causa est. Nostris enim

---

[1] Cicero, *Republic* 5.1.

that was developed in an argument about the state in which the great leaders of the time took part. Cicero, also, speaking in his own person and not in the character of Scipio or someone else, had, at the beginning of the fifth book, quoted the line of the poet Ennius in which he had said:

> The ancient ways maintain the Roman state,
> Its ancient heroes, too.[1]

" This line," says Cicero, " by virtue both of its brevity and of its truth, seems to me to have been such as might come from some oracle. Neither could the men, unless the ways of the state had been what they were, nor those ways unless these men had presided, have established or so long preserved a state with such vast and widespread domains. And so, before any time that we recall, on the one hand the traditional way of life itself supplied outstanding men, and these superior men upheld the ancient way and the institutions of their fathers. Our age, however, having received the republic like a painting high in merit but fading with age, has not only failed to restore it to its former colours but has not taken the trouble even to preserve at least the outline of it and, as it were, the last remains of its design. For what remains of the ancient ways, which, Ennius said, maintained the Roman state? We see them so far sunk in oblivion that not only are they not pursued; men are not even aware that they existed. And what shall I say about our men? Why, the old ways themselves were lost by a dearth of men. Not only must we be held responsible for that great affliction, but we must in a way plead as if in court on a capital charge. It is to our vices, not to any ill fortune, that

223

vitiis, non casu aliquo, rem publicam verbo retinemus, re ipsa vero iam pridem amisimus."

Haec Cicero fatebatur, longe quidem post mortem Africani, quem in suis libris fecit de re publica disputare, adhuc tamen ante adventum Christi; quae si diffamata et praevalescente religione Christiana sentirentur atque dicerentur, quis non istorum ea Christianis inputanda esse censeret? Quam ob rem cur non curarunt dii eorum, ne tunc periret atque amitteretur illa res publica, quam Cicero longe antequam Christus in carne venisset tam lugubriter deplorat amissam? Viderint laudatores eius etiam illis antiquis viris et moribus qualis fuerit, utrum in ea viguerit vera iustitia an forte nec tunc fuerit viva moribus, sed picta coloribus; quod et ipse Cicero nesciens, cum eam praeferret, expressit.

Sed alias, si Deus voluerit, hoc videbimus. Enitar enim suo loco, ut ostendam secundum definitiones ipsius Ciceronis, quibus quid sit res publica et quid sit populus loquente Scipione breviter posuit (adtestantibus etiam multis sive ipsius sive eorum quos loqui fecit in eadem disputatione sententiis), numquam illam fuisse rem publicam, quia numquam in ea fuerit vera iustitia. Secundum probabiliores autem definitiones pro suo modo quodam res publica fuit, et melius ab antiquioribus Romanis quam a posterioribus administrata est; vera autem iustitia non est nisi in ea re publica, cuius conditor rectorque Christus est, si et ipsam rem publicam placet dicere, quoniam eam

---

[1] See below 19.21.

we owe it that we preserve merely the name of a republic, having long since lost the reality."

Such was Cicero's statement of the case, made, to be sure, long after the death of Africanus, whom he made one of the disputants in his books *On the Republic*, but still before the coming of Christ. If such a verdict had been formulated and stated after the heralding and triumph of the Christian religion, who of our opponents would not have thought them attributable to the Christians? Why and for what reason did their gods take no steps to prevent the collapse and loss of that republic which Cicero long before the Incarnation so gloomily laments as lost? Its admirers should consider whether, even in the time of ancient ways and men, true justice flourished in it, or whether perhaps even then its justice was not something kept alive by the old ways, but some lively painting. Even Cicero himself, without knowing it, betrayed the fact when he brought in his " painting."

However, if God wills, we shall examine the matter elsewhere,[1] for in the proper place I shall strive to show that, according to the definitions of Cicero himself, making Scipio his spokesman, when he succinctly laid down what a state is and what a people—definitions supported by many pronouncements both of his own and of characters whom he represented as taking part in that debate—that state never existed, because true justice never resided in it. If we follow, however, definitions easier to justify, there was a commonwealth of a certain sort, and it was better administered by the earlier Romans than the later. True justice, however, exists only in that republic whose Founder and Ruler is Christ, if you please to call it too a republic, since we cannot deny

rem populi esse negare non possumus. Si autem hoc nomen, quod alibi aliterque vulgatum est, ab usu nostrae locutionis est forte remotius, in ea certe civitate est vera iustitia, de qua scriptura sancta dicit: *Gloriosa dicta sunt de te, civitas Dei.*

XXII

Quod diis Romanorum nulla umquam cura fuerit, ne malis moribus res publica deperiret.

SED quod pertinet ad praesentem quaestionem, quamlibet laudabilem dicant istam fuisse vel esse rem publicam, secundum eorum auctores doctissimos iam longe ante Christi adventum pessima ac flagitiosissima facta erat; immo vero nulla erat atque omnino perierat perditissimis moribus. Ut ergo non periret, dii custodes eius populo cultori suo dare praecipue vitae ac morum praecepta debuerunt, a quo tot templis, tot sacerdotibus et sacrificiorum generibus, tam multiplicibus variisque sacris, tot festis sollemnitatibus, tot tantorumque ludorum celebritatibus colebantur; ubi nihil daemones nisi negotium suum egerunt, non curantes quem ad modum illi viverent, immo curantes ut etiam perdite viverent, dum tamen honori suo illa omnia metu subditi ministrarent.

Aut si dederunt, proferatur ostendatur legatur, quas deorum leges illi civitati datas contempserint

---

[1] Psalms 87.3.

that it is a people's estate.   But though this name,
which is current with other associations and meanings,
is perhaps too far removed from common usage, the
fact remains that true justice resides in that city of
which the Holy Scriptures say, " Glorious things are
said of thee, O city of God." [1]

XXII

*That the Roman gods took no care to prevent the
republic from being ruined by bad morals.*

But in regard to the present question, however
admirable they say the republic was or is, by the
admission of their most learned writers it had already
become quite wicked and profligate long before the
coming of Christ; indeed, it no longer existed, and had
utterly perished by its complete moral bankruptcy.
To prevent its destruction, the protecting gods ought
to have made rules of life and conduct their first gift
to the nation that worshipped them in all those
temples, with all those priests and varieties of sacrifice, all those frequent and varied ceremonials, all
those anniversary feasts and all those celebrations of
those important games.   In all this the demons did
nothing but carry on their own business, not concerned how their worshippers lived, or rather, concerned that they should live perniciously, let them
but perform under the domination of fear all
those divine services in honour of the gods.
   If they did, on the other hand, give such rules, let
there be something produced, let there be something
displayed, let there be something read out, to indicate
what laws of the gods were ever given to be dis-

Gracchi ut seditionibus cuncta turbarent, quas
Marius et Cinna et Carbo ut in bella etiam pro-
grederentur civilia causis iniquissimis suscepta et
crudeliter gesta crudeliusque finita, quas denique
Sulla ipse, cuius vitam mores facta describente
Sallustio aliisque scriptoribus historiae quis non
exhorreat? Quis illam rem publicam non tunc perisse
fateatur?

An forte propter huiusce modi civium mores Vergi-
lianam illam sententiam, sicut solent, pro defensione
deorum suorum opponere audebunt:

> Discessere omnes adytis arisque relictis
> Di, quibus imperium hoc steterat?

Primum si ita est, non habent cur querantur de
religione Christiana, quod hac offensi eos dii sui
deseruerint, quoniam quidem maiores eorum iam
pridem moribus suis ab urbis altaribus tam multos ac
minutos deos tamquam muscas abegerunt. Sed
tamen haec numinum turba ubi erat, cum longe antequam mores corrumperentur antiqui a Gallis Roma
capta et incensa est? An praesentes forte dormie-
bant? Tunc enim tota urbe in hostium potestatem
redacta solus collis Capitolinus remanserat, qui etiam
ipse caperetur, nisi saltem anseres diis dormientibus
vigilarent. Unde paene in superstitionem Aegyp-
tiorum bestias avesque colentium Roma deciderat,
cum anseri sollemnia celebrabant.

---

[1] L. Cornelius Cinna and Gnaeus Papirius Carbo were
lieutenants of Marius in the civil war.

[2] Virgil, *Aeneid* 2.351 f.

regarded by the Gracchi when by their partisan bands they caused universal disorder, by Marius and Cinna and Carbo [1] when they moved on to civil wars undertaken for most dishonest reasons, waged ruthlessly and terminated more ruthlessly, or, to top all, by Sulla himself, whose life and character and deeds, as described by Sallust and other historians, were such that—what reader, I ask you, does not shudder at the recital? What reader will not admit that the republic then had perished?

Will they possibly have the audacity to reply in defence of their gods, as they usually do, that they abandoned the city because of the morals of the citizens of this type, and employ the words of the well-known lines of Virgil:

They have withdrawn, deserting shrine and altar; The gods have gone, once mainstay of our power.[2]

First, if this be so, then they have no cause to complain that the Christian religion so offended their gods as to make them abandon Rome, since, as we see, their forefathers had already by their immoral practices driven from the city's altars all those numerous and diminutive gods like so many flies. Really now, where was this crowd of divinities when, long before the ancient morals had decayed, Rome was taken and burned by the Gauls? Were they present then, perhaps, but asleep? For then the whole city was in the hands of the enemy, save only the Capitoline Hill, and this, too, was about to be taken, were it not that the geese at any rate were awake while the gods slept. Hence Rome sank almost to the level of the Egyptians, who worship beasts and birds, when the goose was honoured in annual ceremonies.

Verum de his adventiciis et corporis potius quam animi malis, quae vel ab hostibus vel alia clade accidunt, nondum interim disputo; nunc ago de labe morum, quibus primum paulatim decoloratis, deinde torrentis modo praecipitatis tanta quamvis integris tectis moenibusque facta est ruina rei publicae, ut magni auctores eorum eam tunc amissam non dubitent dicere. Recte autem abscesserant ut amitteretur omnes adytis arisque relictis di, si eorum de bona vita atque iustitia civitas praecepta contempserat. Nunc vero quales, quaeso, dii fuerunt, si noluerunt cum populo cultore suo vivere, quem male viventem non docuerant bene vivere?

XXIII

Varietates rerum temporalium non ex favore aut impugnatione daemonum, sed ex veri Dei pendere iudicio.

Quid quod etiam videntur eorum adfuisse cupiditatibus implendis, et ostenduntur non praefuisse refrenandis, qui enim Marium novum hominem et ignobilem, cruentissimum auctorem bellorum civilium atque gestorem, ut septiens consul fieret adiuverunt atque ut in septimo suo consulatu moreretur senex ne in manus Sullae futuri mox victoris inrueret. Si enim ad haec eum dii eorum non iuverunt, non parum est quod fatentur etiam non propitiis diis suis posse accidere homini istam temporalem, quam nimis

But such accidental evils, evils physical rather than spiritual, that are inflicted by enemies or some other calamity, are not for the moment my theme. My present concern is with the decay of morality, those morals that first dwindled by degrees, but later dashed headlong like a cascade till, though the houses and fortifications still stood intact, the republic was so far gone that their great writers frankly report it as a lost cause. Moreover, the gods had rightly departed to permit its loss, abandoning shrines and altars, if so be the city had ignored their precepts of right living and justice. As it is, though, what value must we set on gods who declined to live with a nation that worshipped them, when, though it led an evil life, they did not instruct it how to lead a good life?

XXIII

That the vicissitudes of this life depend not on the favour or hostility of the demons but on the judgement of the true God.

WHAT about their even, so it seems, assisting in the satisfaction of their lusts and, as is manifest, not sponsoring any restraint of them? Marius, for example, a self-made man not of noble birth, a most bloody inciter and wager of civil wars, was helped by them to reach the consulship seven times and to die, full of years, in his seventh consulship, to prevent his falling into the hands of Sulla, who was soon to be victorious. For if they did not help him to attain these successes, to have the fact admitted is no small gain—the fact that a man, even when not supported by their gods, may reach so high a peak of the

231

diligunt, tantam felicitatem et posse homines, sicut
fuit Marius, salute viribus, opibus honoribus, dignitate
longaevitate cumulari et perfrui diis iratis; posse
etiam homines, sicut fuit Regulus, captivitate servitute inopia, vigiliis doloribus excruciari et emori diis
amicis.   Quod si ita esse concedunt, compendio nihil
eos prodesse et coli superfluo confitentur.

Nam si virtutibus animi et probitati vitae, cuius
praemia post mortem speranda sunt, magis contraria
ut populus disceret institerunt; si nihil etiam in his
transeuntibus et temporalibus bonis vel eis quos
oderunt nocent, vel eis quos diligunt prosunt, ut quid
coluntur, ut quid tanto studio colendi requiruntur?
Cur laboriosis tristibusque temporibus, tamquam
offensi abscesserint, murmuratur et propter eos
Christiana religio conviciis indignissimis laeditur?   Si
autem habent in his rebus vel beneficii vel maleficii
potestatem, cur in eis adfuerunt pessimo viro Mario,
et optimo Regulo defuerunt?   An ex hoc ipsi in-
telleguntur iniustissimi et pessimi?   Quod si propterea magis timendi et colendi putantur, neque hoc
putentur; neque enim minus eos invenitur Regulus
coluisse quam Marius.

worldly success that they love overmuch, and that men like Marius may be blessed in abundance with health, strength, wealth, high offices, respect and long life, and enjoy these blessings all their days, though the gods be wroth with them, and also the fact that men of the stamp of Regulus may be tormented by captivity, bondage, poverty, sleeplessness and pain, and die a cruel death, though the gods be friendly to them. If they grant this point, they confess in brief that the gods bring no advantage and that their worship is superfluous.

For granted that, instead of teaching the qualities of character and the honesty of a life whose rewards must be hopefully sought after death, they rather saw to it that just the opposite lessons were inculcated in the people, granted too that even in the sphere of these temporary and transitory blessings they neither injure any whom they hate nor advance the cause of any whom they love, to what end are they worshipped, to what end do those who are so eager to worship them demand the privilege? Why is there murmuring in periods of hardship and sorrow that they must have withdrawn because they were offended, so that for their sakes the Christian religion becomes the undeserving target of abuse? If, on the other hand, they are capable of doing good or harm in such matters, why did they assist the worst of men, Marius, but fail the best of men, Regulus, in such matters? Should we not conclude from this that they are utterly unjust and wicked? And if that is thought to be reason to fear and worship them the more, let the pagans not think that either, for it is not the case that Regulus worshipped the gods less than Marius.

233

Nec ideo vita pessima eligenda videatur, quia magis Mario quam Regulo dii favisse existimantur. Metellus enim Romanorum laudatissimus, qui habuit quinque filios consulares, etiam rerum temporalium felix fuit, et Catilina pessimus oppressus inopia et in bello sui sceleris prostratus infelix, et verissima atque certissima felicitate praepollent boni Deum colentes, a quo solo conferri potest.

Illa igitur res publica malis moribus cum periret, nihil dii eorum pro dirigendis vel pro corrigendis egerunt moribus, ne periret; immo depravandis et corrumpendis addiderunt moribus ut periret. Nec se bonos fingant quod velut offensi civium iniquitate discesserint. Prorsus ibi erant; produntur, convincuntur; nec subvenire praecipiendo nec latere tacendo potuerunt. Omitto quod Marius a miserantibus Minturnensibus Maricae deae in luco eius commendatus est, ut ei omnia prosperaret, et ex summa desperatione reversus incolumis in Urbem duxit crudelem crudelis exercitum; ubi quam cruenta, quam incivilis hostilique inmanior eius victoria fuerit, eos qui scripserunt legant qui volunt.

Sed hoc, ut dixi, omitto, nec Maricae nescio cui tribuo Marii sanguineam felicitatem, sed occultae potius providentiae Dei ad istorum ora claudenda

---

[1] Q. Caecilius Metellus Macedonicus, conqueror of the Achaean League.
[2] Marius was taken prisoner (88 B.C.) in the marshes of Minturnae, but cowed the soldier who would have slain him.

Nor is it a reason for choosing to live a wicked life, that the gods are thought to have shown more favour to Marius than to Regulus, since Metellus,[1] a man most highly esteemed among the Romans, who had five sons that became consuls, was also fortunate in the goods of this world, while the paragon of vice, Catiline, being reduced to poverty and overthrown in the war brought on by his own crime, was unfortunate. Moreover, the truest and surest good fortune is mainly the portion of the good who worship God, by whom alone it can be bestowed.

Therefore, when that republic was perishing as a result of its evil ways, the gods it worshipped made no move either to direct or to correct its ways that it might not perish. No indeed, they used their influence to deprave and corrupt them that it might perish. Let them not pose as good gods on the ground that they had withdrawn, being offended by the iniquities of the citizens. Without a doubt they were present; they are exposed, they are convicted. They had no power to help by admonition, no power to conceal themselves by silence. I pass over the fact that the compassionate people of Minturnae commended Marius to the goddess Marica in her grove that she might grant him success in every undertaking, and that he escaped from a most desperate situation and returned unharmed to Rome, a ruthless commander of a ruthless army.[2] Let those who wish to know how bloody his victory was, how unworthy of a citizen, and how much more savage than a foe's, read the historical writers.

But as I say, I omit this; and I do not attribute the blood-stained fortune of Marius to Marica, whoever she may be, but rather to the secret prudence of God,

eosque ab errore liberandos qui non studiis agunt sed
haec prudenter advertunt, quia, etsi aliquid in his
rebus daemones possunt, tantum possunt quantum
secreto omnipotentis arbitrio permittuntur, ne magni-
pendamus terrenam felicitatem, quae sicut Mario
malis etiam plerumque conceditur, nec eam rursus
quasi malam arbitremur, cum ea multos etiam pios ac
bonos unius veri Dei cultores invitis daemonibus
praepolluisse videamus, nec eosdem inmundissimos
spiritus vel propter haec ipsa bona malave terrena
propitiandos aut timendos existimemus, quia, sicut
ipsi mali homines in terra, sic etiam illi non omnia
quae volunt facere possunt, nisi quantum illius
ordinatione sinitur, cuius plene iudicia nemo conpre-
hendit, iuste nemo reprehendit.

XXIV

*De Sullanis actibus, quorum se daemones ostentaverint
adiutores.*

SULLA certe ipse, cuius tempora talia fuerunt, ut
superiora, quorum vindex esse videbatur, illorum
comparatione quaererentur, cum primum ad Urbem
contra Marium castra movisset, adeo laeta exta
immolanti fuisse scribit Livius, ut custodiri se Postumius haruspex voluerit capitis supplicium subiturus,
nisi ea, quae in animo Sulla haberet, diis iuvantibus
implevisset.   Ecce non discesserant adytis atque aris

---

[1] Fragment 16, from Book 67.

providing a means to stop their mouths and to free
from error such as are not fanatics but with open
minds give heed to this truth—that, even though the
demons may have some power in these matters, they
have only so much power as they are allowed to have
by the secret ordinance of the Almighty, whereby he
ensures our not greatly valuing earthly good fortune,
which is also commonly granted to bad men like
Marius, and also ensures on the other hand our not
regarding it as a bad thing, since we see that many
religious and good worshippers of the one true God
have also been specially endowed with it despite the
demons; and finally, he ensures our not supposing
that these same utterly unclean demons are to be
propitiated or feared for the sake of these earthly
blessings or evils. For, as wicked human beings on
earth cannot do all they wish, neither can the demons,
except in so far as they are permitted by the decrees
of him whose judgements are by none fully compre-
hended and by none justly reprehended.

XXIV

*On Sulla's deeds in which the demons displayed
themselves as his helpers.*

It is certain that Sulla—whose period was of a sort
to make men compare and regret the earlier period of
which he was held to be the chastiser—when he first
advanced to Rome in his campaign against Marius,
found the entrails so favourable that, as Livy writes,[1]
the diviner Postumius was willing to be held for
execution if Sulla did not make good his hopes with
assistance from the gods. The gods, you see, had not

237

relictis di, quando de rerum eventu praedicebant
nihilque de ipsius Sullae correctione curabant.
Promittebant praesagando felicitatem magnam nec
malam cupiditatem minando frangebant. Deinde
cum esset in Asia bellum Mithridaticum gerens, per
Lucium Titium ei mandatum est a Iove quod esset
Mithridatem superaturus, et factum est.

Ac postea molienti redire in Urbem et suas
amicorumque iniurias civili sanguine ulcisci, iterum
mandatum est ab eodem Iove per militem quendam
legionis sextae, prius se de Mithridate praenuntiasse
victoriam, et tunc promittere daturum se potestatem
qua recuperaret ab inimicis rem publicam non sine
multo sanguine. Tum percontatus Sulla, quae forma
militi visa fuerit, cum ille indicasset, eam recordatus
est quam prius ab illo audierat qui de Mithridatica
victoria ab eodem mandata pertulerat.

Quid hic responderi potest, quare dii curaverint
velut felicia ista nuntiare, et nullus eorum curaverit
Sullam monendo corrigere mala tanta facturum
scelestis armis civilibus qualia non foedarent, sed
auferrent omnino rem publicam? Nempe intelle-
guntur daemones, sicut saepe dixi notumque nobis
est in litteris sacris resque ipsae satis indicant,
negotium suum agere, ut pro diis habeantur et

---

[1] Julius Obsequens, *Prodigies* 116.

departed from the temples and abandoned the shrines, for they made predictions and quite neglected to correct Sulla himself. By forecasts they assured him of great success, nor checked by forewarning the course of his base passion. Later, when he was conducting in Asia the war against Mithridates, through the agency of Lucius Titius[1] there came to him a message from Jupiter saying that he would conquer Mithridates, and so it was in fact.

Afterwards, when he was planning to return to the city to avenge with the blood of citizens his own wrongs and those of his friends, he again received a message from that same Jupiter through the agency of a certain soldier in the Sixth Legion, saying that the god had earlier been harbinger of victory over Mithridates, and now promised to give him such power as would enable him to regain control of the state from his enemies, though not without much bloodshed. Sulla then inquired what shape had appeared to the soldier, and when he had described it, was reminded of the one reported earlier by the man who had brought the message about victory over Mithridates from the same source.

What explanation can there be here for the pains that the gods took to announce such events as if they were fortunate when none of them was at pains to warn and reform Sulla, though by the crime of civil war he was to inflict such injuries on the state as not merely to cripple but to extinguish it altogether? Is it not taken for granted, as I have often said, and as we are warned in our holy scriptures, though the facts speak for themselves, that the demons mind their own business; and that is to pose as gods and be worshipped, to see that shows are provided in their

colantur, ut ea illis exhibeantur quibus hi qui ex-
hibent sociati unam pessimam causam cum eis
habeant in iudicio Dei.

Deinde cum venisset Tarentum Sulla atque ibi
sacrificasset, vidit in capite vitulini iecoris simili-
tudinem coronae aureae. Tunc Postumius haruspex
ille respondit praeclaram significare victoriam iussit-
que ut extis illis solus vesceretur. Postea parvo
intervallo servus cuiusdam Luci Pontii vaticinando
clamavit : " A Bellona nuntius venio, victoria tua est,
Sulla." Deinde adiecit arsurum esse Capitolium.
Hoc cum dixisset, continuo egressus e castris postero
die concitatior reversus est et Capitolium arsisse
clamavit. Arserat autem re vera Capitolium. Quod
quidem daemoni et praevidere facile fuit et celerrime
nuntiare.

Illud sane intende, quod ad causam maxime pertinet, sub qualibus diis esse cupiant qui blasphemant
Salvatorem voluntates fidelium a dominatu daemonum liberantem. Clamavit homo vaticinando : " Victoria tua est, Sulla," atque ut id divino spiritu clamare
crederetur, nuntiavit etiam aliquid et prope futurum
et mox factum unde longe aberat per quem ille
spiritus loquebatur; non tamen clamavit : " Ab
sceleribus parce, Sulla," quae illic victor tam horrenda
commisit, cui corona aurea ipsius victoriae inlustrissi-
mum signum in vitulino iecore apparuit.

Qualia signa si dii iusti dare solerent ac non
daemones impii, profecto illis extis nefaria potius

---

[1] Plutarch, *Sulla* 27.
[2] The goddess of war.
[3] On July 6th, 83 B.C. the Capitol burned. See Platner-
Ashby, *Topographical Dictionary of Ancient Rome* (London,
1929), 299.

honour such that those who offer them become their partners doomed to appear before the judgement seat of God along with them in one damning indictment.

Afterwards, when Sulla had come to Tarentum and had sacrificed there, he saw on the head of the calf's liver the likeness of a golden crown. Then that diviner Postumius interpreted this to mean that there would be a great victory, and ordered that Sulla alone should eat of the vital parts.[1] A little later the slave of a certain Lucius Pontius cried out in a trance, " I come as a messenger from Bellona.[2] The victory is yours, Sulla." Then he added that the Capitol would burn. When he said this, he at once left the camp, but on the next day returned in greater excitement and cried out that the Capitol had burned. The Capitol had, in fact, burned.[3] For a demon it was easy both to foresee this and to report it with all speed.

Note, however, the character of the gods, a point most pertinent to our controversy, under whose sway those wish to live who revile a Saviour by whom the wills of the faithful are freed from slavery to demons. The man cried out in prophecy, " The victory is yours, Sulla," and to make it appear that the cry came by divine inspiration, he also announced that something would shortly happen and presently that it had happened, at a place which was far distant from the mouthpiece of that spirit. But he never cried out, " Refrain from crimes, Sulla! "—crimes so horrible that the victor committed when he arrived, yet he had been shown in a calf's liver a golden crown as the most glorious symbol of Victory herself.

If those who were wont to send such signs had been righteous gods and not wicked demons, then surely

atque ipsi Sullae graviter noxia mala futura monstrarent. Neque enim eius dignitati tantum profuit illa victoria, quantum nocuit cupiditati; qua factum est, ut inmoderatis inhians et secundis rebus elatus ac praecipitatus magis ipse periret in moribus, quam inimicos in corporibus perderet. Haec illi dii vere tristia vereque lugenda non extis, non auguriis, non cuiusquam somnio vel vaticinio praenuntiabant. Magis enim timebant ne corrigeretur quam ne vinceretur. Immo satis agebant ut victor civium gloriosus victus atque captivus nefandis vitiis et per haec ipsis etiam daemonibus multo obstrictius subderetur.

XXV

Quantum maligni spiritus ad flagitia incitent homines,
cum in committendis sceleribus quasi divinam
exempli sui interponunt auctoritatem.

Illinc vero quis non intellegat, quis non videat, nisi qui tales deos imitari magis elegit quam divina gratia ab eorum societate separari, quantum moliantur maligni isti spiritus exemplo suo velut divinam auctoritatem praebere sceleribus? Quod etiam in quadam Campaniae lata planitie, ubi non multo post civiles acies nefario proelio conflixerunt, ipsi inter se prius pugnare visi sunt. Namque ibi auditi sunt

---

[1] Julius Obsequens (*Prodigies* 118) says this occurred between Capua and Volturna and in the consulship of Scipio and Norbanus (85 B.C.).

in those entrails they would have provided evidence rather of evils to come, evils that were abominable and highly injurious even to Sulla. For that victory was not so benignant to his rise in the state as it was malignant to his lust, through which he became so immoderate in his greed, so carried aloft and dashed headlong by his successes that he himself suffered more disaster morally than he inflicted on his enemies corporeally. Here were truly sad, truly deplorable events, of which your far-famed gods gave warning neither by birds, nor by anyone's dream or trance. They had, of course, more to fear from his reform than from his defeat. Reform him indeed! No, they were content if the glorious victor in a civil war might be vanquished and held in bondage by vices unspeakable and so be far more inextricably subject to the demons themselves.

XXV

How strongly the evil spirits incite men to wickedness, when they authorize crimes by displaying their own supposedly divine example.

Who indeed would not conclude from this case, who would not see, unless it be one who prefers to take such gods as his models rather than by divine grace to part company with them, how hard these malevolent spirits strive by their example to furnish a sort of divine authority for crime? For they were even observed once upon a time apparently fighting among themselves at a certain broad plain in Campania where not long afterwards two Roman armies fought each other in abominable conflict. [1] At first

243

primum ingentes fragores, moxque multi se vidisse
nuntiarunt per aliquot dies duas acies proeliari.
Quae pugna ubi destitit, vestigia quoque velut
hominum et equorum, quanta de illa conflictatione
exprimi poterant, invenerunt. Si ergo veraciter
inter se numina pugnaverunt, iam bella civilia
excusantur humana; consideretur tamen quae sit
talium deorum vel malitia vel miseria.

Si autem se pugnasse finxerunt, quid aliud egerunt
nisi ut sibi Romani bellando civiliter tamquam
deorum exemplo nullum nefas admittere viderentur?
Iam enim coeperant bella civilia, et aliquot nefandorum proeliorum strages execranda praecesserat.
Iam multos moverat, quod miles quidam, dum occiso
spolia detraheret, fratrem nudato cadavere agnovit
ac detestatus bella civilia se ipsum ibi perimens
fraterno corpori adiunxit. Ut ergo huius tanti mali
minime taederet, sed armorum scelestorum magis
magisque ardor incresceret, noxii daemones, quos illi
deos putantes colendos et venerandos arbitrabantur,
inter se pugnantes hominibus apparere voluerunt,
nec [1] imitari tales pugnas civica trepidaret affectio,
sed potius humanum scelus divino excusaretur
exemplo.

Hac astutia maligni spiritus etiam ludos, unde
multa iam dixi, scaenicos sibi dicari sacrarique
iusserunt, ut [2] tanta deorum flagitia theatricis canticis

[1] *Dombart:* ne.
[2] *In L* ubi *but with* bi *erased; others* ubi, *but ut is needed, as
witness various MSS. which put it two lines below.*

there were heard loud noises, and then many reported
that they had seen two armies fighting for several
days. When this battle ceased, men also found there
footprints, as it were, of men and horses such as
might have been imprinted there in that conflict. If,
then, the divinities fought with one another in a
genuine battle, human beings have an excuse for
engaging in civil wars. Reflect though how full of
malice or misery such gods must be.

If, however, this battle was a mere pretence on
their part, what was the net result except that the
Romans should seem to be free from sin waging a
civil war, following as they did the example set by the
gods? For the series of civil wars had already
commenced and there had been several cases of
accursed slaughter in abominable battles. Many had
already been deeply moved by the story of a soldier
who, stripping a corpse of its armour, recognized it as
that of his slain brother, then, uttering curses on civil
wars and slaying himself, united his body with this
brother's. Consequently, it was to forestall any
least repentance of the so great evil, and instead to
make the lust for unholy battles rage more and more,
that harmful demons, thought by the Romans to be
worthy of reverent veneration, inasmuch as they held
them to be gods, chose to be seen by men engaged in
civil conflict; they did not want the fellow-feeling of
citizens to shrink from imitating such battles, but
rather chose that the human crime should be excused
by the divine example.

The same guile also motivated these malign spirits
when they ordered the dedication and consecration to
themselves of the performances of which I have
already said a good deal. In these all those disgrace-

atque fabularum actionibus celebrata et quisquis eos fecisse crederet et quisquis non crederet, sed tamen illos libentissime sibi talia exhiberi cerneret, securus imitaretur. Ne quis itaque existimaret in deos convicia potius quam eis dignum aliquid scriptitasse, ubicumque illos inter se pugnasse poetae commemorarunt, ipsi ad decipiendos homines poetarum carmina firmaverunt, pugnas videlicet suas non solum per scaenicos in theatro, verum etiam per se ipsos in campo humanis oculis exhibentes.

Haec dicere compulsi sumus, quoniam pessimis moribus civium Romanam rem publicam iam antea perditam fuisse nullamque remansisse ante adventum Christi Iesu domini nostri auctores eorum dicere et scribere minime dubitarunt. Quam perditionem diis suis non inputant, qui mala transitoria, quibus boni, seu vivant seu moriantur, perire non possunt, Christo nostro inputant, cum Christus noster tanta frequentet pro moribus optimis praecepta contra perditos mores, dii vero ipsorum nullis talibus praeceptis egerint aliquid cum suo cultore populo pro illa re publica, ne periret—immo eosdem mores velut suis exemplis auctoritate noxia corrumpendo egerunt potius ut periret.

Quam non ideo tunc perisse quisquam, ut arbitror, iam dicere audebit, quia " discessere omnes adytis

ful actions of the gods were represented in musical performances and the acting of plays in order that both he who believed the stories and he who did not— for in any case he observed that the gods were highly pleased to see such tales exhibited in their honour— might follow the example set without misgivings. Consequently to prevent anyone supposing that the poets had been insulting the gods in their scribbling, instead of suiting the tale to their real quality, whenever they recorded battles of gods against gods, the gods themselves to deceive mankind supported the poets' compositions by exhibiting to human eyes battles obviously theirs, not merely interpreted by actors on the stage, but enacted in person on the battlefield.

We have been compelled to say these things because their writers had no hesitation in saying and in writing that the utterly corrupt morals of the citizens had already destroyed the Roman republic and that it had quite vanished before the coming of our Lord Jesus Christ. Though they do not impute this destruction to their own gods, yet they impute to our Christ the temporary evils of this life by which good men cannot be destroyed, whether they live or die. They do so in face of the fact that our Christ provides an abundance of maxims in support of the highest morality as opposed to basest immorality, while their own gods never published any such maxims for the nation that worships them, to save their state from destruction. Indeed, they have rather brought about its destruction by corrupting those morals through the hurtful influence of their own example.

No one, I think, will be so bold as to say that the republic perished then because " all the gods departed

arisque relictis di," velut amici virtutibus, cum vitiis
hominum offenderentur; quia tot signis extorum
auguriorum vaticiniorum, quibus se tamquam prae-
scios futurorum adiutoresque proeliorum iactare et
commendare gestiebant, convincuntur fuisse praesentes; qui si vere abscessissent, mitius Romani in
bella civilia suis cupiditatibus quam illorum instiga-
tionibus exarsissent.

XXVI

*De secretis daemonum monitis, quae pertinebant ad
bonos mores, cum palam in sacris eorum omnis
nequitia disceretur.*

QUAE cum ita sint, cum palam aperteque turpi-
itudnes crudelitatibus mixtae, opprobria numinum et
crimina, sive prodita sive conficta, ipsis exposcentibus
te nisi fieret irascentibus etiam certis et statutis
sollemnitatibus consecrata illis et dicata claruerint,
atque ad omnium oculos ut imitanda proponerentur,
spectanda processerint, quid est, quod idem ipsi
daemones, qui se huiusce modi voluptatibus inmundos
esse spiritus confitentur, qui suis flagitiis et facinoribus, sive indicatis sive simulatis, eorumque sibi
celebratione petita ab inpudentibus, extorta a
pudentibus auctores se vitae scelestae inmundaeque
testantur, perhibentur tamen in adytis suis secretis-
que penetralibus dare quaedam bona praecepta de

---

[1] *Sacratis* obviously refers to μύσται. See Souter, *Glossary
of Later Latin*, p. 360, *s.v.* sacramentum [= μυστήριον].
The connecting thought may be that initiates are bound by an
oath not to divulge teachings received in the mysteries.

and left the shrines and altars," as if they were the friends of virtue and were offended by men's vices. The many omens derived from inspection of entrails, from birds, from trances, which they eagerly made use of to vaunt and commend themselves as foreknowing the future and assisting in battle, prove that they were still there. Had they really departed, the Romans in their civil wars would have raged more gently, moved only by their own lusts without the prodding of the gods.

XXVI

Whether the demons gave moral instruction in secret while in their sacrifices wickedness was openly taught.

SINCE this is so, seeing that the mingled obscenities and atrocities, the disgraceful crimes, real or imaginary, of the gods, have been publicly and openly advertised, being consecrated and dedicated to them in fixed and prescribed festivals at their own request, the denial of which would have aroused their anger, and have therefore been presented for all to see, put forward as models to be imitated, why is it that these same demons who, by indulging in pleasures of this kind, acknowledge that they are unclean spirits, and who by their own profligate and wicked deeds, actual or alleged, and by the celebration of these deeds, a thing which the shameless gods requested, but the shamefast granted only by compulsion, testify that they are sponsors of a wicked and polluted life—why are they, nevertheless, generally believed to vouchsafe some good moral precepts to some few, chosen, as it were, to be initiates,[1] in their forbidden shrines and

249

moribus quibusdam velut electis sacratis suis? Quod si ita est, hoc ipso callidior advertenda est et convincenda malitia spirituum noxiorum.

Tanta enim vis est probitatis et castitatis, ut omnis vel paene omnis eius laude moveatur humana natura, nec usque adeo sit turpitudine vitiosa, ut totum sensum honestatis amiserit. Proinde malignitas daemonum, nisi alicubi *se*, quem ad modum scriptum in nostris litteris novimus, *transfiguret in angelos lucis*, non implet negotium deceptionis. Foris itaque populis celeberrimo strepitu impietas impura circumsonat, et intus paucis castitas simulata vix sonat; praebentur propatula pudendis et secreta laudandis; decus latet et dedecus patet; quod malum geritur omnes convocat spectatores, quod bonum dicitur vix aliquos invenit auditores, tamquam honesta erubescenda sint et inhonesta glorianda. Sed ubi hoc nisi in daemonum templis? Ubi nisi in fallaciae diversoriis? Illud enim fit ut honestiores, qui pauci sunt, capiantur; hoc autem, ne plures, qui sunt turpissimi, corrigantur.

Ubi et quando sacrati Caelestis audiebant castitatis praecepta, nescimus; ante ipsum tamen delubrum, ubi simulacrum illud locatum conspiciebamus, universi undique confluentes et ubi quisque poterat stantes

---

[1] 2 Corinthians 11.14.   [2] See above 2.4.

secret inner rooms? If this be so, so much the more crafty is the malice of these pestilent spirits, malice that we must mark well and confute.

For so great is the force of probity and chastity that all or nearly all humanity is moved by the praise of these virtues, nor is any man so depraved by indecency that he has lost all feeling for honesty. Accordingly, the evil designs of the demons, if they do not on occasion, in the familiar words of Scripture,[1] " transform themselves into angels of light," are unsuccessful in their efforts to deceive. Thus it is that foul irreligion makes the welkin ring with the applause of a great multitude where throngs are gathered outside, while the voice of counterfeit chastity is barely audible to a handful on the inside. Indecency is accommodated with a public platform, nobility with a private hearing. Propriety is concealed, impropriety revealed. When evil is seen in action, all are summoned to the spectacle; when good is expressed in words, barely a few are found to give ear, as if things honourable were matter for blushes, things dishonourable for celebration. But where do we find it so, save in the temples of the demons; where, save in the haunts of deceit? For one performance is designed to entrap the better class, who are few; the other performance is designed for the majority, who are utterly vile, to prevent their reform.

Where and when those initiated into the mysteries of Caelestis [2] heard any admonitions to chastity, we do not know. On the other hand, before the very shrine in which her image was placed for all to gaze upon, with one accord we streamed in from all sides and, standing each where he could, we would watch

ludos qui agebantur intentissime spectabamus, in-
tuentes alternante conspectu hinc meretriciam
pompam, illinc virginem deam; illam suppliciter
adorari, ante illam turpia celebrari; non ibi pudi-
bundos mimos, nullam verecundiorem scaenicam
vidimus; cuncta obscenitatis implebantur officia.

Sciebatur virginali numini quid placeret, et exhibe-
batur quod de templo domum matrona doctior repor-
taret. Nonnullae pudentiores avertebant faciem ab
impuris motibus scaenicorum et artem flagitii furtiva
intentione discebant. Hominibus namque vere-
cundabantur, ne auderent impudicos gestus ore libero
cernere; sed multo minus audebant sacra eius, quam
venerabantur, casto corde damnare. Hoc tamen
palam discendum praebebatur in templo, ad quod
perpetrandum saltem secretum quaerebatur in
domo, mirante nimium, si ullus ibi erat, pudore
mortalium, quod humana flagitia non libere homines
committerent, quae apud deos etiam religiose discerent iratos habituri, nisi etiam exhibere curarent.

Quis enim alius spiritus occulto instinctu nequissi-
mas agitans mentes et instat faciendis adulteriis et
pascitur factis, nisi qui etiam sacris talibus oblectatur,
constituens in templis simulacra daemonum, amans in
ludis simulacra vitiorum, susurrans in occulto verba
iustitiae ad decipiendos etiam paucos bonos, fre-

with straining eyes the action of the plays, fixing our eyes now on this side, where a band of harlots was arrayed, now on that, where a virgin goddess stood. The worshippers were praying for her favour, and in her presence obscene rites were celebrated. There we saw no modest mimes, no somewhat more respectable actress; all the requirements of obscenity were fulfilled.

Their learning was to know the pleasure of the virgin goddess; their display of it was such that a matron went home better instructed from the temple. Some, who were more modest, turned their faces from the indecent movements of the actors and learned the art of profligacy by stealthy observation. They were not so bold before human observers as to venture to gaze with frank eyes on immodest gestures; much less did they venture to condemn with chaste heart the rites of the goddess that they worshipped. Yet the thing that was openly enacted in the temple as a lesson to be learned must not be transacted in the home without a quest for privacy at least. Mortal modesty, if any was present, marvelled much that men might not freely indulge in the same ribald acts that they even learned as religious lessons in the worship of gods, whose anger they would feel if they so much as neglected to make a show of such acts.

What else should a spirit be that by secret prompting stirs up the basest minds and is both eager to see adultery committed and gloats on it, once it is committed? Must it not be one that also takes delight in such ceremonials, sets up in temples the counterfeits of demons, loves in plays to see vices counterfeited, one that whispers in secret some words of righteousness to deceive even the few that

quentans in aperto invitamenta nequitiae ad possidendos innumerabiles malos?

XXVII

*Quanta eversione publicae disciplinae Romani diis
suis placandis sacraverint obscena ludorum.*

VIR gravis et philosophaster Tullius aedilis futurus clamat in auribus civitatis, inter cetera sui magistratus officia sibi Floram matrem ludorum celebritate placandam; qui ludi tanto devotius, quanto turpius celebrari solent. Dicit alio loco iam consul in extremis periculis civitatis, et ludos per decem dies factos, neque rem ullam quae ad placandos deos pertineret praetermissam; quasi non satius erat tales deos inritare temperantia quam placare luxuria, et eos honestate etiam ad inimicitias provocare quam tanta deformitate lenire.

Neque enim gravius fuerant quamlibet crudelissima inmanitate nocituri homines, propter quos placabantur, quam nocebant ipsi, cum vitiositate foedissima placarentur. Quando quidem ut averteretur quod metuebatur ab hoste in corporibus, eo modo dii conciliabantur quo virtus debellaretur in mentibus, qui non opponerentur defensores oppugnatoribus

---

[1] The festival of this goddess of the crops in flower was celebrated at Rome on April 28th and May 1st. See Cicero, *Against Verres* 2.5.14.

[2] Cicero, *Catiline* 3.8.

are good, but openly broadcasts advertisements of
vice to gain possession of the wicked, who are more
than can be numbered?

XXVII

*That the obscenity of the propitiatory games did much
to subvert the morals of the republic.*

CICERO, a man of weight and a would-be philosopher, when about to become aedile, proclaims to
the listening city that among the other duties of his
office he must propitiate Mother Flora[1] by celebrating games. These games are regularly the more
devout, the more foully they are celebrated. In
another passage[2] he says, when he was consul and
the state in greatest peril, that the games had been
celebrated for ten days, and that nothing belonging to
the propitiation of the gods had been omitted, as if it
were not better to anger such gods by moderation
than to placate them with excesses, and to provoke
them even to hostility by honest living rather than to
mollify them by so great unseemliness.

For though the cruelty of those men had been
never so harsh who threatened the state, so that, to
escape them, the gods were to be propitiated, yet it
could not have done greater damage than was
already done by the very gods who were propitiated
by most disgustingly vicious exhibitions, forasmuch
as to avert the threatened damage to men's bodies
from the foe gods were placated by means that
wrought the defeat of virtue in men's hearts—the
kind of gods who would not face the foe to defend the
battlements against the attackers until after they had

255

moenium, nisi prius fierent expugnatores morum
bonorum.

Hanc talium numinum placationem petulantissi-
mam inpurissimam inpudentissimam nequissimam
inmundissimam, cuius actores laudanda Romanae
virtutis indoles honore privavit tribu movit, agnovit
turpes fecit infames, hanc, inquam, pudendam
veraeque religioni aversandam et detestandam talium
numinum placationem, fabulas in deos inlecebrosas
atque criminosas, haec ignominiosa deorum vel
scelerate turpiterque facta vel sceleratius turpiusque
conficta oculis et auribus publicis civitas tota discebat,
haec commissa numinibus placere cernebat, et ideo
non solum illis exhibenda, sed sibi quoque imitanda
credebat, non illud nescio quid velut bonum et
honestum, quod tam paucis et tam occulte dicebatur
(si tamen dicebatur), ut magis ne innotesceret, quam
ne non fieret, timeretur.

XXVIII

De Christianae religionis salubritate.

Ab istarum inmundissimarum potestatum tartareo
iugo et societate poenali erui per Christi nomen
homines et in lucem saluberrimae pietatis ab ilal
perniciosissimae impietatis nocte transferri queruntur

succeeded in overthrowing the citadel of morality by their own attack.

This appeasement of such divinities, utterly impudent, impure, shameless, wicked, unclean as it was, of which the performers were by the praiseworthy native virtue of the Romans disqualified for office, removed from the tribal lists, recognized as lewd, stamped as infamous—this appeasement of such divinities, I say, so shameful, so repulsive to true religion, so detestable, these stories of enticement and crime on the part of the gods, these infamous deeds that the gods either criminally and shamefully committed or that were even more criminally and more shamefully presented as fictions to the eyes and ears of the people, in these the whole city was schooled. They took these deeds to be pleasing to the gods, and hence not only believed them to be suitable for exhibition in their honour but also for imitation by themselves. As for whatever supposed good or honourable instruction there may have been, this was given, if at all, to so few and so secretly as to indicate greater fear on their part that it might be disclosed than that it might not be put into practice.

XXVIII

On the wholesomeness of Christianity.

WICKED and ungrateful wretches, enslaved in deep and fast bondage to that sinful spirit, are those who make complaint and murmur when by the name of Christ men are rescued from the hellish yoke of those unclean powers and from their fellowship in punishment, and are transported from the night of utterly

et murmurant iniqui et ingrati et illo nefario spiritu altius obstrictiusque possessi, quia populi confluunt ad ecclesiam casta celebritate, honesta utriusque sexus discretione, ubi audiant quam bene hic ad tempus vivere debeant, ut post hanc vitam beate semperque vivere mereantur, ubi sancta scriptura iustitiaeque doctrina de superiore loco in conspectu omnium personante et qui faciunt audiant ad prae-mium, et qui non faciunt audiant ad iudicium. Quo etsi veniunt quidam talium praeceptorum inrisores, omnis eorum petulantia aut repentina mutatione deponitur, aut timore vel pudore comprimitur. Nihil enim eis turpe ac flagitiosum spectandum imitandumque proponitur, ubi veri Dei aut praecepta insinuantur aut miracula narrantur, aut dona laudantur aut beneficia postulantur.

XXIX

De abiciendo cultu deorum cohortatio ad Romanos.

Haec potius concupisce, o indoles Romana lauda-bilis, o progenies Regulorum, Scaevolarum, Scipio-num, Fabriciorum; haec potius concupisce, haec ab illa turpissima vanitate et fallacissima daemonum malignitate discerne. Si quid in te laudabile natura-liter eminet, non nisi vera pietate purgatur atque perficitur, impietate autem disperditur et punitur. Nunc iam elige quid sequaris, ut non in te, sed in

fatal impiety into the light of utterly wholesome piety. They complain that the masses flock to church in chaste observance with a decorous separation of the sexes, where they are told that it is their duty to live a good life here on earth for a time in order, when it is over, to gain the prize of an eternal life of blessedness. There, from a raised platform visible to all, the Holy Scripture and instruction in righteousness are preached; and those who obey shall hear it to their profit, while those who disobey shall hear it for judgement against them. Although some enter who scoff at such teaching, all their impudence is either abandoned by a sudden change or is suppressed in fear or shame. Nothing lewd and vicious is there presented for observation or imitation. There the teachings of the true God are implanted, or his miracles are recounted, or his mercies are recited, or his benefits are solicited.

XXIX

Exhortation to the Romans to abandon worship of the gods.

DESIRE rather these things, O admirable Roman character, O offspring of men like Regulus, Scaevola, the Scipios and Fabricius. Desire rather these things, segregate them from that utterly vile inanity and utterly deceptive malignity of the demons. If there is in you naturally any special merit, true religion alone can refine and bring it to a perfect state; but irreligion drowns it out and consigns it to punishment. Choose without delay which way you will take, that you may win praise, not in yourself,

Deo vero sine ullo errore lauderis. Tunc enim tibi gloria popularis adfuit, sed occulto iudicio divinae providentiae vera religio quam eligeres defuit. Expergiscere, dies est, sicut experrecta es in quibusdam, de quorum virtute perfecta et pro fide vera etiam passionibus gloriamur, qui usquequaque adversus potestates inimicissimas confligentes easque fortiter moriendo vincentes " sanguine nobis hanc patriam peperere suo."

Ad quam patriam te invitamus et exhortamur ut eius adiciaris numero civium, cuius quodam modo asylum est vera remissio peccatorum. Non audias degeneres tuos Christo Christianisve detrahentes et accusantes velut tempora mala, cum quaerant tempora quibus non sit quieta vita, sed potius secura nequitia. Haec tibi numquam nec pro terrena patria placuerunt. Nunc iam caelestem arripe, pro qua minimum laborabis, et in ea veraciter semperque regnabis. Illic enim tibi non Vestalis focus, non lapis Capitolinus, sed Deus unus et verus

> nec metas rerum nec tempora ponit,
Imperium sine fine dabit.

Noli deos falsos fallacesque requirere ; abice potius atque contemne in veram emicans libertatem. Non sunt dii, maligni sunt spiritus, quibus aeterna tua felicitas poena est. Non tam Iuno Troianis, a quibus carnalem originem ducis, arces videtur invidisse Romanas, quam isti daemones, quos adhuc deos putas,

---

[1] Virgil, *Aeneid* 11.24 f.
[2] *Ibid.* 1.278 f.
[3] Virgil, *Ibid.* 4.234.

but in serving the true God with no deviation. You
had, of course, in those days popular renown, but by
the hidden dispensation of God's providence you had
no opportunity to choose the true faith. Awake, it is
now day, as you have already awakened in the case
of some in whose perfect virtue and even martyrdoms
for the true faith we glory, for they, contending
everywhere against most hostile powers and by their
brave death winning the victory, " have created by
their blood this fatherland for us." [1]

To this fatherland we invite you and urge you to
join the roster of the citizens of the city that offers its
own asylum, so to speak, in a genuine remission of
sins. Do not hearken to your degenerate sons who
asperse Christ and Christians, and denounce their era
as if the times were bad, since the times they require
are not a time of peaceful living, but of carefree
frivolity. You never approved such a goal even for
your earthly fatherland. Lay hold without delay on
the heavenly fatherland, which will cost you but the
slightest toil and will enable you to reign in the true
sense and forever. There thou shalt have no fire of
Vesta, no Capitoline stone, but the one true God

No times, no bounds will set to action
But grant an empire without end.[2]

Do not pursue false and fallacious gods. Abandon
them, rather, and despise them, break away into
true liberty. They are not gods, they are malignant
spirits, for whom your eternal happiness is their
punishment. Juno would appear to have begrudged
the Trojans,[3] from whom you trace your descent
after the flesh, their Roman citadels less than those
demons, whom you still hold to be gods, begrudge the

261

omni generi hominum sedes invident sempiternas.
Et tu ipsa non parva ex parte de talibus spiritibus
iudicasti, quando ludis eos placasti, et per quos
homines eosdem ludos fecisti, infames esse voluisti.
Patere asseri libertatem tuam adversus inmundos
spiritus, qui tuis cervicibus inposuerant sacrandam
sibi et celebrandam ignominiam suam. Actores
criminum divinorum removisti ab honoribus tuis;
supplica Deo vero ut a te removeat illos deos qui
delectantur criminibus suis, seu veris, quod igno-
miniosissimum est, seu falsis, quod malitiosissimum
est.

Bene, quod tua sponte histrionibus et scaenicis
societatem civitatis patere noluisti; evigila plenius!
Nullo modo his artibus placatur divina maiestas
quibus humana dignitas inquinatur. Quo igitur
pacto deos qui talibus delectantur obsequiis haberi
putas in numero sanctarum caelestium potestatum,
cum homines per quos eadem aguntur obsequia, non
putasti habendos in numero qualiumcumque civium
Romanorum?

Incomparabiliter superna est civitas clarior, ubi
victoria veritas, ubi dignitas sanctitas, ubi pax
felicitas, ubi vita aeternitas. Multo minus habet in
sua societate tales deos, si tu in tua tales homines
habere erubuisti. Proinde si ad beatam pervenire
desideras civitatem, devita daemonum societatem.
Indigne ab honestis coluntur, qui per turpes placantur. Sic isti a tua pietate removeantur purgatione

whole race of mankind their everlasting home. And you yourself have given a judgement of no small weight against them when you appeased them with games, yet decreed the men who performed the games to be infamous. Permit your liberty to be vindicated against those unclean spirits who upon your necks placed the yoke of dedicating to them and celebrating their own disgrace. You excluded from your honourable offices the performers of the divine crimes. Pray to the true God that he may exclude from your company those gods who delight in the sins they are charged with—their utter shame is exposed if the charges are true ; their utter malignity, if they are false.

It is well that you of your own accord gave no place in the fellowship of your city to actors and stage performers. But you must be even more alert. The divine majesty is not appeased by these arts that defile human dignity. How can gods who delight in such services be regarded as belonging to the roster of the holy powers of heaven, when the men by whom this worship is performed have not been thought by you worthy of a place, however low, on the roster of Roman citizens ?

Incomparably fairer is that heavenly city where victory is truth, where dignity is holiness, where peace is happiness, where life is eternity. Much less does it have in its fellowship such gods, for you blushed to have such men in yours. Therefore, if you desire to arrive in the blessed city, shun the fellowship of demons. They that are appeased by means of vile men are unworthy to be worshipped by honourable men. Let these gods be excluded from your religious honour by the purging of Christ, as those

Christiana, quo modo illi a tua dignitate remoti sunt notatione censoria.

De bonis autem carnalibus, quibus solis mali perfrui volunt, et de malis carnalibus, quae sola perpeti nolunt, quod neque in his habeant quam putantur habere isti daemones potestatem (quamquam si haberent, deberemus potius etiam ista contemnere quam propter ista illos colere et eos colendo ad illa quae nobis invident pervenire non posse), — tamen nec in istis eos hoc valere, quod hi putant qui propter haec eos coli oportere contendunt deinceps videbimus, ut hic sit huius voluminis modus.

men were excluded from your honourable estate by
the censor's blacklist.

Moreover, where carnal boons, which alone the
wicked desire to enjoy, and carnal evils, which alone
they wish to avoid, are concerned, we shall next show
that even in their case the demons aforesaid do not
have the power they are thought to have (although, if
they did have it, we ought rather to despise these
blessings as well than for the sake of them to worship
the demons and, by worshipping them, disqualify
ourselves for the boons they begrudge us). For
really even in carnal matters they lack the power
that those impute to them who argue that they
should be worshipped for such gains, as we shall see in
the following book, for we must set a limit at this
point to the present book.

BOOK III

LIBER III

I

De adversitatibus, quas solas mali metuunt et quas
semper passus est mundus, cum deos coleret.

IAM satis dictum arbitror de morum malis et animorum, quae praecipue cavenda sunt, nihil deos falsos populo cultori suo quo minus eorum malorum aggere premeretur subvenire curasse, sed potius ut maxime premeretur egisse.

Nunc de illis malis video dicendum quae sola isti perpeti nolunt, qualia sunt fames, morbus, bellum, exspoliatio, captivitas, trucidatio, et si qua similia iam in primo libro commemoravimus. Haec enim sola mali deputant mala, quae non faciunt malos; nec erubescunt inter bona quae laudant ipsi mali esse qui laudant, magisque stomachantur si villam malam habeant quam si vitam, quasi hoc sit hominis maximum bonum, habere bona omnia praeter se ipsum.

Sed neque talia mala, quae isti sola formidant, dii eorum, quando ab eis libere colebantur, ne illis acciderent obstiterunt. Cum enim variis per diversa

BOOK III

I

*On the evils that are all that the wicked fear and that
the world always suffered while it worshipped the
gods.*

ENOUGH has now been said, I think, to show that in
respect to social and personal vices, which are particularly to be avoided, the false gods did nothing
to assist the people that worshipped them to diminish
their oppression by the weight of those evils but
instead took action to increase such oppression to the
utmost.

It is now clear that I must speak about the evils
which alone they are unwilling to endure, such as
famine, disease, war, pillage, captivity, slaughter and
similar calamities that have already been mentioned
in the first book. Evil men regard as evils only those
things which do not make men evil, and they do not
blush to remain evil, in the midst of the good which
they praise, though themselves evil while they
praise. It upsets them more if their countryseat is
faulty than if their life is so, as though the greatest
good for a man were to have everything of his good
save himself.

But their gods did not prevent the occurrence of
those evils which alone they fear, even when they
worshipped them unhampered. At various times and

temporibus ante adventum Redemptoris nostri innumerabilibus nonnullisque etiam incredibilibus cladibus genus contereretur humanum, quos alios quam istos deos mundus colebat, excepto uno populo Hebraeo et quibusdam extra ipsum populum, ubicumque gratia divina digni occultissimo atque iustissimo Dei iudicio fuerunt?

Verum ne nimis longum faciam, tacebo aliarum usquequaque gentium mala gravissima. Quod ad Romam pertinet Romanumque imperium tantum loquar, id est ad ipsam proprie civitatem et quaecumque illi terrarum vel societate coniunctae vel condicione subiectae sunt, quae sint perpessae ante adventum Christi, cum iam ad eius quasi corpus rei publicae pertinerent.

II

An dii, qui et a Romanis et a Graecis similiter colebantur, causas habuerint, quibus Ilium paterentur exscindi.

PRIMUM ipsa Troia vel Ilium, unde origo est populi Romani, (neque enim praetereundum aut dissimulandum est quod et in primo libro adtigi) eosdem habens deos et colens cur a Graecis victum, captum atque deletum est? "Priamo, inquiunt, sunt reddita Laomedontea paterna periuria." Ergo verum est, quod Apollo atque Neptunus eidem Laomedonti mercennariis operibus servierunt? Illis quippe promisisse mercedem falsumque iurasse perhibetur. Miror Apollinem nominatum divinatorem in tanto

---

[1] Virgil, *Aeneid* 4.542; *Georgics* 1.502.

in different places before the coming of our Redeemer, the human race was harassed by countless
and in a few cases even unbelievable misfortunes;
in those days what gods but those did the world worship, except for the one Hebrew nation and apart
from it certain individuals, wherever any were found
worthy of divine grace by the utterly mysterious and
righteous judgement of God?

To shorten the argument, I shall not mention the
very severe calamities suffered by other nations
throughout the world. I shall speak only of such as
befell Rome and the Roman empire, that is, the city
properly so called and any lands that were joined to it
by alliance or subjected by conquest before the
coming of Christ, at a time when they had become
the body, you might say, of the republic.

II

*Whether the gods worshipped alike by Greeks and
Romans were justified in allowing the destruction
of Ilium.*

First of all, Troy or Ilium, from which the Roman
people is sprung (I must not pass over or cloak what I
also touched upon in the first book), possessed and
worshipped the same gods—why then was it conquered, captured, and destroyed by the Greeks?
They say, " Priam paid the penalty for the perjury
of his father Laomedon." [1] Then it is true that
Apollo and Neptune served Laomedon as hired
workers? He promised them pay, you know, according to the tale, and broke his oath. I am surprised
that Apollo, who bears the title of diviner, should have

opificio laborasse nescientem quod Laomedon fuerat
promissa negaturus. Quamquam nec ipsum Neptunum, patruum eius, fratrem Iovis, regem maris,
decuit ignarum esse futurorum. Nam hunc Homerus
de stirpe Aeneae, a cuius posteris Roma est, cum ante
illam urbem conditam idem poeta fuisse dicatur,
inducit magnum aliquid divinantem, quem etiam nube
rapuit, ut dicit, ne ab Achille occideretur,

> cuperet cum vertere ab imo,

quod apud Vergilium confitetur,

> Structa suis manibus periurae moenia Troiae.

Nescientes igitur tanti dii, Neptunus et Apollo,
Laomedontem sibi negaturum esse mercedem struc-
tores moenium Troianorum gratis et ingratis fuerunt.
    Videant ne gravius sit tales deos credere quam diis
talibus peierare. Hoc enim nec ipse Homerus facile
credidit, qui Neptunum quidem contra Troianos,
Apollinem autem pro Troianis pugnantem facit, cum
illo periurio ambos fabula narret offensos. Si igitur
fabulis credunt, erubescant talia colere numina; si
fabulis non credunt, non obtendant Troiana periuria,
aut mirentur deos periuria punisse Troiana, amasse
Romana. Unde enim coniuratio Catilinae in tanta
tamque corrupta civitate habuit etiam eorum gran-
dem copiam quos manus atque lingua periurio aut
sanguine civili alebat? Quid enim aliud totiens
senatores corrupti in iudiciis, totiens populus in
suffragiis vel in quibusque causis, quae apud eum

---

[1] Homer, *Iliad* 20.302–5.   [2] Virgil, *Aeneid* 5.810 f.

toiled away at so great a task, completely unaware that Laomedon was to refuse to pay what he had promised. For that matter Neptune too, his uncle, Jupiter's brother and king of the sea, should not have been blind to future events. For Homer, though the same poet is said to have lived before the founding of Rome, introduces him as divining that from the posterity of Aeneas, by whose descendants Rome was founded, something great would come.[1] He even snatched him up in a cloud, says the poet, that Achilles might not slay him, though, as is admitted in a passage of Virgil,

he wished to overthrow from top to base
Troy's perjured walls, the work of his own hands.[2]

Great gods, then, like Neptune and Apollo, in ignorance that Laomedon would refuse them pay, built the walls of Troy for thanks and for thankless people.

Let them consider whether it is not worse to believe in such gods than to swear falsely by them. For even Homer himself found the story hard to swallow, since he represents Neptune as fighting against the Trojans while Apollo fights for the Trojans, though in the tale both were offended by the fraudulent oath. If, therefore, they believe the stories, let them blush to worship such divinities; if they do not believe the stories, let them not make the Trojan perjury their excuse, or let them wonder why the gods punished the Trojan perjuries but loved those of the Romans. From what source did Catiline's conspiracy in that great and corrupt city draw so abundant a supply of men who lived by hand or tongue on perjury and civil slaughter? What other fault did the senators when bribed in the lawcourts so often commit, or the

contionibus agebantur, nisi etiam peierando peccabant? Namque corruptissimis moribus ad hoc mos iurandi servabatur antiquus, non ut ab sceleribus metu religionis prohiberentur, sed ut periuria quoque sceleribus ceteris adderentur.

III

Non potuisse offendi deos Paridis adulterio, quod inter ipsos traditur frequentatum.

NULLA itaque causa est, quare dii, quibus, ut dicunt, steterat illud imperium, cum a Graecis praevalentibus probentur victi, Troianis peierantibus fingantur irati. Nec adulterio Paridis, ut rursus a quibusdam defenduntur, ut Troiam desererent, suscensuerunt. Auctores enim doctoresque peccatorum esse adsolent, non ultores. " Urbem Romam," inquit Sallustius, " sicuti ego accepi, condidere atque habuere initio Troiani, qui Aenea duce profugi sedibus incertis vagabantur." Si ergo adulterium Paridis vindicandum numina censuerunt, aut magis in Romanis aut certe etiam in Romanis puniendum fuit, quia Aeneae mater hoc fecit. Sed quo modo in illo illud flagitium oderant qui in sua socia Venere non oderant (ut alia omittam) quod cum Anchise commiserat, ex quo Aenean pepererat? An quia illud factum est indignante Menelao, illud autem concedente Vulcano?

---

[1] Sallust, *Catiline* 6.1.

populace when voting or trying cases brought before the assembly? They certainly were guilty of perjury also. For when morals were most corrupt, the ancient practice of the oath was preserved, with the result, not so much that men were restrained from crimes by religious fear, as that perjury was added to the other crimes.

III

That the gods could not have been offended at the adultery of Paris, since they were, it is reported, so often guilty of the same crime.

THERE is consequently no reason for the assumption that the gods, by whom that empire had stood, were at the time when they are proved to have been conquered by the Greeks, angered by the Trojan perjury. Nor were they indignant at the adultery of Paris, as again some say in defence, so that they abandoned Troy. For they are in practice the authors and teachers of vice, not the avengers. " The city of Rome," says Sallust, " as I understand, was founded and inhabited at first by Trojans who, as exiles under Aeneas' leadership, wandered about without fixed homes." [1] If, therefore, the divinities thought fit to exact vengeance for the adultery of Paris, then the punishment should have been visited rather on the Romans or in any case on the Romans too, because Aeneas' mother was the agent. How comes it that they hated the sin in his case when they did not hate it in the case of their colleague Venus, who, not to mention other instances, had committed the sin with Anchises and had borne Aeneas? Is it because in the first instance Menelaus resented it; in the other,

275

Dii enim, credo, non zelant coniuges suas, usque adeo ut eas etiam cum hominibus dignentur habere communes.

Inridere fabulas fortassis existimor nec graviter agere tanti ponderis causam. Non ergo credamus, si placet, Aeneam esse Veneris filium ; ecce concedo, si nec Romulum Martis. Si autem illud, cur non et illud ? An deos fas est hominibus feminis, mares autem homines deabus misceri nefas ? Dura vel potius non credenda condicio, quod ex iure Veneris in concubitu Marti licuit, hoc in iure suo ipsi Veneri non licere. At utrumque firmatum est auctoritate Romana. Neque enim minus credidit recentior Caesar aviam Venerem quam patrem antiquior Romulus Martem.

IV

De sententia Varronis, qua utile esse dixit, ut se
homines diis genitos mentiantur.

DIXERIT aliquis : Itane tu ista credis ? Ego vero ista non credo. Nam et vir doctissimus eorum Varro falsa haec esse, quamvis non audacter neque fidenter, paene tamen fatetur. Sed utile esse civitatibus dicit, ut se viri fortes, etiamsi falsum sit, diis genitos esse credant, ut eo modo animus humanus velut divinae

276

Vulcan consented to it? For the gods, I suppose, are so free from jealousy of their wives that they even condescend to share them with men!

Perhaps I may be thought to ridicule mere myths and not to be treating so weighty a debate with the proper gravity. Then let us take the view, if you like, that Aeneas was not the son of Venus. I grant this, look you, stipulating that Romulus is not to be the son of Mars either. Moreover, is there any reason for accepting one belief and not the other? Does religion permit gods to have intercourse with women, but forbid men to consort with goddesses? A harsh or rather incredible provision it would be that permitted Mars by the right of Venus to do in venery what Venus herself was not permitted to do in her own right. In fact, both cases have the sanction of Rome, for in recent times Caesar believed no less that Venus was among his grandmothers than Romulus long ago believed Mars to be his father.

IV

On Varro's view that it is useful for men to adopt the fiction that they are descended from gods.

SOMEONE will say, " Do you really believe this? " I certainly do not believe it. Why, even Varro, their most learned man, though he does not boldly and assuredly confess that it is false, yet comes near to doing so. He does say that it is expedient in a commonwealth for brave men to believe, though it be a fiction, that they are descended from gods. It is a means whereby the minds of men, inspired by regarding their lineage as founded by a god, may more

277

stirpis fiduciam gerens res magnas adgrediendas praesumat audacius, agat vehementius et ob hoc impleat ipsa securitate felicius. Quae Varronis sententia expressa, ut potui, meis verbis cernis quam latum locum aperiat falsitati, ut ibi intellegamus plura iam sacra et quasi religiosa potuisse confingi, ubi putata sunt civibus etiam de ipsis diis prodesse mendacia.

V

Non probari quod dii adulterium Paridis punierint, quod in Romuli matre non ulti sunt.

SED utrum potuerit Venus ex concubitu Anchisae Aenean parere vel Mars ex concubitu filiae Numitoris Romulum gignere, in medio relinquamus. Nam paene talis quaestio etiam de scripturis nostris oboritur, qua quaeritur, utrum praevaricatores angeli cum filiabus hominum concubuerint, unde natis gigantibus, hoc est nimium grandibus ac fortibus viris, tunc terra completa est.

Proinde ad utrumque interim modo nostra disputatio referatur. Si enim vera sunt, quae apud illos de matre Aeneae et de patre Romuli lectitantur, quo modo possunt diis adulteria displicere hominum, quae in se ipsis concorditer ferunt? Si autem falsa sunt, ne sic quidem possunt irasci veris adulteriis humanis, qui etiam falsis delectantur suis. Huc accedit,

---

[1] Probably taken from M. Terentius Varro's lost *Antiquitatum Libri*.

[2] Genesis 6.4.

boldly embark on tasks of high emprise, carry them
through with greater energy, and so fulfil them with
better success just because of that faith.[1]   You see
what a wide area is opened for falsehood by this
statement of Varro's which I have expressed, as best
I could, in my own words.   We see in this case that
very many beliefs that are now consecrated and
included in religion of a sort may have been fabri-
cated, when lies even about the very gods have been
thought to make citizens better.

V

*That it is not tenable that the gods punished the
adultery of Paris, since they did not punish
adultery in the case of Romulus' mother.*

LET us leave unsettled the question whether Venus
may have conceived from Anchises and borne Aeneas,
or Mars by the conception of Numitor's daughter
have begotten Romulus.   For very much the same
question arises from a passage in our Scriptures also,
the question, that is, whether the apostate angels lay
with the daughters of men, from which union the
whole earth was at that time filled with giants, that is,
excessively large and strong men.[2]

For the present our discussion may be limited
merely to this dilemma : if on the one hand the statement frequently found in their books about Aeneas'
mother and Romulus' father is true, how can the gods
be displeased with men for adulteries which in their
own case they take calmly ?   If, on the other hand,
it is false, not even so can they be angry at real human
adulteries, since they take pleasure in their own,

quoniam, si illud de Marte non creditur, ut hoc quoque de Venere non credatur, nullo divini concubitus
obtentu matris Romuli causa defenditur. Fuit
autem sacerdos illa Vestalis, et ideo dii magis in
Romanos sacrilegum illud flagitium quam in Troianos
Paridis adulterium vindicare debuerunt. Nam et ipsi
Romani antiqui in stupro detectas Vestae sacerdotes
vivas etiam defodiebant, adulteras autem feminas,
quamvis aliqua damnatione, nulla tamen morte
plectebant. Usque adeo gravius quae putabant
adyta divina quam humana cubilia vindicabant.

VI

De parricidio Romuli, quod dii non vindicarunt.

ALIUD adicio, quia, si peccata hominum illis numinibus displicerent, ut offensi Paridis facto desertam
Troiam ferro ignibusque donarent, magis eos contra
Romanos moveret Romuli frater occisus quam contra
Troianos Graecus maritus inlusus; magis inritaret
parricidium nascentis quam regnantis adulterium
civitatis. Nec ad causam, quam nunc agimus, interest, utrum hoc fieri Romulus iusserit aut Romulus
fecerit, quod multi inpudentia negant, multi pudore
dubitant, multi dolore dissimulant.

fictitious though they be. Furthermore, if Mars'
adultery is omitted from their credo, so that Venus'
may also be omitted, the mother of Romulus cannot
plead intercourse with a god to cloak her offence.
She was, moreover, priestess of Vesta and for that
reason the gods should have punished that sacrilegious sin in the case of the Romans more than they
punished the Trojans for the adultery of Paris.
Indeed, the ancient Romans themselves even buried
alive Vestals discovered to be unchaste, while
ordinary women taken in adultery, though they were
sentenced to some punishment, were never put to
death. So much the more seriously did they uphold
the sanctity of shrines considered divine than that of
the marriage bed of mortals.

VI

That the gods did not avenge the fratricide of Romulus.

To adduce another instance, if the sins of men so
aroused the anger of the divinities that enraged at
Paris' deed they abandoned Troy and yielded it to
fire and sword, the slaying of Romulus' brother
should have stirred them more against the Romans
than the deception of the Greek husband stirred
them against the Trojan. Parricide in an infant city
should have angered them more than adultery in one
already lording it. Nor is it relevant to the present
issue whether Romulus ordered the deed to be done
or was himself the agent, a fact that many shamelessly
deny, many shamefastly question and many sorrow-
fully conceal from view.

Nec nos itaque in ea re diligentius requirenda per multorum scriptorum perpensa testimonia demoremur. Romuli fratrem palam constat occisum, non ab hostibus, non ab alienis. Si aut perpetravit aut imperavit hoc Romulus, magis ipse fuit Romanorum quam Paris Troianorum caput; cur igitur Troianis iram deorum provocavit ille alienae coniugis raptor, et eorundem deorum tutelam Romanis invitavit iste sui fratris extinctor?

Si autem illud scelus a facto imperioque Romuli alienum est, quoniam debuit utique vindicari, tota hoc illa civitas fecit quod tota contempsit, et non iam fratrem, sed patrem, quod est peius, occidit. Uterque enim fuit conditor, ubi alter scelere ablatus non permissus est esse regnator. Non est, ut arbitror, quod dicatur quid mali Troia meruerit ut eam dii desererent, quo posset extingui, et quid boni Roma ut eam dii inhabitarent, quo posset augeri; nisi quod victi inde fugerunt et se ad istos, quos pariter deciperent, contulerunt; immo vero et illic manserunt ad eos more suo decipiendos, qui rursus easdem terras habitarent, et hic easdem artes fallaciae suae magis etiam exercendo maioribus honoribus gloriati sunt.

Let us, then, not linger here for research into many writers and the weighing of their evidence in the case. Romulus' brother, all agree, was openly slain, and not by enemies nor by foreigners. Whether Romulus was the agent or the principal only, he was in a truer sense the chief of the Romans than was Paris of the Trojans. Why, then, did that kidnapper of another's wife provoke against the Trojans the wrath of the gods, while that slayer of his own brother rallied to the Romans the protection of the same gods?

If, on the other hand, that crime did not come home to Romulus either as enacted by him or by his order, since the crime should in any case have been dealt with, the city as a whole committed the murder that as a whole it overlooked, so that this way it slew, not its brother, but its father, which is worse. For each was a founder of the city in which one of the two, removed by a crime, was not allowed to be a ruler. In my opinion, there is no answer to the question what punishment Troy deserved for which the gods abandoned her to destruction, or what reward Rome had earned that the gods should take up their residence to ensure her prosperity, unless we say that being vanquished and having fled from Troy, they resorted to the Romans in order to cheat them as well. Not so, however, for they stayed in Troy too in order to cheat as usual those who should once more inhabit those lands, while here at Rome by even greater exercise of their sophistic arts they have boasted still greater honours.

VII

De eversione Ilii, quod dux Marii Fimbria excidit.

CERTE enim civilibus iam bellis scatentibus quid
miserum commiserat Ilium, ut a Fimbria Marianarum
partium homine pessimo everteretur multo ferocius
atque crudelius quam olim a Graecis? Nam tunc et
multi inde fugerunt et multi captivati saltem in
servitute vixerunt; porro autem Fimbria prius edic-
tum proposuit, ne cui parceretur, atque urbem totam
cunctosque in ea homines incendio concremavit.

Hoc meruit Ilium non a Graecis quos sua inritaverat
iniquitate, sed a Romanis quos sua calamitate propa-
gaverat, diis illis communibus ad haec repellenda
nihil iuvantibus seu, quod verum est, nihil valentibus
Numquid et tunc

> Abscessere omnes adytis arisque relictis
> Di,

quibus illud oppidum steterat post antiquos Graecorum ignes ruinasque reparatum?

Si autem abscesserant, causam requiro, et oppida-
norum quidem quanto invenio meliorem, tanto
deteriorem deorum. Illi enim contra Fimbriam
portas clauserant, ut Sullae servarent integram civitatem; hinc eos iratus incendit vel potius penitus
extinxit. Adhuc autem meliorum partium civilium

---

[1] C. Flavius Fimbria, partisan of Marius, who took his own
life in 84 B.C. See Livy, *Epitome* 83; Appian, *Mithridatic
War* 53.

[2] Virgil, *Aeneid* 2.351 f.

VII

*On the destruction of Troy by Fimbria, Marius'
general.*

SURELY we may ask what crime poor Ilium had
committed, when the spate of civil wars had begun,
that it should be destroyed by Fimbria,[1] a wicked
scoundrel of the party of Marius, even more savagely
and cruelly than it was in olden times by the Greeks.
Indeed, many escaped on that occasion and many,
taken captive, at least survived as slaves, while
Fimbria, on the contrary, issued beforehand a directive to spare no one, then by setting fire to it made one
holocaust of the city with all its inhabitants.

Thus was Ilium punished, not by Greeks whom she
had provoked by her own wrongdoing, but by
Romans whose seed had sprung from her disaster,
while the gods in question, who belonged to both
parties, did not help by averting this fate, or else—
and this is the true explanation—they had no power
to help. Did it happen on this occasion too that

All the gods departed from their shrines,
Left altars desolate,[2]

gods who had upheld that same walled city after its
recovery from the fires and devastation of the
Greeks?

Moreover, if they did depart, I demand an explanation, and as I discover a better plea for the citizens, so
much the poorer do I find the argument in defence of
the gods. For the inhabitants had closed their gates
in face of Fimbria to preserve the city intact for Sulla.
This is what enraged him so that he set fire to them,
or rather extinguished them completely. Moreover,

Sulla dux fuit, adhuc armis rem publicam recuperare moliebatur; horum bonorum initiorum nondum malos eventus habuit. Quid ergo melius cives urbis illius facere potuerunt, quid honestius, quid fidelius, quid Romana parentela dignius quam meliori causae Romanorum civitatem servare et contra parricidam Romanae rei publicae portas claudere?

At hoc eis in quantum exitium verterit, adtendant defensores deorum. Deseruerint dii adulteros Iliumque flammis Graecorum reliquerint, ut ex eius cineribus Roma castior nasceretur. Cur et postea deseruerunt eandem civitatem Romanis cognatam, non rebellantem adversus Romam nobilem filiam, sed iustioribus eius partibus fidem constantissimam piissimamque servantem, eamque delendam reliquerunt non Graecorum viris fortibus, sed viro spurcissimo Romanorum? Aut si displicebat diis causa partium Sullanarum, cui servantes urbem miseri portas clauserant, cur eidem Sullae tanta bona promittebant et praenuntiabant? An et hic agnoscuntur adulatores felicium potius quam infelicium defensores?

Non ergo Ilium etiam tunc ab eis cum desereretur eversum est. Nam daemones ad decipiendum semper vigilantissimi, quod potuerunt, fecerunt. Eversis quippe et incensis omnibus cum oppido simulacris solum Minervae sub tanta ruina templi

ulla was still leader of the better faction, for up to his point his object in fighting was to restore the epublic; and as yet these good beginnings of his were unaccompanied by their bad ending. What etter thing could the citizens of that city have done, what more honourable, what more loyal, what more onsistent with their parental obligation to Rome than o preserve the city for the better Roman faction and o close their gates against the murderer by parricide of his fatherland?

Let the defenders of the gods note how great a destruction this brought upon them. Let us grant hat the gods deserted adulterers and abandoned lium to the fires of the Greeks that from her ashes a urer Rome might come to birth. Why did they ater also desert this city bound by consanguinity to he Romans, who was no rebel against her famous laughter Rome, but preserved most steadfast and utiful loyalty to Rome's better faction, and abandon her to destruction, not by the stalwart Greek heroes, ut by the foulest representative of Rome? Or if he gods did not approve the cause of Sulla, in whose nterest the poor wretches had closed their gates to reserve the city, why did they promise and foretell uch successes to that same Sulla? Or do we catch hem once more paying court to the fortunate instead of rallying to defend the unfortunate?

Consequently, Troy was not destroyed that other ime either because it was deserted by the gods. For the demons, ever on the watch for opportunities o deceive, did all that they had power to do. Yes, when all other idols were destroyed and burned with he town, only that of Minerva, so Livy says, is eported to have stood untouched in the vast ruin

illius, ut scribit Livius, integrum stetisse perhibetur
non ut diceretur:

Di patrii, quorum semper sub numine Troia est,

ad eorum laudem, sed ne diceretur:

Excessere omnes adytis arisque relictis
Di,

ad eorum defensionem. Illud enim posse permiss
sunt, non unde probarentur potentes, sed und
praesentes convincerentur.

VIII

An debuerit diis Iliacis Roma committi.

Diis itaque Iliacis post Troiae ipsius documentun
qua tandem prudentia Roma custodienda commiss
est? Dixerit quispiam iam eos Romae habitar
solitos quando expugnante Fimbria cecidit Ilium
Unde ergo stetit Minervae simulacrum? Deinde, s
apud Romam erant quando Fimbria delevit Ilium
fortasse apud Ilium erant quando a Gallis ipsa Rom
capta et incensa est; sed ut sunt auditu acutissim
motuque celerrimi, ad vocem anseris cito redierunt, u
saltem Capitolinum collem, qui remanserat, tueren
tur; ceterum ad alia defendenda serius sunt redir
commoniti.

---

[1] Virgil, *Aeneid* 9.247.
[2] *Ibid.* 2.351. Here the quotation is exact, whereas in th
preceding instance Augustine has used *abscessere* in place o
excessere.
[3] Livy 5.47.4.

of her temple, not that it might be said in their praise

> The country's gods whose presence ever hallows
>   Troy [1]

but that it might not be said in their defence that

> All the gods departed from their shrines,
> Left altars desolate.[2]

So much power they were allowed to exercise, not to demonstrate their puissance, but to make them admit their presence.

VIII

*Whether Rome should have been entrusted to the
Trojan gods.*

So how in any way was it prudent to entrust Rome to the protection of the gods of Ilium after this demonstration in the case of Troy herself? Suppose someone urges that when Ilium fell in the capture by Fimbria, the gods were now familiarly at home in Rome. What, then, made the image of Minerva remain in place? Next we ask, if they were at Rome when Fimbria destroyed Ilium, perhaps they were at Ilium when Rome itself was captured and burned by the Gauls. Having, however, the sharpest hearing and the greatest celerity, they returned at once when the geese cackled,[3] in order to protect at least the Capitoline Hill, which had been spared. Yet the warning came too late for them to return in time to defend anything else.

IX

An illam pacem, quae sub Numae regno fuit, deos praestitisse credendum sit.

Hi etiam Numam Pompilium successorem Romulo adiuvisse creduntur, ut toto regni sui tempore pacem haberet et Iani portas, quae bellis patere adsolent, clauderet, eo merito scilicet quia Romanis multa sacra constituit.

Illi vero homini pro tanto otio gratulandum fuit, si modo id rebus salubribus scisset impendere et perniciosissima curiositate neglecta Deum verum vera pietate perquirere. Nunc autem non ei dii contulerunt illud otium, sed eum minus fortasse decepissent, si otiosum minime repperissent. Quanto enim minus eum occupatum invenerunt, tanto magis ipsi occupaverunt. Nam quid ille molitus sit et quibus artibus deos tales sibi vel illi civitati consociare potuerit, Varro prodit, quod, si Domino placuerit, suo diligentius disseretur loco.

Modo autem quia de beneficiis eorum quaestio est, magnum beneficium est pax, sed Dei veri beneficium est, plerumque etiam sicut sol, sicut pluvia vitaeque alia subsidia super ingratos et nequam. Sed si hoc tam magnum bonum dii illi Romae vel Pompilio

---

[1] See below, 7.34.

IX

Whether the peace in Numa's reign may be attributed to the gods' protection.

THEY are also believed to have helped Romulus' successor, Numa Pompilius, to enjoy peace throughout his reign and to close the gates of Janus, which by custom stand open in time of war; he deserved this boon for, be it noted, he established among the Romans many religious institutions.

No doubt that hero might have claimed our congratulations on being so long free from trouble, if only he had been wise enough to use his freedom for sound enterprises and, instead of utterly unsound niceties of religious research, had with true religion sought to find the true God. In the case as it stands, however, we conclude not that the gods granted him this freedom, but that they might perhaps have deceived him less successfully, had they found him with less free time on his hands, since, the less engaged they found him, the more they engaged his attention themselves. We are informed by Varro what he achieved and what means he used to make gods like that his partners, that is, partners in his commonwealth; and in its proper place, God willing, this matter will be discussed more fully.[1]

The question at the moment, however, is whether they brought any good to the city. Peace is a very good thing indeed, but a good thing that comes from the true God; and like sun, rain, and other vital resources, it is commonly bestowed even on the thankless and the graceless. But suppose it was the gods who granted this great boon, whether to Rome in those days or to Pompilius, why did they never

contulerunt, cur imperio Romano per ipsa tempora
laudabilia id numquam postea praestiterunt? An
utiliora erant sacra, cum instituerentur, quam cum
instituta celebrarentur? Atqui tunc nondum erant,
sed ut essent addebantur; postea vero iam erant,
quae ut prodessent custodiebantur. Quid ergo est,
quod illi quadraginta tres vel, ut alii volunt, triginta
et novem anni in tam longa pace transacti sunt
regnante Numa, et postea sacris institutis diisque
ipsis, qui eisdem sacris fuerant invitati, iam praesidibus atque tutoribus vix post tam multos annos
ab Urbe condita usque ad Augustum pro magno miraculo unus commemoratur annus post primum bellum
Punicum, quo belli portas Romani claudere potuerunt?

X

An optandum fuerit, ut tanta bellorum rabie Romanum
augeretur imperium, cum eo studio, quo sub Numa
actum est, et quietum esse potuisset et tutum.

AN respondent, quod nisi assiduis sibique continuo
succedentibus bellis Romanum imperium tam longe
lateque non posset augeri et tam grandi gloria diffa-
mari? Idonea vero causa! Ut magnum esset imperium, cur esse deberet inquietum? Nonne in
corporibus hominum satius est modicam staturam
cum sanitate habere quam ad molem aliquam

---

[1] In 235 B.C.

bestow it afterwards upon the Roman empire even in her palmier days? Were the sacred institutions more beneficial by virtue of their adoption than by virtue of celebration subsequent to adoption? Yet in the former case they were not yet in being and were adopted to give them being, while in the latter they were already in existence and were safeguarded for the good they could bring. Well, what are we to make of it that those forty-three or, as others prefer, thirty-nine years of Numa's reign passed in such prolonged peace, yet afterwards, when the sacrifices had been established, and the very gods who had been summoned by these same rites were patrons and protectors, in the long period from the founding of the city to the reign of Augustus, barely one year is recorded as a great wonder, shortly after the first Punic War, when the Romans found it possible to close the gates of war? [1]

X

Whether it was desirable for the Roman domain to be increased by such a rage for wars, when it could have been kept secure and peaceful by the aim that was pursued under Numa.

Do they reply that save for constant wars waged in uninterrupted succession, the Roman domain could never have spread so wide or its fame have been so gloriously broadcasted? Isn't that a relevant argument! Why should it have been necessary in order to be a great empire, to be turbulent? Take the human body. Is it not better to have moderate proportions and good health than to attain to some gigantic size with never-ending distresses, and when

giganteam perpetuis adflictionibus pervenire, nec
cum perveneris requiescere, sed quanto grandioribus
membris, tanto maioribus agitari malis?

Quid autem mali esset ac non potius plurimum
boni, si ea tempora perdurarent, quae perstrinxit
Sallustius, ubi ait: " Igitur initio reges (nam in terris
nomen imperii id primum fuit) diversi pars ingenium,
alii corpus exercebant; etiam tum vita hominum sine
cupiditate agitabatur, sua cuique satis placebant."
An ut tam multum augeretur imperium, debuit fieri
quod Vergilius detestatur, dicens:

Deterior donec paulatim ac decolor aetas
Et belli rabies et amor successit habendi?

Sed plane pro tantis bellis susceptis et gestis iusta
defensio Romanorum est, quod inruentibus sibi inpor-
tune inimicis resistere cogebat non aviditas adipiscendae laudis humanae, sed necessitas tuendae
salutis et libertatis. Ita sit plane. Nam " postquam
res eorum," sicut scribit ipse Sallustius, " legibus
moribus agris aucta satis prospera satisque pollens
videbatur, sicut pleraque mortalium habentur, invidia
ex opulentia orta est. Igitur reges populique finitimi
bello temptare; pauci ex amicis auxilio esse, nam
ceteri metu perculsi a periculis aberant. At Romani
domi militiaeque intenti festinare parare, alius
alium hortari, hostibus obviam ire, libertatem patriam
parentesque armis tegere. Post ubi pericula virtute

---

[1] Sallust, *Catiline* 2.1.   [2] Virgil, *Aeneid* 8.326 f.

you attain it, secure no peace but be afflicted with ailments that are greater in proportion to the greater
size of your members?

What evil would there have been, or rather what
good would have been missed, if those times alluded
to by Sallust had endured: " At first the kings (that
term was the first used for the right to rule on earth)
were unlike; some cultivated the mind, others the
body. Men still led lives free from greed; each was
well content with his own." [1] Did the end, so great
an extension of their domain, justify the course that
was taken? To this Virgil bears hostile witness,

> Till by degrees a baser and a drabber age,
> Bringing both rage for war and love of pelf,
> Arrived.[2]

Still, he who would defend the Romans for undertaking and waging such great wars is fully justified in
urging the consideration that, since enemies made
savage inroads on their territory, they were compelled to resist, not by any thirst for the prize of
honour on men's lips, but by the obligation to defend
life and liberty. Fully granted. For, to quote
Sallust himself, " When their state, reinforced by
laws, customs, territory, seemed to be as prosperous
and as powerful as was required, in the usual
course of human events, riches begot envy. In consequence the neighbouring kings and states made
warlike assaults. Only a few friends gave assistance,
for the greater part were terror-stricken and held
aloof from battle. But the Romans, energetic at
home and in the field, made haste, got ready, rallied
one another, faced the enemy, and hedged with arms
their liberty, their fatherland and their parents.

propulerant, sociis atque amicis auxilia portabant
magisque dandis quam accipiendis beneficiis amicitias
parabant." Decenter his artibus Roma crevit.

Sed regnante Numa, ut tam longa pax esset,
utrum inruebant inprobi belloque temptabant, an
nihil eorum fiebat ut posset pax illa persistere? Si
enim bellis etiam tum Roma lacessebatur nec armis
arma obvia ferebantur, quibus modis agebatur, ut
nulla pugna superati, nullo Martio impetu territi
sedarentur inimici, his modis semper ageretur et
semper Roma clausis Iani portis pacata regnaret.
Quod si in potestate non fuit, non ergo Roma pacem
habuit, quamdiu dii eorum, sed quamdiu homines
finitimi circumquaque voluerunt, qui eam nullo bello
provocaverunt; nisi forte dii tales etiam id homini
vendere audebunt, quod alius homo voluit sive
noluit. Interest quidem, iam vitio proprio, malas
mentes quatenus sinantur isti daemones vel terrere
vel excitare; sed si semper hoc possent nec aliud
secretiore ac superiore potestate contra eorum
conatum saepe aliter ageretur, semper in potestate
haberent paces bellicasque victorias, quae semper
fere per humanorum animorum motus accidunt;
quas tamen plerumque contra eorum fieri voluntatem
non solae fabulae multa mentientes et vix veri aliquid

---

[1] Sallust, *Catiline* 6.3.

Afterwards, when they had dispelled the menace by their valour, they went to the aid of friends and allies, and found friends more by conferring than by receiving benefits."[1] In this way Rome grew by honourable means.

What about Numa's reign, then? Was the long peace maintained despite the inroads and attacks of wicked men, or was the continuance of peace due to the non-occurrence of such things? For if Rome was at that time also harassed by wars, yet did not meet force with force of arms, then the means she used to hold her enemies in check, though they were unconquered in battle and undeterred by any war-like move, might always have been used; and thus Rome might have remained at peace for ever and Janus' gates for ever have been closed. If this was not in Rome's power, she therefore enjoyed peace, not at the pleasure of the gods, but at the pleasure of her neighbours on every side and only so long as they did not attack—unless your gods are to be so bold as to put up for sale to one man the decision to do or not to do of another man. There are occasions, to be sure, when the demons, to the extent that they are permitted, may move by fear or excitement such hearts as already have some weakness of their own. But if they always had the power to do so, and if other action were not frequently taken by a less obvious and higher power in opposition to their effort, they would always have peace and victory in war at their discretion, since these almost always come about by motivation of men's minds. Generally, however, peace and victory come about against the will of the gods; it is not only the myths, largely fictitious as they are, containing as they do hardly any truth

297

vel indicantes vel significantes, sed etiam ipsa Romana confitetur historia.

XI

De simulacro Cumani Apollinis, cuius fletus creditus est cladem Graecorum, quibus opitulari non poterat, indicasse.

NEQUE enim aliunde Apollo ille Cumanus, cum adversus Achivos regemque Aristonicum bellaretur, quadriduo flevisse nuntiatus est; quo prodigio haruspices territi cum id simulacrum in mare putavissent esse proiciendum, Cumani senes intercesserunt atque rettulerunt tale prodigium et Antiochi et Persis bello in eodem apparuisse figmento, et quia Romanis feliciter provenisset, ex senatus consulto eidem Apollini suo dona missa esse testati sunt. Tunc velut peritiores acciti haruspices responderunt simulacri Apollinis fletum ideo prosperum esse Romanis, quoniam Cumana colonia Graeca esset, suisque terris, unde accitus esset, id est ipsi Graeciae, luctum et cladem Apollinem significasse plorantem. Deinde mox regem Aristonicum victum et captum esse nuntiatum est, quem vinci utique Apollo nolebat et dolebat et hoc sui lapidis etiam lacrimis indicabat.

---

[1] On the story of the tears see Julius Obsequens, *Prodigies* 87. Livy (43.13) has the story but attributes it to the war with Perseus. The Achaean war ended when Mummius captured Corinth in 146 B.C., that against Aristonicus in Asia when the latter was captured and executed in 129 B.C. Augustine has apparently erred in dating these wars at the same time.

either in word or in symbol, that testify to this, but also the very voice of Roman history itself.

XI

On the statue of Apollo at Cumae, whose tears are said to have portended disaster to the Greeks, because he could not help them.

THAT source and no other reports that the well-known Apollo at Cumae, during the war against the Achaeans and King Aristonicus,[1] wept for four days. When in terror at this portent the soothsayers had adopted the view that this image of the god should be hurled into the sea, the old men of Cumae intervened and reported that a similar portent had been noted in connection with the same statue during the wars with Antiochus and Perseus;[2] and they testified that because the outcome had proved favourable to the Romans, gifts had been sent to that same Apollo of theirs by a decree of the Senate. Then soothsayers who were taken to be more expert were sent for and explained that the weeping of Apollo was a portent favourable to the Romans because Cumae was a Greek colony, and Apollo's weeping had indicated grief and misfortune for his own lands, whence he had been brought, namely, Greece itself. Not long afterwards came the news that King Aristonicus was defeated and taken prisoner, a defeat certainly displeasing and distressing to Apollo, who made it known even by tears from his own stone.

[2] Antiochus the Great, King of Syria, was defeated by Cornelius Scipio in 190 B.C. Perseus, King of Macedon, was conquered by Aemilius Paulus in 167 B.C.

Unde non usquequaque incongrue quamvis fabulosis, tamen veritati similibus mores daemonum describuntur carminibus poetarum. Nam Camillam Diana doluit apud Vergilium et Pallantem moriturum Hercules flevit. Hinc fortassis et Numa Pompilius pace abundans, sed quo donante nesciens nec requirens, cum cogitaret otiosus, quibusnam diis tuendam Romanam salutem regnumque committeret —nec verum illum atque omnipotentem summum Deum curare opinaretur ista terrena, atque recoleret Troianos deos, quos Aeneas advexerat, neque Troianum neque Laviniense ab ipso Aenea conditum regnum diu conservare potuisse—alios providendos existimavit, quos illis prioribus, qui sive cum Romulo iam Romam transierant, sive quandoque Alba eversa, fuerant transituri, vel tamquam fugitivis custodes adhiberet vel tamquam invalidis adiutores.

XII

Quantos sibi deos Romani praeter constitutionem
Numae adiecerint, quorum eos numerositas nihil
iuverit.

Nec his sacris tamen Roma dignata est esse contenta, quae tam multa illi Pompilius constituerat. Nam ipsius summum templum nondum habebat Iovis; rex quippe Tarquinius ibi Capitolium fabrica-

---

[1] Virgil, *Aeneid* 11.836–49.   [2] *Ibid.* 10.464 f.

Which proves that, however mythical the fictions of poets may be, they still present a likeness of truth and depict the behaviour of the demons in a way that is not in all respects inaccurate. In Virgil, Diana grieves for Camilla [1] and Hercules weeps for Pallas soon to die. [2] Perhaps this explains why Numa Pompilius, who enjoyed a generous portion of peace, but did not know or try to discover who granted it, when he considered at leisure to what gods he should commend the safety and sovereignty of Rome—not guessing that it is the true and almighty most high God who gives heed to such earthly matters, but reflecting that the Trojan gods brought by Aeneas had not been able to preserve for any long time either the kingdom of Troy or that of Lavinium founded by Aeneas himself—came to the conclusion that he must add new gods to the earlier roster of those who had either already moved with Romulus to Rome or were some day to move after the fall of Alba Longa; either the new gods were needed to guard the old because they were runagates, or they were needed to reinforce them because they were weaklings.

XII

How many gods the Romans added beyond those founded by Numa and how the multiplicity of gods was of no avail.

Rome did not, however, deign to be content with the shrines and rites established by Numa, though they were so many. For Rome had not as yet her chief temple of Jupiter; it was, of course, King Tarquin

vit; Aesculapius autem ab Epidauro ambivit ad Romam, ut peritissimus medicus in urbe nobilissima artem gloriosius exerceret; mater etiam deum nescio unde a Pessinunte; indignum enim erat, ut, cum eius filius iam colli Capitolino praesideret, adhuc ipsa in loco ignobili latitaret. Quae tamen si omnium deorum mater est, non solum secuta est Romam quosdam filios suos, verum et alios praecessit etiam secuturos. Miror sane, si ipsa peperit Cynocephalum, qui longe postea venit ex Aegypto. Utrum etiam dea Febris ex illa nata sit, viderit Aesculapius pronepos eius; sed undecumque nata sit, non, opinor, audebunt eam dicere ignobilem dii peregrini deam civem Romanam.

Sub hoc tot deorum praesidio, quos numerare quis potest, indigenas et alienigenas, caelites terrestres, infernos marinos, fontanos fluviales, et, ut Varro dicit, certos atque incertos, in omnibusque generibus deorum, sicut in animalibus, mares et feminas?—sub hoc ergo tot deorum praesidio constituta Roma non tam magnis et horrendis cladibus, quales ex multis paucas commemorabo, agitari adfligique debuit.

Nimis enim multos deos grandi fumo suo tamquam signo dato ad tuitionem congregaverat, quibus templa altaria, sacrificia sacerdotes instituendo atque praebendo summum verum Deum, cui uni haec rite gesta debentur, offenderet.

---

[1] The baboon, worshipped as a deity in Egypt. See Lucian, *Toxaris* 28; *Juppiter Tragoedus* 42.

[2] The four generations are Rhea, Zeus, Apollo, Aesculapius.

who erected the Capitolium there. Aesculapius, too, shifted quarters from Epidaurus to Rome so that this most skilled physician might in this noblest city practise his art with greater renown. The Mother of the Gods also came from Pessinus, wherever that may be, for it was hardly fitting that when her son now had his high seat on the Capitoline Hill, she should still be hidden in an obscure spot. If she is the mother of all the gods, however, she not only followed some of her sons to Rome but came before others who were still to follow. I do admire her, if she herself gave birth to Cynocephalus,[1] who long afterwards came from Egypt. Whether even the goddess Fever is one of her daughters is a matter for her great-grandson Aesculapius to decide.[2] But whoever her mother was, I do not suppose that the foreign gods will dare to call baseborn a goddess who is a Roman citizen.

So many were the gods who thus protected Rome, and who can count them : native gods and foreign-born, gods celestial and terrestrial, infernal and marine, fountain gods and river gods, and, as Varro says, gods certain and uncertain, and in every class of gods, as in every kind of animal, the male and the female ? Surely, Rome founded as she was under the protection of so many gods, should not have been assailed and afflicted by such great and terrible calamities, of which I shall mention only a few out of many.

For she had summoned for her protection, by a cloud of her own smoke, as it were by a signal raised, far too many gods in order to establish and provide temples, altars, sacrifices, and priests for them, and in doing so to offend the true and most high God to whom alone such religious service should be rendered.

Et felicior quidem cum paucioribus vixit, sed quanto maior facta est, sicut navis nautas, tanto plures adhibendos putavit; credo, desperans pauciores illos, sub quibus in comparatione peioris vitae melius vixerat, non sufficere ad opitulandum granditati suae. Primo enim sub ipsis regibus, excepto Numa Pompilio, de quo iam supra locutus sum, quantum malum discordiosi certaminis fuit, quod fratrem Romuli coegit occidi!

XIII

Quo iure, quo foedere Romani obtinuerint prima coniugia.

Quo modo nec Iuno, quae cum Iove suo iam

fovebat
Romanos rerum dominos gentemque togatam,

nec Venus ipsa Aeneidas suos potuit adiuvare ut bono et aequo more coniugia mererentur, cladesque tanta inruit huius inopiae, ut ea dolo raperent moxque compellerentur pugnare cum soceris, ut miserae feminae nondum ex iniuria maritis conciliatae iam parentum sanguine dotarentur?

At enim vicerunt in hac conflictione Romani vicinos suos. Quantis et quam multis utrimque

---

[1] Virgil, *Aeneid* 1.282.

Indeed, Rome lived more prosperously with fewer gods, but she adopted the view that in proportion to her size she must enlist more gods, as a larger ship needs more sailors. In my opinion Rome saw no hope in those comparatively few gods under whom she had lived a better life in comparison with her later and worse life, as not being sufficient to provide the needed resources for her greatness. In the first place, even under the kings themselves, with the exception of Numa Pompilius, whom I mentioned above, what a plague of quarrelsome rivalry there must have been to bring about the murder of Romulus' brother!

XIII

The right and the pact whereby the Romans first got
wives.

How does it happen that neither Juno who, with her husband Jupiter, already cherished

The Romans, lords of the world, the race that wears
The toga,[1]

nor Venus herself could give assistance to the sons of Aeneas whereby they might win wives by some good and proper means? Such were the disastrous results of this failure to assist that they seized wives by fraud and were presently forced to fight a battle with their fathers-in-law, so that the poor women, not yet soothed after the wrong done them by their husbands, now for bridal dowry received their fathers' blood.

But in that struggle the Romans conquered their neighbours. Yes, but with how great and with how

vulneribus et funeribus tam propinquorum et confinium istae victoriae constiterunt! Propter unum Caesarem socerum et unum generum eius Pompeium iam mortua Caesaris filia, uxore Pompei, quanto et quam iusto doloris instinctu Lucanus exclamat:

> Bella per Emathios plus quam civilia campos
> Iusque datum sceleri canimus.

Vicerunt ergo Romani, ut strage socerorum manibus cruentis ab eorum filiabus amplexus miserabiles extorquerent, nec illae auderent flere patres occisos, ne offenderent victores maritos, quae adhuc illis pugnantibus pro quibus facerent vota nesciebant. Talibus nuptiis populum Romanum non Venus, sed Bellona donavit; aut fortassis Allecto illa inferna furia iam eis favente Iunone plus in illos habuit licentiae, quam cum eius precibus contra Aenean fuerat excitata.

Andromacha felicius captivata est quam illa coniugia Romana nupserunt. Licet serviles, tamen post eius amplexus nullum Troianorum Pyrrhus occidit; Romani autem soceros interficiebant in proeliis, quorum iam filias amplexabantur in thalamis. Illa victori subdita dolere tantum suorum mortem potuit, non timere; illae sociatae bellantibus parentum suorum mortes procedentibus viris timebant, redeun-

---

[1] Lucan, *Pharsalia* 1.1 f.
[2] Virgil, *Aeneid* 1.8–33.

many wounds and obsequies of both relatives and neighbours were those victories made good! The war of Caesar and Pompey took place between only one father-in-law and his one son-in-law, and that after Caesar's daughter, Pompey's wife, was dead, yet how loud, how justly, prompted by grief, Lucan cries out

> The battle on Emathia's plains in worse
> Than civil war, and crime thus legalized
> We sing.[1]

The Romans conquered therefore, with the result that they used hands bloody with the gore of their fathers-in-law to wrest from unhappy daughters the embraces of love while daughters did not dare lament the death of fathers for fear of offending victorious husbands, and while the fight was still progressing knew not which to pray for. The Roman people owed such marriages not to Venus but to Bellona, or perhaps that infernal fury Allecto had more licence to harm them, now that Juno was aiding them, than she had earlier when she was first roused against Aeneas by Juno's prayers.[2]

Happier was Andromache's captivity than those marriages for the Roman brides. Though she was embraced as a slave, yet after that embrace Pyrrhus slew no Trojan; the Romans, however, still slew in battle fathers-in-law whose daughters they already embraced in the marriage bower. Andromache, though subject to her captor, need only mourn, not fear the death of her people; the Roman brides, mated with combatants as they were, were moved to fear a father's death when their husbands sallied forth, to lament it when they returned, yet had no

307

tibus dolebant, nec timorem habentes liberum nec
dolorem. Nam propter interitum civium propinquorum, fratrum parentum aut pie cruciabantur, aut
crudeliter laetabantur victoriis maritorum.

Huc accedebat quod, ut sunt alterna bellorum,
aliquae parentum ferro amiserunt viros, aliquae
utrorumque ferro et parentes et viros. Neque enim
et apud Romanos parva fuerunt illa discrimina, si
quidem ad obsidionem quoque perventum est civitatis
clausisque portis se tuebantur; quibus dolo apertis
admissisque hostibus intra moenia in ipso foro
scelerata et nimis atrox inter generos socerosque
pugna commissa est, et raptores illi etiam supera-
bantur et crebro fugientes inter domos suas gravius
foedabant pristinas, quamvis et ipsas pudendas
lugendasque victorias.

Hic tamen Romulus de suorum iam virtute desperans Iovem oravit ut starent, atque ille hac occasione nomen Statoris invenit; nec finis esset tanti
mali, nisi raptae illae laceratis crinibus emicarent et
provolutae parentibus iram eorum iustissimam non
armis victricibus, sed supplici pietate sedarent.
Deinde Titum Tatium regem Sabinorum socium
regni Romulus ferre compulsus est, germani consortis
inpatiens; sed quando et istum diu toleraret, qui

liberty either to fear or to lament. For either they were dutifully wrung by the loss of fellow citizens, of relatives, of brothers or of fathers, or they unfeelingly rejoiced in their husbands' victories.

What is more, for war has its vicissitudes, a number of them must have lost husbands by the weapons of a parent, and a number must have lost both parent and husband by the weapons of the two parties. In fact, those decisive encounters were no slight matter even for the Romans if they were really reduced even to seeing their city invested and to defending it behind closed gates; and when their gates were opened by treachery and the enemy was admitted within the walls, there was joined in the very forum an accursed and only too savage battle between fathers-in-law and sons-in-law. The kidnappers were even at times worsted, and, by their often taking refuge among houses, sadly sullied the lustre of their early victories, however true it be that their very victories should also have shamed and saddened them.

At this point, however, Romulus, losing all hope of the valour of his men, prayed to Jupiter that they might be stayed, and from that incident Jupiter took his title as Stayer. Nor would the sorry tale end here, were it not that those kidnapped women darted out with hair dishevelled and, casting themselves before their fathers, disarmed their most just rage, not by victorious weapons but by worshipful entreaty. Then Romulus was forced to put up with Titus Tatius, King of the Sabines, as joint occupant of the throne that he brooked not to share with his own brother. Yet how long could he be expected to suffer this partner either, when a brother, and a twin at that,

fratrem geminumque non pertulit? Unde et ipso interfecto, ut maior deus esset, regnum solus obtinuit.

Quae sunt ista iura nuptiarum, quae inritamenta bellorum, quae foedera germanitatis adfinitatis, societatis divinitatis? Quae postremo sub tot diis tutoribus vita civitatis? Vides quanta hinc dici et quam multa possent, nisi quae supersunt nostra curaret intentio et sermo in alia festinaret.

XIV

De impietate belli, quod Albanis Romani intulerunt, et de victoria dominandi libidine adepta.

QUID deinde post Numam sub aliis regibus? Quanto malo non solum suo, sed etiam Romanorum in bellum Albani provocati sunt, quia videlicet pax Numae tam longa viluerat! Quam crebrae strages Romani Albanique exercitus fuerunt et utriusque comminutio civitatis! Alba namque illa, quam filius Aeneae creavit Ascanius, Romae mater propior ipsa quam Troia, a Tullo Hostilio rege provocata conflixit, confligens autem et adflicta est et adflixit, donec multorum taederet pari defectione certaminum. Tunc eventum belli de tergeminis hinc atque inde

had been too much for him? Thus it came about that Tatius, too, was slain, and Romulus, on his way to be a greater god, became sole ruler.

Strange indeed the law by which they married! Strange the provocation of their war! Strange the basis of their ties of blood, of marriage, of citizenship, of religion! Strange finally their civic life under the tutelage of all those gods! You see the gravity and multiplicity of themes that might engage my eloquence, were it not my purpose to deal with matters still untouched, and were my discourse not intent on other goals.

XIV

On the impiety of the war waged by the Romans against the Albans and on the victory gained through lust for power.

WHAT happened then after Numa under other kings? How great the loss was, not only to the Albans but to the Romans as well, when the Albans were challenged in war! The reason for this was no doubt that the peace of Numa, such was its length, had ceased to be precious. How frequent were the slaughters suffered by both the Roman and the Alban armies, with consequent loss of population on both sides! For Alba, the very Alba founded by Aeneas' son Ascanius, more nearly Rome's mother than Troy herself, was challenged to battle by King Tullus Hostilius; and in the conflict she both inflicted damage and was afflicted herself until both sides wearied of so many struggles in which each was equally a sufferer. It was then determined to base the decision of the war on a conflict between two sets of

fratribus placuit experiri. A Romanis tres Horatii,
ab Albanis autem tres Curiatii processerunt; a
Curiatiis tribus Horatii duo, ab uno autem Horatio
tres Curiatii superati et extincti sunt.

Ita Roma extitit victrix ea clade etiam in certamine
extremo ut de sex unus rediret domum. Cui dam-
num in utrisque, cui luctus, nisi Aeneae stirpi, nisi
Ascanii posteris, nisi proli Veneris, nisi nepotibus
Iovis? Nam et hoc plus quam civile bellum fuit,
quando filia civitas cum civitate matre pugnavit.

Accessit aliud huic tergeminorum pugnae ultimae
atrox atque horrendum malum. Nam ut erant ambo
populi prius amici (vicini quippe atque cognati), uni
Curiatiorum desponsata fuerat Horatiorum soror;
haec postea quam sponsi spolia in victore fratre
conspexit, ab eodem fratre, quoniam flevit, occisa est.
Humanior huius unius feminae quam universi populi
Romani mihi fuisse videtur affectus. Illa quem virum
iam fide media retinebat, aut forte etiam ipsum
fratrem dolens qui eum occiderat cui sororem pro-
miserat, puto quod non culpabiliter fleverit.

Unde enim apud Vergilium pius Aeneas laudabiliter
dolet hostem etiam sua peremptum manu? Unde
Marcellus Syracusanam civitatem recolens eius paulo
ante culmen et gloriam sub manus suas subito con-
cidisse communem cogitans condicionem flendo mise-
ratus est? Quaeso ab humano impetremus affectu,

---

[1] Virgil, *Aeneid* 10.821-4.   [2] See above, 1.6.

triplet brothers, one from each side. From the
Roman side the three Horatii, from the Alban the
three Curiatii advanced. The three Curiatii slew two
of the Horatii, but the one who remained defeated and
put to death the three Curiatii.

Thus Rome emerged as victor, but with such
slaughter even in the final combat that of the six, but
one came home. To whom did the loss on both sides
come, to whom the grief, if not to Aeneas' stock,
Venus' descendants, Jupiter's grandsons? For this,
too, was a worse than civil war when the daughter city
fought with the mother city.

To the death combat of the triplets there was
added another atrocious and shocking catastrophe.
Since both nations had formerly been friendly, being,
of course, both neighbours and relatives, a sister of the
Horatii had been betrothed to one of the Curiatii,
and when she afterwards burst into tears at the sight
of the arms of her betrothed, borne by her victorious
brother as spoils, she was slain by that same brother.
The feeling of this one woman seems to me more
humane than that of the whole Roman people. I do
not think her at fault for weeping over the man to
whom she was bound by half her duty, or perhaps over
the very brother who had slain one to whom he
pledged his sister.

How comes it that good Aeneas, in Virgil, is
praised for his grief over his enemy even though slain
by his own hand? [1] How comes it that Marcellus
shed tears of compassion when he reflected on the
city of Syracuse, how it was a moment ago at the
pinnacle of its fame and had collapsed under his
attack, and went on to contemplate the common lot
of all men? [2] I submit the argument to the verdict

313

ut femina sponsum suum a fratre suo peremptum sine
crimine fleverit, si viri hostes a se victos etiam cum
laude fleverunt. Ergo sponso a fratre inlatam
mortem quando femina illa flebat, tunc se contra
matrem civitatem tanta strage bellasse et tanta hinc
et inde cognati cruoris effusione vicisse Roma
gaudebat.

Quid mihi obtenditur nomen laudis nomenque
victoriae? Remotis obstaculis insanae opinionis
facinora nuda cernantur, nuda pensentur, nuda
iudicentur. Causa dicatur Albae, sicut Troiae
adulterium dicebatur. Nulla talis, nulla similis
invenitur; tantum ut resides moveret

Tullus in arma viros et iam desueta triumphis
Agmina.[1]

Illo itaque vitio tantum scelus perpetratum est socialis
belli atque cognati, quod vitium Sallustius magnum
transeunter adtingit. Cum enim laudans breviter
antiquiora commemorasset tempora, quando vita
hominum sine cupiditate agitabatur et sua cuique
satis placebant: "Postea vero, inquit, quam in Asia
Cyrus, in Graecia Lacedaemonii et Athenienses
coepere urbes atque nationes subigere, libidinem
dominandi causam belli habere, maximam gloriam in
maximo imperio putare," et cetera quae ipse insti-
tuerat dicere.[2] Mihi huc usque satis sit eius verba
posuisse. Libido ista dominandi magnis malis agitat

---

[1] Virgil, *Aeneid* 6.814 f.   [2] Sallust, *Catiline* 2.2.

of human feeling, that a woman may be guiltless who
bewailed her betrothed that was slain by her own
brother, if men have wept for enemies they themselves conquered and have even been praised for it.
Well, then, while that woman was bewailing the death
of her betrothed that was inflicted by her brother,
at that very time Rome was rejoicing that she had
made war on her mother city with such devastation,
and had won a victory by the shedding of so much
kindred blood on both sides.

Why are the words glory and victory used to veil the
truth? Take away the screens of a morbid fashion
and let the naked deeds be examined; let them be
weighed naked, judged naked. Let Alba be indicted, as Troy was indicted for adultery. No such
indictment exists, nothing even like it is found. The
goal of the war was only that

> Tullus might move to arms his sluggish men,
> Urge on to triumph troops unused to fight.[1]

And so it was that such a weakness caused the great
crime of a war between allies and blood relations, a
great weakness that Sallust notes in passing. When
he has touched upon and briefly praised those earlier
days when men lived their lives without cupidity
and each was satisfied with what he had, he says,
" But afterwards, when Cyrus in Asia, and the Lacedaemonians and Athenians in Greece, began to subdue cities and nations, and to consider a lust for
mastery sufficient ground for war, and to think that
the greatest glory belongs to the greatest empire," [2]
and so on with the rest of what he saw fit to say.
For my purpose it is enough to quote only to this
point. This lust for mastery brings many evils upon

et conterit humanum genus. Hac libidine Roma tunc victa Albam se vicisse triumphabat et sui sceleris laudem gloriam nominabat, *quoniam laudatur,* inquit scriptura nostra, *peccator in desideriis animae suae et qui iniqua gerit benedicitur.*

Fallacia igitur tegmina et deceptoriae dealbationes auferantur a rebus, ut sincero inspiciantur examine. Nemo mihi dicat: Magnus ille atque ille, quia cum illo et illo pugnavit et vicit. Pugnant etiam gladiatores, vincunt et ipsi, habet praemia laudis et illa crudelitas; sed puto esse satius cuiuslibet inertiae poenas luere quam illorum armorum quaerere gloriam. Et tamen si in harenam procederent pugnaturi inter se gladiatores, quorum alter filius, alter esset pater, tale spectaculum quis ferret? Quis non auferret? Quo modo ergo gloriosum alterius matris, alterius filiae civitatis inter se armorum potuit esse certamen? An ideo diversum fuit, quod harena illa non fuit, et latiores campi non duorum gladiatorum, sed in duobus populis multorum funeribus implebantur, nec amphitheatro cingebantur illa certamina, sed universo orbi, et tunc vivis et posteris, quo usque ista fama porrigitur, impium spectaculum praebebatur?

Vim tamen patiebantur studii sui dii illi praesides imperii Romani et talium certaminum tamquam theatrici spectatores, donec Horatiorum soror propter

---

[1] Psalms 10.3.

the human race and grinds it down. Rome, conquered on that occasion by this lust, was triumphant at her victory over Alba, and gave the name of glory to the memory of her crime, since, as our Scriptures say, "The wicked wins glory by the desires of his soul, and he who works iniquity is well spoken of." [1]

Away with these deceptive cloaks and fraudulent whitewashings that the facts may be subjected to an honest examination. Let no man say to me: "This or that man is great because he fought with such and such and won." Gladiators also fight, they also are victorious, their cruelty also wins its meed of praise, but I think it better to pay the penalty for any amount of sluggishness rather than to seek the glory granted to those arms. If, however, two gladiators were to advance into the arena to fight, one the son of the other, who could bear the sight? Who would not forbear to see it? How, then, could the contest of arms have been glorious between two cities, one being the mother, the other the daughter? Or does it make a difference that there was no arena, though battlefields much wider than an arena were filled with the corpses, not of two gladiators, but of multitudes belonging to two peoples, and that those contests were not bounded by an amphitheatre but by the whole world, and that it was an impious spectacle upon which those then alive gazed—as will their descendants so long as the report of it is handed down?

Yet those gods who were the patrons of the Roman empire and formed, as it were, the audience when these contests were performed, rested content with the vehemence of their own partisanship until the sister of the Horatii was added by her brother's sword

Curiatios tres peremptos etiam ipsa tertia ex altera
parte fraterno ferro duobus fratribus adderetur, ne
minus haberet mortium etiam Roma quae vicerat.
Deinde ad fructum victoriae Alba subversa est, ubi
post Ilium, quod Graeci everterunt, et post Lavinium,
ubi Aeneas regnum peregrinum atque fugitivum
constituerat, tertio loco habitaverant numina illa
Troiana. Sed more suo etiam inde iam fortasse
migraverant, ideo deleta est. Discesserant videlicet
omnes adytis arisque relictis di, quibus imperium illud
steterat.

Discesserant sane ecce iam tertio, ut eis quarta
Roma providentissime crederetur. Displicuerat enim
et Alba, ubi Amulius expulso fratre, et Roma
placuerat, ubi Romulus occiso fratre regnaverat. Sed
antequam Alba dirueretur, transfusus est, inquiunt,
populus eius in Romam, ut ex utraque una civitas
fieret. Esto, ita factum sit; urbs tamen illa, Ascanii
regnum et tertium domicilium Troianorum deorum,
ab urbe filia mater eversa est; ut autem belli reliquiae
ex duobus populis unum facerent, miserabile coa-
gulum, multus ante fusus utriusque sanguis fuit.

Quid iam singillatim dicam sub ceteris regibus
totiens eadem bella renovata, quae victoriis finita
videbantur, et tantis stragibus iterum iterumque
confecta, iterum iterumque post foedus et pacem
inter soceros et generos et eorum stirpem posterosque

to the tale of two brothers slain—a third victim on the other side to match the three slain Curiatii, that even Rome who conquered might have no fewer deaths. Then as fruit of the victory, came the destruction of Alba, where, after Ilium, which the Greeks destroyed, and after Lavinium, where Aeneas had established a wandering and fugitive kingdom, those Trojan divinities had occupied a third habitation. But perhaps the gods had in their usual fashion also departed from that town, and so it was destroyed. Obviously " the gods had all departed, leaving shrines and altars abandoned, by whom that empire had been maintained."

They had departed, sure enough, and, that, note, for the third time in order that Rome might be the fourth. to be, oh so prudently, entrusted to their keeping. For not only did Alba lose their favour, where Amulius expelled his brother, but Rome gained it, where Romulus slew his brother in order to reign. But before the destruction of Alba, they say, its population was transferred to Rome to make one city of both. Very well, let that be so. Nevertheless, that city, Ascanius' kingdom and the third home of the Trojan gods, a mother city, was destroyed by its daughter. Besides, before the survivors of the war could form one pitiful clot of the two peoples, much blood was shed on both sides.

Why should I tell, war by war, of the constant renewal of the same wars under the other kings—of wars that seemed to end in victories, wars that were again and again terminated by great slaughters, and yet, again and again, after treaties of peace between fathers-in-law and sons-in-law, and their stock and posterity, were enacted once more? No small proof

319

repetita? Non parvum indicium calamitatis huius
fuit, quod portas belli nullus clausit illorum. Nullus
ergo illorum sub tot diis praesidibus in pace regnavit.

XV

Qualis Romanorum regum vita atque exitus fuerit.

IPSORUM autem regum qui exitus fuerunt? De
Romulo viderit adulatio fabulosa, qua perhibetur
receptus in caelum; viderint quidam scriptores
eorum, qui eum propter ferocitatem a senatu dis-
cerptum esse dixerunt subornatumque nescio quem
Iulium Proculum, qui eum sibi apparuisse diceret
eumque per se populo mandasse Romano ut inter
numina coleretur eoque modo populum, qui contra
senatum intumescere coeperat, repressum atque
sedatum. Acciderat enim et solis defectio, quam
certa ratione sui cursus effectam imperita nesciens
multitudo meritis Romuli tribuebat.

Quasi vero si luctus ille solis fuisset, non magis ideo
credi deberet occisus ipsumque scelus aversione etiam
diurni luminis indicatum; sicut re vera factum est
cum Dominus crucifixus est crudelitate atque impietate Iudaeorum. Quam solis obscurationem non ex
canonico siderum cursu accidisse satis ostendit quod
tunc erat pascha Iudaeorum; nam plena luna sollemniter agitur, regularis autem solis defectio non nisi
lunae fine contingit.

---

[1] Livy 1.16.4.

of this unhappy state of things is the fact that none of these kings closed the gates of war. Hence, none of them reigned in peace, though protected by so many gods.

XV

How the Roman kings lived and died.

What, moreover, were the departures of the kings themselves like? Fictitious flattery says of Romulus that he was taken up into heaven. Let certain of their writers see to this, who have stated that his barbarity led the Senate to hew him in pieces,[1] and that a certain Julius Proculus was suborned to say that Romulus had appeared to him and through him commanded the Roman people to worship him among the divinities, and that by this means the people, who had begun to storm against the Senate, were checked and calmed. For an eclipse of the sun had also taken place; and the ignorant populace, not knowing that the mathematical regularity of the sun's own course produced it, gave Romulus' noble deeds the credit.

They might have reflected that, if the sun's eclipse was really evidence of grief, that was rather an argument for the belief that he was murdered; when the light of day withdrew, that was visible evidence of very crime. Compare the actual fact when the Lord was crucified by the cruel and sacrilegious Jews. That the eclipse that then occurred was not caused by the regular movement of the heavenly bodies is clearly shown by the fact that it took place at the passover of the Jews. This festival is celebrated at full moon, but eclipses of the sun regularly occur only in the dark of the moon.

Satis et Cicero illam inter deos Romuli receptionem putatam magis significat esse quam factam, quando et laudans eum in libris de re publica Scipionisque sermone: " Tantum est, inquit, consecutus, ut, cum subito sole obscurato non comparuisset, deorum in numero conlocatus putaretur, quam opinionem nemo umquam mortalis assequi potuit sine eximia virtutis gloria." (Quod autem dicit eum subito non comparuisse, profecto ibi intellegitur aut violentia tempestatis aut caedis facinorisque secretum; nam et alii scriptores eorum defectioni solis addunt etiam subitam tempestatem, quae profecto aut occasionem sceleri praebuit aut Romulum ipsa consumpsit.)

De Tullo quippe etiam Hostilio, qui tertius a Romulo rex fuit, qui et ipse fulmine absumptus est, dicit in eisdem libris idem Cicero, propterea et istum non creditum in deos receptum tali morte, quia fortasse quod erat in Romulo probatum, id est persuasum, Romani vulgare noluerunt, id est vile facere, si hoc et alteri facile tribueretur. Dicit etiam aperte in invectivis: " Illum, qui hanc urbem condidit, Romulum ad deos immortales benivolentia famaque sustulimus," ut non vere factum, sed propter merita virtutis eius benivole iactatum diffamatumque monstraret. In Hortensio vero dialogo cum de solis canonicis defectionibus loqueretur: " Ut easdem, inquit, tenebras efficiat quas effecit in interitu

---

[1] Cicero, *Republic* 2.10.
[2] Cicero, *Catiline* 3.1.
[3] A work preserved only in fragments.

Cicero, too, gives notice that the famous admission of Romulus to the ranks of the gods was rather an act of faith than a fact when, even in praising him in his books on *The Republic* and in the person of Scipio, he says: " Such were his achievements that, suddenly disappearing during an eclipse of the sun, he was believed to have received a place among the gods, a reputation that no mortal could ever have won without unusual renown for virtue." [1] By the phrase " suddenly disappearing " we must surely understand that he was violently removed from sight either by a storm or by a murderous assault, for others of their writers mention besides the sun's eclipse a sudden storm, which certainly either provided an opportunity for the crime or itself swallowed Romulus up.

For that matter, speaking again of Tullus Hostilius, the third king after Romulus, who was likewise destroyed by lightning, the same Cicero says in the same books that he was not believed to have been welcomed among the gods, for all he died so, possibly because the Romans were unwilling that what was agreed (believed, that is) in the case of Romulus should not be made common (cheap, that is), as it would be if it were credited in another case too. Again he speaks plainly in his invectives: " The founder of the city, Romulus, we have exalted to the immortal gods, such is the devotion and renown that he enjoys." [2] For he meant to point out that the thing was not a real event, but a tribute of loyal devotion and propaganda paid to him as the reward of virtue. In the dialogue *Hortensius*,[3] moreover, speaking of the regular eclipses of the sun, he says: " In order to produce the same darkness that was produced at the time of Romulus' passing, which took

323

Romuli, qui obscuratione solis est factus." Certe hic
minime timuit hominis interitum dicere, quia dispu-
tator magis quam laudator fuit.

Ceteri autem reges populi Romani, excepto Numa
Pompilio et Anco Marcio, qui morbo interierunt,
quam horrendos exitus habuerunt! Tullus, ut dixi,
Hostilius, victor et eversor Albae, cum tota domo sua
fulmine concrematus est. Priscus Tarquinius per sui
decessoris filios interemptus est. Servius Tullius
generi sui Tarquinii Superbi, qui ei successit in
regnum, nefario scelere occisus est. Nec " discessere
adytis arisque relictis di " tanto in optimum illius
populi regem parricidio perpetrato, quos dicunt, ut
hoc miserae Troiae facerent eamque Graecis diruen-
dam exurendamque relinquerent, adulterio Paridis
fuisse commotos; sed insuper interfecto a se socero
Tarquinius ipse successit. Hunc illi dii nefarium
parricidam soceri interfectione regnantem, insuper
multis bellis victoriisque gloriantem et de manubiis
Capitolium fabricantem non abscedentes, sed praesentes manentesque viderunt et regem suum Iovem
in illo altissimo templo, hoc est in opere parricidae,
sibi praesidere atque regnare perpessi sunt. Neque
enim adhuc innocens Capitolium struxit et postea
malis meritis Urbe pulsus est, sed ad ipsum regnum,
in quo Capitolium fabricaret, inmanissimi sceleris
perpetratione pervenit.

place when the sun was obscured." Here he
certainly made no bones about it and spoke of the
" passing " as of a human being, for he was engaged
in philosophical discussion rather than in oratorical
compliments.

The other kings of the Roman people, with the
exception of Numa Pompilius and Ancus Marcius,
who died of disease, came to ends that were shocking
indeed. Tullus Hostilius, as I said, the conqueror and
destroyer of Alba, was consumed by lightning with
his whole household. Tarquinius Priscus was slain
by the sons of his predecessor. Servius Tullius was
foully murdered by his son-in-law Tarquinius Super-
bus, who succeeded him on the throne. And when so
great a parricide was committed against Rome's best
king, " the gods did not all depart, leaving shrines and
altars abandoned," as it is said they were driven to
do in poor Troy's case merely by the adultery of Paris,
so that they abandoned it to demolition and incinera-
tion. What is more, Tarquin, the very murderer of
his father-in-law, succeeded him on the throne. This
very parricide who reigned because he slew his
father-in-law, and even boasted of many wars waged
and won, and from the spoils built the Capitoline
Temple, caused no migration of gods; no, they were
at hand, they kept their seats and looked on, they
suffered their king Jupiter to sit at their head as their
king in his most lofty temple, that is, in a shrine
erected by a parricide. For he did not build the
Capitoline Temple while he was still free from guilt,
and afterwards suffer banishment from the city for his
wicked deeds; the very kingdom that he held when
he built the Capitoline Temple, was acquired by
commission of a monstrous crime.

Quod vero eum regno Romani postea depulerunt ac
secluserunt moenibus civitatis, non ipsius de Lucretiae
stupro, sed filii peccatum fuit illo non solum nesciente,
sed etiam absente commissum. Ardeam civitatem
tunc oppugnabat, pro populo Romano bellum gerebat; nescimus quid faceret, si ad eius notitiam
flagitium filii deferretur; et tamen inexplorato
iudicio eius et inexperto ei populus ademit imperium
et recepto exercitu, a quo deseri iussus est, clausis
deinde portis non sivit intrare redeuntem. At ille
post bella gravissima, quibus eosdem Romanos
concitatis finitimis adtrivit, postea quam desertus ab
eis quorum fidebat auxilio regnum recipere non
evaluit, in oppido Tusculo Romae vicino quattuor-
decim, ut fertur, annos privatam vitam quietus habuit
et cum uxore consenuit, optabiliore fortassis exitu
quam socer eius, generi sui facinore nec ignorante
filia, sicut perhibetur, extinctus.

Nec tamen istum Tarquinium Romani crudelem
aut sceleratum, sed superbum appellaverunt, fortasse
regios eius fastus alia superbia non ferentes. Nam
scelus occisi ab eo soceri optimi regis sui usque adeo
contempserunt, ut eum regem suum facerent; ubi
miror, si non scelere graviore mercedem tantam tanto
sceleri reddiderunt. Nec " discessere adytis arisque

And when afterwards the Romans did expel and exclude him from their walled enclosure, the deed of shame with Lucretia was not his fault but his son's; he not only knew nothing of it but was not even there when it was committed. He was then besieging the city of Ardea, carrying on a war in defence of the Roman people. We do not know what he would have done, if news of his son's crime had been brought to his notice. Nevertheless, with no trial of what his verdict would have been, the people deprived him, without examination, of his authority by shutting their gates, as soon as the army, which was ordered to desert him, had been admitted, and did not let him enter when he returned. Yet after the deadliest war, whereby, summoning their neighbours to arms, he had wasted those same Romans, once he had been deserted by those whom he trusted to help him, so that he was too weak to recover his throne, he lived a quiet life as a private citizen for fourteen years, it is said, in the town of Tusculum, near Rome, and lived out his life with his wife. Such an end was probably preferable to his father-in-law's, who had been slain by his son-in-law with the connivance, if report be true, of his own daughter.

Yet our Tarquin, such as he was, the Romans called, not the Cruel, nor the Accursed, but the Proud. Perhaps they found the tyrant's arrogance insufferable because of a pride of their own that matched his. They thought so little of this crime of slaying his father-in-law, their own very good king, that they took him as their king. I wonder whether it was not a greater crime for them to bestow so great a reward on so great a crime. And it did not happen that " the gods did all depart, leaving shrines

relictis di ". Nisi forte quispiam sic defendat istos
deos, ut dicat eos ideo mansisse Romae, quo possent
magis Romanos punire suppliciis quam beneficiis
adiuvare, seducentes eos vanis victoriis et bellis
gravissimis conterentes.

Haec fuit Romanorum vita sub regibus laudabili
tempore illius rei publicae usque ad expulsionem
Tarquinii Superbi per ducentos ferme et quadraginta
et tres annos, cum illae omnes victoriae tam multo
sanguine et tantis emptae calamitatibus vix illud
imperium intra viginti ab Urbe milia dilataverint;
quantum spatium absit ut saltem alicuius Getulae
civitatis nunc territorio comparetur.

XVI

*De primis apud Romanos consulibus, quorum alter
alterum patria pepulit moxque ipse post atrocissima
parricidia a vulnerato hoste vulneratus interiit.*

HUIC tempori adiciamus etiam tempus illud, quo
usque dicit Sallustius aequo et modesto iure agitatum,
dum metus a Tarquinio et bellum grave cum Etruria
positum est. Quamdiu enim Etrusci Tarquinio in
regnum redire conanti opitulati sunt, gravi bello
Roma concussa est. Ideo dicit aequo et modesto iure
gestam rem publicam metu premente, non persua-
dente iustitia.

In quo brevissimo tempore quam funestus ille
annus fuit, quo primi consules creati sunt expulsa
328

and altars abandoned." Perhaps, however, someone will defend those gods by saying that they remained at Rome with intent to punish the Romans by penalties rather than to aid them, as they lured them with empty victories, and crushed them under the staggering burden of their wars.

This was the kind of life the Romans led under the kings in that much praised epoch of the state that expired with the expulsion of Tarquin the Proud after two hundred and forty-three years. At that moment all those victories, bought with so much bloodshed and such great disasters, had scarce expanded the dominion twenty miles from the city. God forbid we should compare so small a domain with that of even any Getulian city of our time.

XVI

On the first Roman consuls, of whom one expelled the other, and presently perished by a wound from a wounded enemy, following a series of blackest murders.

To that epoch let us add also the epoch in which, as Sallust says, equitable and just law still prevailed, that is, until fear of Tarquin and a serious war with Etruria were relieved. For, as long as the Etruscans gave assistance to Tarquin in his attempt to regain the throne, Rome was shaken by a serious war. For this reason, he says, equitable and just law prevailed rather from the pressure of fear than from the influence of justice.

In this very short epoch, how disastrous a year was that in which the first consuls were elected after the

regia potestate! Annum quippe suum non compleverunt. Nam Iunius Brutus exhonoratum eiecit
Urbe collegam Lucium Tarquinium Collatinum;
deinde mox ipse in bello cecidit mutuis cum hoste
vulneribus, occisis a se ipso primitus filiis suis et
uxoris suae fratribus, quod eos pro restituendo
Tarquinio coniurasse cognoverat.

Quod factum Vergilius postea quam laudabiliter
commemoravit, continuo clementer exhorruit. Cum
enim dixisset:

> Natosque pater nova bella moventes
> Ad poenam pulchra pro libertate vocabit,

mox deinde exclamavit et ait:

> Infelix, utcumque ferent ea facta minores.

Quomodolibet, inquit, ea facta posteri ferant id est
praeferant et extollant, qui filios occidit infelix est.
Et tamquam ad consolandum infelicem subiunxit:

> Vincit amor patriae laudumque inmensa cupido.

Nonne in hoc Bruto, qui et filios occidit et a se
percusso hosti filio Tarquinii mutuo percussus super-
vivere non potuit eique potius ipse Tarquinius super-
vixit, Collatini collegae videtur innocentia vindicata,
qui bonus civis hoc Tarquinio pulso passus est quod
tyrannus ipse Tarquinius?

---

[1] Virgil, *Aeneid* 6.820-3.

royal power was expelled!   They did not, to be sure, complete their year, for Junius Brutus thrust from the city in disgrace his colleague, Lucius Tarquinius Collatinus.   Shortly afterward he himself fell in battle at the hands of an enemy, giving as well as receiving wounds, having first slain by his own hands his sons and the brothers of his wife, because he had learned of their conspiring with others to restore Tarquin.

This deed Virgil afterwards mentions with approval, yet instantly shudders at it in the kindness of his heart.   Having said,

> And when a father finds his sons devising wars
> Once more, to save bright freedom, he himself
> Will summon them to execution,[1]

he immediately exclaims,

> Unhappy he, no matter though his deed
> Be celebrated in the days to come.

He means, let men to come judge these deeds in any way they will, that is, let them praise and extol the slayer of his sons, yet he is unhappy.   And then, as if to console the unhappy man, he adds,

> Love of country wins, and boundless appetite for
>   praise.

In the case of this Brutus, who slew his sons and also his enemy, the son of Tarquin, whom, however, he could not himself survive, receiving a blow in return, but rather was survived by Tarquin himself, does not the innocence of his colleague Collatinus appear to have been vindicated, who, though a good citizen, suffered, when this Tarquin was expelled, the same punishment as the tyrannical Tarquin?

331

Nam et idem Brutus consanguineus Tarquinii fuisse perhibetur; sed Collatinum videlicet similitudo nominis pressit, quia etiam Tarquinius vocabatur. Mutare ergo nomen, non patriam cogeretur; postremo in eius nomine hoc vocabulum minus esset, L. Collatinus tantummodo vocaretur. Sed ideo non amisit quod sine ullo detrimento posset amittere, ut et honore primus consul et civitate bonus civis carere iuberetur. Etiamne ista est gloria, Iunii Bruti destestanda iniquitas et nihilo utilis rei publicae? Etiamne ad hanc perpetrandam "vicit amor patriae laudumque inmensa cupido?"

Iam expulso utique Tarquinio tyranno consul cum Bruto creatus est maritus Lucretiae L. Tarquinius Collatinus. Quam iuste populus mores in cive, non nomen adtendit! Quam impie Brutus collegam primae ac novae illius potestatis, quem posset, si hoc offendebatur, nomine tantum privare, et patria privavit et honore! Haec mala facta sunt, haec adversa acciderunt, quando in illa re publica "aequo et modesto iure agitatum est." Lucretius quoque, qui in locum Bruti fuerat subrogatus, morbo, antequam idem annus terminaretur, absumptus est. Ita P. Valerius, qui successerat Collatino, et M. Horatius, qui pro defuncto Lucretio suffectus fuerat, annum illum funereum atque tartareum, qui consules quinque habuit, compleverunt, quo anno consulatus ipsius novum honorem ac potestatem auspicata est Romana res publica.

For the same Brutus is said also to have been of the blood of Tarquin, but what brought down Collatinus, be it noted, was the resemblance of the name, since he was also called Tarquinius. He should, therefore, have been required to give up his name, not his country. Lastly, his name should have been docked of the term, and he called simply Lucius Collatinus. Why did he not lose what he could have lost with no harm? In order that he might be commanded to enjoy no honour, first consul though he was, and no citizenship, good citizen though he was. Is that to pass for glory, such injustice as Junius Brutus', execrable and profitless to the state? Did his " love of country and boundless appetite for fame " force him to do even that?

When the tyrant, Tarquin, was in any case already expelled, Lucius Tarquinius Collatinus, husband of Lucretia, was elected consul along with Brutus. How justly the people gave heed to the character of a citizen, not to his name! How wickedly Brutus deprived both of country and office his colleague in the first holding of that new office, when he might have deprived him of his name only, if that gave offence! These evil deeds were done, these untoward events took place, at a time when " equitable and just law prevailed." Lucretius also, who was elected to replace Brutus, died of disease before the year was out. So Publius Valerius, who succeeded Collatinus, and Marcus Horatius, who filled the vacancy caused by the death of Lucretius, completed that funereal and hellish year which had five consuls, the year in which the Roman republic inaugurated the new office and power of the consulship itself.

XVII

Post initia consularis imperii quibus malis vexata
fuerit Romana res publica, diis non opitulantibus,
quos colebat.

TUNC iam deminuto paululum metu, non quia bella
conquieverant, sed quia non tam gravi pondere urge-
bant, finito scilicet tempore, quo aequo iure ac
modesto agitatum est, secuta sunt quae idem
Sallustius breviter explicat: " Dein servili imperio
patres plebem exercere, de vita atque tergo regio
more consulere, agro pellere et ceteris expertibus
soli in imperio agere. Quibus saevitiis et maxime
faenore oppressa plebes, cum assiduis bellis tributum
et militiam simul toleraret, armata montem sacrum
atque Aventinum insedit, tumque tribunos plebis
et alia iura sibi paravit. Discordiarum et certaminis
utrimque finis fuit secundum bellum Punicum."

Quid itaque ego tantas moras vel scribens patiar,
vel lecturis adferam? Quam misera fuerit illa res
publica, tam longa aetate per tot annos usque ad
secundum bellum Punicum bellis forinsecus inquietare
non desistentibus et intus discordiis seditionibusque
civilibus, a Sallustio breviter intimatum est. Proinde
victoriae illae non solida beatorum gaudia fuerunt,
sed inania solacia miserorum et ad alia atque alia
sterilia mala subeunda inlecebrosa incitamenta
minime quietorum. Nec nobis, quia hoc dicimus,
boni Romani prudentesque suscenseant—quamquam

---

[1] Sallust, *History* 1.11, also quoted above, 2.18.

XVII

The disasters that vexed the Roman republic after the
establishment of the consulship, while no help
was received from the gods they worshipped.

THEN, when little by little alarms subsided, not
because the wars were ended, but because they were
not so serious a burden, that period, we note, came
to an end, in which " equitable and just law prevailed." Then followed the period that Sallust
briefly sketches: " From that time on the patricians
treated the plebs as slaves, ordered them executed
and flogged as the kings had done, drove them from
their land, or behaved like tyrants to the rest who
were landless. The common people, crushed by this
savage treatment and particularly by high rates of
interest, and bearing a double burden of taxation and
military service in the constant wars, withdrew under
arms to the Sacred Hill and to the Aventine, and at
last gained tribunes of the plebs and other rights for
themselves. The end of discord and strife on both
sides was reached only with the Second Punic War." [1]

Why now should I take the time to write, why
should I take the reader's time to read, the whole
story? Sallust has in a nutshell disclosed how
wretched was that republic in the long period of
years up to the Second Punic War when external
wars and internal discords and dissensions never
ceased to cause unrest. The famous victories were,
accordingly, not substantial joys of the fortunate,
but empty comforts of the wretched and alluring
enticements for restless men to make them undergo
fruitless hardships upon hardships. Let not the good
and wise Romans resent our saying this; yet we need

335

de hac re nec petendi sint nec monendi, quando eos
minime suscensuros esse certissimum est. Neque
enim gravius vel graviora dicimus auctoribus eorum et
stilo et otio multum impares; quibus tamen edis-
cendis et ipsi elaboraverunt et filios suos elaborare
compellunt. Qui autem suscensent, quando me
ferrent, si ego dicerem, quod Sallustius ait? " Pluri-
mae turbae, seditiones et ad postremum bella civilia
orta sunt, dum pauci potentes, quorum in gratiam
plerique concesserant, sub honesto patrum aut plebis
nomine dominationes adfectabant; bonique et mali
cives appellati, non ob merita in rem publicam,
omnibus pariter corruptis, sed uti quisque locu-
pletissimus et iniuria validior, quia praesentia de-
fendebat, pro bono ducebatur."

Porro si illi scriptores historiae ad honestam libertatem pertinere arbitrati sunt mala civitatis propriae
non tacere, quam multis locis magno praeconio
laudare compulsi sunt, cum aliam veriorem, quo cives
aeterni legendi sunt, non haberent, quid nos facere
convenit, quorum spes quanto in Deo melior et certior,
tanto maior debet esse libertas, cum mala praesentia
Christo nostro inputant, ut infirmiores imperitiores-
que mentes alienentur ab ea civitate, in qua sola
iugiter feliciterque vivendum est? Nec in deos
eorum horribiliora nos dicimus quam eorum ident-
idem auctores, quos legunt et praedicant, quando

---

[1] Sallust, *History* 1.12.

not ask them nor advise them not to be resentful, when it is most certain that they will have no resentment, for we speak no more severely and mention no more serious faults than their own writers, and we are far from a match for them in style and leisure to write. Nevertheless to get such authors by heart is a task that they have performed and that they compel their children to perform. How would those who are angry with me now put up with me if I were to say what Sallust says? "Frequent riots, party strife, and at last civil wars broke out, while a few powerful men, to whose popularity most citizens had lent support, masquerading as supporters of Senate or people, pursued the goal of tyranny. Both terms, good and bad, were applied to citizens, not for services to the state, since all were equally corrupt; but whatever individual was wealthiest and most strongly entrenched in his lawlessness was counted 'good' because he was a guardian of present conditions." [1]

Furthermore, if those historians thought it the privilege of honourable freedom not to be silent about the blemishes of their state, which in many places they have been forced loudly to praise since they had no other more genuine city (one whose citizens are to be selected for all time), what is it incumbent on us to do, whose freedom ought to be greater as our hope in God is better and surer, when men attribute the evils of this present life to our Christ, in order that the weaker and more innocent-minded may be estranged from that city in which alone a blessed life is to be lived eternally? We say nothing more dreadful against their gods than their own authors, whom they read and cry up, say again and again. Indeed, they are the sources on which we have drawn for some-

quidem et ex ipsis quae diceremus accepimus, et nullo modo dicere vel talia vel cuncta sufficimus.

Ubi ergo erant illi dii, qui propter exiguam fallacemque mundi huius felicitatem colendi existimantur, cum Romani, quibus se colendos mendacissima astutia venditabant, tantis calamitatibus vexarentur? Ubi erant, quando Valerius consul ab exulibus et servis incensum Capitolium cum defensaret occisus est faciliusque ipse prodesse potuit aedi Iovis quam illi turba tot numinum cum suo maximo atque optimo rege, cuius templum liberaverat, subvenire? Ubi erant, quando densissimis fatigata civitas seditionum malis, cum legatos Athenas missos ad leges mutandas paululum quieta opperiretur, gravi fame pestilentiaque vastata est? Ubi erant, quando rursus populus, cum fame laboraret, praefectum annonae primum creavit, atque illa fame invalescente Spurius Maelius, quia esurienti multitudini frumenta largitus est, regni adfectati crimen incurrit et eiusdem praefecti instantia per dictatorem L. Quintium aetate decrepitum a Quinto Servilio magistro equitum cum maximo et periculosissimo tumultu civitatis occisus est?

Ubi erant, quando pestilentia maxima exorta diis inutilibus populus diu multumque fatigatus nova

---

¹ See Livy 3.18.
² See above, 2.16.
³ The prefect was L. Minucius (Livy 4.12 f., 440 B.C.); the dictator, the famous Cincinnatus, then aged 80; the master of the horse, Gaius, not Quintus, Servilius Ahala.

thing to say, and we are by no means capable of putting things as they do or of including everything that they have.

Where, then, were those gods, who are held to deserve worship for the sake of the scanty and treacherous happiness of this world, when the Romans to whom they commended themselves as deserving worship with all the guile of an utterly fraudulent salesman, were harassed by such great calamities? Where were they when the consul Valerius was slain defending the Capitol after it was fired by exiles and slaves,[1] when he found it easier to give aid himself to the temple of Jupiter than it was for that so numerous throng of divinities, with their own greatest and best king, whose temple he had delivered, to come to his aid? Where were they when the city, worn out by the so continually repeated evils of civil strife, was laid waste by dire famine and pestilence at a time when the city was enjoying a short period of calm as it awaited the ambassadors who had been sent to Athens to select laws for adoption?[2] Where were they when again the people were suffering from famine, when they elected for the first time a prefect of the grain supply, and when, as the famine increased, Spurius Maelius, because he distributed grain to the hungry mob, was charged with aspiring to royal power, and at the instance of this same prefect was slain on the authority of the aged dictator, Lucius Quintius, by Quintus Servilius, master of the horse, occasioning thereby a serious and most dangerous riot in the city?[3]

Where were they when, a very great pestilence having arisen, the people in their long and great weariness decreed that lectisternia should be ex-

339

lectisternia, quod numquam antea fecerat, exhibenda
arbitratus est? Lecti autem sternebantur in honorem deorum, unde hoc sacrum vel potius sacrilegium
nomen accepit. Ubi erant, quando per decem con-
tinuos annos male pugnando crebras et magnas
clades apud Veios exercitus Romanus acceperat, nisi
per Furium Camillum tandem subveniretur, quem
postea civitas ingrata damnavit? Ubi erant, quando
Galli Romam ceperunt, spoliaverunt, incenderunt,
caedibus impleverunt? Ubi erant, cum illa insignis
pestilentia tam ingentem stragem dedit, qua et ille
Furius Camillus extinctus est, qui rem publicam
ingratam et a Veientibus ante defendit et de Gallis
postea vindicavit? In hac pestilentia scaenicos ludos
aliam novam pestem non corporibus Romanorum, sed,
quod est multo perniciosius, moribus intulerunt.

Ubi erant, quando alia pestilentia gravis de venenis
matronarum exorta credita est, quarum supra fidem
multarum atque nobilium mores deprehensi sunt
omni pestilentia graviores? Vel quando in Caudinas
furculas a Samnitibus obsessi ambo cum exercitu
consules foedus cum eis foedum facere coacti sunt, ita
ut equitibus Romanis sescentis obsidibus datis ceteri
amissis armis aliisque spoliati privatique tegminibus
sub iugum hostium in vestimentis singulis mitte-

---

[1] This was in 399 B.C.—see Livy 5.13.
[2] The war with Veii lasted 407–396 B.C.—see above, 2.17;
Livy 5.32.
[3] In 390 B.C.—see Livy 5.37–40.
[4] In 365 B.C.—see Livy 7.1.
[5] Livy 8.18.
[6] In 321 B.C.—see Livy 9.3–6.
[7] Livy 10.31.

340

hibited before the useless gods, a new thing never
done before ? [1] They spread couches before the gods
in their honour, from which this sacred or rather
sacrilegious rite got its name. Where were they
when, for ten years in succession, the Roman army by
fighting badly suffered frequent and great disasters
at the hands of the people of Veii, and would have
been destroyed except for the aid at last of Furius
Camillus, whom the thankless city afterwards condemned ? [2] Where were they when the Gauls took,
sacked, burned Rome and filled it with slaughter ? [3]
Where were they when that memorable pestilence
worked such havoc, in which perished that Furius
Camillus, who first defended the thankless republic
from the people of Veii and later recovered it from
the Gauls ? [4] In this pestilence they introduced the
stage performances, another new disease, harmful not
to the bodies of the Romans but, and that is far more
fatal, to their morals.

Where were they when still another serious plague
infected the city, the one which was believed to have
sprung from the poison administered by matrons,
who, in such numbers and so high in rank that it
passes belief, were detected in immorality worse than
any plague ? [5] Or when at the Caudine Forks both
consuls at the head of an army were so beset by the
Samnites that they were forced to make a shameful
treaty with them, six hundred Roman knights being
surrendered as hostages, while the remaining troops,
having lost their arms and been deprived of all other
garments, were forced to pass beneath the yoke, each
garbed in a single piece of clothing ? [6] Or when,
during a severe plague affecting the rest, many in the
army also perished by a stroke of lightning ? [7] Or,

rentur? Vel quando gravi pestilentia ceteris laborantibus multi etiam in exercitu icti fulmine perierunt? Vel quando item alia intolerabili pestilentia Aesculapium ab Epidauro quasi medicum deum Roma advocare atque adhibere compulsa est, quoniam regem omnium Iovem, qui iam diu in Capitolio sedebat, multa stupra, quibus adulescens vacaverat, non permiserant fortasse discere medicinam? Vel cum conspirantibus uno tempore hostibus Lucanis, Bruttiis, Samnitibus, Etruscis et Senonibus Gallis primo ab eis legati perempti sunt, deinde cum praetore oppressus exercitus septem tribunis cum illo pereuntibus et militum tredecim milibus? Vel quando post longas et graves Romae seditiones, quibus ad ultimum plebs in Ianiculum hostili diremptione secesserat, huius mali tam dira calamitas erat, ut eius rei causa, quod in extremis periculis fieri solebat, dictator crearetur Hortensius, qui plebe revocata in eodem magistratu exspiravit, quod nulli dictatori ante contigerat et quod illis diis iam praesente Aesculapio gravius crimen fuit?

Tum vero tam multa bella ubique crebruerunt, ut inopia militum proletarii illi, qui eo, quod proli gignendae vacabant, ob egestatem militare non valentes hoc nomen acceperant, militiae conscriberentur. Accitus etiam a Tarentinis Pyrrhus, rex Graeciae, tunc ingenti gloria celebratus, Romanorum hostis effectus est. Cui sane de rerum futuro eventu consulenti satis urbane Apollo sic ambiguum ora-

---

[1] In 293 B.C.—see Livy 10.47.
[2] In 283 B.C.—see Livy, *Epitome* 12; Orosius 3.22.
[3] In 286 B.C.—see Livy, *Epitome* 11.

likewise, when during another unbearable plague, Rome was forced to invite and bring Aesculapius from Epidaurus, as a physician god, since the many adulteries, for which Jupiter, King of All, now long sitting in the capitol, had found time in his youth, had perchance not allowed him to learn medicine? [1] Or when the Lucanians, Bruttians, Samnites, Etruscans and Senonian Gauls, conspired together so that ambassadors were first slain by them, then an army under a praetor was crushed, seven tribunes and thirteen thousand soldiers being lost with the praetor? [2] Or when, after long and serious civil strife at Rome, in which finally the people plundered the city like an enemy and seceded to the Janiculum, so ominous was the disastrous situation that Hortensius was made dictator, a measure commonly adopted in times of gravest peril, and he, having brought back the people, died still in that same office, a thing that never happened before to any dictator, and that brought a more serious charge against those gods, now that they had Aesculapius among them? [3]

That was the time indeed when wars were so frequent everywhere that to meet the scarcity of soldiers they enrolled for service the proletarians, who had received that appellation because, being too poor to serve as soldiers, they had leisure to beget offspring.[4] Then again Pyrrhus, King of Greece, at that time at the height of his fame, was invited by the Tarentines and became an enemy of the Romans. It was to him, of course, that, when he was inquiring about the outcome of those events, Apollo wittily uttered so ambiguous an oracle that, whichever of the

[4] See Cicero, *Republic* 2.22. Proletarians are those who can only beget offspring (*proles*).

343

culum edidit, ut, e duobus quidquid accidisset, ipse divinus haberetur (ait enim: " Dico te, Pyrrhe, vincere posse Romanos ") atque ita, sive Pyrrhus a Romanis sive Romani a Pyrrho vincerentur, securus fatidicus utrumlibet expectaret eventum. Quae tunc et quam horrenda utriusque exercitus clades! In qua tamen superior Pyrrhus extitit, ut iam posset Apollinem pro suo intellectu praedicare divinum, nisi proxime alio proelio Romani abscederent superiores.

Atque in tanta strage bellorum etiam pestilentia gravis exorta est mulierum. Nam priusquam maturos partus ederent, gravidae moriebantur. Ubi se, credo, Aesculapius excusabat, quod archiatrum, non obstetricem profitebatur. Pecudes quoque similiter interibant, ita ut etiam defecturum genus animalium crederetur. Quid? Hiems illa memorabilis tam incredibili inmanitate saeviens, ut nivibus horrenda altitudine etiam in foro per dies quadraginta manentibus Tiberis quoque glacie duraretur, si nostris temporibus accidisset, quae isti et quanta dixissent! Quid? Illa itidem ingens pestilentia, quamdiu saeviit, quam multos peremit! Quae cum in annum alium multo gravius tenderetur frustra praesente Aesculapio, aditum est ad libros Sibyllinos. In quo genere oraculorum, sicut Cicero in libris de divinatione commemorat, magis interpretibus ut possunt seu volunt dubia coniectantibus credi solet.

Tunc ergo dictum est eam esse causam pestilentiae, quod plurimas aedes sacras multi occupatas privatim

---

[1] The Latin permits the reader to take either *te* or *Romanos* as subject.

[2] Orosius 4.5.

[3] Cicero, *On Divination* 2.54.110–12.

two possible outcomes occurred, he would himself seem to be a diviner (for he said, " I declare, Pyrrhus, that you the Romans have power to conquer "),[1] and so, whether Pyrrhus was to be conquered by the Romans, or the Romans by Pyrrhus, the prophet might await either outcome without anxiety. What dreadful disasters both armies then experienced! Yet in this contest Pyrrhus remained superior, so that he might have said that Apollo was a true diviner as far as his understanding went, had not soon after the Romans come off the better in another battle.

And in the midst of this great military slaughter there arose a deadly plague among the women, for the pregnant women died before the time of delivery. At this point, I suppose, Aesculapius made the excuse that his profession was chief physician, not midwife. Cattle, too, likewise perished in such numbers that it was thought the whole race of animals would become extinct. What about that remarkable winter, so incredibly severe, when snow lay even in the forum dreadfully deep for forty days running and the Tiber also was frozen? If this had happened in our time, what would they have said! What about that other great plague which raged so long and killed so many? Despite the presence of Aesculapius, it was entering its second year far more severe when recourse was had to the Sibylline books.[2] In the case of this kind of oracle, as Cicero tells us in his books *On Divination*,[3] greater faith is put in interpreters who make what guess they can or choose about the application of an ambiguous passage.

In this instance it was said that the cause of the plague was the fact that so many consecrated shrines were occupied for private uses. Thus, for the present,

tenerent; sic interim a magno imperitiae vel desidiae crimine Aesculapius liberatus est. Unde autem a multis aedes illae fuerant occupatae nemine prohibente, nisi quia tantae numinum turbae diu frustra fuerat supplicatum, atque ita paulatim loca deserebantur a cultoribus, ut tamquam vacua sine ullius offensione possent humanis saltem usibus vindicari? Namque tunc velut ad sedandam pestilentiam diligenter repetita atque reparata nisi postea eodem modo neglecta atque usurpata latitarent, non utique magnae peritiae Varronis tribueretur, quod scribens de aedibus sacris tam multa ignorata commemorat. Sed tunc interim elegans non pestilentiae depulsio, sed deorum excusatio procurata est.

XVIII

Quantae clades Romanos sub bellis Punicis triverint frustra deorum praesidiis expetitis.

Iam vero Punicis bellis, cum inter utrumque imperium victoria diu anceps atque incerta penderet populique duo praevalidi impetus in alterutrum fortissimos et opulentissimos agerent, quot minutiora regna contrita sunt! Quae urbes amplae nobilesque deletae, quot adflictae, quot perditae civitates! Quam longe lateque tot regiones terraeque vastatae sunt! Quotiens victi hinc atque inde victores! Quid hominum consumptum est vel pugnantium militum

Aesculapius was freed from the serious charge of ignorance or laziness. Then why were so many shrines occupied without objection by anybody, unless because such great throngs of divinities had for a long time been appealed to without result, and hence the sites were gradually deserted by their worshippers, so that, being unoccupied, it was assumed that they might be reclaimed to serve the needs of men at least without any sin against the gods? For, though at that time they were diligently sought out and put into repair to lay the plague to rest, yet if they had not afterwards through similar neglect and appropriation been lost to view, certainly no one would cite it as evidence of Varro's mighty learning that in discussing sacred shrines he mentions so many that are unfamiliar. Meanwhile, there was procured, not a cessation of the plague, but a neat excuse for the gods.

XVIII

How great were the disasters that crushed the Romans in the Punic wars and were not mitigated by aid implored from the gods.

Now in the Punic wars, when victory long hung in the balance doubtful and undecided between one empire or the other, and two powerful nations were directing their assault upon each other with all their strength and all their resources, how many minor kingdoms were crushed, how many large and noble cities were demolished, how many states were hard smitten or ruined! How many regions far and wide were laid waste! How often were the victors on either side vanquished! How many human beings

vel ab armis vacantium populorum! Quanta vis navium marinis etiam proeliis oppressa et diversarum tempestatum varietate submersa est! Si enarrare vel commemorare conemur, nihil aliud quam scriptores etiam nos erimus historiae. Tunc magno metu perturbata Romana civitas ad remedia vana et ridenda currebat. Instaurati sunt ex auctoritate librorum Sibyllinorum ludi saeculares, quorum celebritas inter centum annos fuerat instituta felicioribusque temporibus memoria neglegente perierat. Renovarunt etiam pontifices ludos sacros inferis et ipsos abolitos annis retrorsum melioribus.

Nimirum enim, quando renovati sunt, tanta copia morientium ditatos inferos etiam ludere delectabat, cum profecto miseri homines ipsa rabida bella et cruentas animositates funereasque hinc atque inde victorias magnos agerent ludos daemonum et opimas epulas inferorum. Nihil sane miserabilius primo Punico bello accidit quam quod ita Romani victi sunt ut etiam Regulus ille caperetur, cuius in primo et in altero libro mentionem fecimus, vir plane magnus et victor antea domitorque Poenorum, qui etiam ipsum primum bellum Punicum confecisset, nisi aviditate nimia laudis et gloriae duriores condiciones quam ferre possent fessis Carthaginiensibus imperasset. Illius viri et captivitas inopinatissima et servitus indignissima, et iuratio fidelissima et mors crudelissima si deos illos non cogit erubescere, verum est quod aerii sunt et non habent sanguinem.

died, whether soldiers in battle or peoples not engaged in warfare! What a huge array of ships were destroyed in naval engagements or sunk amid the vicissitudes of changing weather! If we should try to describe or even mention them, we should become in our own person a mere historian. It was then that, terrified by a new fear, the city of Rome had recourse to vain and ridiculous remedies. By the authority of the Sibylline books, the secular games, celebrated a century before, and then forgotten in happier times, were renewed. The games consecrated to the nether gods were also renewed by the pontiffs, for they, too, had sunk into disuse in the better years of the past.

And no wonder, for when they were renewed, the great abundance of dying men that enriched the gods of the lower world put them too in the mood to enjoy sport, though, to be sure, the venomous wars and blood-stained quarrels, accompanied by deadly victories, now on one side, now the other, themselves provided great sport for demons and rich banquets for the nether gods. No doubt, in the First Punic War nothing more lamentable occurred than the Roman defeat in which that Regulus was taken captive whom I mentioned in the first and second books, a man incontestably great, previously a victor and a conqueror of the Carthaginians, who would even have brought that first Punic War to an end, had not his excessive appetite for praise and glory impelled him to exact from the wearied Carthaginians terms too harsh for them to bear. If this man's unexpected captivity and his most undeserved enslavement, his fidelity to his oath and his most cruel death, do not force the aforesaid gods to blush, it must be true that they are made of air and have no blood.

349

Nec mala illo tempore gravissima intra moenia defuerunt. Nam exundante nimis ultra morem fluvio Tiberino paene omnia urbis plana subversa sunt, aliis impetu quasi torrentis inpulsis, aliis velut stagno diuturno madefactis atque sublapsis. Istam deinde pestem ignis perniciosior subsecutus est, qui correptis circa forum quibusque celsioribus etiam templo Vestae suo familiarissimo non pepercit, ubi ei veluti vitam perpetuam diligentissima substitutione lignorum non tam honoratae quam damnatae virgines donare consuerant. Tunc vero illic ignis non tantum vivebat, sed etiam saeviebat. Cuius impetu exterritae virgines sacra illa fatalia, quae iam tres, in quibus fuerant, presserant civitates, cum ab illo incendio liberare non possent, Metellus pontifex suae quodam modo salutis oblitus inruens ea semiustus abripuit. Neque enim vel ipsum ignis agnovit, aut vero erat ibi numen quod non etiam, si fuisset, fugisset. Homo igitur potius sacris Vestae quam illa homini prodesse potuerunt. Si autem a se ipsis ignem non repellebant, civitatem, cuius salutem tueri putabantur, quid contra illas aquas flammasque poterant adiuvare? Sicut etiam res ipsa nihil ea prorsus potuisse patefecit.

Haec istis nequaquam obicerentur a nobis, si illa sacra dicerent non tuendis his bonis temporalibus

Nor was there any lack in that period of the most serious disasters within the walls. For when the Tiber overflowed its usual banks and covered almost all the lower areas in the city, some buildings were carried away by the violence of what was almost a torrent, others, when soaked, as of course they were when the overflow persisted, collapsed. This destruction was followed by an even more fatal fire that, when it had fastened on certain of the higher buildings about the forum, did not even spare its own peculiar temple of Vesta, where the Virgins, not so much honoured as condemned, were wont to confer on fire a life eternal by ceaselessly replenishing it with wood. At that time truly the fire there was not merely living; it was raging. When the virgins, terrified by its attack, were unable to save from the flame those fateful images that had already overthrown three cities in which they had resided, the pontiff Metellus, forgetful in a way of his own safety, rushed in and rescued them, being himself half consumed by fire. For neither was he himself recognized by the fire, nor was there in truth any deity there that would not, if it had been there at all, have fled with the rest. It was rather the case, then, that a human being had power to aid the holy appurtenances of Vesta than that these things had power to aid a human being. Moreover, if they did not protect themselves from the flames, what help could they bring against those floods and flames to the city over whose safety they were thought to mount guard? Just so the actual event reveals that they had no power whatever.

These objections on our part would have no point if they maintained that these religious practices were instituted, not to secure temporal blessings, but as

351

instituta, sed significandis aeternis, et ideo, cum ea, quod corporalia visibiliaque essent, perire contingeret, nihil his rebus minui, propter quas fuerant instituta, et posse ad eosdem usus denuo reparari. Nunc vero caecitate mirabili eis sacris quae perire possent fieri potuisse existimant ut salus terrena et temporalis felicitas civitatis perire non posset. Proinde cum illis etiam manentibus sacris vel salutis contritio vel infelicitas inruisse monstratur, mutare sententiam, quam defendere nequeunt, erubescunt.

XIX

De afflictione belli Punici secundi, qua vires utrius-
que partis consumptae sunt.

Secundo autem Punico bello nimis longum est com-memorare clades duorum populorum tam longe secum lateque pugnantium, ita ut his quoque fatentibus, qui non tam narrare bella Romana quam Romanum impe-rium laudare instituerunt, similior victo fuerit ille qui vicit. Hannibale quippe ab Hispania surgente et Pyrenaeis montibus superatis, Gallia transcursa Alpibusque disruptis, tam longo circuitu auctis viribus cuncta vastando aut subigendo torrentis modo Italiae faucibus inruente quam cruenta proelia gesta sunt, quotiens Romani superati! Quam multa ad hostem oppida defecerunt, quam multa capta et

symbols of the eternal, and that therefore, though the corporeal and visible objects chanced to perish, yet no damage was done to the realities which they had been established to serve, and new provision could be made to supply the same service. As it is, so remarkable is their blindness, they suppose that by the action of perishable objects of worship the earthly safety and the temporal felicity of a state could be kept imperishable. Accordingly, when it is shown that, even while those sacred objects lasted, they suffered either crushing blows to their welfare or invasions of ill fortune, they blush to change the opinion that they are unable to defend.

XIX

Of the scourge of the Second Punic War whereby the resources of both sides were exhausted.

As for the Second Punic War, it would be too long a task to enumerate all the disasters experienced by the two nations in their wide-ranging contest with one another—such disasters that, as even those freely acknowledge whose aim is not so much a narrative of the wars of Rome as a eulogy of Rome's dominion, the conquering nation was more like one conquered. When Hannibal, as we know, left his source in Spain, crossed the Pyrenees mountains, traversed Gaul, burst through the Alps and, while making so long a circuit, increased his strength by plundering or subduing everything as he went, sweeping through the passes into Italy like a flood, what bloody battles were waged, how many times were the Romans defeated! How many towns went over to the enemy, how many were captured and overwhelmed! How

oppressa! Quam dirae pugnae et totiens Hannibali
Romana clade gloriosae! De Cannensi autem
mirabiliter horrendo malo quid dicam, ubi Hannibal,
cum esset crudelissimus, tamen tanta inimicorum
atrocissimorum caede satiatus parci iussisse perhibetur? Unde tres modios anulorum aureorum
Carthaginem misit, quo intellegerent tantam in illo
proelio dignitatem cecidisse Romanam, ut facilius eam
caperet mensura quam numerus, atque hinc strages
turbae ceterae tanto utique numerosioris, quanto
infimioris, quae sine anulis iacebat, conicienda
potius quam nuntianda putaretur.

Denique tanta militum inopia secuta est, ut Romani
reos facinorum proposita inpunitate colligerent, servitia libertate donarent atque illis pudendus non tam
suppleretur quam institueretur exercitus. Servis
itaque, immo, ne faciamus iniuriam, iam libertis, pro
Romana re publica pugnaturis arma defuerunt.
Detracta sunt templis, tamquam Romani diis suis
dicerent: " Ponite quae tam diu inaniter habuistis,
ne forte aliquid utile inde facere possint nostra
mancipia, unde nostra numina facere non potuistis."
Tunc etiam stipendiis sufficiendis cum defecisset
aerarium, in usus publicos opes venere privatae, adeo
unoquoque id quod habuit conferente, ut praeter
singulos anulos singulasque bullas, miserabilia dignitatis insignia, nihil sibi auri senatus ipse, quanto
magis ceteri ordines tribusque relinquerent. Quis
ferret istos, si nostris temporibus ad hanc inopiam

ill-omened were the engagements that so often by
a Roman disaster brought glory to Hannibal! What
shall I say too of the surprisingly shocking loss at
Cannae when Hannibal, cruel in the extreme as he
was, nevertheless had his fill of the slaughter of his
worst enemies and, it is said, gave orders that they
should be spared? From the carnage he sent three
pecks of gold rings to Carthage to signify that so
great a proportion of the Roman nobility had fallen
in that battle that it was easier to grasp it by measure
than by number, and that the frightful slaughter of
the common soldiers, the more in number as lower in
social rank, who lay there dead without rings, must
rather be guessed at than precisely reported.

Then so great a dearth of soldiers ensued that the
Romans by promising freedom from punishment
gathered in the criminal classes and manumitted
slaves, and used these classes, not as replacements,
but created from them a new army to be ashamed of.
And so these slaves, or rather, not to wrong them,
these men now freedmen, lacked arms to fight for the
Roman republic, so arms were taken down from the
temples, as if the Romans should say to their gods,
" Lay down what you have so long kept to no purpose, preventing our slaves from making some use of
objects that you, our gods, were unable to use." At
that time the public treasury also lacked funds for
paying the soldiers, and private resources were sold
for public purposes, as each individual contributed
what he had, to such an extent that except for one
ring each and one amulet, pitiable marks of rank, even
the senators left themselves no gold. How much more
was this true of the other orders and the tribes! If
in our time they were to be reduced to this poverty,

355

cogerentur, cum eos modo vix feramus, quando pro
superflua voluptate plura donantur histrionibus quam
tunc legionibus pro extrema salute conlata sunt?

XX

*De exitu Saguntinorum, quibus propter Romanorum
amicitiam pereuntibus dii Romani auxilium non
tulerunt.*

Sed in his omnibus belli Punici secundi malis nihil
miserabilius ac miserabili querella dignius quam
exitium Saguntinorum fuit. Haec quippe Hispaniae
civitas amicissima populi Romani, dum eidem populo
fidem servat, eversa est. Hinc enim Hannibal fracto
foedere Romanorum causas quaesivit quibus eos
inritaret ad bellum. Saguntum ergo ferociter obside-
bat; quod ubi Romae auditum est, missi legati ad
Hannibalem, ut ab eius obsidione discederet. Contempti Carthaginem pergunt querimoniamque depo-
nunt foederis rupti infectoque negotio Romam
redeunt. Dum hae morae aguntur, misera illa civitas
opulentissima, suae rei publicae Romanaeque caris-
sima, octavo vel nono a Poenis mense deleta est.

Cuius interitum legere, quanto magis scribere,
horroris est. Breviter tamen eum commemorabo; ad
356

who would be able to bear up under their reproaches, unbearable as they now are, when, to gratify an unnecessary taste, larger sums are bestowed on actors than were then collected for the legions fighting for the last chance of survival?

XX

Of the destruction of the Saguntines, who perished by reason of their friendship for Rome, yet received no aid from the Roman gods.

Among all these disasters of the Second Punic War, however, none was more pitiable or more deserving of pitiable lament than the destruction of the Saguntines. This Spanish city was, be it noted, on the friendliest of terms with the Roman people and was destroyed while preserving its loyalty to them. For when Hannibal had broken his treaty with the Romans, he turned to them for grounds to stir the Romans to war. Accordingly, he fiercely invested Saguntum, and when this was learned at Rome, ambassadors were sent to Hannibal to call upon him to lift the siege. When no attention was paid to them, they moved on to Carthage, and there laid a complaint that the treaty had been broken, then, unsuccessful in their mission, returned to Rome. While time was wasted in this way, that wretched city, for all its great wealth, precious as it was both to itself and to the Roman republic, was destroyed by the Carthaginians in the eighth or ninth month of the siege.

Horrible it is to read of its fate, much more to write of it, but I shall briefly touch upon it because it has a

rem quippe quae agitur multum pertinet. Primo
fame contabuit; nam etiam suorum cadaveribus a
nonnullis pasta perhibetur. Deinde omnium fessa
rerum, ne saltem captiva in manus Hannibalis perveniret, ingentem rogum publice struxit, in quem
ardentem ferro etiam trucidatos omnes se suosque
miserunt. Hic aliquid agerent dii helluones atque
nebulones, sacrificiorum adipibus inhiantes et falla-
cium divinationum caligine decipientes; hic aliquid
agerent, civitati populi Romani amicissimae sub-
venirent, fidei conservatione pereuntem perire non
sinerent.

Ipsi utique medii praefuerunt, cum Romanae rei
publicae interiecto foedere copulata est. Custodiens
itaque fideliter, quod ipsis praesidibus placito iunxe-
rat, fide vinxerat, iuratione constrinxerat, a perfido
obsessa oppressa consumpta est. Si ipsi dii tempestate atque fulminibus Hannibalem postea Romanis
proximum moenibus terruerunt longeque miserunt,
tunc primum tale aliquid facerent. Audeo quippe
dicere honestius illos pro amicis Romanorum ideo
periclitantibus ne Romanis frangerent fidem et nullam
opem tunc habentibus, quam pro ipsis Romanis, qui

close bearing on the subject in hand. In the first place, the city was wasted by famine; for some authors report that she even dined on the corpses of her own citizens. Thereupon, weary of the whole story, that she might at least escape falling captive into Hannibal's hands, she officially built a huge funeral pyre, to which as it blazed all consigned themselves and their families, after butchery by the sword as well. Here those gods should have done something, gormandizers and parasites that they were, whose mouths were agape for the fat of sacrificial victims while they maintained the cheat by a fog of treacherous predictions. Here they should have acted, should have supported a state most friendly to the Roman people, should not have let it be destroyed, when destruction menaced it for keeping faith.

They had indeed themselves officiated as mediators when that alliance was established by the signing of a treaty with the Roman republic. A city faithfully preserving the alliance which under their patronage it had agreed to form, pledged its fidelity, and bound itself with an oath, then was besieged, crushed and destroyed by a violator of oaths. If it really was the gods who later, when Hannibal was at the very walls of Rome, terrified him with lightning and storm and drove him far away, they should have done the like on that first occasion at the siege of Saguntum. Indeed, I venture to say that it would have been more to their credit if they had been able to produce a raging tempest in defence of friends of the Romans who were in jeopardy for keeping faith with the Romans, and who at that time had no resources with which to fight, than it was to do so on behalf of the Romans

pro se pugnabant atque adversus Hannibalem opulenti erant, potuisse tempestate saevire.

Si ergo tutores essent Romanae felicitatis et gloriae, tam grave ab ea crimen Saguntinae calamitatis averterent; nunc vero quam stulte creditur, diis illis defensoribus Romam victore Hannibale non perisse, qui Saguntinae urbi non potuerunt, ne pro eius periret amicitia, subvenire! Si Saguntinorum Christianus populus esset et huius modi aliquid pro fide evangelica pateretur, quamquam se ipse nec ferro nec ignibus corrupisset, sed tamen si pro fide evangelica excidium pateretur, ea spe pateretur, qua in Christum crediderat, non mercede brevissimi temporis, sed aeternitatis interminae. Pro istis autem diis, qui propterea coli perhibentur, propterea colendi requiruntur, ut harum labentium atque transeuntium rerum felicitas tuta sit, quid nobis defensores et excusatores eorum de Saguntinis pereuntibus respondebunt, nisi quod de illo Regulo extincto? Hoc quippe interest, quod ille unus homo, haec tota civitas; utriusque tamen interitus causa conservatio fidei fuit. Propter hanc enim ad hostes et redire ille voluit, et noluit ista transire.

Conservata ergo provocat deorum iram fides? An possunt et diis propitiis perire non solum quique

themselves, who were fighting on their own behalf
and were rich in resources against Hannibal.

If, therefore, they were guardians of Roman
prosperity and glory, they should have kept it free
from this great blot of the Saguntine disaster. As it
is, how stupid to believe that through the defence of
these gods Rome did not perish at the hands of a
victorious Hannibal, when they were unable to suc-
cour the city of Saguntum and save it from destruction in the cause of Roman friendship! If the
people of Saguntum had been Christian, and had
suffered an experience of this kind in loyalty to the
Gospel—though in that case it could not have sought
self-destruction, whether by fire or sword, but suppose
in any case that it had suffered destruction in loyalty
to the Gospel—it would have suffered with that hope
wherewith it had believed in Christ, not hope of a
momentary reward, but of a reward for an age without
limit. Where those gods are on trial, however, who
are held to be objects of worship for one end, and are
demanded as proper objects of worship for one end,
namely, the safeguarding of happiness in this unstable, transitory life, what will those who speak to
defend or excuse them plead concerning the destruction of the Saguntines except what they said about
the death of Regulus? There is, to be sure, a
difference in the two cases, because one instance
involves a single human being, the other a whole city,
but in both cases the cause of destruction was the
keeping of faith. For this was his motive for going
back to his enemies and also the city's for not going
over to hers.

Does the keeping of faith provoke the anger of the
gods? Or is it possible that not only individuals but

homines, verum etiam integrae civitates? Utrum volunt, eligant. Si enim fidei servatae irascuntur illi dii, quaerant perfidos a quibus colantur; si autem etiam illis propitiis multis gravibusque cruciatibus adflicti interire homines civitatesque possunt, nullo fructu felicitatis huius coluntur. Desinant igitur suscensere, qui sacris deorum suorum perditis se infelices esse factos putant. Possent enim illis non solum manentibus, verum etiam faventibus non sicut modo de miseria murmurare, sed sicut tunc Regulus et Saguntini excruciati horribiliter etiam penitus interire.

XXI

Quam ingrata fuerit Romana civitas Scipioni liberatori suo et in quibus moribus egerit, quando eam Sàllustius optimam fuisse describit.

Porro inter secundum et postremum bellum Carthaginiense, quando Sallustius optimis moribus et maxima concordia dixit egisse Romanos (multa enim praetereo suscepti operis modum cogitans), eodem ipso ergo tempore morum optimorum maximaeque concordiae Scipio ille Romae Italiaeque liberator eiusdemque belli Punici secundi tam horrendi, tam exitiosi, tam periculosi praeclarus mirabilisque con-

---

[1] Sallust, *History* 1.8, 22.

even whole cities may perish, though the gods be propitious to them? Let our opponents take their choice in this dilemma. If, on the one hand, the gods are angered by the keeping of faith, let them look for faithless men to worship them; if, on the other, men and states can perish visited by many and terrible torments, though the gods be propitious to them, their worship does not yield a return in this sort of happiness. Let those who think that their misfortunes are due to the cessation of rites in honour of their gods, cease to be angry, for it is possible that even if the gods were not only still here, but were also well disposed, they might be, not as now merely whining that they are wretched, but, like Regulus and the Saguntines in the past, even perishing to extinction after ghastly tortures.

XXI

Of the ingratitude of Rome to its deliverer Scipio and of its morals in the period described as best by Sallust.

REMEMBERING the limits of the work I have undertaken, I pass by many events and arrive at the period between the second and the last war with Carthage, an epoch in which, according to Sallust,[1] the Romans lived with the highest morality and greatest harmony. Well, in that same time of highest morality and greatest harmony, the famous Scipio, the liberator of Rome and Italy, and the one who with remarkable prestige had brought to a close that same Second Punic War, which was at once so dreadful, so disastrous and so fraught with perils, the conqueror of

363

fector, victor Hannibalis domitorque Carthaginis,
cuius ab adulescentia vita describitur diis dedita
templisque nutrita, inimicorum accusationibus cessit
carensque patria, quam sua virtute salvam et liberam
reddidit, in oppido Linternensi egit reliquam com-
plevitque vitam, post insignem suum triumphum
nullo illius urbis captus desiderio, ita ut iussisse
perhibeatur ne saltem mortuo in ingrata patria funus
fieret. Deinde tunc primum per Gnaeum Manlium
proconsulem de Gallograecis triumphantem Asiatica
luxuria Romam omni hoste peior inrepsit. Tunc
enim primum lecti aerati et pretiosa stragula visa
perhibentur; tunc inductae in convivia psaltriae et
alia licentiosa nequitia.

Sed nunc de his malis, quae intolerabiliter homines
patiuntur, non de his, quae libenter faciunt, dicere
institui. Unde illud magis, quod de Scipione commemoravi, quod cedens inimicis extra patriam, quam
liberavit, mortuus est, ad praesentem pertinet
disputationem, quod ei Romana numina, a quorum
templis avertit Hannibalem, non reddiderunt vicem,
quae propter istam tantummodo coluntur felicitatem.
Sed quia Sallustius eo tempore ibi dixit mores optimos
fuisse, propterea hoc de Asiana luxuria commemorandum putavi, ut intellegatur etiam illud a Sallustio
in comparationem aliorum temporum dictum, quibus
temporibus peiores utique in gravissimis discordiis

---

[1] A small town on the Campanian coast.
[2] Cn. Manlius Vulso, as proconsul, commanded an expedition
against the Galatians or Gallogreeks in 189 B.C.

Hannibal and the captor of Carthage, whose whole
life is described as devoted from youth up to the gods
and nourished in their temples, after his remarkable
triumph yielded to the accusations of his enemies and,
bereft of his native city, that he had kept safe and
independent by his valour, took up his abode in the
town of Linternum[1] and there ended his days, moved
by so little desire for that city after his resplendent
triumph that he is said to have given orders that not
even after death should his funeral be held in his
thankless fatherland. Soon for the first time Asiatic
luxury, worse than any armed foe, crept into Rome
through the agency of the proconsul Gnaeus Manlius,
who triumphed over the Gallogreeks.[2] Then it was
that for the first time beds of bronze and costly
coverings are said to have made their appearance;
then harp girls were introduced into banquets, as
well as other licentious profligacies.

It was, however, my intention to speak, not of these
evils that men do with right good will, but of those
that they suffer past all bearing. One reason why
the case of Scipio, who, as I mentioned above, withdrew in face of his enemies and died beyond the
borders of his fatherland that he had liberated, is the
more relevant to the present discussion, is that those
Roman divinities, who are worshipped solely for the
sake of temporal happiness, made him no such return
for driving Hannibal from their temples. But, since
Sallust says that morality was then at its highest
peak, I thought it well to make the point about
Asiatic luxury, that it may be understood that even
what Sallust says is true only in comparison with
other times, during which morals were certainly
worse, inasmuch as factions were more violent. For

mores fuerunt. Nam tunc, id est inter secundum et
postremum bellum Carthaginiense, lata est etiam lex
illa Voconia, ne quis heredem feminam faceret, nec
unicam filiam. Qua lege quid iniquius dici aut cogi-
tari possit, ignoro. Verum tamen toto illo intervallo
duorum bellorum Punicorum tolerabilior infelicitas
fuit. Bellis tantummodo foris conterebatur exercitus,
sed victoriis consolabatur; domi autem nullae, sicut
alias, discordiae saeviebant.

Sed ultimo bello Punico uno impetu alterius
Scipionis, qui ob hoc etiam ipse Africani cognomen
invenit, aemula imperii Romani ab stirpe deleta est,
ac deinde tantis malorum aggeribus oppressa Romana
res publica, ut prosperitate ac securitate rerum, unde
nimium corruptis moribus mala illa congesta sunt,
plus nocuisse monstretur tam cito eversa, quam prius
nocuerat tam diu adversa Carthago.

Hoc toto tempore usque ad Caesarem Augustum,
qui videtur non adhuc vel ipsorum opinione gloriosam,
sed contentiosam et exitiosam et plane iam enervem
ac languidam libertatem omni modo extorsisse
Romanis et ad regale arbitrium cuncta revocasse et
quasi morbida vetustate conlapsam veluti instaurasse
ac renovasse rem publicam; toto ergo isto tempore
omitto ex aliis atque aliis causis etiam atque etiam
bellicas clades et Numantinum foedus horrenda
ignominia maculosum; volaverant enim pulli de
cavea et Mancino consuli, ut aiunt, augurium malum

---

[1] The Lex Voconia, passed in 169 B.C., at the instigation of
the tribune of the people, Q. Voconius Saxa.

[2] C. Hostilius Mancinus concluded a treaty with the
Numantians in 137 B.C. but this was repudiated by the Senate,
and Mancinus was surrendered at his own desire to the
Numantians but they refused to receive him—see Livy,
Epitome 54; Velleius Paterculus 2.1; Orosius 4.5.

then it was, between the second and the last war with Carthage, that the notorious Voconian law [1] was also passed, which forbade a man to name a woman as heir, not even an only daughter. If any law could be stated or even conceived more unjust than this one, I do not know what. But it is true that in all this interval between the two Punic wars any difficulties were less burdensome. The army was harassed only by foreign wars, and was comforted by victories; at home too there were no such furious conflicts as at other times.

But when in the last Punic War, Rome's rival in imperialism was destroyed root and branch in one charge by another Scipio, who thereby gained the surname of Africanus, from then on the Roman republic was so overwhelmed by ills piled on ills that in her days of prosperity and security, which were the source from which, as morals yielded to corruption, those ills accumulated, Rome stands out as more hurt by Carthage in so speedy a fall, than in so long an opposition previously.

In the whole period down to Caesar Augustus, who appears in every way to have wrested from the Romans that liberty which was no longer even in their own eyes glorious, but rather productive of discord and destruction, and now quite feeble and inert, and who reintroduced the totalitarian absolutism of kings, and, as it were, restored and renewed the republic when it was sunk in senile decay—in this whole period I pass over military disasters again and again suffered for one cause or another, as well as the treaty of Numantia stained by ghastly disgrace, for the sacred chickens, so they say, had flown from their coop and made a bad omen for the consul Mancinus,[2] as if in

fecerant; quasi per tot annos, quibus illa exigua
civitas Romanum circumsessa exercitum adflixerat
ipsique Romanae rei publicae terrori esse iam coeperat, alii contra eam alio augurio processerunt.

XXII

*De Mithridatis edicto, quo omnes cives Romanos, qui
intra Asiam invenirentur, iussit occidi.*

SED haec, inquam, omitto, quamvis illud nequaquam tacuerim, quod Mithridates rex Asiae ubique in
Asia peregrinantes cives Romanos atque innumerabili
copia suis negotiis intentos uno die occidi iussit; et
factum est. Quam illa miserabilis rerum facies erat,
subito quemque, ubicumque fuisset inventus, in agro
in via in oppido, in domo in vico in foro, in templo in
lecto in convivio inopinate atque impie fuisse truci-
datum! Quis gemitus morientium, quae lacrimae
spectantium, fortasse etiam ferientium fuerunt!
Quam dura necessitas hospitum non solum videndi
nefarias illas caedes domi suae, verum etiam per-
petrandi, ab illa blanda comitate humanitatis repente
mutatis vultibus ad hostile negotium in pace pera-
gendum, mutuis dicam omnino vulneribus, cum percussus in corpore et percussor in animo feriretur!

all those years in which that little city had, though invested, plagued the Roman army, and had now begun to be a terror to the Roman republic itself, other commanders had taken the field against it with some other augury.

XXII

Of Mithridates' edict that all Roman citizens found in the province of Asia should be slain.

THESE things, however, I omit, as I say, though of one thing I must speak, how Mithridates, King of Asia, gave an order for the massacre on a single day of all the Roman citizens dwelling abroad anywhere in Asia, of whom there were great numbers all minding their own business, and this was done. What a pathetic sight it was when suddenly, where each man was found, in a field, on a road, in a town, at home, in a street, in a market-place, in a temple, in bed, at a banquet, he was without warning and without regard for the gods treacherously butchered! What groans there were from the dying, what tears from the witnesses, even perhaps from those who dealt the blow themselves! How harsh was the necessity laid upon the hosts, not only of beholding this wicked slaughter in their homes, but even of engaging in it themselves, as suddenly their faces shifted from a mild and kind expression of friendship to take part in the hostile business that was to be transacted in time of peace, where those who wounded were, putting it quite correctly, wounded in return; the smitten was cut in his physical body, but the smiter was cut to the heart.

Num et isti omnes auguria contempserant? Num
deos et domesticos et publicos, cum de sedibus suis ad
illam inremeabilem peregrinationem profecti sunt,
quos consulerent, non habebant? Hoc si ita est, non
habent cur isti in hac causa de nostris temporibus
conquerantur; olim Romani haec vana contemnunt.
Si autem consuluerunt, respondeatur, quid ista pro-
fuerunt, quando per humanas dumtaxat leges nemine
prohibente licuerunt.

XXIII

*De interioribus malis, quibus Romana res publica
exagitata est, praecedente prodigio, quod in rabie
omnium animalium quae hominibus serviunt fuit.*

SED iam illa mala breviter, quantum possumus, com-
memoremus, quae quanto interiora, tanto miseriora
exstiterunt, discordiae civiles vel potius inciviles, nec
iam seditiones, sed etiam ipsa bella urbana, ubi tantus
sanguis effusus est, ubi partium studia non contionum
dissensionibus variisque vocibus in alterutrum, sed
plane iam ferro armisque saeviebant; bella socialia,
bella servilia, bella civilia quantum Romanum
cruorem fuderunt, quantam Italiae vastationem
desertionemque fecerunt!

Namque antequam se adversus Romam sociale
Latium commoveret, cuncta animalia humanis usibus
subdita, canes equi, asini boves, et quaeque alia
pecora sub hominum dominio fuerunt, subito efferata

---

[1] The Social War broke out in 90 B.C.

Had all these slain also despised the auguries? When they set out from their homes upon that route never to be retraced, had they no private and public gods to consult? If they had not, our opponents have no reason to complain about our era in this respect. Long have the Romans despised the auguries as empty of significance. If, on the other hand, they did make inquiry of the omens, the question waits for an answer, what good such things did when they were not forbidden—not at least, that is, by man-made enactments.

XXIII

Of internal disasters by which the Roman republic was afflicted after a prodigy that appeared in the madness of all useful animals.

Now let us mention as briefly as possible those disasters that were the more lamentable as they were the more internal. I mean the conflicts called civil, which are, however, really uncivil, now no longer partisan riots only, but downright wars as well within the city, when so much blood was shed, when party spirit raged, not now showing itself by wrangling in the assemblies and by the exchange of discordant shouts, but by the open clash of steel and arms. What a sea of Roman blood the social wars, the servile wars, the civil wars poured out! How great the area of Italy that they devastated and made desolate!

Before Latium, an ally, started the Social War [1] against Rome, all the animals domesticated to man's service—dogs, horses, asses, oxen and all other livestock that are under man's dominion—suddenly became wild and, forgetting the gentle ways of

371

et domesticae lenitatis oblita relictis tectis libera
vagabantur et omnem non solum aliorum, verum
etiam dominorum aversabantur accessum, non sine
exitio vel periculo audentis, si quis de proximo
urgeret. Quanti mali signum fuit, si hoc signum fuit,
quod tantum malum fuit, si etiam signum non fuit!
Hoc si nostris temporibus accidisset, rabidiores istos
quam sua illi animalia pateremur.

XXIV

De discordia civili, quam Gracchiae seditiones
excitaverunt.

INITIUM autem civilium malorum fuit seditiones
Gracchorum agrariis legibus excitatae. Volebant
enim agros populo dividere, quos nobilitas perperam
possidebat. Sed iam vetustam iniquitatem audere
convellere periculosissimum, immo vero, ut res ipsa
docuit, perniciosissimum fuit. Quae funera facta
sunt, cum prior Gracchus occisus est! Quae etiam,
cum alius frater eius non longo interposito tempore!
Neque enim legibus et ordine potestatum, sed turbis
armorumque conflictibus nobiles ignobilesque neca-
bantur. Post Gracchi alterius interfectionem Lucius
Opimius consul, qui adversus eum intra Urbem arma
commoverat eoque cum sociis oppresso et extincto
ingentem civium stragem fecerat, cum quaestionem
haberet iam iudiciaria inquisitione ceteros persequens,

---

[1] See Julius Obsequens, *Prodigies* 54; Orosius 5.18.
[2] Tiberius Gracchus was tribune of the plebs in 133 B.C., his
brother Gaius in 123 B.C.
[3] An interval of ten years.
[4] He was consul in 121 B.C.

domestication, left their shelters and wandered at large; they resented the approach, not of strangers only, but even of their own masters, not without death or danger to the bold man who came close to compel them.[1] Of how great an evil this was a portent, if it was a portent; a thing that was a great evil in itself, even if it were not a portent to boot! Had this happened in our day, we should find our critics more rabid against us than they found their animals against them.

XXIV

Of the civil dissension that the partisan movements of the Gracchi stirred up.

First on the list of civil disorders came the party strife stirred up by the agrarian legislation of the Gracchi, for they wanted to divide among the populace the land that the nobles wrongly possessed.[2] But to dare to attack an ancient wrong was a very ticklish business, or rather, it was utterly fatal, as the event showed. What mourning for the dead there was when the elder Gracchus was slain! And the same later when another Gracchus his brother was slain not long after![3] Not by laws and orderly processes, but by armed mobs in conflict, were noble and ignoble done to death. After the assassination of the younger Gracchus, the consul Lucius Opimius,[4] who had taken up arms against him within the city and, after defeating and slaying him with his confederates, had massacred a huge number of the citizens, held an investigation, using a judicial examination this time to hound the rest, and is said

tria milia hominum occidisse perhibetur. Ex quo intellegi potest, quantam multitudinem mortium habere potuerit turbidus conflictus armorum, quando tantam habuit iudiciorum velut examinata cognitio. Percussor Gracchi ipsius caput, quantum grave erat, tanto auri pondere consuli vendidit; haec enim pactio caedem praecesserat. In qua etiam occisus est cum liberis Marcus Fulvius consularis.

XXV

De aede Concordiae ex senatus consulto in loco seditionum et caedium condita.

Eleganti sane senatus consulto eo ipso loco, ubi funereus tumultus ille commissus est, ubi tot cives ordinis cuiusque ceciderunt, aedes Concordiae facta est, ut Gracchorum poenae testis contionantum oculos feriret memoriamque compungeret. Sed hoc quid aliud fuit quam inrisio deorum, illi deae templum construere, quae si esset in civitate, non tantis dissensionibus dilacerata conrueret? Nisi forte sceleris huius rea Concordia, quia deseruerat animos civium, meruit in illa aede tamquam in carcere includi.

Cur enim, si rebus gestis congruere voluerunt, non ibi potius aedem Discordiae fabricarunt? An ulla

---

[1] M. Fulvius Flaccus, consul in 125 B.C.

[2] This great temple to Concord, not the first in Rome, was probably built soon after 367 B.C., and what Opimius did was to restore it—see Platner-Ashby, *Topographical Dictionary of Ancient Rome* (London 1929), 138–40.

[3] See Plutarch, *C. Gracchus* 47.

to have executed three thousand men. We may judge by these figures the enormous number that may well have perished in the riotous armed conflict, seeing that what passed as a judicial inquest produced so many condemnations. The assassin of Gracchus sold the head of his victim to the consul for its weight in gold, for this had been agreed on in advance of the slaying. In this massacre was slain also Marcus Fulvius, a man of consular rank, together with his children.[1]

XXV

Of the temple of Concord erected by a decree of the Senate on the site where so many riots and massacres had taken place.

CERTAINLY it was a matter of great refinement, the decree of the Senate whereby a temple of Concord was built on the very spot where the fatal battle of the mobs was joined, where so many citizens of all ranks had fallen, in order that this witness to the vengeance meted to Gracchus might strike the eyes and goad the memory of those who addressed the assembly.[2] Surely, though, this was but a mockery of the gods, to build a temple to that goddess who, had she been in the body politic, would not have allowed it to collapse torn by such great dissensions? Or perhaps Concord was to blame for this crime, because she had deserted the hearts of the citizens, and she deserved the penalty of being shut up in that shrine as it were in a prison.

If they wanted to suit the shrine to the historical background, why did they not rather erect on that spot a temple to Discord?[3] Or is there any reason

375

ratio redditur, cur Concordia dea sit, et Discordia dea
non sit, ut secundum Labeonis distinctionem bona sit
ista, illa vero mala? Nec ipse aliud secutus videtur
quam quod advertit Romae etiam Febri, sicut Saluti,
templum constitutum. Eo modo igitur non solum
Concordiae, verum etiam Discordiae constitui debuit.
Periculose itaque Romani tam mala dea irata vivere
voluerunt nec Troianum excidium recoluerunt originem ab eius offensione sumpsisse. Ipsa quippe quia
inter deos non fuerat invitata, trium dearum litem
aurei mali suppositione commenta est; unde rixa
numinum et Venus victrix, et rapta Helena et Troia
deleta. Quapropter, si forte indignata, quod inter
deos in Urbe nullum templum habere meruit, ideo
iam turbabat tantis tumultibus civitatem, quanto
atrocius potuit inritari, cum in loco illius caedis, hoc
est in loco sui operis, adversariae suae constitutam
aedem videret!

Haec vana ridentibus nobis illi docti sapientesque
stomachantur, et tamen numinum bonorum malorum-
que cultores de hac quaestione Concordiae Dis-
cordiaeque non exeunt, sive praetermiserint harum
dearum cultum eisque Febrem Bellonamque praetu-
lerint, quibus antiqua fana fecerunt, sive et istas
coluerint, cum sic eos discedente Concordia Discordia
saeviens usque ad civilia bella perduxerit.

---

[1] See above, 2.11.

See above, 2.14.

[3] Discord is personified frequently in Virgil, e.g. *Aeneid*
6.280, 7.702.

why Concord should be a goddess, but Discord not, why we should not employ Labeo's distinction and view one as a good goddess, the other as an evil one? [1] He seems to have had no other evidence than that he noticed in Rome a temple dedicated to Fever, as well as one to Health.[2] By this analogy therefore a temple should have been founded not only to Concord, but also to Discord.[3] Thus the Romans to their peril chose to live under the menace of so evil a goddess unplacated, and never reflected that the tale of Troy and its destruction begins with the resentment of Discord. You know, of course, that when she was not invited with the other gods, she contrived to set three goddesses disputing by placing before them the golden apple. Hence the quarrel of the deities, the victory of Venus, the kidnapping of Helen and the destruction of Troy. It follows that if she was perhaps offended because she of all the gods had obtained no temple in the city, and was therefore already upsetting the state with such great tumults, she may well have been far more fiercely aroused when she saw erected a temple to her adversary on the spot where that slaughter—the spot where her handiwork, that is—had taken place!

When we have our fun with such inanities, those learned and sapient men are bilious, yet, since they do worship pairs of good and bad divinities, they cannot extricate themselves from this dilemma about Concord and Discord; either they overlooked the worship of these goddesses and preferred to them Fever and Bellona, to whom they dedicated shrines in ancient times, or they have worshipped them too, though Concord thus abandoned them and Discord raging led them all the way to civil wars.

XXVI

De diversis generibus belli, quae post conditam
aedem Concordiae sunt secuta.

PRAECLARUM vero seditionis obstaculum aedem
Concordiae, testem caedis suppliciique Gracchorum,
contionantibus opponendam putarunt. Quantum ex
hoc profecerint, indicant secuta peiora. Laborarunt
enim deinceps contionatores non exemplum devitare
Gracchorum, sed superare propositum, Lucius Saturninus tribunus plebis et Gaius Servilius praetor et
multo post Marcus Drusus, quorum omnium seditionibus caedes primo iam tunc gravissimae, deinde
socialia bella exarserunt, quibus Italia vehementer
adflicta et ad vastitatem mirabilem desertionemque
perducta est. Bellum deinde servile successit et bella
civilia.

Quae proelia commissa sunt, quid sanguinis fusum,
ut omnes fere Italae gentes, quibus Romanum
maxime praepollebat imperium, tamquam saeva
barbaries domarentur! Iam ex paucissimis, hoc est
minus quam septuaginta, gladiatoribus quem ad
modum bellum servile contractum sit, ad quantum
numerum et quam acrem ferocemque pervenerit,
quos ille numerus imperatores populi Romani supera-
verit, quas et quo modo civitates regionesque vasta-
verit, vix qui historiam conscripserunt satis explicare

---

[1] L. Appuleius Saturninus, tribune 102 B.C., re-elected 100
B.C.
[2] C. Servilius Glaucia, praetor 100 B.C.
[3] M. Livius Drusus, tribune 91 B.C.

XXVI

On the various kinds of wars which followed the erection of the temple of Concord.

WHAT moved them, however, to set up the temple of Concord was the belief that, being a memorial of the death and punishment of the Gracchi, it would face the orators in the assemblies as a conspicuous barrier to broiling. How much good it did them, let the worse times which followed decide. For from then on the orators bent their efforts, not to fight shy of the example of the Gracchi, but to outbid their programme, as did Lucius Saturninus, the tribune of the people,[1] Gaius Servilius, the praetor,[2] and much later, Marcus Drusus,[3] all of whom stirred up broils that kindled the flames, first of bloody riots, serious enough from the start, then of the social wars that furiously scourged Italy and left her a startling spectacle of devastation and solitude. Next came the Servile War [4] and the civil wars.

What battles were joined, what blood was shed, with the result that almost all the peoples of Italy, to whom the Roman dominion was chiefly indebted for its success, were subdued like some savage barbarous country! Historians have hardly found a satisfactory answer to the question how a conflict begun by a very small number, that is, fewer than seventy gladiators, was expanded into a servile war by the addition of a huge number of fierce and cruel men, who thereafter defeated many a general of the Roman people and devastated cities and whole districts. This was not

[4] See Livy, *Epitome* 69; Diodorus Siculus 36.1; Appian, *Civil War* 1.116–120; Florus 3.20; Orosius 5.24; Plutarch, *Crassus* 8–11.

potuerunt.   Neque id solum fuit servile bellum, sed et
Macedoniam provinciam prius servitia depopulata
sunt et deinde Siciliam oramque maritimam.   Quanta
etiam et quam horrenda commiserint primo latro-
cinia, deinde valida bella piratarum, quis pro magnitudine rerum valeat eloqui?

XXVII

De bello civili Mariano atque Sullano.

Cum vero Marius civili sanguine iam cruentus multis
adversarum sibi partium peremptis victus Urbe pro-
fugisset, vix paululum respirante civitate, ut verbis
Tullianis utar, " superavit postea Cinna cum Mario.
Tum vero clarissimis viris interfectis lumina civitatis
extincta sunt.   Ultus est huius victoriae crudelitatem
postea Sulla, ne dici quidem opus est quanta deminu-
tione civium et quanta calamitate rei publicae."   De
hac enim vindicta, quae perniciosior fuit, quam si
scelera quae puniebantur inpunita relinquerentur, ait
et Lucanus:

> Excessit medicina modum nimiumque secuta est,
> Qua morbi duxere manum.   Periere nocentes;
> Sed cum iam soli possent superesse nocentes.

---

[1] For slave revolts in Sicily see T. Mommsen, *History of
Rome*, tr. by W. P. Dickson (Everyman Library 1921) 4.74 f.
It is possible that Augustine is confusing a slave revolt led
by Andronicus in Asia in 132 with the revolt of Andriscus,
pseudo-Philip, in 149 B.C., on whom see *Oxford Classical
Dictionary* (Oxford 1949), pp. 52 f.

the only servile war, for the whole province of Macedonia was laid waste by a slave rebellion, as were Sicily later and the sea-coast of Italy.[1] Whose eloquence can cope adequately with the facts, the number and the horror of their acts of brigandage, and, soon to follow, the wars waged stoutly by the pirates?[2]

XXVII

On the civil war of Marius and Sulla.

WHEN Marius, already stained with the blood of many citizens, slain because they belonged to the opposing party, was beaten and fled from the city, the state was barely breathing again when, to use Cicero's words, " Cinna afterwards made himself master in company with Marius. Then, in truth, the most noble citizens were slain and the lights of the city were put out. Sulla afterwards avenged the ruthlessness of this conquest. How many citizens were lost and what disaster the republic suffered we may forbear even to mention." [3] Of this vengeance, which was more deadly than any failure to punish the crimes for which punishment was exacted, Lucan says :

The remedy forsook due measure, went
Too far with wholesome knife where foul disease
Was guide. 'Tis true, the victims all had sinned ;
But by that time alone were sinners able to
    survive.[4]

[2] The Asiatic pirates, long a problem, were finally crushed by Pompey in 67 B.C.
[3] Cicero, *Catiline* 3.10, 24.
[4] Lucan, *Pharsalia* 2.142–4.

Illo bello Mariano atque Sullano exceptis his, qui
foris in acie ceciderunt, in ipsa quoque Urbe cadaveribus vici plateae fora, theatra templa completa
sunt, ut difficile iudicaretur, quando victores plus
funerum ediderint, utrum prius ut vincerent, an
postea quia vicissent; cum primum victoria Mariana,
quando de exilio se ipse restituit, exceptis passim
quaqua versum caedibus factis caput Octavii consulis
poneretur in rostris, Caesares a Fimbria domibus
trucidarentur suis, duo Crassi pater et filius in conspectu mutuo mactarentur, Baebius et Numitorius
unco tracti sparsis visceribus interirent, Catulus
hausto veneno se manibus inimicorum subtraheret,
Merula flamen Dialis praecisis venis Iovi etiam suo
sanguine litaret. In ipsius autem Marii oculis
continuo feriebantur, quibus salutantibus dexteram
porrigere noluisset.

XXVIII

*Qualis fuerit Sullana victoria, vindex Marianae
crudelitatis.*

Sullana vero victoria secuta, huius videlicet vindex
crudelitatis, post tantum sanguinem civium, quo fuso
fuerat comparata, finito iam bello inimicitiis viventibus

---

[1] Cn. Octavius, consul 90 B.C., an early victim of Marius.

[2] L. Caesar, consul 90 B.C., and his brother Strabo Vopiscus,
both put to death by Marius' orders in 87 B.C.

[3] See above, 3.7.

[4] P. Crassus took his life after seeing his son slain before his
eyes in 87 B.C.

[5] Both were partisans of Sulla, executed by Marius in 87 B.C.

In that war between Marius and Sulla, not to mention those who fell in combat outside the walls, within the city itself the compounds, the squares, the markets, the theatres, the temples, were so full of corpses that it was hard to decide in which period the victors slew more men, before the victory to achieve it, or after it because they had achieved it. For on the first occasion, when Marius was victorious and won his own return from exile, not to mention any butcheries perpetrated generally on all sides, the head of the consul Octavius [1] was exposed on the rostra; the Caesars [2] were assassinated by Fimbria [3] in their own houses, the two Crassi,[4] father and son, were slaughtered in each other's sight; Baebius and Numitorius [5] perished and were dragged by the hooks after their viscera had been scattered abroad; Catulus [6] drank poison, and so escaped the violence of his enemies; Merula,[7] the flamen of Jupiter, cut his veins and so rendered a libation to Jupiter of his own blood. Moreover, those whose greetings Marius refused to accept by offering his right hand were at once cut down before his very eyes.

XXVIII

*On the nature of Sulla's victory, which avenged Marius'
cruelty.*

Then followed the victory of Sulla, which no doubt was vengeance for Marius' cruelty, but, after so much blood of citizens had been shed to procure that victory, even when the war was ended, in time of peace, since enmities survived, there

---

[6] Q. Lutatius Catulus, consul 102 B.C.

[7] In the temple of Jupiter Capitolinus in 87 B.C.

crudelius in pace grassata est. Iam etiam post Marii
maioris pristinas ac recentissimas caedes additae
fuerant aliae graviores a Mario iuvene atque Carbone
earundem partium Marianarum, qui Sulla imminente
non solum victoriam, verum etiam ipsam desperantes
salutem cuncta suis aliis caedibus impleverunt. Nam
praeter stragem late per diversa diffusam obsesso
etiam senatu de ipsa curia, tamquam de carcere,
producebantur ad gladium. Mucius Scaevola pontifex, quoniam nihil apud Romanos templo Vestae
sanctius habebatur, aram ipsam amplexus occisus est,
ignemque illum, qui perpetua virginum cura semper
ardebat, suo paene sanguine extinxit. Urbem
deinde Sulla victor intravit, qui in villa publica non
iam bello, sed ipsa pace saeviente septem milia
deditorum (unde utique inermia) non pugnando, sed
iubendo prostraverat.

In Urbe autem tota quem vellet Sullanus quisque
feriebat, unde tot funera numerari omnino non
poterant, donec Sullae suggereretur sinendos esse
aliquos vivere, ut essent quibus possent imperare qui
vicerant. Tunc iam cohibita quae hac atque illac
passim furibunda ferebatur licentia iugulandi, tabula
illa cum magna gratulatione proposita est, quae
hominum ex utroque ordine splendido, equestri
scilicet atque senatorio, occidendorum ac proscri-
bendorum duo milia continebat. Contristabat numerus, sed consolabatur modus; nec quia tot cade-

---

[1] They were consuls in 82 B.C.

[2] See Cicero, *On the Orator* 1.39.180; *On Duties* 3.15.62;
Livy, *Epitome* 86; Florus 3.21.

[3] The only building in the Campus Martius before the end
of the Republic. The number of persons slaughtered is given
variously.

were more cruel orgies still. Even before, after the original, and the then still very recent, butcheries of the elder Marius, others more dire were added to them by Marius the younger and Carbo,[1] members of the same Marian party, who, when Sulla was about to fall upon them, despairing not only of victory but even of life itself, filled the whole scene with new butcheries of their own. Not satisfied with slaughter spread afar on all sides, they even laid siege to the senate, and senators were led forth from the senate house itself, as from a prison, to the sword. Mucius Scaevola, the pontiff,[2] sought shelter in the temple of Vesta, than which in the eyes of the Romans no shrine was more sacred, yet though he embraced the altar itself, he was slain, and with his blood almost put out that fire which ever burned under the unremitting care of the virgins. Then the victorious Sulla entered the city and in the Public Villa,[3] when no longer war but very peace was raging, laid low, not by giving battle but by giving an order, seven thousand who had surrendered, and so were certainly unarmed.

Throughout the whole city, too, each partisan of Sulla struck whom he pleased, with the result that the deaths were so many they could not be counted, until it was intimated to Sulla that a few ought to be allowed to live that there might be some subjects for the conquerors to rule. Then the furious licence to slaughter, now here, now there, at random was checked, and there was great thanksgiving when the list was published for the slaying and proscription of two thousand men of the two noble ranks, that is, of the equestrian and senatorial orders. The number on this list caused grief, but any limit brought comfort. Sorrow for the many doomed to fall

385

bant tantum erat maeroris, quantum laetitiae quia ceteri non timebant.

Sed in quibusdam eorum, qui mori iussi erant, etiam ipsa licet crudelis ceterorum securitas genera mortium exquisita congemuit. Quendam enim sine ferro laniantium manus diripuerunt, inmanius homines hominem vivum quam bestiae solent discerpere cadaver abiectum. Alius oculis effossis et particulatim membris amputatis in tantis cruciatibus diu vivere vel potius diu mori coactus est. Subhastatae sunt etiam, tamquam villae, quaedam nobiles civitates; una vero, velut unus reus duci iuberetur, sic tota iussa est trucidari. Haec facta sunt in pace post bellum, non ut acceleraretur obtinenda victoria, sed ne contemneretur obtenta. Pax cum bello de crudelitate certavit et vicit. Illud enim prostravit armatos, ista nudatos. Bellum erat, ut qui feriebatur, si posset, feriret; pax autem, non ut qui evaserat viveret, sed ut moriens non repugnaret.

XXIX

De comparatione Gothicae inruptionis cum eis cladibus quas Romani vel a Gallis vel a bellorum civilium auctoribus acceperunt.

QUAE rabies exterarum gentium, quae saevitia barbarorum huic de civibus victoriae civium comparari potest? Quid Roma funestius taetrius amariusque
386

weighed less than joy for the rest, who were now exempt from fear.

Yet in the case of some who were sentenced to death, even the rest in their security, ruthless though it made them, were moved to lamentation. A man was torn apart by the naked hands of the executioners; yes, human beings tore a living human being apart more pitilessly than wild beasts are wont to tear a corpse that has been thrown out. Another had his eyes gouged out and his limbs cut off piece by piece, so that he was forced amid these cruel tortures to remain a long time living, or rather a long time dying. Certain famous cities were put under the auctioneer's hammer like so many estates, but one was sentenced to be executed whole, as if a single criminal were being condemned to death. These things were done in time of peace, after a war, not that victory might be more speedily won, but that, being won, it might not be held cheap. Peace vied with war in cruelty and won, for the war slaughtered armed men, while peace slew the disarmed. War allowed him who was struck to strike if he could; peace, however, decreed, not that he who had escaped might live, but that he might not, as he died, fight back.

XXIX

A comparison of the Gothic invasion with the disasters to which the Romans were subjected by the Gauls or by the authors of the civil wars.

What fury of foreign nations, what savagery of barbarians, can be compared with this victory of citizens over citizens? What attack that Rome saw

vidit, utrum olim Gallorum et paulo ante Gothorum
inruptionem an Marii et Sullae aliorumque in eorum
partibus virorum clarissimorum tamquam suorum
luminum in sua membra ferocitatem? Galli quidem
trucidaverunt senatum, quidquid eius in Urbe tota
praeter arcem Capitolinam, quae sola utcumque
defensa est, reperire potuerunt; sed in illo colle
constitutis auro vitam saltem vendiderunt, quam etsi
ferro rapere non possent, possent tamen obsidione
consumere. Gothi vero tam multis senatoribus
pepercerunt, ut magis mirum sit quod aliquos peremerunt.

At vero Sulla vivo adhuc Mario ipsum Capitolium,
quod a Gallis tutum fuit, ad decernendas caedes
victor insedit, et cum fuga Marius lapsus esset fero-
cior cruentiorque rediturus, iste in Capitolio per
senatus etiam consultum multos vita rebusque privavit. Marianis autem partibus Sulla absente quid
sanctum cui parcerent fuit, quando Mucio civi sena-
tori pontifici aram ipsam, ubi erant ut aiunt fata
Romana, miseris ambienti amplexibus non pepercerunt? Sullana porro tabula illa postrema, ut
omittamus alias innumerabiles mortes, plures iugu-
lavit senatores, quam Gothi vel spoliare potuerunt.

was more lamentable, more revolting, more galling? Which was worse, the Gallic invasion long ago and the recent invasion of the Goths, or the ferocity of Marius, of Sulla and of other most distinguished men, as if their own eyes were to attack their own limbs? The Gauls, to be sure, slaughtered whatever senators they could find in the city outside the Capitoline citadel, which alone was in any case defended, but at least they sold life in return for gold to those who were established on that hill, though they might still have drained that life by a siege, even if they could not shear it with the sword. The Goths, on the other hand, spared so many senators that the surprising thing is rather that they slew any at all.

Yet Sulla, while Marius still lived, set up his headquarters as victor in that very Capitol, which was safe from the Gauls, in order to issue his bloody orders there, and when Marius took flight and escaped, though destined to return fiercer and more bloody, Sulla in the Capitol, even making a decree of the senate his instrument, deprived many of life and property. Then, in the absence of Sulla, what did the Marian party regard as inviolate, when they did not spare Mucius, a citizen, senator, pontiff, grasping in pitiful embrace the very altar where, as they say, the destiny of Rome resides? And, furthermore, that final proscription list of Sulla, to say nothing of other countless deaths, dispatched more senators than the Goths were able even to plunder.

XXX

*De conexione bellorum, quae adventum Christi
plurima et gravissima praecesserunt.*

Qua igitur fronte, quo corde, qua inpudentia, qua
insipientia vel potius amentia illa diis suis non
inputant, et haec nostro inputant Christo? Crudelia
bella civilia, omnibus bellis hostilibus, auctoribus
etiam eorum fatentibus, amariora, quibus illa res
publica nec adflicta, sed omnino perdita iudicata est,
longe ante adventum Christi exorta sunt, et scelera-
tarum concatenatione causarum a bello Mariano
atque Sullano ad bella Sertorii et Catilinae (quorum a
Sulla fuerat ille proscriptus, ille nutritus), inde ad
Lepidi et Catuli bellum (quorum alter gesta Sullana
rescindere, alter defendere cupiebat) inde ad Pompei
et Caesaris (quorum Pompeius sectator Sullae fuerat
eiusque potentiam vel aequaverat vel iam etiam
superaverat; Caesar autem Pompei potentiam non
ferebat, sed quia non habebat, quam tamen illo victo
interfectoque transcendit), hinc ad alium Caesarem,
qui post Augustus appellatus est, pervenerunt, quo
imperante natus est Christus.

Nam et ipse Augustus cum multis gessit bella
civilia, et in eis etiam multi clarissimi viri perierunt
inter quos et Cicero disertus ille artifex regendae rei
publicae. Pompei quippe victorem Gaium Caesarem,
qui victoriam civilem clementer exercuit suisque

---

[1] In 78 B.C.   [2] In 63 B.C.
[3] In 77 B.C.

XXX

*On the long series of most disastrous wars which
preceded the coming of Christ.*

How brazen are they, therefore, how senseless, how
shameless, how foolish, or rather how mad, when they
fail to attribute those events to their own gods, and
yet do attribute these recent slaughters to our
Christ! Those cruel civil wars, which were more
painful, by the admission of their own authors, than
all their foreign wars, and by which the Republic was
judged, not merely to have been plagued, but utterly
destroyed, began long before the coming of Christ.
The chain of cause and effect linked crime to crime.
The wars of Marius and Sulla led to the wars of
Sertorius [1] and Catiline,[2] of whom the former was
proscribed and the latter nursed by Sulla. This
led to the war of Lepidus and Catulus,[3] of whom the
one wished to abolish, the other to defend the acts of
Sulla. This led to the wars of Pompey and Caesar,
of whom Pompey had been a partisan of Sulla, whose
power he had now equalled or even surpassed.
Caesar, however, could not brook the power of
Pompey, but only because he did not have it himself;
yet he soared higher still, when Pompey was conquered and slain. The series of wars then arrived at
another Caesar, afterwards called Augustus, in whose
reign Christ was born.

For Augustus himself waged civil wars with many
men and in them too many of the most famous men
perished, among them that eloquent master of the art
of governing a state, Cicero. Gaius Caesar, as we
know, after his victory over Pompey, adopted a policy
of clemency to the vanquished citizens, granting life

391

adversariis vitam dignitatemque donavit, tamquam regni adpetitorem quorundam nobilium coniuratio senatorum velut pro rei publicae libertate in ipsa curia trucidavit. Huius deinde potentiam multum moribus dispar vitiisque omnibus inquinatus atque corruptus adfectare videbatur Antonius, cui vehementer pro eadem illa velut patriae libertate Cicero resistebat. Tunc emerserat mirabilis indolis adulescens ille alius Caesar, illius Gai Caesaris filius adoptivus, qui, ut dixi, postea est appellatus Augustus. Huic adulescenti Caesari, ut eius potentia contra Antonium nutriretur, Cicero favebat, sperans eum depulsa et oppressa Antonii dominatione instauraturum rei publicae libertatem, usque adeo caecus atque inprovidus futurorum, ut ille ipse iuvenis, cuius dignitatem ac potestatem fovebat, et eundem Ciceronem occidendum Antonio quadam quasi concordiae pactione permitteret et ipsam libertatem rei publicae, pro qua multum ille clamaverat, dicioni propriae subiugaret.

XXXI

Quam inpudenter praesentia incommoda Christo inputent, qui deos colere non sinuntur, cum tantae clades eo tempore quo colebantur extiterint.

Deos suos accusent de tantis malis, qui Christo nostro ingrati sunt de tantis bonis. Certe quando

and position to his opponents. He was charged, however, with aiming at monarchy; hence certain noble senators formed a conspiracy and slew him, to vindicate the liberty of the state, so they said, in the Senate House itself. Then as candidate to succeed to his dominant position appeared a man of very different moral standards, a man befouled and wasted by every kind of vice, Antony. He was strongly resisted by Cicero in the name of that same liberty of the fatherland. By that time a youth of remarkable character had emerged, the other Caesar aforesaid, adopted son of Gaius Caesar, who was, as I said, afterwards called Augustus. This young Caesar was favoured by Cicero in order that his power might grow in opposition to Antony. Cicero hoped that when Antony's tyranny had been repulsed and stamped out, Caesar would restore liberty to the Republic, so blind and unable to foresee the future was he. For that young man, whose career and influence he was fostering, left that same Cicero to be assassinated by Antony when he made a treaty of so-called friendship with him, and enslaved to his own authority that very liberty of the Republic in defence of which Cicero had often sounded an alarm.

XXXI

On the effrontery of those who, because the worship of the gods is not allowed, attribute the present troubles to Christ, though such great disasters occurred when the gods were worshipped.

Let them score evils so great against their own gods, they who will not thank our Christ for such great bounties. Sure it is that when these evils took

illa mala fiebant, calebant arae numinum Sabaeo thure sertisque recentibus halabant, clarebant sacerdotia, fana renidebant, sacrificabatur ludebatur furebatur in templis, quando passim tantus civium sanguis a civibus non modo in ceteris locis, verum etiam inter ipsa deorum altaria fundebatur. Non elegit templum, quo confugeret Tullius, quia frustra elegerat Mucius. Hi vero qui multo indignius insultant temporibus Christianis, aut ad loca Christo dicatissima confugerunt, aut illuc eos ut viverent etiam ipsi barbari deduxerunt.

Illud scio et hoc mecum quisquis sine studio partium iudicat, facillime agnoscit (ut omittam cetera quae multa commemoravi et alia multo plura quae commemorare longum putavi): si humanum genus ante bella Punica Christianam reciperet disciplinam et consequeretur rerum tanta vastatio, quanta illis bellis Europam Africamque contrivit, nullus talium, quales nunc patimur, nisi Christianae religioni mala illa tribuisset. Multo autem minus eorum voces tolerarentur, quantum adtinet ad Romanos, si Christianae religionis receptionem et diffamationem vel inruptio illa Gallorum vel Tiberini fluminis igniumque illa depopulatio vel, quod cuncta mala praecedit, bella illa civilia sequerentur. Mala etiam alia, quae usque adeo incredibiliter acciderunt, ut inter prodigia numerarentur, si Christianis temporibus accidissent,

---

[1] Virgil, *Aeneid* 1.416 f.

place, the altars of the gods were warm " with Sabaean incense and fragrant with fresh garlands," [1] the priesthoods were held in honour, the shrines were bright and shining, there were sacrifices, there were games, there were frenzies in the temples in those days when all that blood of citizens was shed on all sides by citizens, not only in all other places but even among the altars of the gods. Cicero did not choose to seek refuge in a temple, because Mucius had so chosen in vain. Those, on the other hand, who with much less excuse make the Christian era a target for abuse, either fled for refuge to the places most hallowed to Christ, or were even conducted thither by the barbarians themselves to preserve their lives.

Now, not to rehearse again the other disasters, many of which I have recounted, omitting many more as too tedious to recall, this one thing I know, and anyone whose judgement is not warped by zeal for his party will easily see it too: if the human race had accepted the teaching of Christ before the Punic wars, and such great destruction of property had followed as then afflicted Europe and Africa in those wars, there is no one of those who belabour us who would have attributed those evils to anything but the Christian religion. Much less would their cries be matter for patience, as far as pertains to the Romans, if the Christian religion had been accepted and broadcast before that invasion of the Gauls, or before the destructive floods of the River Tiber, or the conflagrations that laid Rome waste, or the greatest of all evils, the civil wars. Other evils too, so unbelievable when they occurred that they were listed among prodigies, if they had happened to the Christian era, at

quibus ea nisi Christianis hominibus tamquam crimina
obicerent? Omitto quippe illa, quae magis fuerunt
mira quam noxia, boves locutos, infantes nondum
natos de uteris matrum quaedam verba clamasse,
volasse serpentes, feminas et gallinas et homines in
masculinum sexum fuisse conversas et cetera huius
modi, quae in eorum libris non fabulosis, sed historicis,
seu vera seu falsa sint, non inferunt hominibus per-
niciem, sed stuporem.

Sed cum pluit terra, cum pluit creta, cum pluit
lapidibus (non ut grando appellari solet hoc nomine,
sed omnino lapidibus), haec profecto etiam graviter
laedere potuerunt. Legimus apud eos Aetnaeis
ignibus ab ipso montis vertice usque ad litus proximum decurrentibus ita mare ferbuisse, ut rupes
urerentur, ut pices navium solverentur. Hoc utique
non leviter noxium fuit, quamvis incredibiliter mirum.
Eodem rursus aestu ignium tanta vi favillae scripserunt oppletam esse Siciliam, ut Catinensis urbis
tecta obruta et pressa dirueret; qua calamitate
permoti misericorditer eiusdem anni tributum ei
relaxavere Romani. Lucustarum etiam in Africa
multitudinem prodigii similem fuisse, cum iam esset
populi Romani provincia, litteris mandaverunt; con-
sumptis enim fructibus foliisque lignorum ingenti
atque inaestimabili nube in mare dicunt esse
deiectam; qua mortua redditaque litoribus atque hinc
aere corrupto tantam ortam pestilentiam, ut in solo
regno Masinissae octingenta hominum milia perisse
referantur et multo amplius in terris litoribus

whom would the reproach have been cast, as if they were our crimes, but at the Christian people? Note that I pass over prodigies that were more surprising than harmful, oxen speaking, infants yet unborn crying out certain words from their mothers' wombs, serpents flying, hens and women changed into males, and other similar events that appear in their works, not of fiction but of history. Whether they are true or false, they bring no disaster to men, but only cause astonishment.

But when it rained earth, when it rained chalk, when it rained stones (not hailstones so called, but real stones), these things could certainly do even severe damage. We have read in their books that the fires of Etna, flowing from the top of the mountain to the adjoining shore, so caused the sea to boil that rocks were burned and the pitch in ships was melted. This in any case was no light damage, however incredibly strange. Again, they relate that in the same fiery burst of flames Sicily was buried under so great a quantity of ashes that the houses of Catina were wrecked when the ashes piled up and weighed them down. Moved to mercy by this calamity, the Romans lightened their tribute for that year. In Africa, which by that time had become a Roman province, they record that there was also a prodigious number of locusts which, when the fruit and the leaves of trees had been eaten up, were hurled, they say, into the sea in one huge and incalculable cloud. When they were cast up dead on the shore and the air was polluted with them, there arose such a pestilence that in the Kingdom of Masinissa alone eight hundred thousand people are said to have perished, and many more in the districts

proximis. Tunc Uticae ex triginta milibus iuniorum, quae ibi erant, decem milia remansisse confirmant.

Talis itaque vanitas, qualem ferimus eique respondere compellimur, quid horum non Christianae religioni tribueret, si temporibus Christianis videret? Et tamen diis suis ista non tribuunt, quorum cultum ideo requirunt, ne ista vel minora patiantur, cum ea maiora pertulerint a quibus antea colebantur.

bordering on the sea. Of the thirty thousand troops then at Utica, they assert that only ten thousand survived.

Given the kind of silliness accordingly that we must put up with, and to which we are compelled to make a reply, suppose it saw such events in the Christian era, which of them would it not lay to the charge of the Christian religion? Yet they do not charge the disasters I have mentioned to their own gods, but demand the privilege of worshipping them to escape present disasters that are actually less, though those greater disasters fell to the lot of such as formerly worshipped them.

THE LOEB CLASSICAL LIBRARY

VOLUMES ALREADY PUBLISHED

Latin Authors

AMMIANUS MARCELLINUS. Translated by J. C. Rolfe. 3 Vols.

APULEIUS: THE GOLDEN ASS (METAMORPHOSES). W. Adlington (1566). Revised by S. Gaselee.

ST. AUGUSTINE: CITY OF GOD. 7 Vols. Vol. I. G. E. McCracken. Vols. II and VII. W. M. Green. Vol. III. D. Wiesen. Vol. IV. P. Levine. Vol. V. E. M. Sanford and W. M. Green. Vol. VI. W. C. Greene.

ST. AUGUSTINE, CONFESSIONS OF. W. Watts (1631). 2 Vols.

ST. AUGUSTINE, SELECT LETTERS. J. H. Baxter.

AUSONIUS. H. G. Evelyn White. 2 Vols.

BEDE. J. E. King. 2 Vols.

BOETHIUS: TRACTS and DE CONSOLATIONE PHILOSOPHIAE. Rev. H. F. Stewart and E. K. Rand. Revised by S. J. Tester.

CAESAR: ALEXANDRIAN, AFRICAN and SPANISH WARS. A. G. Way.

CAESAR: CIVIL WARS. A. G. Peskett.

CAESAR: GALLIC WAR. H. J. Edwards.

CATO: DE RE RUSTICA. VARRO: DE RE RUSTICA. H. B. Ash and W. D. Hooper.

CATULLUS. F. W. Cornish. TIBULLUS. J. B. Postgate. PERVIGILIUM VENERIS. J. W. Mackail.

CELSUS: DE MEDICINA. W. G. Spencer. 3 Vols.

CICERO: BRUTUS and ORATOR. G. L. Hendrickson and H. M. Hubbell.

[CICERO]: AD HERENNIUM. H. Caplan.

CICERO: DE ORATORE, etc. 2 Vols. Vol. I. DE ORATORE, Books I and II. E. W. Sutton and H. Rackham. Vol. II. DE ORATORE, Book III. DE FATO; PARADOXA STOICORUM; DE PARTITIONE ORATORIA. H. Rackham.

CICERO: DE FINIBUS. H. Rackham.

CICERO: DE INVENTIONE, etc. H. M. Hubbell.

CICERO: DE NATURA DEORUM and ACADEMICA. H. Rackham.

CICERO: DE OFFICIIS. Walter Miller.

CICERO: DE REPUBLICA and DE LEGIBUS. Clinton W. Keyes.

CICERO: DE SENECTUTE, DE AMICITIA, DE DIVINATIONE. W. A. Falconer.

CICERO: IN CATILINAM, PRO FLACCO, PRO MURENA, PRO SULLA. New version by C. Macdonald.

CICERO: LETTERS TO ATTICUS. E. O. Winstedt. 3 Vols.

CICERO: LETTERS TO HIS FRIENDS. W. Glynn Williams, M. Cary, M. Henderson. 4 Vols.

CICERO: PHILIPPICS. W. C. A. Ker.

CICERO: PRO ARCHIA, POST REDITUM, DE DOMO, DE HARUSPICUM RESPONSIS, PRO PLANCIO. N. H. Watts.

CICERO: PRO CAECINA, PRO LEGE MANILIA, PRO CLUENTIO, PRO RABIRIO. H. Grose Hodge.

CICERO: PRO CAELIO, DE PROVINCIIS CONSULARIBUS, PRO BALBO. R. Gardner.

CICERO: PRO MILONE, IN PISONEM, PRO SCAURO, PRO FONTEIO, PRO RABIRIO POSTUMO, PRO MARCELLO, PRO LIGARIO, PRO REGE DEIOTARO. N. H. Watts.

CICERO: PRO QUINCTIO, PRO ROSCIO AMERINO, PRO ROSCIO COMOEDO, CONTRA RULLUM. J. H. Freese.

CICERO: PRO SESTIO, IN VATINIUM. R. Gardner.

CICERO: TUSCULAN DISPUTATIONS. J. E. King.

CICERO: VERRINE ORATIONS. L. H. G. Greenwood. 2 Vols.

CLAUDIAN. M. Platnauer. 2 Vols.

COLUMELLA: DE RE RUSTICA. DE ARBORIBUS. H. B. Ash, E. S. Forster and E. Heffner. 3 Vols.

CURTIUS, Q.: HISTORY OF ALEXANDER. J. C. Rolfe. 2 Vols.

FLORUS. E. S. Forster. CORNELIUS NEPOS. J. C. Rolfe.

FRONTINUS: STRATAGEMS and AQUEDUCTS. C. E. Bennett and M. B. McElwain.

FRONTO: CORRESPONDENCE. C. R. Haines. 2 Vols.

GELLIUS. J. C. Rolfe. 3 Vols.

HORACE: ODES and EPODES. C. E. Bennett.

HORACE: SATIRES, EPISTLES, ÁRS POETICA. H. R. Fairclough.

JEROME: SELECTED LETTERS. F. A. Wright.

JUVENAL and PERSIUS. G. G. Ramsay.

LIVY. B. O. Foster, F. G. Moore, Evan T. Sage, and A. C. Schlesinger and R. M. Geer (General Index). 14 Vols.

LUCAN. J. D. Duff.

LUCRETIUS. W. H. D. Rouse. Revised by M. F. Smith.

MANILIUS. G. P. Goold.

MARTIAL. W. C. A. Ker. 2 Vols. Revised by E. H. Warmington.

MINOR LATIN POETS: from PUBLILIUS SYRUS to RUTILIUS NAMATIANUS, including GRATTIUS, CALPURNIUS SICULUS, NEMESIANUS, AVIANUS and others, with " Aetna " and the " Phoenix." J. Wight Duff and Arnold M. Duff.

Minucius Felix. Cf. Tertullian.

Ovid: The Art of Love and Other Poems. J. H. Mosley. Revised by G. P. Goold.

Ovid: Fasti. Sir James G. Frazer

Ovid: Heroides and Amores. Grant Showerman. Revised by G. P. Goold

Ovid: Metamorphoses. F. J. Miller. 2 Vols. Vol. 1 revised by G. P. Goold.

Ovid: Tristia and Ex Ponto. A. L. Wheeler.

Persius. Cf. Juvenal.

Pervigilium Veneris. Cf. Catullus.

Petronius. M. Heseltine. Seneca: Apocolocyntosis. W. H. D. Rouse. Revised by E. H. Warmington.

Phaedrus and Babrius (Greek). B. E. Perry.

Plautus. Paul Nixon. 5 Vols.

Pliny: Letters, Panegyricus. Betty Radice. 2 Vols.

Pliny: Natural History. 10 Vols. Vols. I–V and IX. H. Rackham. VI.–VIII. W. H. S. Jones. X. D. E. Eichholz.

Propertius. H. E. Butler.

Prudentius. H. J. Thomson. 2 Vols.

Quintilian. H. E. Butler. 4 Vols.

Remains of Old Latin. E. H. Warmington. 4 Vols. Vol. I. (Ennius and Caecilius) Vol. II. (Livius, Naevius Pacuvius, Accius) Vol. III. (Lucilius and Laws of XII Tables) Vol. IV. (Archaic Inscriptions)

Res Gestae Divi Augusti. Cf. Velleius Paterculus.

Sallust. J. C. Rolfe.

Scriptores Historiae Augustae. D. Magie. 3 Vols.

Seneca, The Elder: Controversiae, Suasoriae. M. Winterbottom. 2 Vols.

Seneca: Apocolocyntosis. Cf. Petronius.

Seneca: Epistulae Morales. R. M. Gummere. 3 Vols.

Seneca: Moral Essays. J. W. Basore. 3 Vols.

Seneca: Tragedies. F. J. Miller. 2 Vols.

Seneca: Naturales Quaestiones. T. H. Corcoran. 2 Vols.

Sidonius: Poems and Letters. W. B. Anderson. 2 Vols.

Silius Italicus. J. D. Duff. 2 Vols.

Statius. J. H. Mozley. 2 Vols.

Suetonius. J. C. Rolfe. 2 Vols.

Tacitus: Dialogus. Sir Wm. Peterson. Agricola and Germania. Maurice Hutton. Revised by M. Winterbottom, R. M. Ogilvie, E. H. Warmington.

Tacitus: Histories and Annals. C. H. Moore and J. Jackson. 4 Vols.

TERENCE. John Sargeaunt. 2 Vols.

TERTULLIAN: APOLOGIA and DE SPECTACULIS. T. R. Glover. MINUCIUS FELIX. G. H. Rendall.

TIBULLUS. Cf. CATULLUS.

VALERIUS FLACCUS. J. H. Mozley.

VARRO: DE LINGUA LATINA. R. G. Kent. 2 Vols.

VELLEIUS PATERCULUS and RES GESTAE DIVI AUGUSTI. F. W. Shipley.

VIRGIL. H. R. Fairclough. 2 Vols.

VITRUVIUS: DE ARCHITECTURA. F. Granger. 2 Vols.

Greek Authors

ACHILLES TATIUS. S. Gaselee.

AELIAN: ON THE NATURE OF ANIMALS. A. F. Scholfield. 3 Vols.

AENEAS TACTICUS. ASCLEPIODOTUS and ONASANDER. The Illinois Greek Club.

AESCHINES. C. D. Adams.

AESCHYLUS. H. Weir Smyth. 2 Vols.

ALCIPHRON, AELIAN, PHILOSTRATUS: LETTERS. A. R. Benner and F. H. Fobes.

ANDOCIDES, ANTIPHON. Cf. MINOR ATTIC ORATORS.

APOLLODORUS. Sir James G. Frazer. 2 Vols.

APOLLONIUS RHODIUS. R. C. Seaton.

APOSTOLIC FATHERS. Kirsopp Lake. 2 Vols.

APPIAN: ROMAN HISTORY. Horace White. 4 Vols.

ARATUS. Cf. CALLIMACHUS.

ARISTIDES: ORATIONS. C. A. Behr. Vol. I.

ARISTOPHANES. Benjamin Bickley Rogers. 3 Vols. Verse trans.

ARISTOTLE: ART OF RHETORIC. J. H. Freese.

ARISTOTLE: ATHENIAN CONSTITUTION, EUDEMIAN ETHICS, VICES AND VIRTUES. H. Rackham.

ARISTOTLE: GENERATION OF ANIMALS. A. L. Peck.

ARISTOTLE: HISTORIA ANIMALIUM. A. L. Peck. Vols. I.–II.

ARISTOTLE: METAPHYSICS. H. Tredennick. 2 Vols.

ARISTOTLE: METEOROLOGICA. H. D. P. Lee.

ARISTOTLE: MINOR WORKS. W. S. Hett. On Colours, On Things Heard, On Physiognomies, On Plants, On Marvellous Things Heard, Mechanical Problems, On Indivisible Lines, On Situations and Names of Winds, On Melissus, Xenophanes, and Gorgias.

ARISTOTLE: NICOMACHEAN ETHICS. H. Rackham.

4

ARISTOTLE: OECONOMICA and MAGNA MORALIA. G. C. Armstrong (with METAPHYSICS, Vol. II).

ARISTOTLE: ON THE HEAVENS. W. K. C. Guthrie.

ARISTOTLE: ON THE SOUL, PARVA NATURALIA, ON BREATH. W. S. Hett.

ARISTOTLE: CATEGORIES, ON INTERPRETATION, PRIOR ANALYTICS. H. P. Cooke and H. Tredennick.

ARISTOTLE: POSTERIOR ANALYTICS, TOPICS. H. Tredennick and E. S. Forster.

ARISTOTLE: ON SOPHISTICAL REFUTATIONS.
On Coming to be and Passing Away, On the Cosmos. E. S. Forster and D. J. Furley.

ARISTOTLE: PARTS OF ANIMALS. A. L. Peck; MOTION AND PROGRESSION OF ANIMALS. E. S. Forster.

ARISTOTLE: PHYSICS. Rev. P. Wicksteed and F. M. Cornford. 2 Vols.

ARISTOTLE: POETICS and LONGINUS. W. Hamilton Fyfe; DEMETRIUS ON STYLE. W. Rhys Roberts.

ARISTOTLE: POLITICS. H. Rackham.

ARISTOTLE: PROBLEMS. W. S. Hett. 2 Vols.

ARISTOTLE: RHETORICA AD ALEXANDRUM (with PROBLEMS. Vol. II). H. Rackham.

ARRIAN: HISTORY OF ALEXANDER and INDICA. Rev. E. Iliffe Robson. 2 Vols. New version P. Brunt.

ATHENAEUS: DEIPNOSOPHISTAE. C. B. Gulick. 7 Vols.

BABRIUS AND PHAEDRUS (Latin). B. E. Perry.

ST. BASIL: LETTERS. R. J. Deferrari. 4 Vols.

CALLIMACHUS: FRAGMENTS. C. A. Trypanis. MUSAEUS: HERO AND LEANDER. T. Gelzer and C. Whitman.

CALLIMACHUS, Hymns and Epigrams, and LYCOPHRON. A. W. Mair; ARATUS. G. R. Mair.

CLEMENT OF ALEXANDRIA. Rev. G. W. Butterworth.

COLLUTHUS. Cf. OPPIAN.

DAPHNIS AND CHLOE. Thornley's Translation revised by J. M. Edmonds: and PARTHENIUS. S. Gaselee.

DEMOSTHENES I.: OLYNTHIACS, PHILIPPICS and MINOR ORATIONS I.–XVII. AND XX. J. H. Vince.

DEMOSTHENES II.: DE CORONA and DE FALSA LEGATIONE. C. A. Vince and J. H. Vince.

DEMOSTHENES III.: MEIDIAS, ANDROTION, ARISTOCRATES, TIMOCRATES and ARISTOGEITON I. and II. J. H. Vince.

DEMOSTHENES IV.–VI: PRIVATE ORATIONS and IN NEAERAM. A. T. Murray.

DEMOSTHENES VII: FUNERAL SPEECH, EROTIC ESSAY, EXORDIA and LETTERS. N. W. and N. J. DeWitt.

DIO CASSIUS: ROMAN HISTORY. E. Cary. 9 Vols.

DIO CHRYSOSTOM. J. W. Cohoon and H. Lamar Crosby. 5 Vols.

DIODORUS SICULUS. 12 Vols. Vols. I.–VI. C. H. Oldfather. Vol. VII. C. L. Sherman. Vol. VIII. C. B. Welles. Vols. IX. and X. R. M. Geer. Vol. XI. F. Walton. Vol. XII. F. Walton. General Index. R. M. Geer.

DIOGENES LAERTIUS. R. D. Hicks. 2 Vols. New Introduction by H. S. Long.

DIONYSIUS OF HALICARNASSUS: ROMAN ANTIQUITIES. Spelman's translation revised by E. Cary. 7 Vols.

DIONYSIUS OF HALICARNASSUS: CRITICAL ESSAYS. S. Usher. 2 Vols. Vol. I.

EPICTETUS. W. A. Oldfather. 2 Vols.

EURIPIDES. A. S. Way. 4 Vols. Verse trans.

EUSEBIUS: ECCLESIASTICAL HISTORY. Kirsopp Lake and J. E. L. Oulton. 2 Vols.

GALEN: ON THE NATURAL FACULTIES. A. J. Brock.

GREEK ANTHOLOGY. W. R. Paton. 5 Vols.

GREEK BUCOLIC POETS (THEOCRITUS, BION, MOSCHUS). J. M Edmonds.

GREEK ELEGY AND IAMBUS with the ANACREONTEA. J. M. Edmonds. 2 Vols.

GREEK LYRIC. D. A. Campbell. 4 Vols. Vol. I.

GREEK MATHEMATICAL WORKS. Ivor Thomas. 2 Vols.

HERODES. Cf. THEOPHRASTUS: CHARACTERS.

HERODIAN. C. R. Whittaker. 2 Vols.

HERODOTUS. A. D. Godley. 4 Vols.

HESIOD AND THE HOMERIC HYMNS. H. G. Evelyn White.

HIPPOCRATES and the FRAGMENTS OF HERACLEITUS. W. H. S. Jones and E. T. Withington. 4 Vols.

HOMER: ILIAD. A. T. Murray. 2 Vols.

HOMER: ODYSSEY. A. T. Murray. 2 Vols.

ISAEUS. E. W. Forster.

ISOCRATES. George Norlin and LaRue Van Hook. 3 Vols.

[ST. JOHN DAMASCENE]: BARLAAM AND IOASAPH. Rev. G. R. Woodward, Harold Mattingly and D. M. Lang.

JOSEPHUS. 10 Vols. Vols. I.–IV. H. Thackeray. Vol. V. H. Thackeray and R. Marcus. Vols. VI.–VII. R. Marcus. Vol. VIII. R. Marcus and Allen Wikgren. Vols. IX.–X. L. H. Feldman.

JULIAN. Wilmer Cave Wright. 3 Vols.

LIBANIUS. A. F. Norman. 3 Vols. Vols. I.–II.

LUCIAN. 8 Vols. Vols. I.–V. A. M. Harmon. Vol. VI. K. Kilburn. Vols. VII.–VIII. M. D. Macleod.

LYCOPHRON. Cf. CALLIMACHUS.

Lyra Graeca, J. M. Edmonds. 2 Vols.

Lysias. W. R. M. Lamb.

Manetho. W. G. Waddell.

Marcus Aurelius. C. R. Haines.

Menander. W. G. Arnott. 3 Vols. Vol. I.

Minor Attic Orators (Antiphon, Andocides, Lycurgus, Demades, Dinarchus, Hyperides). K. J. Maidment and J. O. Burtt. 2 Vols.

Musaeus: Hero and Leander. Cf. Callimachus.

Nonnos: Dionysiaca. W. H. D. Rouse. 3 Vols.

Oppian, Colluthus, Tryphiodorus. A. W. Mair.

Papyri. Non-Literary Selections. A. S. Hunt and C. C. Edgar. 2 Vols. Literary Selections (Poetry). D. L. Page.

Parthenius. Cf. Daphnis and Chloe.

Pausanias: Description of Greece. W. H. S. Jones. 4 Vols. and Companion Vol. arranged by R. E. Wycherley.

Philo. 10 Vols. Vols. I.–V. F. H. Colson and Rev. G. H. Whitaker. Vols. VI.–IX. F. H. Colson. Vol. X. F. H. Colson and the Rev. J. W. Earp.

Philo: two supplementary Vols. (*Translation only.*) Ralph Marcus.

Philostratus: The Life of Apollonius of Tyana. F. C. Conybeare. 2 Vols.

Philostratus: Imagines; Callistratus: Descriptions. A. Fairbanks.

Philostratus and Eunapius: Lives of the Sophists. Wilmer Cave Wright.

Pindar. Sir J. E. Sandys.

Plato: Charmides, Alcibiades, Hipparchus, The Lovers, Theages, Minos and Epinomis. W. R. M. Lamb.

Plato: Cratylus, Parmenides, Greater Hippias, Lesser Hippias. H. N. Fowler.

Plato: Euthyphro, Apology, Crito, Phaedo, Phaedrus, H. N. Fowler.

Plato: Laches, Protagoras, Meno, Euthydemus. W. R. M. Lamb.

Plato: Laws. Rev. R. G. Bury. 2 Vols.

Plato: Lysis, Symposium, Gorgias. W. R. M. Lamb.

Plato: Republic. Paul Shorey. 2 Vols.

Plato: Statesman, Philebus. H. N. Fowler; Ion. W. R. M. Lamb.

Plato: Theaetetus and Sophist. H. N. Fowler.

Plato: Timaeus, Critias, Clitophon, Menexenus, Epistulae. Rev. R. G. Bury.

Plotinus: A. H. Armstrong. 7 Vols. Vols. I.–III.

PLUTARCH: MORALIA. 16 Vols. Vols I.–V. F. C. Babbitt. Vol. VI. W. C. Helmbold. Vols. VII. and XIV. P. H. De Lacy and B. Einarson. Vol. VIII. P. A. Clement and H. B. Hoffleit. Vol. IX. E. L. Minar, Jr., F. H. Sandbach, W. C. Helmbold. Vol. X. H. N. Fowler. Vol. XI. L. Pearson and F. H. Sandbach. Vol. XII. H. Cherniss and W. C. Helmbold. Vol. XIII 1–2. H. Cherniss. Vol. XV. F. H. Sandbach.

PLUTARCH: THE PARALLEL LIVES. B. Perrin. 11 Vols.

POLYBIUS. W. R. Paton. 6 Vols.

PROCOPIUS H. B. Dewing. 7 Vols.

PTOLEMY: TETRABIBLOS. F. E. Robbins.

QUINTUS SMYRNAEUS. A. S. Way. Verse trans.

SEXTUS EMPIRICUS. Rev. R. G. Bury. 4 Vols.

SOPHOCLES. F. Storr. 2 Vols. Verse trans.

STRABO: GEOGRAPHY. Horace L. Jones. 8 Vols.

THEOCRITUS. Cf. GREEK BUCOLIC POETS.

THEOPHRASTUS: CHARACTERS. J. M. Edmonds. HERODES, etc. A. D. Knox.

THEOPHRASTUS: ENQUIRY INTO PLANTS. Sir Arthur Hort, Bart. 2 Vols.

THEOPHRASTUS: DE CAUSIS PLANTARUM. G. K. K. Link and B. Einarson. 3 Vols. Vol. I.

THUCYDIDES. C. F. Smith. 4 Vols.

TRYPHIODORUS. Cf. OPPIAN.

XENOPHON: CYROPAEDIA. Walter Miller. 2 Vols.

XENOPHON: HELLENCIA. C. L. Brownson. 2 Vols.

XENOPHON: ANABASIS. C. L. Brownson.

XENOPHON: MEMORABILIA AND OECONOMICUS. E. C. Marchant. SYMPOSIUM AND APOLOGY. O. J. Todd.

XENOPHON: SCRIPTA MINORA. E. C. Marchant. CONSTITUTION OF THE ATHENIANS. G. W. Bowersock.